HANDBOOK FOR EFFECTIVE
DEPARTMENT LEADERSHIP

HANDBOOK FOR EFFECTIVE DEPARTMENT LEADERSHIP

CONCEPTS AND PRACTICES IN TODAY'S SECONDARY SCHOOLS

THOMAS J. SERGIOVANNI

University of Illinois

Allyn and Bacon, Inc.   Boston   London   Sydney

Copyright © 1977 by ALLYN AND BACON, Inc.,
470 Atlantic Avenue, Boston, Massachusetts 02210.

LIBRARY OF CONGRESS CATALOGING IN PUBLICATION DATA

Sergiovanni, Thomas J
  Handbook for effective department leadership.

  Includes bibliographical references and index.
  1. Departmental chairmen (High schools)—Handbooks,
manuals, etc. I. Title.
LB2822.S44   373.1'2'013   76-43015
ISBN 0-205-06747-6

10 9 8 7 6 5 4   85 84 83 82 81 80

CONTENTS

PREFACE

This book is a practical guide for effective department leadership in today's secondary schools. It is addressed primarily to the men and women who now occupy or are preparing to occupy positions as department chairpersons in our junior and senior high schools. The natural complementary audience is school principals and other administrators who markedly influence the course of the chairpersonship. Together, they can use the book to evaluate the breadth and scope of the chairpersonship and to redefine the role effectively.

Reference is not made to the middle school or to chairpersonship alternatives such as division heads and unit leaders. The intent is not to deny these movements, or to take issue with them, but to simplify matters by speaking singularly to the more prevalent secondary school chairperson. Significant benefits can be derived from organizing differently; indeed the middle school is a promising development. Whatever the choice of a particular school, one point remains clear—effectiveness depends upon a viable middle-level leadership. Participants in this leadership are designated here as chairpersons but the concepts and practices suggested seem equally applicable to other middle-level leadership roles.

Each chapter is divided into two parts: one deals with concepts underlying the topics under consideration; the other illustrates practices. An assumption basic to this concepts/practices approach is that a consideration of practices alone is limited; concepts must enlighten specific situations and circumstances. This approach provides a combination that can increase the chairperson's basic understanding of his or her job, can help him or her to adopt and revise present practices and to develop new ones.

This concepts/practices approach makes the book particularly suitable for use in staff development and other school district in-service programs. Though not designed specifically for classroom use as a textbook, some university instructors might find the approach attractive for use in supervision and curriculum leadership courses.

A number of practitioners and professors contributed ideas, comments, and suggestions as this book was developed. The following deserve special mention: Bruce Altergott, William Campbell, Janet Eyler, Anthony Gregorc, Ben Harris, Carl Johnson, Allan Maclean, Richard MacFeeley, Lloyd McCleary, Thomas McGreal, Howard Mehlinger, Robert Metcalf, Verner Ohst, Gene Schmidt, Robert Wheat, James Wicklund, and Shiela Wilson. Lee Babcock and Jane Feilen were patient typists.

Being a chairperson is a difficult and demanding task, but the rewards are great. Perhaps this book will make the going a bit easier. I would appreciate ideas, reactions, suggestions, and illustration of practices from chairpersons and others who use this book.

Please write to me directly at 333 Education, University of Illinois, Urbana 61801. University instructors are also cordially invited to share their ideas about the book and experiences in using it in their courses. Such feedback will help me keep abreast of current developments and will assist in preparing future editions of this book.

Thomas J. Sergiovanni

HANDBOOK FOR EFFECTIVE DEPARTMENT LEADERSHIP

PART ONE

NEW LEADERSHIP
FOR THE
JUNIOR AND SENIOR
HIGH SCHOOL

LEADERSHIP ROLES IN THE SECONDARY SCHOOL

❧ CONCEPTS ❧

This book is intended to help department chairpersons in junior and senior high schools to become more effective. Such increased effectiveness depends upon the chairperson's ability to increase his level, quantity, and quality of leadership. Modern chairpersons have important leadership functions to perform, many which have been abandoned by those in other roles and some which are new to today's complex secondary school. The chairperson's role is changing and leadership demands are increasing. Changes in the chairperson's role depend upon the status and changes of other school roles such as principal, central office coordinator or supervisor, and classroom teacher. Therefore, before one can adequately understand demands for leadership which chairpersons face, he or she needs to understand changes that are taking place in other key roles.

Today's principal would make excellent copy for novelists, soap opera writers, and amateur psychologists. Plot details would vary with each writer's imagination but the bones of each story would probably remain the same. The new principal often begins his career with an idealistic view of his or her job—a view that includes exaggerated expectations for his ability to provide the school with leadership in general and educational leadership in particular. Feelings of guilt are common as principals find that increasing efforts are consumed in the school's management and organizational affairs, in dealing with the school's outside faces such as the district central office, the school community, and the general community at large; decreasing efforts are spent on educational programs and instructional matters. But the principal is supposed to be an educational leader, so he is often told.

The gap between reality and ideal has personal consequences for the principal and organizational consequences for the school. In reconciling this gap, some principals may become cynical and withdraw completely from educational matters. Others cope with the educational leadership functions establishing elaborate administrative controls over educational program decision-making. Administrative controls often take the form of a rigidly standardized curriculum, heavily bureaucratic course development and approval procedures, common testing and grading procedures and a system of impersonal supervision and evaluation. A paper curriculum and procedural school which can be readily managed often takes the place of a living curriculum and dynamic school.

EDUCATIONAL LEADERSHIP

Principals should not turn away from educational program matters, but should view their educational responsibilities anew. Perhaps the principal should view his role as that of an *educational statesman* rather than educational leader in its usual sense. As an educational statesman, the principal is primarily concerned with:

- overall educational program
- basic philosophy, working assumptions, values and beliefs
- general goals and objectives
- broad structure and design for education
- assessment of community needs and their relationship to school interests and activities

The educational statesman ought to be able to communicate the school's mission and work to outside forces and to argue successfully for adequate resources to support the school's educational program because of what it is, what it stands for, and what it does.

 The principal is responsible for developing educational policy and shaping the school's broad educational posture.

Educational leadership is directly concerned with the development and articulation of educational programs and includes a high concern for:

curriculum and teaching objectives
educational encounters
teaching styles, methods and procedures
classroom learning climates
teacher, student and program evaluation
curriculum content, coordination and scope
alternatives and options
pattern of teacher and student influence
lesson and unit planning
scheduling
grouping
structure of knowledge
curriculum and teaching innovation

Most of these activities are beyond reasonable expectations for principals and unless delegated to the chairperson level do not get adequate attention in the typical junior and senior high school. As a statesman, the principal is concerned with educational leadership activities at a different level. He exercises this leadership by raising issues, testing ideas, providing information, and evaluating for consistency with the overall policy and philosophy of the school. School policy and philosophy are themselves evaluated and redefined as statesmanship and leadership functions interact.

If chairpersons are to assume increased responsibility for educational leadership, two conditions need to be met:

 They need to expand their present role emphasis on instructional leadership in subject areas

They need to be provided with more responsibility and authority than that which is presently available

The first condition is more controversial than the second though we see the two conditions as being interdependent. As long as the chairperson operates only as an instructional leader in a given subject area, he will not get or deserve more responsibility and authority. Expanding his instructional leadership role will require additional responsibility and authority.

INSTRUCTIONAL LEADERSHIP

Instructional leadership refers to leadership given to one specific content area, discipline or subject matter area exclusive of others. A science department chairperson who works with staff in developing science curriculum, science objectives and science teaching methods without attention to, concern for, or participation in similar activities focused on the entire junior or senior high school educational program is only exercising instructional leadership. Instructional leadership is concerned with only a small part of what happens to students. Educational leadership is concerned with students as they interact with the total school educational program.

 Instructional leadership is an important part of educational leadership but in itself is not equivalent to educational leadership.

Delegating responsibility and autonomy to chairpersons who only operate as instructional leaders may be more harmful educationally than maintaining more centralized control. What may result is the establishment of several powerful but uncoordinated city-states, each out to maximize its own position and, given our present climate of limited resources, usually at the expense of others. This situation can lead to an inordinate amount of competition, conflict, and curriculum fragmentation. Students lose the most from this sort of limited instructional leadership.

Educational leadership and its more limited component, instructional leadership in subject areas, are exercised within a complex organization. Further, the exchange of

5

leadership requires that chairpersons interact with teachers and other groups engaged in the work of the school. To function effectively, educational workers require some direction and coordination, some map of what is ahead, and a supply of adequate resources. Educational leadership is not independent of other school expressions and demands but rather takes place as part of an interdependent complex leadership system. Each component of the system defines an important leadership role for the chairperson. Chairperson leadership roles include organizational, supervisory and administrative leadership as well as educational and instructional leadership.

ORGANIZATIONAL LEADERSHIP

Secondary schools differ in size and organizational setting and though schools which resemble the red brick house of old are still functioning in many rural areas, the typical secondary school of today is a relatively complex organization. Decisions must be made, people and material coordinated, records kept, communications channeled, innovations discovered and implemented, steps and procedures followed, power and authority distributed, tasks assigned, schedules developed, specifications honored and integrated, staff recruited, positions allocated, and resources must be obtained and distributed. These characteristics are common to most complex organizations; leaders, regardless of the kind of organization from which they come, need to be able to deal with such concerns in ways which keep the concerns subservient to the organization's goals. To do so is to express *organizational leadership*.

The naive vision of educational leadership often does not take into account its interdependence with organizational leadership. Educational leadership takes place in a complex organizational setting and its success usually depends upon one's knowledge of and ability to influence this setting.

Organizational leadership should not be confused with organizational drift. We drift when we become victims of and reactors to the organizational setting. The setting determines our goals, decisions, and activities. We are leading, as opposed to reacting, when this organizational setting becomes subservient to our purposes and to the educational goals we seek to achieve. If left to drift, schools like most other organizations become survival-oriented, obsessed with maintaining a state of stability. Routine, predictability, and reliability are prized while uncertainty, innovation, ambiguity, and stress are forces to be overcome. Buffers are erected to protect the school from hostile and potentially hostile outsiders. Internally, status systems are developed to protect administrators from teachers, and teachers from students. A mechanistic mentality sets in which is manifested in precisely defined roles, obligations, duties, and relationships for students, teachers, chairpersons, and administrators; detailed regulations are prescribed to increase predictability in and programming of behavior for teachers and students; decisions which are varied and unpredictable are funneled to the top while decision-making is standardized at lower levels in order to insure reliability and control of thought and action; and a concern for processing the largest number of students as efficiently as possible in terms of personnel, money, equipment, and space becomes paramount. All of these features describe the attempt to reduce ambiguity, risk, and uncertainty in the rigidly structured, highly programmed, excessively bureaucratic school.

The negative consequences of permitting schools to organize in a manner which ensures their own inclinations for survival, as opposed to using schools as vehicles for achieving human goals, will be discussed in Chapter 3. In a general sense, however, the less evidence of people in schools being concerned with *why, for what purpose,* and *who benefits* when decisions are made by school officials and teachers, the greater the danger of schools and classrooms within schools drifting into this mechanistic mentality. Purpose is an enemy of mechanistic organizations.

Consider, for example, the question of who benefits from decisions that teachers or school officials make. Take a moment to develop a mental image of a grid, similar to that presented below, for recording the prime beneficiaries of decisions that have been made recently in your school. At the top of the grid list several of the possible prime beneficiaries. In the grid used in this example, administrators, students, teachers, the school as an organization, parents, local industry, society, and the universities are listed as possible beneficiaries. On the left side of the grid mentally list a half dozen or so decisions. As a decision is listed, go across the top of the grid and check off the prime beneficiary.

PRIME BENEFICIARY

DECISION	ADMIN-ISTRA-TORS	STU-DENTS	TEACH-ERS	SCHOOL	PARENTS	INDUS-TRY	UNIVER-SITIES	SOCIETY
Ability grouping			√					
Hall passes	√			√				
Lesson plans			√	√				
Required courses							√	

FIGURE 1-1. PRIME BENEFICIARY GRID

Some examples might be:

1. The decision to group students by ability. Reason: students are easier to teach. Prime beneficiary: the teacher.
2. The decision to require hall passes for students. Reason: students are easier to regulate and control. Prime beneficiary: the administration and the school as an efficiently operated organization.
3. The decision to require daily lesson plans. Reason: in case of absence, the substitute knows what to do. Prime beneficiary: the teacher and the school as an efficiently operated organization.
4. The decision to require three units of math for graduation. Reason: to meet university entrance requirements. Prime beneficiary: the university.

The decisions themselves are not being disputed but the basis upon which such decisions are often made is worth considering. If one makes a long enough list of decisions and if he is being reasonably candid, it soon becomes embarrassingly clear that most decisions are made without regard for educationally sound purposes but for reasons relating to the smooth, safe, efficient, and reliable operation of the school as an organization.

"The objectives must determine the organization or else the organization will determine the objectives" was the wording in *Cardinal Principles of Secondary Education* in 1918. These words are as important now for the junior and senior high schools as they were decades ago. In summary, effective educational leadership depends upon the chairperson being able to establish that schools as organizations are designed to serve people, goals, and activities and not the other way around. It is in this sense that educational and organizational leadership are interdependent, each nourishing the other.

SUPERVISORY LEADERSHIP

Educational organizations are essentially human organizations. Unlike industrial organizations where the main resources are raw materials, machinery, technology, and patents, the school's most important and expensive resources are its teachers, supervisors and administrators. About four out of five dollars spent on education wind up in the pockets of educational workers. Further, despite well-intended efforts to the contrary, teaching is a relatively private activity. Teachers work alone most of the time and their performance remains invisible to other teachers and educational workers. What teachers say they do, what the department agrees to do, and what the school requires teachers to do are the public agendas of teaching, but the hidden agenda of what actually goes on in the classroom is largely up to individual teachers. Teachers can and do perform when necessary for chairpersons and principals but the reality of teaching is that once the classroom door is closed, teachers can do pretty much as they please providing they are not noticeably violating basic rules of order.

The challenge of working with teachers to improve education lies in identification and commitment. Like it or not, the chairperson finds himself dependent upon his staff's identification with and commitment to department and school goals if he hopes to have these objectives realized in any real sense.

Chairpersons express *supervisory leadership* when they work directly with teachers, either one at a time or in groups, and in a fashion which obtains their identification with and commitment to agreed-upon objectives. Goals may focus on staff personal and professional development, department and classroom learning climates, teaching methods and activities, evaluation, and similar concerns associated with the improvement of educational experience for students. Further, supervisory leadership is much more concerned with action, change, movement, and improvement than it is with control, order, checking, and rating.

As teachers experience effective supervisory leadership, they should become more committed to department and school goals, more motivated to work, more sure of where they are going, more confident in themselves, and more satisfied with their jobs because of the kind and quality of work they do. These are the chairperson's objectives as he provides supervisory leadership in his school.

ADMINISTRATIVE LEADERSHIP

A school's effectiveness depends upon its ability to adapt to its external environment and at the same time to maintain itself internally. The spirit of a school's adapting to its external environment is implicit in our previous discussion of educational, organizational, and supervisory leadership. Schools respond to societal and individual needs by developing and evaluating goals, moving educational programs forward, developing more effective and efficient educational and organizational structures, and by promoting staff growth and development. These are important keys to effective functioning in a changing world.

The gains which schools make through leadership need to be consolidated and incorporated into the structure, so that schools can function in many areas with some reliability and without constant attention. People need to know, for example, where materials are, how classes will be scheduled, what records should be kept, when and where meetings will take place, how to apply for personal leave days, who to call when sick, how the composition of students has changed in the last five years, and how to order supplies. An information system needs to be provided and maintained so that more rational decisions can be made. Operating procedure, policy, or rules structure needs to be provided so that fairly routine decisions can be made without much time or effort. Some mechanism needs to be developed so that teachers are not involved in decisions which do not interest them.

One could justly argue that the *maintenance* of an information system and of a routine decision-making system are not expressions of leadership. Yet administrative functions are badly in need of leadership in the sense that more efficient systems need to be developed and existing systems need to be evaluated to ensure that they are helping rather than hindering the work of teachers and the pursuit of objectives. Administrative functions, such as the accumulation and storage of information and the establishment of rules and procedures, tend to proliferate. As new information is required for storage, old information continues to be stored and as new rules are developed and implemented, old rules continue to be enforced.

Chairpersons seem particularly burdened by administrative functions and maintenance chores passed down from administrators and up from teachers. Much of the administrative work is of dubious value to the department and school and the remainder needs to be mastered more efficiently. Administrative leadership for the chairperson then has two directions—developing efficient ways to handle information and routine decision-making, and evaluating existing administrative procedures in an attempt to reduce them substantially. If chairpersons are not able to master the administrative side of their jobs, they will not have either the time or energy to exercise their broader leadership functions.

TEAM LEADERSHIP

Differences between educational and organizational leadership have been discussed, with the former concerning the total educational program and the latter concerning program as defined by a specific content area or discipline. Where departments are generally considered as separate entities and chairpersons are often concerned primarily with the welfare of their own departments, educational leadership is difficult to implement.

The chairperson's use of educational leadership is dependent upon the development of a *leadership team* in the school. Team leadership is deceptively similar to cabinet, curriculum council, and executive committee structures which presently exist in many junior and senior high schools. Team leadership is similar in its arrangement but different in its assumptions. It requires that cabinets and councils discard the popular bargaining model of decision-making where one party wins and another loses. It also requires that cabinets and councils disregard narrow views of the school's educational program and instead work to reduce curriculum fragmentation. The success of team leadership depends upon

 the development of mutual support and trust among chairpersons and between them and the principal,

the acknowledgment that chairpersons are interdependent, with each becoming more effective individually as the group becomes more effective,

the development of a commitment to understanding, appreciating, and working toward an intellectually and humanistically rich educational program for the whole school

In summary, departments need to be viewed as interdependent parts of a total school program and chairpersons need to become part of a cadre responsible for educational leadership in the school. The principal is an important and influential member of this team and brings to it concern for the school's overall posture, its basic philosophy, its basic assumptions, its goals and objectives, and its broad structure and design. In this book team leadership is considered as an important, albeit distinct, part of the chairperson's supervisory leadership responsibilities.

THE CHAIRPERSON'S LEADERSHIP ROLE

How simple life would be if it were possible to provide chairpersons with an assortment of leadership hats—one for each emphasis described above. But leadership emphasis is rarely expressed in a pure form and few situations require only one emphasis. As the chairperson's leadership responsibilities are summarized below, interdependencies among the emphases become apparent.

The effective chairperson works:

to achieve school and department educational objectives	Educational Leadership
through teachers who identify with and are committed to these objectives	Supervisory Leadership
within a department and school structure which supports the objectives and facilitates the work of teachers	Organizational Leadership
over an extended period of time	Administrative Leadership
in cooperation with other chairpersons and the principal	Team Leadership

This book seeks to build the chairperson's potential and competencies for exercising leadership. In Chapter 2 attempts are made to define more specifically the chairperson's role and to develop a set of objectives to guide his work. Additional chapters examine each of the leadership emphases—educational, organizational, supervisory, administrative and team—the building blocks to effectiveness for chairpersons.

☙ CHAPTER ONE ❧

☙ PRACTICES ❧

How do you presently function as a department chairperson and how do your co-workers function? How do you spend your time? What are your most important leadership responsibilities? Are you satisfied with those tasks and responsibilities you are presently emphasizing? Being able to describe and understand your present leadership roles and the tasks and responsibilities which actually consume most of your time is a good starting point in planning and developing a program for your own professional development as a leader in your school.

In this section you will have an opportunity to examine what is expected of you as a department leader, what levels of competency you now have and areas in which you may need to develop. Further, you will have an opportunity to explore how your job goals and demands fit with your broader personal and career goals. The chairperson's role is not for everyone and the sooner you understand what you are getting into, the better able you will be to either accept the challenge of the position or opt out.

Included in Section B are discussions of competencies for chairpersons (with a self-evaluation checklist), and personal and career planning (including a life goal inventory). Further, a short checklist of problems common to the chairperson's role is provided.

COMPETENCIES FOR CHAIRPERSONS

Competencies are descriptions of tasks and performances that are considered essential for successful implementation of a given role. Included here is a self-evaluation checklist of competencies, adapted from lists developed for supervisors and administrators.* Review the list carefully. For each competency indicate if it is important to your leadership role as you understand it, if you are satisfied with the time you spend in this area, if you are satisfied with your present performance level, and if you need in-service help in this area. Review your ratings with your principal. Do not assume that this is a complete list. Add other competencies statements which you and your principal feel should be included.

*Ben Harris and John King, *Professional Supervisory Competencies, Competency Specifications for Instructional Leadership Personnel.* Special Education Supervisor Training Project, University of Texas at Austin, Rev., 1975, and Lloyd McCleary and Kenneth McIntyre, "Competency Development and University Methodology," *The Principal's Search.* Washington, D.C.: National Association of Secondary School Principals, 1972, pp. 53–68.

SAMPLE COMPETENCIES FOR CHAIRPERSONS:
SELF-EVALUATION CHECKLIST

EDUCATIONAL LEADERSHIP	THIS IS IMPORTANT TO MY LEADERSHIP ROLE		I AM SATISFIED WITH THE AMOUNT OF TIME I SPEND ON THIS		I AM SATISFIED WITH MY LEVEL OF COMPETENCE AND PERFORMANCE		I NEED IN-SERVICE HELP ON THIS	
	YES	NO	YES	NO	YES	NO	YES	NO
1. *Setting Instructional Goals* Given a mandate to clarify major goals of instruction, you can lead groups of parents, citizens, specialized personnel, teachers, and pupils through a series of discussions, presentations, training sessions, and other experiences to produce a report showing some of the most important instructional goals on which there is agreement.								
2. *Designing Instructional Units* You can design instructional units which specify targets and objectives, instructional sequences, a variety of appropriate teaching/learning activities, materials, and evaluative procedures.								
3. *Developing and Adapting Curricula* Having secured innovative curricula developed outside the school or district, you can adapt the curricula to meet the needs of a student or student group, and make them available to local personnel for use in guiding instructional planning.								
4. *Evaluating and Selecting Learning Materials* Given expressed needs for learning materials, you can develop a set of evaluative criteria and procedures to determine the quality, utility, and availability of learning materials, and can organize and conduct review sessions where teachers and other personnel can apply the criteria to new materials and make recommendations for acquisitions in needed areas.								
5. *Evaluating the Utilization of Learning Resources* Given an array of learning resources currently available for use, you can design and conduct a study to determine the extent and appropriateness of their utilization, and based on the results of that study, can make recommendations for the improved utilization of specific learning resources in specific ways.								

	THIS IS IM-PORTANT TO MY LEADER-SHIP ROLE		I AM SATISFIED WITH THE AMOUNT OF TIME I SPEND ON THIS		I AM SATIS-FIED WITH MY LEVEL OF COM-PETENCE AND PER-FORMANCE		I NEED IN-SERVICE HELP ON THIS	
EDUCATIONAL LEADERSHIP	YES	NO	YES	NO	YES	NO	YES	NO
6. *Producing Learning Materials* Given learning needs and a curricular design to meet those needs, you can arrange for the production of the necessary learning materials to complement, fulfill, and/or enhance the aims of the curriculum.								
7. *Supervising in a Clinical Mode* Given a teacher experiencing difficulties within a classroom, you can lead the teacher through a clinical cycle using classroom observation data, non-directive feedback techniques, and various planning and in-service experiences to produce significantly improved teacher behavior.								
8. *Planning for Individual Growth* Given a teacher and data concerning various facets of his/her on-the-job performance, you can assist the teacher in establishing individual professional growth plans which include objectives for change in classroom practices, a schedule of experiences sequenced for continuous stimulation and growth, criteria specified for interim and terminal evaluation, and a specified period for accomplishing the objectives.								
SUPERVISORY LEADERSHIP								
1. *Building a Healthy Climate* You know and are able to employ model(s) that identify organizational conditions important to the building of self-actualization in the staff and the satisfaction of ego needs of individuals.								
2. *Team Building* You know about and are able to employ procedures for establishing organizational goals, clarifying roles, planning and otherwise providing structure in order for individuals to relate to each other in cooperative and supporting ways.								
3. *Resolving Conflict* You know about and are able to work through con-								

SUPERVISORY LEADERSHIP	THIS IS IM-PORTANT TO MY LEADER-SHIP ROLE		I AM SATISFIED WITH THE AMOUNT OF TIME I SPEND ON THIS		I AM SATIS-FIED WITH MY LEVEL OF COM-PETENCE AND PER-FORMANCE		I NEED IN-SERVICE HELP ON THIS	
	YES	NO	YES	NO	YES	NO	YES	NO

flict situations with students, parents, teachers, and others related to school activity involving role conflict, value conflict, goal conflict, and interpersonal conflict.

4. *Making Decisions*
You know about and are able to apply decision-making models, and, through participatory procedures, develop with the students and staff rational approaches to problem solving; focusing both on problem content and on process.

5. *Planning and Organizing Meetings*
You know about and are able to plan and operate meetings which are effective because they get the job done and at the same time build staff identity and commitment to group decisions.

6. *Recruiting and Selecting Personnel*
You know about and are able to engage in a variety of selective recruitment activities, and can secure a list of several possible applicants from various sources, can systematically secure and validate relevant information on the applicants by conducting personal interviews, by checking with previous employers, and by using other selection procedures, and can prepare a set of recommendations for filling the vacancies with the applicants who will best fulfill job requirements.

7. *Assigning Personnel*
You know about and are able to analyze the needs, expectations, and composition of existing staff groups in various units, and, based on that analysis, you can prepare and justify recommendations for assigning and reassigning staff members to positions for optimum educational opportunity.

8. *Bringing About Change*
You know about and are able to build a change strategy which takes into account human factors helping or hindering change, level of acceptance needed from teachers for successful implementation and a realistic appraisal of the amount and kind of influence you have as a change facilitator.

ORGANIZATIONAL LEADERSHIP	THIS IS IM-PORTANT TO MY LEADER-SHIP ROLE		I AM SATISFIED WITH THE AMOUNT OF TIME I SPEND ON THIS		I AM SATIS-FIED WITH MY LEVEL OF COM-PETENCE AND PER-FORMANCE		I NEED IN-SERVICE HELP ON THIS	
	YES	NO	YES	NO	YES	NO	YES	NO

1. *Revising Existing Structures*
   Having determined the strengths and weaknesses of an existing organizational structure, you can propose carefully reasoned or research-supported changes, which may include the alteration of assignments, of the use of staff time, of the required reporting patterns, or of the allocation of resources to improve efficiency, productivity, and morale, and, in so doing, improve efficiency.

2. *Assimilating Programs*
   Given a successful instructional program operating within a department, center, classroom, or other unit, you can design a plan for the smooth integration of the entire program or selected components thereof into a larger system, prepare a timetable and assignments for the transferring of responsibilities, and assure that the instructional improvement evidenced in the program is continued in the system to which it is transferred.

3. *Monitoring New Arrangements*
   Given the task of implementing a new organizational arrangement, you can determine reporting procedures, compare actual operations with planned developments, and when necessary, make recommendations to modify operations to bring them into agreement with formulated plans.

4. *Developing a Staffing Plan*
   Given a new project proposal which specifies budget, general objectives, and operational procedures, you can describe essential staff positions to be filled, develop job descriptions for each, and specify the competencies required of the individuals who will fill the positions.

5. *Informing the Public*
   You can establish, promote and maintain favorable impressions of public school programs among community members by disseminating school information through the public media, by speaking to public and school groups, by conferring with parents and other interested individuals, and by meeting, as necessary, with community groups and leaders.

17

	THIS IS IM-PORTANT TO MY LEADER-SHIP ROLE		I AM SATISFIED WITH THE AMOUNT OF TIME I SPEND ON THIS		I AM SATIS-FIED WITH MY LEVEL OF COM-PETENCE AND PER-FORMANCE		I NEED IN-SERVICE HELP ON THIS	
ORGANIZATIONAL LEADERSHIP	YES	NO	YES	NO	YES	NO	YES	NO

6. *Student Discipline*
You can establish adequate control of the student body and provide necessary disciplinary rules with the help and cooperation of teachers, parents and students.

7. *Policies and Procedures*
You know about and are able to establish a system of policies and procedures, linked to and justified by educational goals and purposes, which facilitates and frees teachers to work more effectively and which sets high standards for that work.

ADMINISTRATIVE LEADERSHIP

1. You know about and are able to employ managerial planning tools and procedures in administering your department.

2. You can organize, supervise, and manage the financial affairs of the department.

3. You are familiar with the projected budgetary needs of your school, including salary, operation and maintenance costs.

4. You know the financial situation of your school and can analyze cost by student, grade, by total enrollment, by number graduating, and by number failed or dropping out. You are aware of implications for your department.

5. You can plan the department's educational program in accordance with the available facilities and equipment.

6. You can apply rational decision making models and procedures in the administration of department programs.

7. You are able to keep accurate records of purchasing needs, inventories, expenditures and other business functions,

PERSONAL AND CAREER PLANNING

A professional career in educational administration and supervision can be demanding and the chairperson's role, if one takes his leadership responsibilities seriously, can be particularly demanding. Being an effective leader requires a commitment in time and energy which may well conflict with your other goals and aspirations. On the other hand leadership effectiveness may open new horizons to you professionally through career advancement and may also provide you with increased personal satisfaction.

In this discussion you are provided with a life goal inventory which may help you to understand better the professional and personal goals you seek, and how these goals interact with each other.

Some people prefer to avoid thinking about what they value in life and what they hope to achieve as persons and as professionals. Since the pursuit of one goal often means the neglect of another, some individuals would rather avoid than face up to goal conflict. Without goals one can never fail; thus fear of failure encourages avoidance of confronting goals. But it is unlikely that one can face up to what his job is and what it can become without facing up to what one seeks and values in life both personally and professionally. Further, this sort of painstaking analysis should help you answer the question—is the job of chairperson for me?

LIFE GOAL INVENTORY*

The purpose of this inventory is to give you an outline for looking at your life goals systematically. Your concern here should be to describe as fully as possible your aims and goals in all areas of your life. Consider all goals that are important to you, whether they are relatively easy or difficult to attain. Be honest with yourself. Having fun and taking life easy are just as legitimate life goals as being president. You will have a chance to rate the relative importance of your goals later. Now you should try to just discover *all* of the things that are important to you.

To help make your inventory complete, we have listed general goal areas on the following categories. They are:

A. Career satisfaction
B. Status and respect
C. Personal relationships
D. Leisure satisfactions
E. Learning and education
F. Spiritual growth and religion

*This personal and career planning exercise is an abridged version from David Kolb, Irwin Rubin, and James McIntyre, *Organizational Psychology: An Experiential Approach* (Englewood Cliffs, N.J.: Prentice-Hall, Inc., 1971), pp. 277-288. © 1971. Reprinted by permission.

These categories are only a general guide; feel free to change or redefine them in the way that best suits your own life. The unlabeled area is for whatever goals you think of that do not seem to fit into the other categories.

Fill out your own goals in the various sections of this inventory, making any redefinitions of the goal areas you feel necessary. Ignore for the time-being the three columns on the right-hand side of each page. Directions for filling out these columns appear at the end of the inventory.

A. Career Satisfaction

General Description: Your goals for your future job or career, including specific positions you want to hold. (Examine carefully your present or future role as a chairperson. Review that aspiration or status with other career and personal goals you select.)
Individual Redefinition:

SPECIFIC GOALS	IMPORTANCE (H,M,L)	EASE OF ATTAINMENT (H,M,L)	CONFLICT WITH OTHER GOALS (YES OR NO)
1.			
2.			
3.			

B. Status and Respect

To what groups do you want to belong? What are your goals in these groups? To what extent do you want to be respected by others? From whom do you want respect?
Individual Redefinition:

SPECIFIC GOALS	IMPORTANCE (H,M,L)	EASE OF ATTAINMENT (H,M,L)	CONFLICT WITH OTHER GOALS (YES OR NO)
1.			
2.			
3.			

C. Personal Relationships

Goals in your relationships with your colleagues, parents, friends, people in general.

Individual Redefinition:

SPECIFIC GOALS	IMPORTANCE (H,M,L)	EASE OF ATTAINMENT (H,M,L)	CONFLICT WITH OTHER GOALS (YES OR NO)
1.			
2.			
3.			

D. Leisure Satisfactions

Goals for your leisure time and pleasure activities—hobbies, sports, vacations; interests you want to develop.
Individual Redefinition:

SPECIFIC GOALS	IMPORTANCE (H,M,L)	EASE OF ATTAINMENT (H,M,L)	CONFLICT WITH OTHER GOALS (YES OR NO)
1.			
2.			
3.			

E. Learning and Education

What would you like to know more about? What skills do you want to develop? To what formal education do you aspire?
Individual Redefinition:

SPECIFIC GOALS	RATINGS		
1.			
2.			
3.			

F. Spiritual Growth and Religion

Goals for peace of mind, your search for meaning, your relation to the larger universe, religious service, devotional life.
Individual Redefinition:

SPECIFIC GOALS	RATINGS		

G. Other Personal Goals

Definition:

SPECIFIC GOALS	RATINGS		

DIRECTIONS FOR RATING GOALS

Now that you have completed the inventory, go back and rate the importance of each goal according to the following scheme:

H — Compared to my other goals this goal is very important.
M — This goal is moderately important.
L — A lot of other goals are more important than this one.

According to the following scheme, rate each goal on the probability that you will reach and/or maintain the satisfaction derived from it.

H — Compared with my other goals, I easily reach and maintain goal.
M — I reach and maintain this goal with moderate difficulty.
L — It would be very difficult to reach this goal.

In the last rating space, write whether or not (Yes or No) the goal is in conflict with any of your goals. Then fill out the Goal Conflicts sheet which follows.

Goal Conflicts

List the goals that are in conflict with one another. Which ones are the most serious? Which will require your personal attention to be resolved?

1.

2.

3.

4.

5.

Anticipating Conflicts

One of the major deterrents to goal accomplishment is the existence of conflict between goals. The person who ignores the potential conflicts between job and family, for instance, will probably end up abandoning goals because of the either/or nature of many decisions.

The cross-impact matrix is one method of anticipating possible conflicts. List your goals on both axes of the matrix in order of priority (Goal 1 is first on both horizontal and vertical axes). The next step is to estimate the potential impact of the vertical goal statements on the horizontal, using the following symbols:

(+) for a helpful impact ("working on Goal 1 will help me with Goal 3")
(−) for a hindering impact ("working on Goal 2 will make it more difficult to accomplish Goal 5")
(o) for no impact of any kind

Think about your goal statements carefully as you do this. Try to think of all possible conflict situations and enter them.

FIGURE 1-2. THE CROSS-IMPACT MATRIX*

	GOAL 1	GOAL 2	GOAL 3	GOAL 4	GOAL 5	GOAL 6	GOAL 7	GOAL 8
GOAL 1								
GOAL 2								
GOAL 3								
GOAL 4								
GOAL 5								
GOAL 6								
GOAL 7								
GOAL 8								

List conflicts in order of importance:
1.
2.
3.
4.
5.

*This portion of the personal and career planning exercise is from Kolb *et al.*, *op. cit.*, 2nd ed., 1974, p. 307.

Removing Obstacles

What personal shortcomings will keep me from achieving my goals?

1. _____

2. _____

3. _____

4. _____

What obstacles in the world will keep me from achieving my goals?

1. _____

2. _____

3. _____

4. _____

What can I do to eliminate or lessen the effect of any of these obstacles or short-comings? (Note that you need not eliminate the block entirely. Anything you can do to lessen the force of the obstacle will start you moving toward your goal.)

OBSTACLE	WHAT CAN I DO ABOUT IT?
_____	_____
_____	_____
_____	_____
_____	_____
_____	_____
_____	_____
_____	_____
_____	_____

What specific things can I do which will move me toward my goals?

1. _____

_____

_____

2. _____

_____

_____

3. _____

_____

_____

4. _____

_____

_____

5. _____

_____

_____

Circle the one which you are going to emphasize the most.

WHO CAN HELP ME ACHIEVE MY GOALS?   WHAT WILL I ASK OF THEM?

1. _____   _____

_____   _____

_____   _____

_____   _____

_____   _____

_____   _____

2. _____   _____

   _____   _____

   _____   _____

   _____   _____

   _____   _____

PROBLEMS THAT OFTEN ACCOMPANY THE CHAIRPERSON'S ROLE*

Chairpersons, particularly individuals new to this role, are often concerned with the following problems.* To what extent do they concern you? What can you do about them? Why not discuss some of these problems with your principal?

COMMON PROBLEMS	DOES THIS PROBLEM AFFECT YOU?
1. *You may feel uneasy* Many factors contribute to a general feeling of uneasiness in a leadership position. Introspection may lead to self-doubt as to your capability of handling the work. Although your principal and department members have expressed confidence in you, you may still have lingering doubts about your suitability for the role.	YES NO
2. *Your job specifications seem fuzzy* As you move up in the hierarchy, you will receive less explicit directions to guide and control your behavior. Innovation and independence are expected. Job security (tenure), which came with teaching, may not support you as a chairperson. More is expected of you as you move upward, and much of it will be after regular hours. Also, the results of bad decisions and poor performance are greater and more noticeable. If you were unprepared for a class presentation, the students knew. But if you miss a budget deadline, many people know and various activities may be delayed.	YES NO
3. *The higher you go, the less specialized your job tasks* Schools employ teachers as specialists. Department chairpersons are more than specialists. They are generalists, which means they must subordinate their special skills and acquire the broader orientation of the school's operation and problems. You may have been a master teacher of U.S. History, but you'll now have to see the social sciences, the whole school's curriculum, and how to work with adults in addition to teachers. Your inability to adjust from a specialist to a generalist role, and the responsibilities that accompany it, can cause you problems.	YES NO
4. *You are having difficulty deciding whether you are primarily a teacher or administrator* You cannot be everything to everybody. Yet, most school organization structures	

*This list of problems was suggested and elaborated by Anthony Gregorc.

identify the chairperson as part teacher and part supervisor. Teachers will expect you to represent them and listen (without telling) to their complaints against the administration. Meanwhile, the administration will want you to carry out their decisions and possibly evaluate your teachers. At times a tug of war develops and the chairperson pleads, "How can I win?" YES NO

5. *You are having difficulty handling confidential information*
As a chairperson, you will be subject to a growing number of increasingly complex constraints. Often ideas, concerns, or confidential information will be available to you on a "need to know" basis. You may even have to use this information in a decision. Because of this, you may occasionally feel frustration because you are unable to share the information. This often endangers your credibility with teachers. YES NO

6. *Sometimes decisions you make cause hard feelings among the staff or in other chairpersons*
All leaders at some time are forced to decide whether they should make a popular decision or uphold their own ideals or official duties at the expense of being liked. This can be a tough position but must be faced. YES NO

7. *You are not accepted as "one of the gang" any more*
Being a leader is going to separate you somewhat from your staff. Even if you want to be "one of the boys," they probably won't let you. This phenomenon occurs even if you were promoted from the ranks. YES NO

8. *You are having trouble filling another's shoes*
Unless a position was newly created, you had a predecessor. Depending upon his nature and style, there are remaining expectations on the minds of other people. He may have been indirect and subtle. You may be direct and open. There may be a certain amount of shock until your style becomes familiar. It may take some people a while to adjust. YES NO

DEFINING THE CHAIRPERSON'S ROLE

✿ CONCEPTS ✿

The chairperson's job can be described as to what he does, his position in the school, and what he is to accomplish. All of these should be parts of the chairperson's job description but the emphasis which each receives has much to do with helping and hindering his effectiveness as a leader. This chapter considers definitions of the chairperson's role and how they relate to his effectiveness. This chapter's purpose is to help chairpersons move away from viewing their jobs primarily as completing a set of tasks or fulfilling a set of relationships, to the view of combining these elements with a major concern for accomplishing objectives.

HOW JOB DESCRIPTION CAN HINDER EFFECTIVENESS

Job descriptions are such a part of the organization and life of school, business, and army that to suggest they may be more harmful than helpful is heresy. The problem in relationship to leadership effectiveness is not the idea of a job description but the way it is written and therefore the way it tends to focus job performance. Most job descriptions emphasize what the chairperson is to do but not what he is to accomplish. Exhibit A is a job description from a typical suburban high school.[1] It relies heavily on defining the job in terms of what the chairperson does by using such phrases as: conducts department meetings, visits classrooms, recommends materials for acquisition, attends formal meetings, implements administrative directives, orients teachers to policy, encourages enrollment in professional groups, develops plans, establishes standards, answers inquiries regarding courses, and prepares evaluation.

Such job descriptions map out the territory for the chairperson but reveal little about why he engages in these activities.[2] Further, a chairperson can fulfill each of the demands listed above and still be ineffective. He can conduct department meetings which lull people to sleep, he can visit classrooms and terrorize teachers, he can recommend material that requires busy work from students; he can attend formal meetings and think only of himself and his department; he can implement administrative directives rigidly; he can develop plans that remove discretion from teachers; he can establish uniform standards for all or he can conduct department meetings that produce creative decision; he can visit classrooms and help teachers achieve their objectives; he can recommend materials that encourage students to be thoughtful; he can attend formal meetings and work to build an integrated high school educational program; he can implement administrative directives flexibly; he can develop plans that involve people and facilitate their work; he can establish standards that help teachers to grow and develop as persons and professionals. What the chairperson does is important but alone it is not sufficient to judge his effectiveness. When the purpose of the activity and the outcome of the activity are included, one now has an effective job description.

EXHIBIT A

WEST SUBURBAN HIGH SCHOOL

Job Description for Department Chairpersons

The role of a Department Chairperson is one of both teacher and administrator. A Department Chairperson will spend part of each day in the classroom as a teacher. The remainder of each day, he will spend supervising his department. The Department Chairperson is an important member of an administrative team, including the Building Principal and the Dean of Students, which is responsible for the daily operation and control of the departments within the school.

The Department Chairperson serves teachers and students by creating and maintaining superior standards in teaching and learning. He induces needed change within his department while coordinating instruction therein. He integrates instructional plans with other departments and maintains constructive working relations with the administration as he works to establish more effective ways of individualized instruction.

While it is recognized that responsibility for the functions of the position rests with the Department Chairperson, it is also evident that the effectiveness of the position and the morale of the department is likely to hinge on the degree to which he involves teachers and students.

The Department Chairperson is directly responsible to the principal of the building in which he serves for attainment of the purposes of the school.

SPECIFIC DUTIES OF THE DEPARTMENT CHAIRMAN

A. Administrative Duties
1. Conducts regularly scheduled departmental meetings and holds supplementary meetings as may be necessary. A typewritten agenda and summary of each meeting will be submitted to the Building Principal and all other persons as directed by the Building Principal.

2. Visits classrooms, observes and evaluates the teachers of his department at work. On the basis of these visits, prepares a written report of his observations, discusses this report and his observations with the observed teacher. Confers as necessary with the Building Principal regarding the results of these observations and the report.

3. Recommends the acquisition of new or additional materials of instruction and textbooks for his department and assists as needed in the scheduling and coordinated usage of these materials.

4. Recommends to the Building Principal individual teaching assignments for the members of his department and presents a preliminary teaching schedule for his department.

5. Interviews candidates for departmental positions in accordance with instructions supplied by the Assistant to the Superintendent.

6. Responsible for certifying an annual inventory of instructional supplies and equipment, preparing a departmental budget request, approving all departmental requisitions, supervising the maintenance of department equipment, working with assigned personnel in the formulation of projects and/or request for available federal or state subsidies.

7. Attends formal meetings with building administrators so as to promote the integration of learning experiences of the students and the elimination of needless duplication of effort and experience.

8. Responsible to the Building Principal for taking all necessary "first steps" to correct each situation of error within his department whether such situations involve teacher error, student error or teacher-student error.

9. Responsible for all other duties assigned by the Building Principal or the Superintendent.

B. *Staff Personnel Duties*
   1. Responsible for the methods and procedures initiated by the staff members within his department.

   2. Discusses and implements administrative directives with his department and directs all necessary actions thereto.

   3. Orients teachers to departmental policy and other necessary details for the proper indoctrination within the department.

   4. Encourages and stimulates enrollment in professional groups and attendance at professional meetings.

   5. Works with departmental members in developing long-range plans for the department, planning and writing necessary course guides, and other methods of improving the total program of instruction.

   6. Supervises student teachers assigned to his department.

   7. Recommends to the guidance department the level placement of all students enrolled in his department after consultation with the classroom teacher.

   8. Assists counselors by advising procedures for individual students.

   9. Checks all progress cards sent out by teachers in his department.

   10. Gives all necessary assistance to substitute teachers serving in his department and supplies the assistant to the superintendent with a written evaluation of each substitute employed.

11. Delegates duties, as necessary, to accomplish departmental projects and goals.

12. Confers with individual teachers of his department as often as necessary in order to assure himself that his department is working within the guidelines of administrative directives.

C. *Student Personnel Duties*

1. Responsible for establishing standards and evaluating progress to determine the degree of achievement and need for curricular change.

2. Makes provision for testing programs within his department and is responsible for its design, execution, and distribution.

3. Responsible for recommending the initiation of all pilot courses.

4. Supervises the entrance of pupils or pupil work into school-approved contests and co-curricular activities pertaining to his department.

5. Works closely with the Dean of Students and counselors on matters of student discipline which may arise within his department.

D. *Curriculum Duties*

1. Answers all inquiries regarding courses of study.

2. Determines the need for modification and updating of the total departmental program through constant evaluation which involves the usage of all available objective data.

3. Prepares written evaluations, outlines summaries of particular courses as required by the board of education.

4. Aids in the preparation of in-service courses.

5. Integrates the work of the department into the total instructional program of the school.

6. Participates in formal meetings with the Building Principal and the curriculum committee.

7. Suggests books, magazines or pamphlets to be purchased by the school librarian.

8. Nominates and evaluates instructional materials and equipment to be purchased by the audio-visual director and the director of telecommunications.

HOW POSITION DESCRIPTIONS CAN HINDER EFFECTIVENESS

In many junior and senior high schools position descriptions are used singly, or, as in Exhibit A, in combination with job description to describe and define the chairperson's role. A position description focuses on the chairperson's organizational and interpersonal position in the school. Position descriptions are part of organizational charts and are characterized by such phrases as: responsible to the principal, approves requests from teacher, checks student progress cards, authorizes field trips, cooperates with central office supervisors, advises the counseling department, and reports to the assistant principal.

As with job descriptions, position descriptions alone are not very helpful except in those schools where rapid staff turnover prevails. Their value increases considerably when "why" and "for what purpose" questions are answered for each of the specified relationships.

How the Job Is Presently Conceived

The West Suburban High School job description, Exhibit A, represents a typical conception of the chairperson's job today. The description details an assortment of duties and responsibilities, many of which exceed chairpersons' present authority and influence. The job is seen as carrying out a series of functions with few hints provided as to what the objectives of tasks should be. Item A2 of Exhibit A, for example, states that the chairperson is expected to visit classrooms and file evaluation reports, but the anticipated outcome of such visits—their effect on teachers, students, instructional strategies and curriculum—is not mentioned. The possibilities for educational, organizational, supervisory and administrative leadership are built into the job description but they are seen more as duties than possibilities.

As in most job descriptions, administrative duties are listed first and educational duties toward the end. The chairperson's job is often seen as a pressure valve by the administration. Principals, their assistants, and many central office administrators are subjected to strong demands for administrative control from their superiors and from outside forces. Relief from this pressure is often sought by emphasizing administrative control at the chairperson level. Thus, pressing for meetings, checking department agendas, having evaluation reports filed, seeking promptness and thoroughness in materials, and budget requests and department discipline get top priority as job descriptions are developed.

It is not surprising that when chairpersons are asked to describe their role as it ought to be, they respond differently.

Chairpersons are likely to give prime importance to their instructional leadership and educational leadership responsibilities. Further, they typically feel they need more authority, more say, and more freedom to work in educational matters.

Role clarification for the chairperson position is needed and will come about as chairpersons, teachers, and administrators:

 focus less on chairpersons' duties and more on what chairpersons should accomplish

see the chairpersons' role as less of a safety valve for administrative and clerical functions and more as a comprehensive leadership role.

35

Apparent and Real Leadership Effectiveness

Leadership effectiveness can be deceptive. Some chairpersons are conscientious but seem not to be getting anywhere. Others may appear to be disorganized, but their departments are exciting places. One's accomplishments and objectives are associated with *leadership* effectiveness. How one looks and the images he projects are associated with *apparent* effectiveness. A third kind of effectiveness is *personal* effectiveness.

 Apparent effectiveness refers to those behaviors which give a person an air of effectiveness. A chairperson appears effective when he is usually on time, has a well planned agenda, responds promptly to requests, gets reports in on time, has a tidy desk or office, is good at public relations, makes quick decisions.

These characteristics may or may not be related to actual leadership effectiveness. Alone, they are not sufficient descriptions of the chairperson's job or adequate criteria for evaluation.

 Personal effectiveness refers to satisfying one's private objectives rather than department or school objectives.

A chairperson who wants to become the principal and who is progressing toward this end is being personally effective. One who successfully competes with a rival for power is personally effective. One who dominates department activities because of his own insecurity is personally effective. Sometimes personal effectiveness benefits the department and school and other times it does not. When it does, the chairperson is being an effective leader and at the same time reaping personal benefits. When it does not, the chairperson is being selfish and his actions are regressive to the school.

 Real leadership effectiveness is the extent to which the chairperson achieves objectives which are important to his department and school. Depending upon the emphasis, this effectiveness can be a result of educational, organizational, supervisory, administrative or team leadership. Sometimes the leader looks effective too and this is apparent effectiveness. Sometimes the leader reaps personal gains as a result of his success and this is personal effectiveness. But apparent effectiveness and personal effectiveness are not always leadership effectiveness.

Objectives Are Situationally Determined

Leadership by objectives, supervision by objectives, and management by objectives are the logical conclusions to the argument that what is needed is more concern with what the chairperson achieves than with his duties or his personality. This is not to say that leadership by objectives means the development of detailed performance criteria or detailed measurable objectives. Such specific objectives are appropriate on occasion but by and large the intention is more general. Often the only result is an awareness of what is being accomplished as chairpersons execute their duties.

Objectives for chairpersons are situationally specific. That is, they need to be developed as a result of interaction with local needs, philosophy, and assumptions, and in cooperation with teachers and administrators. Many objectives can be gained from this book but their appropriateness for a given chairperson depends on the specifics of his situation.

Criteria for Worthwhile Action

In the absence of specific objectives, chairpersons need to develop guidelines for deciding when one set of actions may be more worthwhile than others. Even when specific objectives are known, certain actions which define the way chairpersons work to achieve the objectives are more worthwhile or appropriate than others. Being concerned only with achieving the objectives is not enough, for some ways of operating are more acceptable than others and indeed some ways of operating are not acceptable at all.

Chairpersons will have clear objectives in mind sometimes, only general notions in mind other times. One might, for example, be working with a science teacher to help him manage more effectively six groups of students each working at different health stations, or to explore general possibilities of individualizing instruction. In each case, certain ways of working with this teacher are better than others.

Presented below is a list of criteria which chairpersons can use to plan and evaluate the worth of their behaviors as they work with teachers. Similar lists could be constructed for use in working with students, in deciding teaching strategies, and in working on organizational and administrative matters.[3]

All things being equal, one activity is more worthwhile than another if it:

—shows that the chairperson has confidence and trust in teachers.
—permits teachers to make informed choices in carrying out the activity and to reflect on the consequences of their choices.
—encourages teachers to discuss important things about their jobs with the chairperson.
—seeks teachers' ideas and opinions and makes use of them.
—builds positive attitudes toward department and school goals.
—increases the amount of responsibility felt by each member of the department for achieving department and school goals.
—generates favorable and cooperative attitudes by teachers toward other members of the department and school.
—results in relatively high satisfaction throughout the department with regard to membership in the department and school, supervisor, and one's own accomplishment.

—increases the amount of interaction and communication aimed at achieving department and school goals.

—helps teachers understand that teachers and schools exist to serve students and not the other way around.

—encourages teachers to willingly share information with others.

—shows that the chairperson knows and understands problems faced by teachers.

—permits teachers to exert a great deal of influence on department and school goals, methods and activities.

—increases the amount of information available to teachers.

—involves teachers fully in decisions related to their work.

—can be accomplished successfully by teachers at different levels of ability and with different interests.

—assumes that teachers are willing and able to give top performance if provided the opportunity to do so.

—recognizes the importance of authority vested in one's competencies and abilities rather than in one's school position or rank.

—reasonably stretches and challenges teachers.

—assumes that teachers are improvable and are interested in self-development as persons and professionals.

—helps teachers feel important, needed, useful, successful, proud, and respected.

—assumes that teachers prefer meaningful and important work to being idle, but idleness rather than routine or busy work.

One should not be deluded that all teachers are able to respond to these criteria. But most teachers can respond appropriately and many others can learn to respond. In judging the worthwhileness of activities chairpersons need to assume that all teachers can operate under these principles, but be prepared to make exceptions as they find individuals who cannot. It is important to note that the criteria are not abandoned but that individuals are exempted. Exceptions can be handled by helping teachers to learn how to respond, by releasing those who cannot respond after help, and by reassigning those who cannot be released to responsibilities where student contact is minimal, where working as an interdependent member of a team is not essential, and where their jobs can be structured to permit efficient close supervision. Suitable jobs might include working under supervision in instructional technology, curriculum administration, and media administration.

The list of criteria presented provides a set of statements, assumptions, and beliefs which can help chairpersons judge the worth of their actions apart from the accomplishment of specific objectives. Given the presence of specific objectives, a list of criteria such as this can help chairpersons select appropriate ways to achieve these objectives. What validates criteria? What makes one set of actions, behavior and activities more worthwhile than others? Some of the criteria are validated by values one holds about the nature of education, how schools should be operated and ways in which administrators and supervisors should behave. Other criteria are validated by theories, concepts and ideas from the social sciences.

Social Sciences as a Basis for Action

In discussing effectiveness the emphasis has been on the chairperson and his role. Yet effectiveness is related to the entire school, how that school is organized and operated, its effects on people and their feelings and the extent to which the school accomplishes its objectives. Chairpersons can provide the necessary building blocks of individual effectiveness to help the school become more effective as an organization.

In understanding how chairpersons contribute to school effectiveness, one needs to understand the relationships among three important sets of variables:

 Actions which chairpersons and administrators take and patterns of control and influence which they establish. This is an initiating, causal, or ACTION set of variables.

Feelings, attitudes, values and commitments of teachers and others as they react to the action variables. This is a mediating, intervening, or HUMAN EFFECTS set of variables.

Performance of people and effects on the school. This is an end-result, output or SCHOOL SUCCESS set of variables.

The relationships among these sets of variables are just beginning to be understood. A common practice that is now suspect is for administrators to work from action variables directly to school success variables. Social science theorists suggest that the attainment of school success variables is dependent upon the health of the school's human resources as reflected in teachers' skills, trust, support, commitment, and motivation.[4] The extent to which these human effects variables are positively or negatively affected is in turn dependent upon the ways in which action variables are expressed.

Inadequate theories of school effectiveness assume that the action variables directly affect the school success variables. For example, the way in which a chairperson involves teachers in decision-making directly improves their performance on the job.

An adequate theory of school effectiveness assumes that the human effects variables directly affect the school success variables. Action variables directly affect human effects variables and therefore only indirectly affect school success variables. For example, the way in which a chairperson involves teachers in decision-making increases or

39

decreases their identification with and commitment to objectives. It is this degree of identification and commitment that affects their performance on the job.

ACTION VARIABLES	HUMAN EFFECTS VARIABLES	SCHOOL SUCCESS VARIABLES
Leadership behavior Leadership assumptions Administrative strategies Department and school structure re: rules and regulations, formalization, flexibility, centralized decision-making, status systems Distribution and use of authority Department and school goals and objectives Educational program organization Teaching technology	Attitudes Perceptions Commitment levels Performance expectations Motivational forces Loyalty Satisfaction Values and goals Work group traditions	Quantity and quality of teacher performance Absence and turnover rates School-community relationships Teacher-administrator relationships Similar categories for students

The action variables are broader in scope than immediate chairperson behaviors. These behaviors are both cause and result of building a broader organizational and management system for the school.

There are at least two categories of objectives for chairpersons.

1) Objectives directly related to the school success variables, as:

Teachers will provide more options and alternatives for students.
Teachers will concentrate more on teaching concepts and structures of subjects and less time on teaching facts and information.
Teacher attendance at school will improve.

2) Objectives related to the human effects variables, as:

Teachers will find teaching to be more challenging and interesting.
Teachers will become more committed to individualizing instruction.
Teachers will increase their confidence and trust in the chairperson.

Human effects variables and school success variables in operation are often not distinguishable. As a chairperson works to help teachers develop more options, he does it in a way which increases their commitment to individualized instruction. This helps them find their jobs more challenging, and increases their confidence and trust in him. The more successful he is in meeting human effects objectives, the more successful he will be in meeting the options objectives. He could, of course, ignore the human effects variables and work directly at establishing options, but probably he will meet resistance.

The criteria proposed for judging worthwhile activities are based on the assumption that regardless of what the objectives are, they need to be pursued by chairpersons in a way which builds positive human effects.

ENDNOTES

1. Exhibit A is an edited document from a suburban Chicago high school of about 2,000 students.

2. W. J. Reddin's book *Managerial Effectiveness* (New York: McGraw-Hill, 1971), contributed much to thought on the relationship between job descriptions and leadership effectiveness.

3. This discussion of worthwhile activities was influenced by conversations with James Raths. See, for example, his article "Teaching without Specific Objectives," *Educational Leadership,* 28, 1971, pp. 714–20.

4. This discussion is based on Rensis Likert's theory of organizational effectiveness. See his *The Human Organization: Its Management and Value* (New York: McGraw-Hill, 1967). For an application and extension of this theory to schools see Thomas J. Sergiovanni and Robert J. Starratt, *Emerging Patterns of Supervision: Human Perspectives* (New York: McGraw-Hill, 1971), pp. 15–24, and Thomas J. Sergiovanni and Fred D. Carver, *The New School Executive: A Theory of Administration* (New York: Dodd, Mead, 1973), pp. 55–118.

❦ CHAPTER TWO ❦

❦ PRACTICES ❦

The chairperson's role has been traditionally defined through the job description, which continues to be an effective tool for sketching the chairperson's responsibilities and the behaviors expected of him. The job description should be considered the broad outline for the chairperson. But job descriptions alone often put the emphasis in the wrong places. As we tried to establish in the Concepts section of this chapter, doing is not equated with effectiveness. This section tries to help you to be more concerned with your effectiveness than with just what you do, and to help you further quality of your decisions and actions.

In this section we propose job targets and leadership by objectives as additional ways to define the chairperson's role. Identifying those key-results areas within one's job is an important part of the target-setting approach and an analysis of this technique is included. However, it is not always possible to find all of the important targets. Thus accompanying the use of key-results areas must be some framework for judging decisions and activities both in the absence and presence of targets. *Such judgments should be made on the basis of a leadership platform which serves to determine when one decision or activity is more worthwhile than others.*

Included in Section B are:

A principal's view of the chairperson's role
An analysis of key-results areas for chairpersons and the relationship of these
    areas to job targets
Leadership-targets questions
Target-setting worksheet
Guidelines for setting priorities and managing time
A position statement from the National Council of Social Studies
An inventory for charting department effectiveness

A PRINCIPAL'S VIEW

Principals can influence not only the content, scope and nature of the chairperson's job description but the operational job description as shown in the chairperson's daily activities. A high school principal prepared the following statement. He shares his views on why teachers seek the role of chairperson, what it takes to be successful, and how he sees the chairperson functioning. Several principals have read this statement and all agreed that the views expressed are not atypical.

Some of the views expressed may be helpful to you as you come to grips with why you sought the chairpersonship, what it requires from you and the key dimensions of your own role. Further, your principal's expectations for your behavior and his views of the chairperson's role are critical determiners of your effectiveness. This statement is intended therefore to focus your attention on your principal's view of your role.

1. To what extent is your principal likely to share the views presented here?
2. Do you know the views of your principal?
3. To what extent do you agree with this principal's statement?
4. To what extent do you agree with the views of your principal?
5. If this principal is "telling it like it is," do you still find the chairperson's role attractive?

So You Want To Be A Department Chairperson*

In my twenty-three years of administrative experience—as a high school principal for fourteen of those years and nine years as assistant superintendent working with four high schools—I have known many department chairpersons. I have worked with them directly and indirectly. I have known them professionally and socially. I have promoted them, fired them, praised them, criticized them—and because of these experiences feel that I have some ideas for what makes a good department chairperson.

I have entitled this article "So You Want to Be a Department Chairperson," and have elected to divide it into three parts. The first part will explore the question: "Why do you want to be a department chairperson," second, "What it takes to be a chairperson," and third, "What is the *real* role of the department chairperson?"

WHY DO YOU WANT TO BE A DEPARTMENT CHAIRPERSON? There are a number of reasons why a teacher aspires to the position of department chairperson. I will list most of them keeping in mind that they are not in any particular order because individuals vary in their reasons.

Stepping Stone. Some aspiring chairpersons feel the only road to an administrative position is to first be in charge of a department. Some chairmen become deans, then assistant principals, principal. Of course, there are others who become teachers again.

Goal Accomplishment. Teachers who feel strongly about their subject-matter goals believe that the way to improve the education of students enrolled in classes in their department is to be in charge so as to direct the activities.

*By Robert Wheat.

Financial Improvement.   More money is a major reason. Department chairpersons today are increasing their annual salaries from $1,000 to $2,000.

Lighter Teaching Load.   In many school districts department chairpersons teach a reduced number of classes. This appeals to many teachers who feel they can do a more effective job if they have to deal with a smaller number of students.

Feeling of Prestige.   There is always that desire to have mother say, "My son, the department chairman."

And the list goes on.   A mistaken notion that the job is less demanding than teaching, a longing for more "lounge-time," a desire for the personal coffee pot in the office of the department chairman, a more convenient time to get a haircut, first on the list to work the "paid" activities—these could be some of the reasons that have never surfaced in the research of "why do you want to be a chairperson?"

WHAT IT TAKES TO BE A CHAIRPERSON.   Chairpersons come in assorted sizes. They vary in dress, looks, attitudes, background; possibly no two are alike in all respects. If they are all different, what then is required to be a chairperson? And again, not in order of priority.

Knowledge of Subject Matter.   Although this is probably the most overrated trait, it is still an important one. He or she must command respect from his teachers and one way is to be knowledgeable in the field. I say that this is "probably overrated" because it will vary by departments. Most English department chairpersons "know" English— literature, grammar, speech. Very few department chairpersons in foreign language know another language except the one they are teaching. Physical education chairpersons are also not entirely trained in all activities, and recently another dimension has been added with the combination of boys' and girls' athletics. Athletic directors, who are also physical education chairpersons, have a distinct advantage in a personal way by being in charge of all facilities, but may spread themselves too thinly because of the number of activities in today's comprehensive high schools. Dual or even trio chairpersons—girls, boys, and athletic director—may create problems that could be studied further.
Science chairpersons may have similar difficulties, as do chairpersons in business education and industrial arts in regard to knowing the subject matter in their respective departments, while social studies, guidance, and possibly home economics usually experience fewer problems in this needed trait.

Successful Teaching Experience.   Department chairpersons, as other persons in education, cannot accurately measure the total learning experiences of the students, but they can possibly determine what may be valid methods of teaching. They *can,* if they have experience in the classroom in a variety of ways over a period of time. Just as I feel that a guidance counselor cannot be successful in counseling, as we know it in the high school today, unless he or she has had a good classroom background, I feel a chairperson cannot be effective in that role if he or she has not been thought of as a top-notch teacher.

Cooperative Attitude. The anti-establishment teacher will not make a good chairperson. The supervisor of a department may be classified as "neither fish nor fowl" but must learn to play the part of both when required to do so. The chairperson is the right hand of the principal for that department. They are a two-person team in many situations. The chairperson is also a teacher and will be identified with the teachers in many activities.

Ability to Organize. Just as a high school principal, or any other administrator is sometimes placed in the role of a clerk, so is the department chairperson. Notes to teachers, making out requisitions, taking inventory, filing purchase orders, approving invoices, answering memos from the administration are only a few of the duties that require an organized person. Attention to details falls into this category, and there is no substitute for this trait. If a chairperson does not have it he will fail because of criticism from all directions, above and below.

Strong Commitment to Education. This does not necessarily mean a "rah rah" guy for the State Education Association or the local union. But it does mean that he is convinced that a job needs to be done in the schools today and he can do it by working hard. It does mean less lounge time, but not necessarily abstinence. It does require longer hours—meeting with the teachers in the department, or the administration, or students, or parents, or the board of education, or citizens. It means attending professional conferences, sometimes at his own expense. It requires reading on his own, not just for a credit in a college class, and attempting to promote in-service training for others.

And Lots of Other "What It Takes." I suppose a book could be written on this part of the paper, but many of the traits are those required of all "successful" persons. Lest we forget good grooming, using "Scope," proper attire—these are important because of the close contact a chairperson has with so many different persons on a daily basis. A chairperson is more than a teacher in many, many ways—this he cannot forget.

WHAT IS THE REAL ROLE OF THE DEPARTMENT CHAIRPERSON? Some of the areas have been touched on in the preceding paragraphs. The real role is a complicated one. School districts have gone on strike because of differences of opinion as to what the chairperson should or should not be—or do.

The chairperson is limited in many ways in what he may accomplish. He can write course outlines, aims, objectives, goals. He can write, but not achieve, because his principal, his superintendent, and his board of education usually determine the final outcome. If he is a good salesman, a new course may be added—or dropped. He is not "god" in his department—this a new chairperson must be willing to accept.

Supplies and equipment seem to be major items discussed each year. Sometimes the chairperson can determine the amounts, but the usual procedure is for him to discuss the "type." Department chairmen do not *appropriate* monies for their department, they accept the budget allotment. This sometimes can be a true test of what role the chairperson plays. Does he blame the administration and board by declaring, "It's not my fault, teachers. I asked for all that you want"? Was he a successful salesman at budget time?

Department chairpersons for the most part do not enjoy one important role—that of the evaluator. Chairpersons do not like to "hire and fire," especially the latter, and yet in most schools the principal (back to that right hand again) depends almost entirely on the recommendation of the chairperson. It is an expected duty, and regardless of the personal feeling of the chairperson about face-to-face "conflict" in some instances, it is a job that has to be done. A poor teacher that is retained in the department because of the attitude "I don't want to hurt anybody" may cause the chairperson many problems, sometimes covering a period of many years.

Possibly this third phase of this paper could be summarized by listing the roles or duties a chairperson may be called upon to assume, and as educators like to repeat, not in order of priority. Many of these activities come about because of the leadership role of the chairperson with other teachers in the school, even if the duties by nature are not part of the assigned job.

1. evaluate teachers
2. make out requisitions
3. file purchase orders
4. approve invoices
5. take inventory
6. submit budget requests
7. approve conference and travel requests
8. recommend teachers for summer school
9. attend administrative meetings with principal
10. recommend textbooks for adoption
11. serve on in-service institute committees
12. submit "end of year" departmental report
13. participate in "opening of school" activities
14. recommend curriculum revisions
15. serve on negotiating committees
16. make oral reports at board of education meetings
17. participate in parental conferences
18. make sure teachers in department turn in report cards
19. interview prospective teachers
20. attend "open house" activities in a leadership role
21. in multi-high school districts coordinate with other chairpersons
22. assist guidance department in preparing orientation booklets
23. advise teachers on disciplinary cases
24. sit in as a representative on grievances filed
25. be involved in activities sponsored by State High School Association

26. subscribe to professional journals in subject area
27. advise librarian on books and periodicals needed for resource materials
28. insure a procedure for audio-visual equipment use in the department
29. design key system accounting for special lab desks, filing cabinets, equipment in department
30. check over lesson plan books if used in the school

The department chairpersons probably are assigned additional duties in their own districts, but the preceding list should be representative. It should be emphasized that mere participation in these jobs does not necessarily guarantee a successful and effective chairperson. The school supervisor in this role is not unlike his counterparts in industry in many respects. Success depends on how well he relates to all levels, but especially his fellow teachers and his building administration, namely the high school principal.

KEY-RESULTS AREAS IN YOUR ROLE

Effectiveness in your job as chairperson requires performing critical tasks and achieving important targets. Critical and important are the words to remember because you will not have unlimited time to be all things to everyone. Indeed each task you pursue competes for your time and talent with other tasks. Effectiveness, you will find, is determined less by the number of tasks you complete and more by the importance of these tasks. Peter Drucker states the case this way:*

Effective executives concentrate on the few major areas where superior performance will produce outstanding results. They force themselves to set priorities and stay with their priority decisions. They know that they have no choice but to do first things first—and second things not at all. The alternative is to get nothing done.

Some areas of your job are more important than others and within these areas certain tasks are more critical than others. Identifying these key areas where results will greatly affect department and school goals is a critical aspect of defining one's role and of adopting a leadership targets orientation to one's job.

Determining Your Key-Results Areas

Determining key-results areas for your role is a cooperative enterprise for the chairpersons as a group, the school principal and perhaps coordinators and supervisors from the central office. Key-results areas for any one particular chairpersonship will be somewhat like others but should also be different enough to account for such variances as

*Peter Drucker, *The Effective Executive* (New York: Harper and Row, 1966), p. 24.

department objectives, types of students, kind of staff, pattern or flow of work, scheduling, and setting.

In beginning to think about your key-results areas, ask yourself the following questions:

1. What does the chairperson's position contribute (to the school) which is different than other positions?

2. Why is this position needed at all?

3. If the chairperson's position were eliminated *completely,* what would change?

4. As chairperson what authority do I really have? In what areas?

5. What would change in the department or school if I were maximally effective as a chairperson?

6. How would I know without anyone telling me when I am being effective?

7. How do I actually spend my time?

8. How would I like to spend my time?

9. What are the two or three most critical things that my principal expects of me?

10. What are the two or three most critical things that the teachers expect of me?

From Key-Results Areas to Job Targets

Five broad key-results areas can be identified for your role: educational, organizational, supervisory, administrative and team leadership. Within each of these broad areas, specific key-results areas need to be defined. Each area then becomes the basis for identifying your general responsibilities, goals and objectives. From there, targets are selected for focus in a given time, perhaps every three months, semester or year. As one pursues a target, probable outcomes are then determined in order to aid the planning of programs and activities. At the end of the agreed-upon time, a review of outcomes and activities can identify what was accomplished and can help select new targets for the next time.

One should also try to discover, define, and describe outcomes that were not originally anticipated. This process, from identifying key-results areas to describing both anticipated and unanticipated outcomes for a given time, takes place within a framework of decisions which are consistent with one's leadership platform and the department's educational platform (the latter concept is discussed in Chapters 5 and 10). The cycle looks like this:

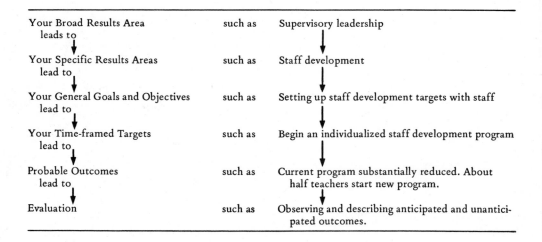

Your Broad Results Area leads to	such as	Supervisory leadership
Your Specific Results Areas lead to	such as	Staff development
Your General Goals and Objectives lead to	such as	Setting up staff development targets with staff
Your Time-framed Targets lead to	such as	Begin an individualized staff development program
Probable Outcomes lead to	such as	Current program substantially reduced. About half teachers start new program.
Evaluation	such as	Observing and describing anticipated and unanticipated outcomes.

EXAMPLES OF KEY-RESULTS AREAS. Key-results areas and job targets for three broad results areas are shown schematically below. These are provided to show you how one might proceed through the cycle and to suggest a format for recording and analyzing results areas, targets and outcomes. As one moves from left to right in the three sample schematics, the less applicable to your situation will likely be the given suggestions. Specific targets are situationally determined and must come from you as you establish department needs.

For each of your broad results areas, it is important to go through each of the three steps shown in the schematic. You should clearly establish your broad key-results areas, specific results areas, and general goals and objectives. Specific targets within a given time frame, however, should be selected with careful attention to time constraints.

KEY RESULTS AREAS AND JOB TARGETS—EDUCATIONAL LEADERSHIP AREA

MY BROAD RESULTS AREA	MY SPECIFIC RESULTS AREA	MY GENERAL GOALS AND OBJECTIVES	MY TARGETS FOR THIS YEAR	PROBABLE OUTCOMES OR RESULTS
1.0 Educational Leadership Area	1.1 Goals, Objectives, Curriculum			
	1.2 Educational Platform	1.21 Maintenance of Commitment	1.211	1.2211 Change in platform statements
			1.212	1.2212 Change in classroom practices
		1.22 Evaluation for Relevance	1.221 Staff review of individualized instruction platform statements	
			1.222 Examine grading practices for consistency with platform	
	1.3			
	1.4 Clinical Supervision	1.41 Staff acceptance and participation in C.S.	1.411 Introduce new teachers to the process of C.S.	1.4121
			1.412 Establish group responsibility for implementing	1.4122 At least two teachers will begin C.S. together
		1.42	1.421	
			1.422	
	1.5			

Evaluation:

1. Describe the outcomes. To what extent were predicted outcomes achieved? Can you give examples or show evidence of their achievement?

2. What outcomes *not* predicted were observed?

51

KEY RESULTS AREAS AND JOB TARGETS—SUPERVISORY LEADERSHIP AREA

MY BROAD RESULTS AREA	MY SPECIFIC RESULTS AREA	MY GENERAL GOALS AND OBJECTIVES	MY TARGETS FOR THIS YEAR	PROBABLE OUTCOMES OR RESULTS
2.0 Supervisory Leadership Area	2.1 Staff, morale, satisfaction			
	2.2 Staff development	2.21 Review S.D. needs	2.211	2.2211 50% participation
			2.212	2.2212 S.D. program individualized
		2.22 Set S.D. targets with staff	2.221 Begin individualized S.D. program	
			2.222 Reduce current program	
	2.3			
	2.4 Personnel function	2.41 Recruitment	2.411 Develop job specs for new position	2.4121 Staff will participate in interview
			2.412 Involve staff in screening & selection	2.4122 Staff will participate in selection
		2.42 Orientation	2.421	
			2.422	

Evaluation:

1. Describe the outcomes. To what extent were predicted outcomes achieved? Can you give examples or show evidence of their achievement?

2. What outcomes *not* predicted were observed?

KEY RESULTS AREAS AND JOB TARGETS—ORGANIZATIONAL LEADERSHIP AREA

MY BROAD RESULTS AREA	MY SPECIFIC RESULTS AREA	MY GENERAL GOALS AND OBJECTIVES	MY TARGETS FOR THIS YEAR	PROBABLE OUTCOMES OR RESULTS
3.0 Organizational Leadership Area	3.1 Shared decision-making	3.21 Evaluating department meetings	3.211	3.2211 Teachers will suggest agenda items
			3.212	3.2212 Teacher talk at meetings will increase
	3.2 Department meetings	3.22 Increase faculty participation and commitment	3.221 Develop open agenda system	
			3.222 Elect or appoint moderator to "chair" meetings	
	3.3	3.41 Continuous review of policies and procedures	3.411 Compare policies for consistency with educational platform	3.4121 Students will criticize & suggest re: policies in question
	3.4 Policies and procedures		3.412 Get students' reaction to Dept. independent study and elective policies	
	3.5	3.42	3.421	3.4122 Students will comply willingly with policies
			3.422	

Evaluation:

1. Describe the outcomes. To what extent were predicted outcomes achieved? Can you give examples or show evidence of their achievement?

2. What outcomes *not* predicted were observed?

53

KEY RESULTS AREAS AND JOB TARGETS—_____ AREA

MY BROAD
RESULTS
AREA

MY SPECIFIC
RESULTS
AREA

MY GENERAL
GOALS AND
OBJECTIVES

MY TARGETS
FOR THIS
YEAR

PROBABLE
OUTCOMES OR
RESULTS

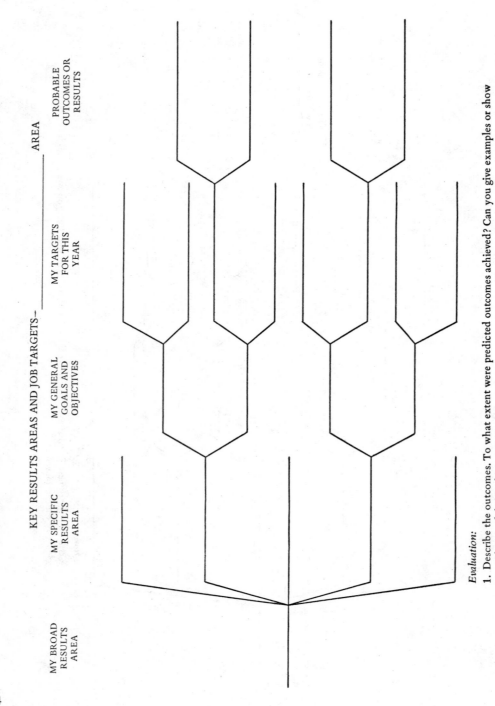

Evaluation:

1. Describe the outcomes. To what extent were predicted outcomes achieved? Can you give examples or show evidence of their achievement?

2. What outcomes *not* predicted were observed?

54

DEFINING THE CHAIRPERSON'S ROLE: PRACTICES

It is better to select a few targets and give them adequate attention than to select many targets which can only be dealt with superficially. You will learn more about time management later in this section.

Guidelines for Evaluating Specific Results Areas

The answers to the following questions should help you to determine the appropriateness of specific results areas selected.

1. Is there agreement within your department as to the importance of specific results areas?

2. Is there agreement among department chairpersons?

3. Is there agreement with your principal?

4. Do the specific results areas lead to the establishment of job targets?

5. Are specific results areas within the limits of your authority and responsibility?

6. Are the specific results areas within the limits of your competence?

LEADERSHIP TARGETS QUESTIONS

Much attention has been given to the concept of management by objectives (MBO) in recent education literature.* Our discussion of target setting for chairpersons fits within the general MBO concept but differs in a number of respects. MBO requires a system-wide or at least school-wide commitment to setting planned, linked objectives at

---

*The general source most often quoted is George Odiorne, *Management by Objectives* (New York: Pitman, 1965). More specific is Steven Knezevich, *Management by Objectives and Results* (Washington, D.C.: AASA National Academy for School Executives, 1973).

all levels. Desirable as this may be, the reality is that system-wide efforts are difficult to implement and are not widespread.

Here is a simplified way in which chairpersons, alone, with their principal, or with other chairpersons, may focus on targets.

1. What is the target-setting approach?
   The target-setting approach is how the chairperson, after analyzing the broad key-results areas in his job, notes specific results areas and tasks he intends to perform or targets he intends to accomplish, and his anticipated results.

2. What can the target-setting approach do?
   Four important benefits of target-setting are: an expanded and enriched description of one's job; direction and purpose for the chairperson, subordinates and superiors; the establishment of priorities for the management of the chairperson's time; and evaluation and feedback for the chairperson.

3. What can't target-setting do?
   Target-setting will not make the ineffective chairperson effective, but can make the effective chairperson more effective. Target-setting is not a substitute for competence, compassion, leadership ability, or commitment.

4. Is it necessary that targets be set so that outputs are measurable? Are targets the same as behavioral objectives?
   Targets and anticipated results descriptions need not follow any particular set of rules. Sometimes one needs operational and measurable performance objectives; at other times, more general statements of intents are needed. Often, you will not even be sure of the results you seek. This statement is unorthodox but it describes a common and acceptable predicament.
   Consider, for example, the chairperson dissatisfied with present grading practices. He might set as a target the establishment of informal meetings with students and teachers to discuss the problem together. True believers in performance objectives might propose that the chairperson state, "Students and teachers will discuss the problem together," or, "Five alternatives will be generated," but the substantive outcomes in which we are interested defy being nailed down and indeed await discovery in the process of the meetings.

TARGET-SETTING WORKSHEET

Use this worksheet to plan or effect steps and activities needed to reach targets. The worksheet asks you to specify your target and your action plans, and to keep a record of estimated and actual time spent in various stages of your plans and total time spent as you pursue a particular target. Further, the worksheet enables you to link the target to your broad results areas, and to evaluate each step in your plan.

Use the worksheet to:

1. Plan and evaluate strategies and steps needed to achieve your targets.
2. Schedule and calendar your plan.
3. Record the estimated and actual time spent on various stages of your plan, and the total time spent.
4. Keep a yearly record of time you spend on targets in each of your specific and broad key-results areas. Use the yearly record to contrast actual time spent with your intents and priorities.

TARGET-SETTING WORKSHEET

My Target: _____

My Outcomes, Results: _____

My Completion Date: _____

Check Appropriate Broad Key-Results Areas.	
Educational	_____
Organizational	_____
Supervisory	_____
Administrative	_____
Team	_____

Approximate Time in Hours Needed _____ My Specific Key-Results Area _____

STEPS I NEED TO TAKE THINGS I NEED TO DO	EST. TIME	BEGIN WHEN	FINISH WHEN	WHAT WILL THIS STEP ACCOMPLISH?	ACTUAL TIME	ACTUAL RESULTS
1.						
2.						
3.						
4.						
5.						

Total Time on This Target ➔ | Keep a continuous record of time spent by results areas.

GUIDELINES FOR SETTING PRIORITIES AND MANAGING TIME

The complex components of leadership effectiveness are difficult to reduce to simple plans. But maximum effectiveness is impossible without adequate planning and management of time. As a chairperson, you join a cadre of educational workers who work hard and competently for long hours on seemingly endless tasks. Indeed, it may be virtually impossible to find more time to put into the job—to meet present and new demands—without dangerously eroding personal and family life.

Chances also are, you are not as effective as you could or should be. This statement may seem unfair. Even though, when one is at the limit of investment in his job he is unlikely to find additional time, he still can increase his effectiveness by managing time more efficiently.

Time Management

To be realistic, time management will increase one's effectiveness substantially, but not by 100 percent or even by 50 percent. Even the most effective chairperson only partially controls his time. You control your time when it is discretionary time to be used according to your judgment, that is, when it is yours to decide how it will be invested or spent. You do not control your time when you are reacting to others, to your environment, to situations and conditions determined by others, or when you are engaged in routine organizational tasks and demands programmed for you by the larger school environment within which you work. These sorts of demands on your time will not go away.

The effective chairperson spends about two-thirds of his time on uncontrolled events; the other one-third is spent at his discretion. He controls about one-third of his time.

Let's assume that you manage to increase your time control from 10 to 15 percent. How much more effective are you likely to be? A 5 percent increase in time control should result in a 10 percent increase in effectiveness. Shooting for a 30 percent time control ought to be your goal. This is attainable and realistic and upon reaching it there will be a noticeable change in your effectiveness.

Setting Priorities

Increasing your time control is only part of your problem. Once you obtain more discretionary time, how do you use it wisely to maximize benefits for yourself and your school? This involves planning.

Perhaps the most important principle of good planning is the setting of priorities. (Refer back to Peter Drucker's advice, p. 48.)

Priority setting depends upon understanding the key-results areas in your job and your major purposes. Chairpersons sometimes treat these issues as academic questions. One could develop a list of critical job components, purposes, and outcomes for the chairpersonship and even incorporate them into a totally unrealistic job description. What is important is not what one says his purposes are but what purposes are inferred from what he does and how he spends his time.

If you are serious about beginning a time management and planning program, the first step is to find out what your real job components, purposes, and outcomes are by inferring them from what you do and from how you spend your time. Keep a detailed log of your activities over several weeks.

Analysis of such logs often suggests that chairpersons are doers of tasks rather than managers or supervisory leaders of people. In discussions with chairpersons too little distinction is often made between doing and supervisory leadership. You merely do tasks if your activities could be delegated to another individual. You provide leadership when you help others to develop personally and professionally, to improve their performance, to adopt new ways of working, to learn, to solve problems. Leadership has to do with getting results through people. The effective chairperson is one who obtains planned results through people.

The way schools operate, the tasks are often crisis-oriented; frequently by default they become top priority. Sometimes the tasks are systems-oriented; they take priority because delays upset the bureaucratic system. For example, a chairperson plans to spend time with a teacher who is experimenting with an individually-paced chemistry program. But he receives an urgent request to prepare a two-year staff needs projection for the principal. Then a parent calls to request a meeting that afternoon. Apparently, a teacher detained his youngster for writing obscene words on his note book and the parent feels that this represents an infringement of free speech. The first instance is systems-oriented. Lack of response to this request upsets someone else's timetable. The second instance is crisis-oriented. Many chairpersons seem programmed to respond immediately to pressure from the school community.

Consider the following propositions: 1) Top priority needs to go to leadership functions, not to doing tasks; 2) One important way to lead more is by doing less; and 3) In any administrative role which contains leadership responsibilities, increased effectiveness is associated with doing less.

It is unrealistic to assume that the doing side of your job is going to disappear, but you will not attend properly to the leadership side of your job without establishing priorities linked to the analysis of your job's major components and key-results areas.

Try keeping a log to determine how you spend your time. This will permit you by inference to establish what the actual components, purposes, and outcomes of your job are.

Then analyze your key-results areas and determine your major purposes. Base your priorities upon the difference between your inferences and your ideals. Priorities should be few, perhaps no more than three primary and six secondary priorities for the year. Having too many priorities may be worse than having none.

Focus on your leadership responsibilities and leave the doing tasks to the 60 percent of time you don't control. Avoid setting objectives in areas of routine activity. Administering the teacher evaluative program is a routine function and does not call for an objective. Helping teachers to set targets for themselves or teaching them to use self-evaluation methods and activities, however, are practices which qualify as leadership objectives.

Rational analysis is important to the development of priorities but courage may be even more important to the process. Indeed, courage in selecting priorities is the ingredient which distinguishes ordinary leaders from great leaders. In selecting priorities Peter Drucker advises:*

> *Pick the future against the past; Focus on opportunity rather than on problems; Choose your own direction—rather than climb on the bandwagon; and aim high, aim for something that will make a difference, rather than for something that is "safe" and easy to do.*

Once priorities are established, set a specific time for planning. Priorities give us general guidelines—they suggest the major avenues to our work. Plans suggest the specifics with which we will deal within a general time. The success of any planning depends upon the establishment of regular times for planning. A yearly plan ought to be developed with monthly times set aside for developing an operational plan. This process needs to be supplemented by a weekly planning session. Friday is good for weekly planning; it permits stock-taking for the previous week and a projection of next week's activities.

*Ibid, p. 111.

From a planning session should come a written sketch or outline of projected targets and activities. A written plan is more binding, less apt to be forgotten, than mental plans. Further, a written plan enables stock-taking at the end of the planning time frame. Plans should be kept simple enough to be readily understood by most teachers or others with whom you work. Yearly plans will be more comprehensive than monthly or weekly plans. Weekly plans should be kept to one page whenever possible.

In summary, the yearly plan speaks to priorities, broad goals, and major anticipated accomplishments. The monthly plan is a time map for carrying out your yearly plan. The weekly plan is an operational plan from which you work.

Written plans should deal with the "whats," "hows," and "whens." The "whats" refer to objectives, targets, outcomes, or goals that you seek. The "hows" are strategies for achieving these anticipated outcomes. The "whens" refer to the development of a schedule or a timetable for implementing your strategy.

For additional help, refer to Leadership Targets and to the Target-Setting Work Sheet. See also the concepts and practices section of the Administrative Leadership chapter (Chapter 8), particularly for help in scheduling your time.

A REPRESENTATIVE POSITION STATEMENT

To help yourself identify role dimensions, read position papers available from professional organizations, such as the following statement.* Similar statements are likely to be available from the professional organization which represents your teaching area.

Supervision In Social Studies—A Position Statement

The interaction between teachers and students is the most vital element of an educational system. Supervision is justifiable only to the extent that it facilitates this interaction. Supervision in social studies appears in different forms, among these are the department chairman and the social studies supervisor. If supervisory personnel are to be helpful to the classroom teacher they must be well-qualified, their task must be defined clearly and they must operate under optimal conditions. The following standards for social studies supervisors have been adopted by the Social Studies Supervisors Association of the National Council for the Social Studies.

A. *Qualifications*
 1. The supervisor or chairperson should be an individual who has demonstrated a high degree of competency in teaching social studies.
    a. The department chairperson should be the initial contact for the social studies teacher in matters of personnel, curriculum, media, and overall teaching conditions.

---

*"Standards for Social Studies Supervisors," Section A: *Qualifications and Conditions of Employment.* From the Constitution of Social Studies Supervisors Association of the National Council for the Social Studies.

b. The department chairperson should encourage and support innovative teachers by providing them with materials and assistance.

c. The department chairperson should disseminate information concerning recent research and pertinent developments in social studies education.

d. The department chairperson should schedule regular departmental meetings with agendas developed cooperatively with the teachers.

e. The department chairperson should prepare with teachers a departmental budget, and submit it to the school administration.

f. The department chairperson should participate in the interviewing and hiring of new teachers for the department.

g. The department chairperson should ensure that social studies teachers are assigned appropriately.

h. The department chairperson should participate in the evaluation of teachers in the department for tenure recommendations or other purposes. This evaluation should be based on the standards of the National Council for the Social Studies.

i. The department chairperson should initiate in-service education programs for teachers.

j. The department chairperson should encourage teachers to take advantage of educational opportunities by budgeting support in such ways as substitute teachers and reimbursement of expenses.

k. The department chairperson should be involved in the selection of members of the department for special rewards and educational opportunities.

2. The social studies supervisor should assume responsibility in the following areas:

a. The supervisor should hold explanatory conferences with individual teachers and groups of teachers to assess the status of social studies teaching within his or her area of influence.

b. The supervisor should initiate and sustain new programs which reflect current trends.

c. The supervisor should be prepared to assist local schools or districts in innovative efforts by assisting them in obtaining funds and expert consultation.

d. The supervisor should assist in the establishment of a coordinated kindergarten-through-grade-twelve social studies program, especially at the local level.

Conditions of Employment

1. Teachers should have a voice in the selection of their department chairperson.

2. The social studies department chairperson should teach at least one class daily. The maximum number of classes taught will depend on department size; if there are more teachers, he or she will have fewer teaching responsibilities.

3. The social studies department chairperson must have one duty-free period for lunch, one period for preparation, and one period for supervisory duties daily. Supervisory periods should be increased at the rate of one period per

61

eight teachers in the department. Teaching responsibilities would be reduced accordingly.

4. The social studies supervisor has broad responsibilities which should be clearly defined prior to employment. An adequate number of staff members should be provided to assist in the performance of these responsibilities.

5. The supervisor should receive a twelve-month appointment. During the summer the supervisor should plan and conduct creative and stimulating in-service programs directed toward the improvement of both teaching and curriculum.

6. The supervisor should attend local, state, and national meetings of professional organizations with all expenses paid. Attendance will enable the supervisor to fulfill responsibilities as an innovator and disseminator of information.

DEPARTMENT EFFECTIVENESS INVENTORY

It should be clear that department effectiveness is no accident, but takes careful planning and determined effort. This inventory can help you to assess your department's present effectiveness and to determine what remains to be done.

Positive responses to less than half the items suggest that much work needs to be done. It might be useful to ask teachers to respond to the inventory and to use their responses as a basis for discussion and department planning. The inventory can serve as a needs assessment checklist to help you identify specific key-results areas and targets. Periodically checking the inventory can help provide you with a progress record.

Department Inventory*

I. *DOES THE DEPARTMENT HAVE AN INNOVATIVE CLIMATE?*

YES   NO

____ ____ 1. Do department members feel that trying out new approaches, materials, and techniques is the "thing to do"?

____ ____ 2. Do department meetings focus largely on substantive issues?

____ ____ 3. Do most teachers in the department borrow and share ideas for the classroom during the semester?

____ ____ 4. Do teachers talk about their teaching areas when they get together informally at school?

____ ____ 5. Do most department members know what their colleagues are doing?

____ ____ 6. Do teachers sit in on each other's classes?

____ ____ 7. Is the department open to student input about course offerings and teaching methods?

*Adapted from a checklist developed by Janet Eyler and included in *A Handbook for Departmental Leadership in Social Studies.* Indiana University, Social Studies Development Center, 1975, pp. 17–20.

—— —— 8. Nearly all of the teachers in the department would agree with my assessment.

—— —— 9. My principal would agree with my assessment.

II. ARE DEPARTMENT MEMBERS SKILLED AT SOLVING PROBLEMS TOGETHER?

YES   NO

—— —— 1. Is the department sensitive to needs for change, so that important decisions are made carefully and problems are considered before a crisis is present?

—— —— 2. Is a lot accomplished when the department meets?

—— —— 3. Does the group face important issues?

—— —— 4. Does the department generate a variety of solutions before narrowing consideration to one or two?

—— —— 5. Do all members of the group make important contributions?

—— —— 6. When conflicts arise, are they resolved by testing the suggestions, looking for evidence, seeking more information?

—— —— 7. Is there a systematic procedure for tackling problems and tasks?

—— —— 8. Do department members frequently solve problems or accomplish goals by working with colleagues?

—— —— 9. Nearly all of the teachers in the department would agree with my assessment.

—— —— 10. My principal would agree with my assessment.

III. IS THE DEPARTMENT PART OF AN INFORMATION NETWORK?

YES   NO

—— —— 1. Are department members active in teaching-area professional organizations?

—— —— 2. Does the department receive professional journals and newsletters?

—— —— 3. Does the department have a plan for seeing that newsletters, journals or other sources of new input get to members for whom they might be relevant?

—— —— 4. Does the department have easy access to a resource center of materials for classroom use?

—— —— 5. Are teachers in the department in contact with their teaching-area counterparts in other schools?

—— —— 6. Do members attend workshops, conventions, and other opportunities for professional growth?

—— —— 7. Does the department have a professional library in the building?

—— —— 8. Are there resource personnel available who can track down articles and materials relevant to projects undertaken by the department?

—— —— 9. Does the department receive news of opportunities and information about teaching materials from a district coordinator or supervisor?

_____ _____ 10. Nearly all of the teachers in the department would agree with my assessment.

_____ _____ 11. My principal would agree with my assessment.

IV. *DOES THE SCHOOL STRUCTURE SUPPORT INNOVATIVE TEACHING?*

A. *Does the department make major decisions about its program?*

YES   NO

_____ _____ 1. Does the department have a budget of its own?

_____ _____ 2. Does the department contribute significantly to decisions involving major reorganization or curriculum change?

_____ _____ 3. Does the department choose the materials used in its classrooms?

_____ _____ 4. Does the department plan course offerings?

_____ _____ 5. Does the department determine or influence the nature of in-service day activities?

_____ _____ 6. Does the department have a voice in selection of a department head?

_____ _____ 7. Does the department take an active part in interviewing and hiring new members?

B. *Does the department have resources for working together?*

YES   NO

_____ _____ 1. Does the department have a place to work together?

_____ _____ 2. Is time allotted for frequent department meetings?

_____ _____ 3. Do department members (at least those teaching the same subject) have a simultaneous free period?

_____ _____ 4. Is time provided for in-service days or other continuing education?

_____ _____ 5. Does the department head have extra time and other support for carrying out his duties?

_____ _____ 6. Are secretarial help and adequate duplicating equipment provided for teachers producing supplementary materials?

_____ _____ 7. Does the system provide financial support and/or release time to teachers who wish to attend professional conferences or to visit other schools?

_____ _____ 8. Can department members order supplementary materials for the classroom or library?

_____ _____ 9. Does the library provide a good collection of teaching area resources for students?

_____ _____ 10. Does the building design provide instructional flexibility?

_____ _____ 11. Are there facilities for conferring with students individually?

C. *Are the school and district climate supportive?*

YES   NO

—— —— 1. Do the principal and staff clearly support innovation?

—— —— 2. Is the supervisor's office a useful source of ideas and information?

—— —— 3. Does the local press usually respond positively to developments in the schools?

—— —— 4. Do teachers feel that the community is proud of its schools?

—— —— 5. Does the school inform parents about innovations and activities?

—— —— 6. Nearly all of the teachers in the department would agree with my assessment.

—— —— 7. My principal would agree with my assessment.

SCORECARD

Below 28 You have your work cut out for you.

29–39 You are making progress.

40–49 Your department has the climate needed for effective functioning.

Over 49 Your department is a bell-ringer.

PART TWO

THE CHAIRPERSON'S ORGANIZATIONAL LEADERSHIP FUNCTIONS

CHAPTER THREE

UNDERSTANDING THE SCHOOL AS A FORMAL ORGANIZATION

CONCEPTS

We live in an organized world and the world is full of organizations. "Children are born into the physical confines of large medical organizations—hospitals—spend much of their growing years in even larger organizations—schools—and graduate, most of them, into the employ of even larger businesses or government organizations. Many of our large high schools are as populous as small towns, universities are veritable cities, and multinational corporations are virtual native states."[1]

Understanding how organizations work is necessary if chairpersons are to exercise their leadership responsibilities. In this chapter, we shall examine organizations' key aspects that relate to the chairperson's work. These are: (1) the characteristics of bureaucracy as applied to schools; (2) who benefits from the organization, and (3) how control is obtained and power expressed. Concepts and principles are examined with reference to organizational theory and as they apply to modern junior and senior high schools.

THE COMPLEX ORGANIZATION: BEAUTY OR BEAST?

Some see the modern organization as a beautiful accomplishment; others see a beast which dehumanizes man's spirit. Chairpersons should not be advocates or enemies of organizations but should accept the reality that most secondary schools are fairly complex organizations and as such provide us with benefits and costs. Certain goals, objectives, and educational activities can only be pursued in an organized setting but others suffer because of this organized setting. Are the benefits worth the cost? Can the costs be lived with? Are the benefits of long-term value? Are some costs so high that benefits need to be foresaken?

The relevant organizational principle is that *form should follow function*. Form follows function when the school is organized in a way which helps the goals and activities of people. Function follows form when the work of people is modified to fit the structure of the organization. But the real relationship between form and function is not direct. The two interact constantly, each making demands on the other. At any given moment function may be determined by form demands, but over the long haul chairpersons need to keep the balance in favor of form following function. Organizational structure is the central nervous system of the school; when it is functioning properly, it permits the school to perform a variety of related motions and activities—often simultaneously.

But there are limits. Some activities are modified or prohibited because they make disintegrating demands on the school's organizational structure. For example, take the principles of individualized instruction and teacher autonomy. The secondary school can and should increase its capability to provide individualized education for youngsters and to provide teachers with autonomy. But these increases cannot reach the point that a separate school is created for each student or teacher. To do so would destroy the school as an organized institution.

 Form should follow function but without disintegration of form. Education takes place in an organized setting which should be responsive to organizational goals and functions.

When the relationship between form and function is one-to-one, the school as an organization disintegrates. A one-to-one relationship may be best ideally, but is not practical in a system of mass education committed to providing services to all secondary-age youth.

When function follows form, man often has lost control of the organization. Mindlessness, meaninglessness, passivity, and alienation are the by-products of such schools. When critics damn the schools for being too bureaucratic, dehumanizing, and mechanistic, they refer to schools where function usually follows form.

In this chapter organizational structure is accepted as a necessity which could be beautiful or beastly, depending upon the extent to which people control or are controlled by the organization, and depending upon the extent to which organizational form, processes, and schedules are designed to facilitate school functions, goals and activities.

BUREAUCRACY AND SCHOOLS

Bureaucracy is a loaded word that frequently conjures negative images. Yet there is no single image of bureaucracy. Organizations such as schools have certain bureaucratic characteristics with some characteristics more obvious than others. All secondary schools are bureaucracies and some are much more bureaucratic than others. Max Weber believed that "the decisive reason for the advance of bureaucratic organization has always been its purely technical superiority over other forms of organization."[2]

The characteristics of bureaucratic organizations are:

1. Use of a division of labor and of specific allocations of responsibility
2. Reliance on fairly exact, hierarchical levels of graded authority
3. Administrative thought and action based on written policies, rules and regulations
4. Impersonal, universal application of the bureaucratic environment to all inhabitants
5. Development of longevity of administrative careers.[3]

Max Abbott applies these bureaucratic characteristics to schools as follows[4]:

1. The school organization has clearly been influenced by the need for specialization and the factoring of tasks. The division of the school into elementary and secondary units; the establishment of science, mathematics, music, and other departments within a school; the introduction of guidance programs and psychological services; indeed, the separation of the administrative function from the teaching function, all represent responses to this need.
2. The school organization has developed a clearly defined and rigid hierarchy of authority. Although the term "hierarchy" is seldom used in the lexicon of the educational administrator, the practices to which it refers are prevalent. The typical organization chart is intended specifically to clarify lines of authority and channels of communication. Even in the absence of such a chart, school employees have a clear conception of the nature of the hierarchy in their school systems. In fact, rigid adherence to hierarchical principles has been stressed to the point that failure to adhere to recognized lines of authority is viewed as the epitome of immoral organizational behavior.
3. The school organization has leaned heavily upon the use of general rules to control the behavior of members of the organization and to develop standards which would assure reasonable uniformity in the performance of tasks. Whether they have taken the form of policy manuals, rules and regulations, staff handbooks, or some other type of document, general rules have been used extensively to provide for the orderly induction of new employees into the organization and to eliminate capricious behavior on the part of all school personnel, including administrators and members of boards of education.
4. Despite frequent proclamations regarding togetherness and democracy, the school organization has made extensive application of Weber's principle of impersonality in organizational relationships. Authority has been established on the basis of rational considerations rather than charismatic qualities or traditional imperatives; interpersonal interactions have tended to be functionally specific rather than functionally diffuse; and official relationships have been governed largely by universalistic as contrasted with particularistic considerations. Thus, by operating in a spirit of "formalistic impersonality," the typical school system has succeeded, in part, in separating organizational rights and obligations from the private lives of individual employees.
5. Employment in the educational organization has been based upon technical competence and has constituted for most members a professional career. Promotions have been determined by seniority and by achievement; tenure has been provided; and fixed compensation and retirement benefits have been assured.

Each of the characteristics of bureaucracy is designed and used to bring about desirable consequences but the danger of undesirable and unanticipated consequences also exists.

WHO BENEFITS?

Peter Blau and Richard Scott have developed a system of classifying organizations on the basis of who are the prime *beneficiaries* of organizational activity.[5] They identify four categories of persons who could be the prime beneficiaries:

1. The members or *rank and file* participants—in the case of the school, *teachers.*
2. The *owners or managers* of the organization—in the case of the school, *administrators and supervisors.*
3. The *clients,* those people technically outside the organization who yet have regular, direct contact with it—in the case of the schools, the *students.*
4. The *public at large* or members of the society in which the organization exists—in the case of the schools, the *community, state,* and *nation.*

The prime beneficiary is not the only beneficiary. Teachers, students, administrators, and community: all are potential beneficiaries but in any given situation one group receives the prime benefits.

Four types of organizations can be identified upon the basis of prime beneficiary.

 Mutual benefit associations whose primary beneficiaries are members (teachers) and who work hard at maintaining internal democratic control for members.

Business concerns whose primary beneficiaries are owners and managers (the administration) and who work hard at maintaining efficiency of operations.

Professional organizations whose prime beneficiaries are clients (students) and whose members work hard at providing professional services to clients.

Commonweal organizations whose primary beneficiary is the public (community) which works hard to maintain external democratic control.

The school possesses characteristics of each of the types, but when the emphasis is on winning teacher rights and benefits, on making the job easier, on building barriers which protect teachers, the school looks most like a mutual benefit association. When the emphasis is on increasing and protecting administrative rights and prerogatives, and on operating by administrative images and directions, the school looks more like a business organization. When the emphasis is on meeting community demands and pressures, the school looks more like a commonweal organization. When the emphasis is on serving the educational, social, and emotional needs of students, the school looks most like a professional organization.

Most educators will agree that the school should be more like a professional organization where teachers, administrators, and the public benefit but where the prime beneficiary is the student. In operation, however, students may not be the prime beneficiaries.

Refer to the Prime Beneficiary Grid (p. 7). A similar grid can be constructed to evaluate student behavior codes, faculty handbooks, department standard operating procedures and other policies which characterize the department and schools. Policies and rules provide efficient and reliable guidelines for decision-making and communicate minimum expectations to school participants. But they need to be flexible, responsive to human needs, and consistent with and supportive of school objectives.

Tension exists between each of the potential beneficiaries and no school can function without benefits to each of the groups discussed. The most tense and difficult of the four is working to manifest the school as a professional organization. Students are a relatively powerless group and cannot compete equally for benefits without the direct intervention of adult advocates. Chairpersons can play a key role as advocates of students as prime beneficiaries.

POWER AND AUTHORITY

Amitai Etzioni classifies organization on the basis of the type of power and authority most often used to make lower-level participants comply. He identifies three types of power[6]:

Coercive power where lower-level participants are forced to comply. If they do not comply, they will suffer physical, social, career, psychological, or other losses.

Utilitarian power where lower-level participants are provided with extrinsic rewards for complying, such as money, grades, favoritism, and promotion.

Normative power where lower-level participants comply for intrinsic reasons: they agree with what needs to be done, think it is important, think it is right, and usually find it personally rewarding to comply.

Organizations which rely on coercive power usually have goals and purposes which require order and reliability from lower-level participants, and achieve these goals through routine tasks. Most lower-level participants are alienated from such organizations, and probably would not participate if they did not have to. Concentration camps, prisons, and custodial mental hospitals are usually classified as coercive organizations.

Organizations which rely on utilitarian power usually have economic goals and purposes. These purposes are pursued as long as participants find it worth their while to participate. Most of such involvements are calculated. Participants function as long as they obtain extrinsic rewards, and cease to participate when they no longer need or obtain these rewards. Business firms and unions are usually classified as utilitarian.

Organizations which rely heavily on normative power usually have cultural purposes. Lower-level participants pursue these goals because they identify and believe in them and obtain personal satisfaction from them. They are committed to these purposes and participate because of their commitment. Schools, universities, and hospitals are often cited as examples of normative organizations.

By charting junior and senior high schools known to you on Figure 3–1, one can determine whether they are most like coercive, utilitarian, or normative organizations. One can begin charting schools by identifying the type of power most often used to obtain compliance from teachers or from students. Follow the arrows to the right; first identify goals and activities most often engaged in by teachers or students, and then move to the right and left. Or first identify the level of identity or involvement of teachers or students at work in the school, then move to the left.

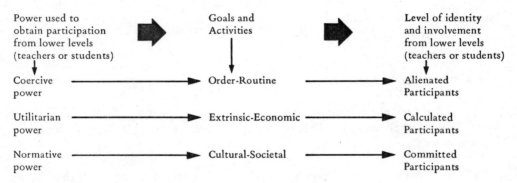

FIGURE 3-1. THE USE OF POWER IN THE SECONDARY SCHOOL

Many schools rely heavily on coercive power to obtain compliance from teachers and students. Coercion is seen as necessary because the goals are seen as standardized, routine, and even distasteful. The presumption that youngsters are not supposed to like school work results in large numbers of alienated lower-level participants.

Many schools rely on utilitarian power to persuade or bribe students and teachers to participate. When extrinsic rewards are not forthcoming participation slows down. Students who work primarily for grades don't work when grades are not at stake and teachers who work on a curriculum project primarily for extra pay or favoritism don't work when money and "points" are not at stake.

Many schools rely primarily on normative power and work to build identity and commitment of teachers and students to goals and purposes. It is assumed that if the work is important, relevant, and meaningful enough, and if teachers and students identify enough with purposes, then they will freely engage in work activities.

Coercive, utilitarian, and normative powers all have a place in junior and senior high schools but the primary long-term use of one or another results in different conse-quences for individuals and the schools. Primary use of coercive power results in alienated teachers and students. Schools cannot operate successfully for long periods when its clients and workers are alienated. Primary use of utilitarian power results in teachers and students adopting a "what's in it for me?" philosophy in deciding whether to participate or not. Such a philosophy is inconsistent with what secondary schools try to teach youngsters. Primary use of normative power does not preclude occasional use of coercive or utilitarian power but does recognize that in the long run what people do because of commitment has lasting value for them individually and for the school as an organization.

BUREAUCRATIC AND PROFESSIONAL VALUES

It is important that junior and senior high schools increase their capacity to operate as professionally-oriented organizations. But schools are bureaucracies too and education takes place in an organized setting. Bureaucracies can be mechanistically or professionally oriented but as they move toward professionalism, value conflicts arise.

Certain values of professionalism conflict with expectations which are normally held for people who work in organized settings. Professionals claim that their occupation requires expertise, specialized knowledge and skills acquired only through training. They claim autonomy, the right to decide how to work without interference from administrative and lay restrictions. They claim a commitment for their profession which is higher than loyalty to a specific school. They claim a responsibility for maintaining professional standards of work.[7]

AS A PROFESSIONAL THE TEACHER IS EXPECTED TO STRESS:	BUT AS A BUREAUCRAT THE TEACHER IS EXPECTED TO STRESS:
uniqueness of student problems and needs	uniformity in dealing with student problems and needs
change, innovation, research	rules, regulations, procedures
achievement of goals	efficiency in operation
particularistic application of rules	universalistic application of rules
skill based on present knowledge	skill based on past practice
ability authority	hierarchical authority
loyalty to the profession and students	loyalty to the school, its administration and trustees[8]

Serious conflict often arises from gaps between bureaucratic and professional expectations. No easy solutions resolve this conflict but its intensity diminishes as chairpersons accept and acknowledge the professional claims of teachers, and as teachers recognize that they work not independently but as members of work teams linked to other teams in a complex organization.

PROBLEMS WITH DELEGATING AUTHORITY

As schools develop a professional orientation, delegating authority and decentralizing decision-making will increase. This desirable trend is not without its problems. Delegation can lead to dysfunctional consequences for the school. Some of these are illustrated in Figure 3-2, which is based on the work of Selznick.[9]

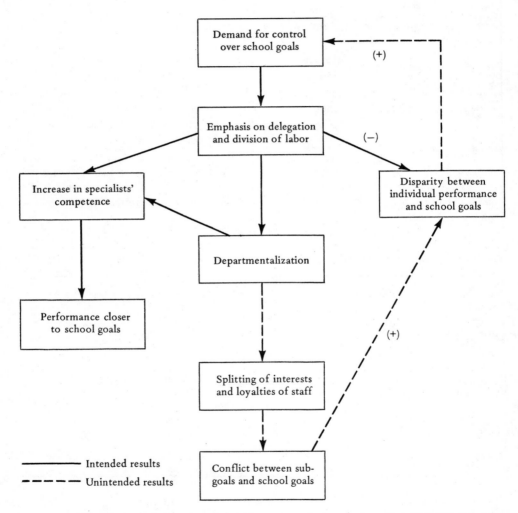

FIGURE 3-2. PROBLEMS WITH DELEGATING AUTHORITY. FROM THOMAS SERGIOVANNI AND ROBERT STARRATT, *EMERGING PATTERNS OF SUPERVISION: HUMAN PERSPECTIVES* (NEW YORK: McGRAW-HILL, 1971). ADAPTED FROM JAMES G. MARCH AND HERBERT A. SIMON, *ORGANIZATIONS* (NEW YORK: JOHN WILEY, 1958), p. 43.

In this figure, the school attempts to increase its control over achieving school goals by delegating authority to the departmental level. It does this hoping to obtain better decisions by placing decision-making prerogatives closer to those with specialized competence. An unanticipated consequence of delegating authority to departments often is the splitting of staff interests and loyalties. Teachers and chairpersons begin to think only in terms of their own goals, which may conflict with the goals of the whole school. This conflict between department and school goals could actually increase the disparity between performance and school effectiveness. Interestingly, the school often reacts to this disparity by increasing its emphasis on delegation with the same hopes that it had originally.

In delegating authority to departments in junior and senior high schools, it is important to be aware of possible unintended consequences, including: the substitution of department goals for school goals, increasing competition among departments, curriculum fragmentation, and isolation of staff.

Delegation, of course, has many desirable consequences; chairpersons play a key role of highlighting the desirable while checking the undesirable. Much will depend upon the extent to which chairpersons see themselves as a leadership cadre who care about and are responsible to the whole school, rather than as barons of competing city-states.

SUMMARY

This overview of organizations is intended to help chairpersons begin to understand the complexities and subtleties of the environment within which they work. The facts of life are that the modern secondary school contains a number of professional and bureaucratic characteristics which must be successfully managed. The school is characterized by professional work which takes place in an organized setting. The quality of one's organizational leadership will be measured by his effectiveness in manipulating the organizational structure and environment in ways which enrich the school's professional work. Awareness of who benefits from school decisions, and understanding of the exercise of power in managing the relationship between structure and function, can help the chairperson.

ENDNOTES

1. H. Randolph Bobbit, Jr., Robert Breinholt, Robert Doktor, and James McNaul, *Organizational Behavior: Understanding and Prediction* (Englewood Cliffs, New Jersey: Prentice-Hall, Inc., 1974), p. 1.

2. Max Weber, "Bureaucracy," in Hans Gerth and C. Wright Mills (eds.), *From Max Weber* (New York: Oxford University Press, 1946), p. 214.

3. Max Weber, *Theory of Social and Economic Organizations*, trans. by A. M. Henderson and T. Parsons (New York: Oxford University Press, 1947), pp. 333–336.

4. Max G. Abbott, "Hierarchical Impediments to Innovation in Educational Organization," in M. G. Abbott and John Lovell (eds.), *Change Perspectives in Educational Administration* (School of Education, Auburn University, 1965), pp. 44–45.

5. Peter M. Blau and W. Richard Scott, *Formal Organizations* (San Francisco, Calif.: Chandler Publishing Company, 1962), pp. 42–45.

6. Amitai Etzioni, *A Comparative Analysis of Complex Organizations* (New York: Free Press, 1961).

7. Teaching is not a profession in the true sense of the word though many professionals work in schools as teachers. Some consider teaching to be a semi-profession where work is more craftlike than the established professions and where work takes place in an organized setting with superordinate and subordinate relationships as opposed to the more individual activities of established professionals. See, for example, Amitai Etzioni (ed.), *The Semi-Professionals and Their Organizations* (New York: The Free Press, 1969).

8. Ronald Corwin, "Professional Persons in Public Organizations," *Educational Administrative Quarterly*, Vol. 1, No. 3, 1965, p. 7.

9. P. Selznick, *TVA and the Grass Roots* (Berkeley: University of California Press, 1949). Figure 3–2 is adapted from James G. March and Herbert Simon, *Organizations* (New York: John Wiley, 1958), pp. 36–47 and appears in Thomas J. Sergiovanni and Robert Starratt, *Emerging Patterns of Supervision* (New York: McGraw-Hill, 1971), p. 57.

☙ PRACTICES ❧

Where is the line between formalizing department affairs to provide reasonable expectations and support for people, and formalizing affairs to program behavior and stifle imagination? Secondary schools tend to over-organize; educational goals and functions become subordinate to organizational structures and procedures. Yet some stability, some notion of standards, and some routinization is necessary in any organized society and can help teachers and other professionals to work.

In the concepts section of this chapter some safeguards were suggested to help ensure that in your school, form does follow function. In this section areas are discussed where a degree of formalization in your department is necessary and could be helpful. This section contains:

Suggestions for establishing policies and procedures
Guidelines for effective policies
Procedures for handling requests for new courses and projects
Request for new course form
Curriculum project proposal form
Suggestions for handling complaints over controversial issues
A sample policy for handling complaints
The National Council for Teachers of English Document, "Citizens' Report for
    Reconsideration of a Work"
Suggestions for handling grievances from teachers

ESTABLISHING POLICIES AND PROCEDURES

One of your responsibilities as chairperson will be to help establish, administer and evaluate school policies and procedures. If yours is a fairly large junior or senior high school, consider establishing supplementary policies and procedures at the department level. Perhaps the most important principle for establishing and implementing policies and procedures is that they should help you and other professionals in the school to be more effective in working with students. Policies should facilitate progress toward job targets; they should free people to work more effectively; and they should be justified by educational goals. Unfortunately this is not always so. Sometimes policies and procedures are limiting; sometimes they place personal ease over educational goals and purposes; sometimes they violate due process; and sometimes they are out of date. Review the following questions and answers, and guidelines for effective policies as you evaluate your policies and consider others for adoption.

Department and School Policies and Procedures: Questions and Answers

What are policies? Policies are principles, guidelines, or general rules of action set up by the school or the department.

How are policies different than procedures? Procedures are detailed instructions which specify what teachers are to do given certain circumstances. The school or department may have certain policies relating to school discipline and additional procedures which specify actions to be followed in handling a specific situation such as a student suspension.

Must all policies be accompanied by procedures? No, this is not possible or desirable. Some programming of the activities of teachers and other school participants is necessary to ensure reliable responses to certain problems. This is particularly important where due process is a concern or where state and federal guidelines must be met. But the number of situations for which procedures exist can easily get out of hand. Remember that organizations exist to help people accomplish objectives, and not the other way around. A plethora of procedures robs people of decision-making prerogatives and may well result in a lack of sensitivity to the uniqueness of situations. "Canned" decision-making assumes that all problems can be fitted to the specified steps; often this is not the case.

What are the advantages of policies? Policies help communicate the overall character of a department or school. They bring a needed consistency to decisions, which helps to establish a sense of common values. Policies should exist not only to guide management and personnel decisions but educational program and teaching decisions as well. See the discussion of educational platform which appears in Chapter 9 for examples of policies of this type. Further, by helping to pre-decide some issues, policies prevent time-consuming, repetitive, and routine study of problems. Policies also provide a certain amount of proxy power which equips teachers with organizational authority to act.

May department policies and procedures be different than school policies and procedures or those of other departments? Yes. Certain department policies and procedures frequently need to differ from those of other departments or of the school. The nature, setting, and work of departments, the number and type of personnel, the clients, equipment, and schedules are by no means standard in most secondary schools. Consider for example the differences which exist among these four departments: Distributive Education, English, Physical Education, and Science. But differences in policies and procedures does not mean they should contradict each other. Often departments develop "implementing" policies and procedures which are different by departments but consistent with the school's general policies.

Guidelines for Effective Policies

1. First and foremost, make sure that policies reflect school and department goals, plans, and educational platform.
2. Submit all policies to periodic evaluation by applying the "who benefits" test. See the concepts section of this chapter.
3. Don't consider policies as sacred rules cast in stone and as part of the school's legacy. Do consider policies as guidelines or tools for implementing educational program and reaching goals. Provide for periodic review of policies. Change those no longer current or those not serving the school's purposes. Policies should be useful, complete, and concise.
4. Be sure that policies together represent an identifiable and consistent pattern. Contradictory policies threaten the credibility of the policy system.
5. Distinguish between policies and procedures. Policies help people think about their decisions and actions. Procedures tell them what to decide and how to behave. Procedures should be few and cover only areas where standard behavior is critical.
6. Put your policies in writing. This tests their clarity and usefulness.
7. Communicate policies and make them available.

PROCEDURES FOR HANDLING REQUESTS FOR NEW COURSES AND PROJECTS

One challenging task for chairpersons is learning the difference between making policies and procedures which lead to orderly planning and growth, innovation and creativity and making policies and procedures which force conformity, stifle creativity, and lead to unduly programed behavior. In his studies of what constitutes an effective work group, Likert observes:*

> The group knows the value of 'constructive' conformity and knows when to use it and for what purposes. Although it does not permit conformity to affect adversely the creative efforts of its members, it does expect conformity on mechanical and administrative matters to save the time of members and to facilitate the group's activities. The group agrees, for example, on administrative forms and procedures, and once they have been established, it expects its members to abide by them until there is good reason to change them.

When dealing with educational program matters the stakes are particularly high and no ordinary set of policies or procedures will do. The object is not to specify what a person will do but to establish expected standards of excellence. This section provides sample forms for handling requests for new courses and proposals for curriculum projects.

*Rensis Likert, *New Patterns of Management* (New York: McGraw-Hill, 1961), p. 168.

Notice that the emphasis in each case is on establishing standards. Proposers are expected to plan and reason out courses and projects characterized by attention to objectives, concepts, and evaluation. Additional data, such as anticipated scheduling, financial, time and personnel demands are also included. Notice also that the samples are designed to ensure that the ideas being proposed have been adequately discussed in preliminary stages, and that formal proposals are shared not only within the school but with other schools in the district and with the central office.

REQUEST FOR A NEW COURSE

REQUESTED BY THE _____ DEPT.   DATE _____

1. This course will be called _____ ; it will serve _____ grade students. Briefly describe the content on the back of this sheet. Give examples of (a) purposes and anticipated outcomes, (b) major concepts and topics, (c) types of activities with which students will be engaged, (d) evaluation procedures, and (e) curriculum materials or books to be used.

2. Prerequisites (list below):

3. This course will be: _____ Elective _____ Required _____ One semester _____ Two semesters

4. This course will be (please check one):
   _____ an addition to the department's offering
   _____ a replacement for _____
   _____ a pilot study

5. This course will require (please check appropriate spaces):
   _____ the adoption of a new textbook (complete new textbook request form)
   _____ the use of a text previously adopted and in use
   _____ the use of a fee card for course materials (complete fee card request form)

6. This course will require (please check appropriate spaces):
   _____ specialized organization of teacher time
   _____ specialized room arrangements or equipment (explain on back of sheet)
   _____ specialized student grouping or sectioning

7. The format for teaching this course will be essentially:
   _____ lecture-discussion (large group)   _____ independent study
   _____ lecture-discussion (small group)   _____ laboratory
   _____ seminar   _____ field study
   other _____ .

8. To what extent does this course conflict with the intents and content of other courses in your department, courses offered by other departments?

9. Has this proposed course been discussed with other members of your department?
   _____ Yes   _____ No

10. If approved this course will begin _____
                                              (semester-year)

	RECOMMEND DEFERRED	APPROVED	NOT APPROVED
CHAIRPERSON	_____	_____	_____

COMMENTS:

THE CHAIRPERSON'S ORGANIZATIONAL LEADERSHIP FUNCTIONS

	RECOMMEND DEFERRED	APPROVED	NOT APPROVED
CURRICULUM COUNCIL OR CHAIRPERSON GROUP	_____	_____	_____

COMMENTS:

CURRICULUM COUNCIL OR CHAIRPERSON GROUP	_____	_____	_____

COMMENTS:

PRINCIPAL	_____	_____	_____

COMMENTS:

CURRICULUM PROJECT PROPOSAL FORM

School Year 19____ – 19____

PROJECT TITLE _____

SCHOOL _____ DEPT. _____ DATE _____

FACULTY MEMBERS RECOMMENDED FOR THE PROJECT _____

PROPOSED PROJECT DIRECTOR _____

1. Project Outline

2. Project Objectives

3. Review of previous curriculum projects. Please list previously completed curriculum development projects which relate to this curriculum project.

4. Project Schedule
STARTING DATE _____
ESTIMATED HOURS NEEDED FOR THIS PROJECT _____
     The project will be completed on or before _____ unless a time extension is granted by the principal. If the project is not completed on the approved date, funds will be withdrawn.

5. Will the project involve the teaching of controversial material? If yes, prepare a rationale for including this material and attach to this proposal. Refer to your department's policies for teaching controversial material.

6. Will this project require financial assistance? ____ Yes ____ No. If yes, complete the following:

ESTIMATED COSTS	APPROVED MAXIMUM (TO BE COMPLETED BY PRINCIPAL)
MATERIALS_____	_____
SALARIES _____	_____
MISC. _____	_____
TOTAL _____	_____

Describe proposed expenditures on a separate sheet of paper.

7. Evaluation. How will this project be evaluated?

8. IMPLEMENTATION
Date for implementation
Plan for implementation (e.g., announcement of course, selection of students, etc.)

Needed facilities and/or equipment which exceed those of a standard classroom.

9. Additional comments

9. Additional comments (Cont'd.)

Project submitted by:_____   _____
                                                              Date

Approved by:_____   _____
                              Department Chairman   Date

Approved by curriculum council
or chairperson group:_____   _____
                                                              Date

Approved by:_____   _____
                                    Principal   Date

After building level approvals, all proposals are to be sent to the District for circulation to other principals and department chairpersons.

Upon completion of curriculum development project, copies of the final report shall be submitted to the Department Chairman, the Principal and the Director of Curriculum and Instruction.

Requisitions for all payments shall be prepared by the appropriate building personnel and submitted through the usual channels to the Director of Curriculum and Instruction.

CURRICULUM PROJECT: FINAL REPORT OR
END-OF-YEAR PROGRESS REPORT

I. School and Department concerned: _____

II. Project title: _____

_____

III. Have completed project drafts been filed with the following:

    YES   NO

   _____ _____   1. Director of Curriculum and Instruction

   _____ _____   2. Building Principal

   _____ _____   3. Department Chairman

IV. If not, please submit a statement explaining why copies have not been filed.

V. If project will not be completed, please provide information relative to situation and any future implications for this project or a similar one.

VI. Final Summary (Write this brief description carefully. Include objectives, a description of the project, evaluation procedures, and outcomes.)

Handling Complaints Over Controversial Issues

It is difficult to avoid controversy over what should be taught, with what materials, and how. Some controversy signals a healthy, responsive educational program, innovative staff, and a desire to help youngsters to cope with differences of opinion, to search out their own values, and to function as adults in our free society. But complaints are made, inquiries are made, and information is sought by parents. How controversies are handled often determines whether the issue becomes resolved or aggravated. Departments should not seek to avoid controversy but rather should plan strategies for handling such areas. Provided below are sample forms and suggestions for developing policies relating to teaching potentially controversial material and for handling complaints.

SUGGESTIONS FOR DEVELOPING A POLICY ON TEACHING POTENTIALLY CONTROVERSIAL MATERIAL

1. In planning to teach materials which may be controversial, develop a clear rationale for their study. Consider, for example, why the particular material, topics, or issues were chosen. Know how this material fits into your educational program. Be able to justify how exposing students to this material helps achieve program or unit objectives.
2. Put this rationale in writing and file it in the department office. Make this rationale available to the principal or other appropriate administrators in case a complaint develops.
3. Place in the same file examples of curriculum materials, classroom assignments, quizzes, and other documents used to teach the material.
4. Be sure that as teachers deal with controversial issues they do so in a professional manner. They should state issues plainly. They should focus on issues and not personalities and on points of view, not on who says what. Discussions should be orderly and teachers should clarify positions rather than advocate them. Teachers should protect (without embarrassing) students who hold minority views.
5. A mechanism should be provided for excusing students from discussions if for any legitimate reason parents so request. This mechanism should be unobtrusive—that is, students should not be unduly singled out for being excused.
6. When unanticipated controversial issues arise teachers should deal with them forthrightly, following the suggestions listed in (4) above.

SUGGESTIONS FOR DEVELOPING A POLICY DEALING WITH COMPLAINTS ABOUT CONTROVERSIAL MATERIAL

1. When you receive a complaint, consider it legitimate. Try to find out the exact complaint. Make sure that you and the individual or group making the complaint are discussing the same issue. This is an important step which permits you an opportunity to "model" behavior you would like to see in the person making the complaint—tolerance, acceptance, fair play, and focusing on issues, not personalities.

2. Make sure that the complaint is concerned with educational program content or teaching method and not with personality characteristics of a given teacher.

3. Discuss the complaint with the individual politely, fairly, and with understanding. If you want him to show these characteristics, you need to establish them first.

4. Provide the individual with a written rationale for dealing with the material under complaint. (See above, Suggestions for Developing a Policy on Teaching Potentially Controversial Material.)

5. Make every reasonable effort to respond to the complaint and to resolve the objection but *do not* compromise goals, objectives, and educational program platform dimensions which are a part of your department's program.

6. If the individual persists in his complaint, call upon other community members for assistance. It is important that the individual know that other opinions exist. Avoid embarrassing the individual. Often "loss of face" forces the person to see the controversy as a war which requires a winner and a loser. Your best bet is to treat the problem as a misunderstanding which can be resolved with both sides winning with dignity.

7. If the complaint goes this far, you should have building administrators and central office specialists involved.

8. Be sure that the individual making the complaint has thoroughly read and studied the material under question.

9. Invite the individual to visit the classroom where materials are being used or issues are being discussed.

10. Your best bet is to stick to the issues at hand and avoid reacting personally to the complaint or reacting personally to the individual making the complaint.

11. You will not always be right! Sometimes individuals have legitimate complaints which should be honored!

What to do if the complainer persists? Assuming that you feel your position is justifiable, you should ask the individual to submit his complaint in a formal statement in writing. His statement should be responded to in writing. Now it is necessary for the Superintendent to be involved. Assuming you have the support of the Superintendent, the Board of Education should then conduct a formal hearing. This hearing will probably span several meetings, all of which should be well publicized. Careful minutes should be taken and the press should be invited. The purpose of these meetings is to win popular support for your point of view.

If you find that public support is not forthcoming, you should carefully reconsider the issues at stake. Perhaps your position is faulty. Perhaps it can be compromised without serious loss to principles you value. Perhaps you are convinced that your view must prevail. If the latter is the case, request help from such agencies as:

Your local, state and national education association or union
The National Council for Teacher Education
The subject matter association with which you must identify

The American Civil Liberties Union
Your state bar association
The legal agency of your state department of education
Nearby colleges and universities (try in particular the administration and super-
vision department of your state university).

A Sample Policy for Handling Complaints

The following policy statements and set of procedures are from a large suburban
high school. Consider carefully the policy statements, the form letter, and the format for
formally receiving complaints. To what extent is this approach consistent with the policy
development suggestions provided earlier? What additions or deletions would you
suggest? Use this example to help elicit discussion in your school as you evaluate present
policies and procedures and as you formulate new ones.

SAMPLE PROCEDURES FOR HANDLING COMPLAINTS

Members of the community will continue to have the privilege to examine and to criticize constructively the methods and the materials of instruction. To gain insight into classroom procedures, visitors, particularly parents, are entitled to an explanation by the chairperson, have the right to ask questions until the chairperson feels that all pertinent information has been given, and may be given copies of available instructions, lists, or schedules used in the unit.

Parents and other residents of the district have the right to visit the class once, at such a time as may be determined by the principal in consultation with the teacher. After that, the teacher may recommend to his department chairperson that the visitations be terminated. Exclusions of any visitor will be determined by the department in consultation with the principal. If the parent or visitor is excluded, he may have access to all available materials of instruction which have been used in the class. He shall not, however, have the right to request that the proceedings of the class be recorded in any way.

If a resident of our district wishes to question the use of the instructional materials of a unit or course, he may request from the principal's office a questionnaire designed to make clear the points in question.

(Sample of Form Letter)

Dear _____ :

Your interest in the curriculum, materials, and objectives of _____ School is greatly appreciated by the faculty and me. We strive to keep our program abreast of the best current thinking and research in the field of modern secondary school education. We are open at all times to perceptive criticism and suggestions from concerned parents and friends.

We ask you to complete the enclosed questionnaire as completely and conscientiously as your time permits. Members of our staff have spent considerable time in determining the nature of the materials needed for our courses, and the elimination of any of them should be carefully justified.

Your completed questionnaire should be mailed to:

> The Office of the Principal
> School _____
> Address _____
> _____
> _____

We will inform you within a reasonable time of decisions resulting from your action.

Sincerely yours,

_____
Principal

_____
Chairperson

Questionnaire to be completed by any resident of the _____ High School attendance area who questions the use of particular instructional materials.

Name _____ Date _____

Address _____

Name of Organization Represented _____

Position in Organization _____

1. What is the nature of the material in question: (check one)
   a. Text regularly used in class _____
      Title _____
   b. Supplementary book used in class at option of teacher _____
      Title _____
   c. Library book _____
      Title _____
   d. Other _____
      Explain:

2. I have carefully examined this material. If it is a book, I have read it in its entirety: Yes_____ No_____

3. I am well acquainted with the course in which this material is used, and with its place in the curriculum: Yes_____ No_____
   a. If the answer to Number 3 is *no*:
      a. I would like a conference with the teacher of the course: Yes_____ No_____
      b. I would like a conference with the department chairperson: Yes_____ No_____

4. I am now or have been a certified:
   a. Teacher _____
   b. Librarian _____
   c. School Administrator_____
   d. Psychologist or Counselor_____
   e. None of these. I am presently employed as _____
      _____
      _____

5. I question the use of this book or other material for the following reason: (Be clear and specific. Attach further statements to this form if you consider them necessary.)

Citizen's Request for Reconsideration of a Work: NCTE

The National Council for Teachers of English suggests the use of the form, "Citizen's Request for Reconsideration of a Work"* for handling objections to texts, books, and other printed materials. They note that the form provides serious objectors with an opportunity to think through their complaints systematically, and also discourages "idle censors." The following advantages of using the form are cited:

formalizes the complaint,

indicates specifically the book or books in question,

identifies the complainant,

suggests the size of his backing,

requires the complainant to think through his objections (items 1–3),

causes him to evaluate the work for other groups than merely the one he first had in mind (item 4),

establishes his familiarity with the work (item 5),

gives him an opportunity to consider his criticism about the work and the teacher's purpose in using the work (items 6–8), and

gives him an opportunity to suggest alternative actions (items 9 and 10)

*From *The Student's Right to Read,* National Council of Teachers of English, Urbana, Ill. 1972, p. 18.

CITIZEN'S REQUEST FOR RECONSIDERATION OF A WORK

Hardcover _____

Author _____ Paperback _____

Title _____

Publisher (if known) _____

Request initiated by _____

Telephone _____ Address _____

City _____ Zip Code _____

Complainant represents
_____ himself/herself
_____ (name organization)_____
_____ (identify other group)_____

1. To what in the work do you object? Please be specific; cite pages. _____
_____

2. What of value is there in this work? _____
_____

3. What do you feel might be the result of reading this work? _____
_____

4. For what age group would you recommend this work? _____
_____

5. Did you read the entire work?_____What pages or sections?_____
_____

6. Are you aware of the judgment of this work by critics?_____
_____

7. Are you aware of the teacher's purpose in using this work? _____
_____

8. What do you believe is the theme or purpose of this work? _____
_____

9. What would you prefer the school do about this work?
_____ Do not assign or recommend it to my child
_____ Withdraw it from all students
_____ Send it back to the English department for reevaluation

10. In its place, what work of equal value would you recommend that would convey as valuable a picture and perspective of a society or a set of values?_____
_____
_____

_____
(Signature of complainant)

HANDLING COMPLAINTS AND GRIEVANCES FROM TEACHERS

Since complaints and grievances often result from actions and policies which affect the teacher day by day, the chairperson is unusually vulnerable. If one sees complaints as reflections on himself, one is likely to respond in a defensive manner. Instead, see grievances as opportunities to communicate with teachers, to clarify roles and responsibilities, and to check on the nature of school rules and regulations. Be careful to avoid viewing complaints as personal battles between you and teachers; rather, look for constructive ways to confront and resolve problems. Occasionally, invite or sponsor a complaint in order to check out or test a set of rules you believe to be questionable.

In schools where a union or association contract governs the handling of grievances, the following general steps are usually followed. Be sure to check your own contract for specific steps.

1. In the first step, the teacher who feels he has a grievance or complaint discusses his problem directly with his superior—usually the department chairperson.
2. If the problem cannot be worked out at this level, the teacher may then take the matter up with the principal. In a large high school where access to the principal may be difficult or formal, the teacher seeks the assistance of the association's or union's building representative in contacting the principal. The matter is then considered by all three or by the representative and the principal.
3. If the matter is not resolved at this level, the building representative takes the complaint to either the personnel administrator of the district or to the superintendent.
4. If the problem is still not resolved, the next step is arbitration or voluntary mediation.

THE DEPARTMENT AS AN EFFECTIVE WORK GROUP

🜋 CONCEPTS 🜋

SIZING UP YOUR DEPARTMENT

One can size up a department by examining eight critical items:

1. The amount of enthusiasm and commitment which exists for department goals and purposes
2. The quantity and quality of teacher contribution to the department
3. The quality of listening to each other by teachers
4. The amount of creativity exhibited in problem solving
5. Ways in which conflict and disagreements are handled
6. The quality and nature of leadership
7. The methods and means of making decisions
8. The ways in which departments evaluate their performance.[1]

Using these critical items, several descriptions of departments at work are provided below. These descriptions are adapted from W. J. Reddin, 3-D Team Mode Theory.[2] Which of these descriptions is most like the department with which you are affiliated? Would other members of the department agree? Would your principal agree?

PROBLEM-SOLVING DEPARTMENT. Such a department attempts to examine problems as intensively as possible and thus reach an optimal solution to which all are committed. Due consideration is given both to the task at hand and the feelings of department members. Ideas are of high quality and relevant to the task. When a department operates this way, the chairperson usually functions as an executive.

PRODUCTIVE DEPARTMENT. Here, the immediate task is the primary concern. Contributions come from those who push for their own ideas. Disagreement occurs frequently but is usually useful. Discussions in the productive department may be dominated by a few members but their leadership is beneficial. Evaluation aims at making the department more efficient. The chairperson usually functions as a benevolent autocrat.

CREATIVE DEPARTMENT.   Focuses primarily on developing its members and their ideas. Much attention is paid to the minority opinion, to incorporate the ideas of all members in the decision. Disagreement, although rare, is looked into closely so that benefit is derived from it. Evaluation of the department's efforts usually is aimed at improving department creativity. The chairperson usually functions as a developer.

PROCEDURAL DEPARTMENT.   Follows procedures and established patterns. Creativity and contributions, although forthcoming within defined procedures, are sound. Members listen politely and disagreement is handled in a formal manner. Leadership is routine. Evaluation usually amounts to a comparison of the department's efforts with those of other departments. Evaluation is, however, functional. The chairperson usually functions as a bureaucrat.

MIXED DEPARTMENT.   Tries to compromise between getting the task done and sparing people's feelings. The result is less effective than above. The department lacks focus on the problem, its members' comments are often irrelevant and attempts at creativity usually fail. Disagreement exists but serves no useful purpose. Leadership is often absent when needed and present when not needed. Evaluation is weak. When a department operates this way the chairperson usually functions as a compromiser.

FIGHT DEPARTMENT.   Characterized by conflict and argument. The conflict is not functional as contributions and creativity are usually blocked by argumentive department members. Leadership is dominated by one or two noisy individuals. Disagreement sometimes becomes personal rather than objective. Evaluation of the department's efforts usually amounts to attacks on department members. The chairperson usually functions as an autocrat.

DEPENDENT DEPARTMENT.   Here the by-word is harmony. More attention is paid to avoiding conflict than to discussing the problem. Everyone can be expected to agree with most contributions and creative ideas are blocked when they are seen as possible criticisms of members or of the department as a whole. Disagreement, even when obviously functional, is avoided. Leadership sometimes evolves, but it is usually friendly and weak. Evaluation of the department's efforts is usually in the form of compliments. When a department operates this way the chairperson usually functions as a missionary.

DEPARTMENT IN FLIGHT.   Displays little interest in getting the job done. Conflict is minimal because of the energy it requires. Creativity and contributions are low and leadership appears to be absent. The characteristic decision is a rewording of the original problem. Rarely is any effort made to evaluate or improve performance. The chairperson usually functions as a deserter.

Departments may operate very close to one of Reddin's descriptions most of the time, but most departments shift operating styles occasionally to meet certain issues. The problem-solving, productive, creative and procedural departments are indeed different in operating styles but nevertheless each is effective in its own way. On the other hand, the mixed, fight, dependent and flight departments, although different in operating styles, are each ineffective.

Chairpersons' leadership styles associated with each of the department descriptions will be described in the next chapter, which deals specifically with leadership skills and behavior. As the topic of leadership is discussed and related to department descriptions, it will be seen that each effective leadership style has a corresponding ineffective style and each effective department description can be matched to an ineffective description.

What Is an Effective Group?

Many departments in junior and senior high schools are better characterized as collections of individuals rather than as groups. A collection of teachers may qualify as a physical group if located in the same area of the building, or as a department group if they all teach in the same academic area, but it does not follow that they qualify as a psychological group. Members of a psychological group

share common purposes

interact with each other

perceive themselves to be a group

obtain satisfaction of their needs as a result of group membership

When a department gets together, one can only be sure that a physical group is assembled. If some of the teachers share common goals, interact with each other, share a group identity and get needs met as a result of membership, then a psychological group exists within a physical group. Psychological groups are concerned with both body and spirit; physical groups are concerned only with body.

Whether most teachers are merely physical members or are psychological members of the department may depend largely upon whether their needs are met as a result of group membership. Teachers tend to become marginal group members or withdraw from the group when rewards cease or are not worth the contributions they are making to the group. In return for rewards teachers are expected to provide the group with loyalty, effort, and interest.

The development of the department as a psychological group is a critically important first step but not totally effective. Psychological groups are not necessarily work groups. Consider, for example, a group of teachers who share a common purpose, the maintenance of things the way they are; who interact regularly, to discredit change attempts in their school; who identify together as a group, the regulars; and who find group membership comforting and satisfying, a mutual protection society. This group certainly is a psychological group but probably is not an effective work group. In summary,

 A physical group is a collection of individuals.

A psychological group is a collection of individuals who share common purposes, interact with each other, perceive themselves to be a group, and find group membership rewarding.

Effective work groups are always psychological groups, but psychological groups are not always effective work groups.

Formal and Informal Groups

The junior or senior high school department is a *formal group* established and defined by the school to achieve certain objectives. These are organizationally defined and concern the work which is considered necessary for the school to function effectively.

Teachers are hired and fitted into the formal group structure with the expectation that their activities will help the group perform its assigned tasks. But "the whole teacher" reports to school each day and he brings with him needs which are not ordinarily work-defined. He needs to interact, to belong, to be accepted, to be respected, and to feel safe. Informal groups often emerge to fulfill these needs.

Chairpersons usually consider informal groups as enemies of the formal group, as distractions from the utilization of departmental energies toward goals and tasks. This is often true. Informal groups frequently develop objectives which compete with or are opposed to departmental objectives.

 Informal group objectives and activities, however, are not naturally opposed to those of the formal group.

Whether or not conflict exists between informal and formal group structures depends upon the amount of identity and commitment among teachers toward formal goals and tasks. When identity and commitment are high, the informal group structures are put to work on behalf of the department. When identity and commitment are low, competing informal objectives are established. In the first case social or teacher-comfort objectives might take precedence over educational or student-centered objectives and the department could begin to resemble a country club. The emergence of opposing objectives could result in bickering, argument, and sabotage.

A working group needs interaction effectiveness capabilities and task effectiveness capabilities. Interaction effectiveness refers to the group's ability to provide for its members' needs which are not work-defined. Belonging, acceptance and security needs are examples. Task effectiveness refers to the group's ability to pursue such activities as promoting, defining, and accomplishing school-related objectives.

A group is unlikely to be successful in its tasks unless it possesses the capacity for interaction effectiveness, which increases as communication frequency among department members increases. Frequency of communication depends upon how much department members share common values and beliefs, feel comfortable with and trust each other, and interact with each other.

Task effectiveness increases as task identification and commitment among department members increase. Task identity and commitment in turn depend upon the opportunities which teachers have to accept responsibility, to participate in decision-making, to influence department direction, procedures and outcomes, in essence to become shareholders in the department corporation. In summary,

 The effective department work group is a psychological group and therefore members share common purposes, interact with each other, have a group identity, and find membership satisfying. The group is characterized by high interaction effectiveness.

In addition, the common purposes which members share are consistent with department objectives, and interaction usually concerns itself with job-defined tasks, purposes, and activities. There is high identity with and commitment to department objectives and task effectiveness is high.

Characteristics of Effective Work Groups

Rensis Likert identifies three important characteristics of members in effective work groups: they have a high degree of group loyalty, they have effective interaction skills, and they have high performance goals.

Groups so characterized are found to be consistently more productive, display higher group morale, and return more satisfaction to members than groups which lack these characteristics. A more descriptive list of properties of effective work groups, all of which are proposed by Likert, is presented below. Probably no work group has all of these properties, but they are worthy targets for chairpersons. Further, each property is worthy of discussion and analysis by department members as they consider their own contribution to building group effectiveness.

Here are the properties and performance characteristics of the highly effective group[3]:

1. The members are skilled in the various leadership and membership roles and functions required for interaction between leaders and members and between members and other members.
2. The group has been in existence sufficiently long to have developed a relaxed working relationship among all its members.
3. The members of the group are attracted to it and are loyal to its members, including the leader.
4. The members and leaders have a high degree of confidence and trust in each other.

5. The values and goals of the group are a satisfactory integration and expression of the relevant values and needs of its members. They have helped shape these values and goals and are satisfied with them.

6. The members of the group are highly motivated to abide by the major values and to achieve the important goals of the group. Each member will do all that he reasonably can, and at times all in his power, to help the group achieve its central objectives. He expects every other member to do the same. This high motivation springs, in part, from the basic motive to achieve and maintain a sense of personal worth and importance. Being valued by a group whose values he shares, and deriving a sense of significance and importance from this relationship, leads each member to do his best. He is eager not to let the other members down. He strives hard to do what he believes is expected of him.

7. All the interaction, problem-solving, decision-making activities of the group occur in a supportive atmosphere. Suggestions, comments, ideas, information, criticisms are all offered with a helpful orientation. Similarly, these contributions are received in the same spirit. Respect is shown for the point of view of others both in the way contributions are made and in the way they are received. There are real and important differences of opinion, but the focus is on arriving at sound solutions and not on exacerbating and aggravating the conflict.

8. The leader of each work group exerts a major influence in establishing the tone and atmosphere of that work group by his leadership principles and practices.

9. Each member accepts willingly and without resentment the goals and expectations that he and his group establish for themselves. These goals are high enough to stimulate each member to do his best, but not so high as to create anxieties or fear of failure. In an effective group, each person can exert sufficient influence on the decisions of the group to prevent it from setting unattainable goals for any member while setting high goals for all. The goals are adapted to the member's capacity to perform.

10. The leader and the members believe that each group member can accomplish "the impossible." These expectations stretch each member to the maximum and accelerate his growth. When necessary, the group tempers the expectation level so that the member is not broken by a feeling of failure or rejection.

11. When necessary or advisable, other members of the group will give a member the help he needs to accomplish successfully the goals set for him. Mutual help is a characteristic of highly effective groups.

12. The supportive atmosphere of the highly effective group stimulates creativity. The group does not demand narrow conformity as do the work groups under authoritarian leaders. No one has to "yes the boss," nor is he rewarded for such an attempt. The group attaches high values to new, creative approaches and solutions to its problems and to the problems of the organization of which it is a part. The motivation to be creative is high when one's work group prizes creativity.

13. The group knows the value of "constructive conformity" and knows when to use it and for what purposes. Although it does not permit conformity to affect adversely the creative efforts of its members, it does expect conformity on mechanical and administrative matters to save the time of members and to

facilitate the group's activities. The group agrees, for example, on administrative forms and procedures; once they have been established, it expects its members to abide by them until there is good reason to change them.

14. There is strong motivation on the part of each member to communicate fully and frankly to the group all the information which is relevant and of value to the group's activity. This stems directly from the member's desire to be valued by the group and to get the job done. The more important to the group the member feels an item of information to be, the greater is his motivation to communicate it.

15. There is high motivation in the group to use the communication process so that it best serves the interests and goals of the group.

16. Just as there is high motivation to communicate, there is correspondingly strong motivation to receive communications.

17. In the highly effective group, there are strong motivations to try to influence other members as well as to be receptive to influence by them.

18. The group processes of the highly effective group enable the members to exert more influence on the leader and to communicate far more information to him, including suggestions as to what needs to be done and how he could do his job better, than is possible in a man-to-man relationship.

19. The ability of the members of a group to influence each other contributes to the flexibility and adaptability of the group. Ideas, goals, and attitudes do not become frozen if members are able to influence each other continuously. Although the group is eager to examine any new ideas and methods which will help it do its job better, and is willing to be influenced by its members, it is not easily shifted or swayed. Any change is undertaken only after rigorous examination of the evidence. This stability in the group's activities is due to the steadying influence of the common goals and values held by the group members.

20. In the highly effective group, individual members feel secure in making decisions which seem appropriate to them because the goals and philosophy of operation are clearly understood by each member and provide him with a solid base for his decisions. This unleashes initiative and pushes decisions down while still maintaining a coordinated and directed effort.

21. The leader of a highly effective group is selected carefully. His leadership ability is so evident that he would probably emerge as a leader in any unstructured situation.

Shared Decision-Making

Rensis Likert's list of properties of effective groups suggests the importance to department effectiveness of interaction effectiveness among teachers. A key to success is putting the efforts of interaction effectiveness to work on behalf of department objectives and tasks. The extent to which this occurs depends directly upon the extent to which teachers identify with and are committed to department objectives and tasks.

Shared decision-making in departments is an important incentive to building this identity and commitment. Slogans advocating shared decision-making are not new to chairpersons. Such approaches have the potential for effectiveness but often result in disappointment for teachers and chairpersons alike. Some view shared decision-making as being "wishy washy," a sign of weakness or indecisiveness in the chairperson. Often teachers refer to departments operated this way as "groups of incompetents appointed by the unwilling to do the unnecessary." "A camel is a horse which was put together by a committee," is often repeated.

The alternative to shared decision-making is for chairpersons to assume complete decision-making responsibility. This procedure has appeal to many teachers who are uninterested and uninvolved, particularly if decisions do not affect them very much. Most teachers, however, want to be involved in department and school decisions they see as being important and are interested in their work and in the affairs of their departments. The absence of shared decision-making soon results in dissatisfaction of teachers and in the development of competing or opposing informal group objectives.

Chairpersons have no viable alternative to shared decision-making if they wish to enjoy group identity and commitment to department objectives and tasks. Further, most problems facing departments are complex, and shared decision-making often provides the necessary specialized knowledge, creative ideas, and alternative testing required for sound solutions.

 Two major reasons why shared decision-making does not work are the use of such approaches at the wrong time and lack of agreement among department members on how such an approach should operate. Shared decision-making works sometimes but not at others.

The next chapter describes several styles of leadership which chairpersons may use and the circumstances under which they are effective and ineffective. One of these circumstances has particular relevance to shared decision-making: the extent to which the nature of the problem or the tasks to be decided are important to teachers. For example, teachers will probably not want to be bothered with shared decision-making on routine management issues but will probably wish to be involved in decisions relating to teaching strategies.

Uncertainty about how shared decision-making should take place or lack of agreement about how it operates is difficult but not insurmountable. One of the goals of the chairperson should be to help the department work better as a problem-solving group. Group effectiveness cannot and should not be a side issue, but should be discussed regularly as a proper agenda item. One approach to improving problem-solving capabilities is for the department to develop a shared decision-making model. Such a model would of course be subject to requirement and revision as needed.

Building a Department-Shared Decision-Making Model

The building of an initial decision-making model is a task probably best tackled head-on. Several meetings will need to be planned, each taking a one- to two-hour block of time. Membership, influence, and control patterns, group norms, and operating procedures are the primary issues which need to be discussed and settled by the group as a decision-making model is developed. Questions relating to these issues are provided below.

1. *Membership Questions.* Who will be members of the department decision-making group? Will teacher aides, part-time faculty and specialties be included? What about the principal, other administrators and supervisors, students, and parents?

2. *Influence and Control Questons.* What weight should be accorded each member? Does everyone have an equal vote? Can the chairperson veto certain decisions or all decisions? What decisions will be made by chairpersons outside of the shared decision-making model? What decisions will be made by individuals, the group, with students?

3. *Group Norm Questions.* Will attendance be voluntary or mandatory? How will the group deal with silence, apathy, and conflict? Will the group encourage diverse opinions or "group think"? What are the essentials which everyone must accept and what are the areas where diversity is welcomed?

4. *Operating Procedures Questions.* Who will chair the group? How will the agenda be set? Who can provide input? How will priorities be set? Who will call meetings? How will issues be settled? What roles will voting and consensus seeking play? How will decisions be reversed or changed?

These additional questions might help a department get started in developing a shared decision-making model[4]:

Should all members of the decision-making groups be involved in all decisions?
How can responsibility and accountability for decisions be legally shared by the chairperson?
Is it legitimate for some decisions to be made by someone else? Which decisions?
How does information get fed into the decision-making body?
Will standing committees or ad hoc committees be used?
How is sufficient information to be gathered on which to base a decision?
Should the principal, chairperson or others have veto power over decisions made by the group?
How often should the decision-making group meet?
How are priorities for decision-making established?
Should decision-makers implement as well as determine policy and procedures?
Should decisions be made on the basis of a majority vote?
Is co-leadership possible?
What shall be the size of the decision-making groups?
How can one vote and maintain personal anonymity?
How are new members oriented to the decision-making process?

Fear is the initial reaction of principals and chairpersons to the prospects of developing a shared decision-making model. This fear focuses primarily on possible loss of control and power over teachers. At first glance this procedure does seem to "give teachers everything." Experience in developing such models, however, reveals that teachers are not interested in becoming administrators or in stripping principals and chairpersons of management prerogatives. Though early attempts at developing a model often result in teachers' assuming ambitious responsibilities, they quickly come to see these as burdens piled upon existing teaching duties. Teachers soon realize they do not wish to become administrators, but they do want opportunities to contribute ideas to the solution of problems, to learn more of what is expected of them and of what others are doing, and to influence the course of decisions which have relevance to their professional work. This is exactly what chairpersons want, too. Shared decision-making is a means to this end and the result of properly developed and executed decision-making models is high teacher identification and commitment to department objectives and improved performance.

Cooperation and Competition Among Departments

In Chapter 3 some organizational characteristics of modern junior and senior high schools were discussed. Particular attention was given to the problems of overspecialization, which often leads to competing subgoals among departments. Actually many principals and chairpersons prefer a system of organization based on competing departments. Principals often take a "survival of the fittest" attitude in distributing resources, with the strongest, most vocal, most powerful department obtaining more resources than others. Chairpersons point out that competition among departments builds spirit within departments and adds zest to organizational life.

The effects of inter-group competition within and between groups is a thoroughly researched area. In summarizing a number of studies Schein describes the effects[5]:

A. What happens *within* each competing group?
1. Each group becomes more closely knit and elicits greater loyalty from its members; members close ranks and bury some of their internal differences.
2. Group climate changes from informal, casual, playful to work and task-oriented; concern for members' psychological needs declines while concern for task accomplishment increases.
3. Leadership patterns tend to change from more democratic toward more autocratic; the group becomes more willing to tolerate autocratic leadership.
4. Each group becomes more highly structured and organized.
5. Each group demands more loyalty and conformity from its members in order to be able to present a "solid front."

B. What happens *between* the competing groups?
1. Each group begins to see the other groups as the enemy, rather than merely a neutral object.
2. Each group begins to experience distortions of perception—it tends to perceive only the best parts of itself, denying its weaknesses, and tends

to perceive only the worst parts of the other group, denying its strengths; each group is likely to develop a negative stereotype of the other ("they don't play fair like we do").

3. Hostility toward the other group increases while interaction and communication with the other group decrease; thus it becomes easier to maintain negative stereotypes and more difficult to correct perceptual distortions.

4. If the groups are forced into interaction—for example, if they are forced to listen to representatives plead their own and the others' cause in reference to some task—each group is likely to listen more closely to its own representative and not to listen to the representative of the other group, except to find fault with his presentation; in other words, group members tend to listen only for that which supports their own position and stereotype.

Inter-group competition breeds some beneficial effects within groups. Indeed within the department the smell of battle builds cohesiveness and provides an incentive to focus on tasks. But as one department becomes more effective as a result of competition, the departments as a collection are less effective. In battle, for every winner there is a loser. The consequences of winning and losing as a result of inter-group competition are described by Schein[6]:

C. What happens to the *winner?*
1. Winner retains cohesion and may become even more cohesive.
2. Winner tends to release tension, lose its fighting spirit, become complacent, casual, and playful (the "fat and happy" state).
3. Winner tends toward high intragroup cooperation and concern for members' needs, and low concern for work and task accomplishment.
4. Winner tends to be complacent and to feel that winning has confirmed the positive stereotype of itself and the negative stereotype of the "enemy" group; there is little basis for re-evaluating perceptions, or re-examining group operations in order to learn how to improve them.

D. What happens to the *loser?*
1. If the situation permits because of some ambiguity in the decision, there is a strong tendency for the loser to deny or distort the reality of losing; instead, the loser will find psychological escapes like "The judges were biased," "The judges didn't really understand our solution," "The rules of the game were not clearly explained to us."
2. If loss is accepted, the losing group tends to splinter, unresolved conflicts come to the surface, fights break out, all in the effort to find the cause for the loss.
3. Losing group is more tense, ready to work harder, and desperate to find someone or something to blame: the leader, itself, the judges who decided against them, the rules of the game (the "lean and hungry" state).
4. Loser tends toward low intragroup cooperation, low concern for members' needs, and high concern for recouping by working harder.
5. Loser tends to learn a lot about itself as a group because positive stereotype of itself and negative stereotype of the other group are upset by the loss,

forcing a re-evaluation of perceptions; as a consequence, loser is likely to reorganize and become more cohesive and effective, once the loss has been accepted realistically.

Occasionally, particularly in the short run, the positive effects of interdepartment competition may outweigh the negative, but as a long-term strategy interdepartmental cooperation makes more sense.

Interdepartmental cooperation requires that chairpersons see themselves as a cadre of individuals committed to educational and team leadership rather than isolated local administrators concerned exclusively with specialized instructional leadership. In this effort,[7]

 Greater emphasis needs to be given to total school effectiveness and the role of departments in contributing to it. Departments should be rewarded on the basis of their contribution to the total school effort rather than on individual effectiveness.

Opportunities for interaction and communication should be provided to enable departments to discuss intergroup coordination. School rewards should be distributed to departments partly on the basis of the extent to which they help each other.

Opportunities for rotation of members among groups or departments should be provided to stimulate mutual understanding and empathy.

Less emphasis needs to be placed on competition between departments for organizational rewards and on win-lose strategies. More emphasis needs to be placed on pooling resources by departments to maximize school effectiveness with rewards shared equally by cooperating departments.

Conflict Within Departments

Two characteristics of schools make them particularly susceptible to conflict among members of departments; schools are basically *value enterprises* and they operate in an economy of *scarce resources*. In values conflict members often disagree over appropriate educational goals and means, over appropriate student-teacher relationships, and over similar questions where one's position relates to attitude, beliefs, and philosophy. In scarce resources conflict individuals compete for the same thing, not enough of which seems to exist to satisfy everyone's desires. Some examples of scarce resources might be money, prime scheduling times, desirable students, high status courses, and positions of responsibility. Values conflict and scarce resources conflict are often intermingled and it is not unusual for each or both to contribute to interpersonal conflict, personality clashes, and even vendettas among teachers and between departments.

Conflict within a department can be devastating if left uncontrolled but conflict also can be a sign of independence, life, and health for a department. If teachers are relatively independent, feel free to express their opinion, and care about department goals and activities, then they will often have strong feelings about such matters. In this context, conflict seems like a normal and fruitful characteristic of the healthy department.

The chairperson has a number of options in developing strategies to deal with conflict within his department.

 One way of dealing with conflict is a *separated strategy*. Here the chairperson ignores, avoids or postpones dealing with the conflict issue at hand.

A second way is a *win/lose strategy*. Here one confronts conflict either by using sheer force or by using parliamentary procedures with the intent that as conflict is resolved there will be a winner and a loser.

A third way is a *win/win strategy*. Here the chairperson works to resolve conflict so that it is not necessary for losses to occur to any of the individuals involved.

Examples of separated strategies are[8]:

1. *Avoidance.* The costs of confrontation are seen to be too great. The odds of winning are stacked up too sharply against us. Conflict is avoided.
2. *Procrastination.* It is assumed that the passage of time will help resolve the conflict. Conflict is postponed with the hope that everything will work out.
3. *Co-existence.* It is assumed that individuals in conflict have approximately equal power; therefore, further conflict is likely to bring mutual loss. Individuals are in a holding pattern and when one side sees an imbalance of power in his favor, he is likely to move to a win/lose strategy.

Examples of win/lose strategies are:

4. *Fight.* It is assumed that the individuals engaged in conflict are independent; they don't need each other. Indeed each side believes that it would be better off without the other. In fight, the most able side wins and the costs are borne by the losers. The losers typically do not accept the decision of the winners and often immediately begin plotting and preparing for the next opportunity to fight. They have lost the battle but still hope to win the war. There often seems no end to the fight cycle.
5. *Third Party.* Like co-existence, each side of the conflict is equally powerful but they find themselves actively engaged in a win/lose struggle. A stalemate ensues and a third party is asked to decide the issue. Losers seldom feel that justice has been done as a result of third party intervention and while hostility may not continue as openly as it does for losers in fight, it exists nonetheless.
6. *Vote.* This is a parliamentary form of fighting. This procedure results in winners and losers but feelings are suppressed more and effects of losing are weaker. Further, the vote at least legitimately binds the losers to the decision of the winners. Voting causes lots of problems for chairpersons, particularly when the vote is close. A 6-to-5 decision may legally be the green light to

move ahead but nearly half the department has formally declared itself as opposed to the decision. The formal declaration of one's position often makes it difficult to subsequently become supportive of the decision.

7. *Compromise.* It is assumed that a partial victory for both sides is better than none at all; therefore bargaining takes place to "split the difference." Ideally, both sides give up something of lesser value to obtain something of greater value. In many circumstances compromise decisions may be the best we can do but they rarely are best in terms of developing optimal solutions to problems.

Examples of win/win strategies are:

8. *Consensus.* This strategy depends on the willingness of individuals to back off for personal interest after a certain point and at the same time avoiding backing off too easily. Its intent is to bring all parties to a mutually satisfying position on the problem under study. Consensus is only possible when there is an overriding commitment to the department and its members. Each individual argues his point not to win it necessarily but because he believes that his input and that of others will help develop a strong solution to the problem at hand.

9. *Third alternative.* This strategy is often a natural outgrowth of the consensus strategy. As each party in the conflict examines his ideas in relation to others, a third alternative emerges which is substantially different than options presently being considered. This third alternative is seen as beneficial to each of the parties in the conflict. Third alternatives often emerge accidentally but they need to be sought more deliberately.

10. *Mutual benefit.* This strategy differs from the others in that the intention of each person in the group is to work at solutions which will be of most benefit to others. In this strategy the department is seen as the winner and each individual in the group benefits from the winning. Competition is keen, value conflicts are real and differences exist with regard to the distribution of scarce resources. In each case these are exploited so that decisions that are reached as a group are better than any one individual's decision.

Any of the strategy types described above might be appropriate in one situation but inappropriate in another. Most will agree that the win/win strategies are usually the best, but circumstances do not always permit conflict to be resolved without losses to someone. Further, the issues may be such that resolving them in a way in which everyone is a winner may result in a solution which costs too much: it may not be educationally sound or students may incur the losses.

Strategies 4–10 might be viewed as a continuum, with those closer to mutual benefit being more productive to the department than those toward fight. Chairpersons probably should start with 10 in dealing with conflict, sliding down as far as they dare as it becomes necessary. When the costs of sliding further down toward fight are too great, but "better" strategies are not possible, the chairperson might wish to consider one of the three separated strategies described.

ENDNOTES

1. W. J. Reddin, 3-D Team Mode Theory as summarized in "Team Style Diagnosis Test" Instructions—Team Consensus Method. Managerial Effectiveness Ltd., Box 1012, Fredericton, N. B., Canada, 1972.

2. *Ibid.*

3. Adapted from Rensis Likert, *New Patterns of Management* (New York: McGraw-Hill, 1961), pp. 166–69.

4. Dr. Joseph Bechard of the Urbana, Illinois School District No. 116 was generous in sharing materials on shared decision-making which he has developed and used in practice.

5. Edgar Schein, *Organizational Psychology* (Englewood Cliffs, N. J.: Prentice-Hall, 1965), p. 81.

6. *Ibid.*, p. 82.

7. *Ibid.*, p. 85.

8. Adapted from Charles W. Miller and Robert Richardson, "Learning to Use Conflict" mimeo, undated.

Developing an effective work group among the teachers in your department, a critical aspect of your team leadership responsibilities, largely determines the extent to which you are effective in other leadership areas. Review, for example, your analysis of your key results areas and targets in the practices section of Chapter 2. Examine the competencies you selected from the list provided in the practices section of Chapter 1. Chances are, most of the competencies and key results areas you selected require that your department operate at a high level of effectiveness. In the first section of this chapter the critical components of an effective work group were described. Meetings are important to this effectiveness. In this section, suggestions and guidelines are provided to help you build department effectiveness particularly within the context of meetings. Included in this section are:

> Guidelines for avoiding unnecessary meetings
> Suggestions for meeting more effectively
> Building the agenda for meetings
> An agenda proposal form
> An agenda schedule worksheet
> A meeting evaluation checklist
> Some notes on seating arrangements
> Guidelines for meeting with the public
> A planning and evaluation checklist for public meetings
> Evaluating the human side of group functioning

AVOIDING UNNECESSARY MEETINGS

Meetings are an important part of the chairperson's job. In the concepts section of this chapter the needs were stressed for developing an effective work team, shared decision-making, and a mutual support system. These characteristics are not likely to happen without frequent formal and informal meetings. As one begins to develop an effective work group, meetings will be frequent, but as effectiveness increases, fewer meetings will be needed. Peter Drucker's comments, below, raise the issue of excessive meetings. Review his comments in light of these questions:

1. Does Drucker imply that all meetings are a waste of time?
2. Do departments and other groups in your school meet too often, just right, or not enough?
3. What percentage of meetings do you consider a waste of time?
4. Would the teachers in your department respond similarly? How would they respond?
5. Do some parts of the meetings held in your department seem to be more useful than others? What parts go well?
6. How often do you meet informally with teachers?
7. How often do you attend "other than department" meetings?
8. Is the issue Drucker raises one of meeting more—or less—or is the issue one of meeting more effectively?

Meetings Can Be Time-wasters*

Meetings are by definition a concession to deficient organization. For one either meets or one works. One cannot do both at the same time. In an ideally designed structure (which in a changing world is of course only a dream) there would be no meetings. Everybody would know what he needs to do his job. Everyone would have the resources available to him to do his job. We meet because people holding different jobs have to cooperate to get a specific task done. We meet because the knowledge and experience needed in a specific situation are not available in one head, but have to be pieced together out of the experience and knowledge of several people.

There will always be more than enough meetings. Organization will always require so much working together that the attempts of well-meaning behavioral scientists to create opportunities for "cooperation" may be somewhat redundant. But if executives in an organization spend more than a fairly small part of their time in meeting, it is a sure sign of mal-organization.

Every meeting generates a host of little follow-up meetings—some formal, some informal, but both stretching out for hours. Meetings, therefore, need to be purposefully directed. An undirected meeting is not just a nuisance; it is a danger. But above all, meetings have to be the exception rather than the rule. An organization in which everybody meets all the time is an organization in which no one gets anything done. Wherever a time log shows the fatty degeneration of meetings—whenever, for instance, people in an organization find themselves in meetings a quarter of their time or more—there is time-wasting mal-organization.

As a rule, meetings should never be allowed to become the main demand on an executive's time. Too many meetings always bespeak poor structure of jobs and the wrong organizational components. Too many meetings signify that work that should be in one job or in one component is spread over several jobs or several components. They signify that responsibility is diffused and that information is not addressed to the people who need it.

Often meetings become an excuse for getting on with one's work rather than a means to accomplish this work. One carefully-planned meeting may be worth several of

*Excerpts from Peter Drucker, *The Effective Executive* (New York: Harper and Row, 1967), pp. 44, 45.

the type described by Drucker. You can avoid unnecessary meetings by planning the meetings you do have. Share Drucker's comments with groups with whom you meet regularly. Use his comments to raise the issue of excessive meetings. Help them understand that meeting more effectively is a substitute for meeting more often.

Suggestions for Meeting More Effectively

The best way to cut down on the number of meetings you attend or conduct is to get more out of them. But effective meetings should not only be seen as profitable in the sense that objectives are achieved and tasks are accomplished. Effective meetings are also stimulating, enjoyable, and interesting to teachers. Earlier, it was suggested that though psychological groups are not always effective work groups, effective work groups *are* always psychological groups. Keep this in mind as you review the following suggestions for planning and conducting department meetings:

1. *Identify and record a set of goals or targets for the year's department meetings.* These goals or targets should be related to your key results areas and the yearly targets you set for yourself (see the second section of Chapter 2). A tentative yearly schedule of topics and activities might then be distributed to all department members.

2. *Plan carefully for each meeting.* Your plans should focus less on particular solutions to problems than on facilitating solutions. If you decide beforehand on *the* way to solve a particular problem, you probably don't need a meeting. Your responsibility is to help the group solve problems and you do this by providing the necessary structure, resources, and environment. Planning includes setting targets for meetings, building an agenda, preparing the physical setting, obtaining faculty involvement, preparing a record-keeping system, and arranging for evaluation of meetings.

3. *Be concerned with the physical setting for your meetings.* Teachers generally come to meetings in addition to their assignments and only rarely as a substitute for an assignment. So effort should be made to provide a comfortable setting, but one which is also conducive to getting the work done.
   Provide for adequate seating, ventilation and refreshments. Prepare to start and finish on time. Being organized, having materials ready, using a blackboard or a felt pen pad also help.

4. *Prepare and distribute an agenda to all department members before each meeting.* Teachers should participate in developing the agenda. Guidelines for developing an agenda, and for obtaining and using teacher input are provided in the next part of this section.

5. *Develop and display objectives for each meeting.* These purposes should be communicated to department members on the agenda, which is circulated, and again on a blackboard or felt pen pad. Purposes are important to help structure the meeting and to provide for a means of evaluating progress during and after the meeting.

6. *Keep "administrivia" time to a minimum.* Announcements and other routines which do not require elaboration or reactions should be made through

115

memos. No more than 20 percent of the meeting time should be spent on such routines (ten to twelve minutes per hour).

7. *Use a moderator to chair department meetings.* A moderator is a person elected by the department who assumes responsibility for operating meetings. Moderators could also be selected, meeting by meeting, on a rotating basis. The chairperson is still responsible for planning meetings, agenda building, evaluating, and for administering decisions made at meetings. The use of a moderator offers a number of advantages. The chairperson is in a position to listen to others and to participate, idea for idea, with others on an equal basis. Communications tend to free up and department members are likely to participate willingly. The chairperson might "chair" the meeting for the first ten minutes dealing with routine matters, then join the group as a participant, leaving the chairing to the moderator for the problem-solving discussions.

8. *Involve staff in planning, agenda building, problem-solving and evaluation.* Department members should help outline yearly goals and individual meeting targets and participate as much as possible in other aspects of planning and operating meetings. You and your department constitute a team; you are in it together; and you need each other if you see department effectiveness as more than doing one's job in a satisfactory but routine fashion.

9. *Keep a record of department meetings.* A detailed summary of each meeting is well worth the effort. Such a record might contain department positions, reactions to curricular materials, policies and activities agreed upon, and procedures adopted, all important for future reference. Each year, the record should be reviewed, policy-oriented and procedural statements should be extracted and, after careful review by department members, made a part of the department's policies and procedures or if appropriate, a part of the department's educational program platform (see Chapter 10 for a discussion of educational program platform).

10. *Provide a mechanism for evaluating meetings.* Evaluation is an important but overlooked aspect of building effectiveness into meetings. Meetings should be evaluated on a regular basis and evaluation should become an important part of the planning and agenda-building cycle. A checklist for evaluating meetings is provided later in this section.

The kind of leadership you bring to meetings will influence effectiveness. Of particular importance will be your actual behavior in the meeting after the planning and arranging suggested above. You want to operate so as not to force department members to compete with you, or to vie for your attention. Competing or patronizing behavior can be expected from group members if you are the center of the group's activity. Shifting the focus from *yourself* to the group problems and targets will require a break from tradition. The following principles might be helpful to you as you work to shift the focus.

1. *Avoid competing with department members.* You have good ideas and they should be expressed. But if you are inclined to contribute your ideas before others, chances are you will favor yours and others are likely to accept them because of your authority. As a general rule, give precedence to the ideas of every other member before presenting yours. Probably you will hear some ideas not likely to be offered if you contribute first. Further, often the ideas

you have are proposed by others in the group, and that helps in their ultimate adoption.

2. *Listen to your department members.* Practice paraphrasing in your own words to make sure you understand the ideas of others to their satisfaction. This requires that you avoid making judgments, tuning out or projecting your own ideas or otherwise not fully comprehending what others are saying.

3. *Avoid putting others on the defensive.* This requires that you assume most members' contributions to have value and that you work to discover this value. Often the wildest idea has within it some insights from which all can benefit.

4. *Keep the tone of the meeting at a high peak.* The amount of energy or excitement present in a group depends upon factors beyond your control. Being tired, sick or pressed for time are examples. But you can contribute much to the group's tone. If you are interested, alert and working hard, this modelling is likely to affect others. Keep the meeting pace brisk. Don't try to be a professional clown but show that you have a sense of humor. Occasionally humor tends to have a rejuvenating effect on group interest and effort. Have high expectations for members to participate: ask them challenging questions, give them responsibilities, expect them to be prepared.

5. *Get participation from everyone.* It is easy to "play" to the few people who tend to be talkative. But you need everyone's ideas. Let the group know this. Seek out the quieter members but don't embarrass them. If they don't respond, move on to another person. As you prepare for your next meeting, give the less talkative members more formal responsibility.

6. *Keep an on-going record of the group's progress.* Keep notes during the meeting. Do this by writing on an easel or blackboard which is visible to all group members. Indicate what has been accomplished and when you are moving on to the next step. When the group gets involved in discussion, restate where you think the group is and have them comment. This on-going record can be kept by the moderator, if you choose to use one, or by another member of the group. Rotating this responsibility among group members keeps them interested, particularly in the continuity of issues from meeting to meeting. If, for example, it is my responsibility to record next week, I had better be alert to events occurring this week for many may carry over.

BUILDING THE AGENDA FOR DEPARTMENT MEETINGS

An agenda is a tool used to inform group members what is expected of them during a meeting and what the meeting will try to accomplish. The intent of the agenda is to guide activities discussion in an orderly fashion. But the real merits of the agenda are its effects on group members before the meeting gets underway. Knowing beforehand what items will be discussed helps individuals to prepare for meetings, to assemble needed materials, to do some thinking and perhaps visit with others. Further, if the agenda is cooperatively constructed, it provides a unique and effective way to build identity and commitment to group meetings and to increase interest and participation. Interest, participation, identity and commitment are participant qualities essential to successful meetings.

Two approaches to agenda building are proposed below—an open approach and a structured agenda. Each shares in high involvement of teachers in the process of agenda building and each can result in a well planned, orderly meeting to which teachers are committed. Which method will be best for you and your department? Why not try each to see which you and teachers in your department prefer?

Guide to Building an Agenda—Open Approach

The open approach to agenda building provides more participation of staff. The staff assumes a full 75 percent of responsibility for this task. This approach is suggested by the following steps:

1. Identify a high traffic area for department faculty members but one not generally accessible to large numbers of students. A department office, professional library or resource room might be a good choice.
2. Place in this area a large blackboard, felt pen pad, or piece of brown wrapping paper mounted on a wall.
3. Have teachers write on this display space agenda items they wish to have considered following these procedures.
   a) The name of the initiator or proposer must be placed next to the agenda item.
   b) An estimate of the amount of meeting time needed for dealing with the item should be included. Indicate the total time scheduled for the meeting to give teachers some sense of priority and to discourage them from offering unimportant items.
   c) A priority rating should be provided for each item. The person should indicate high (next meeting), medium (within three meetings) or low (as time permits) priority.
4. As teachers review the items during the agenda building process, have them write their names next to items in which they are most interested. This will permit them to identify other similarly interested teachers with whom they might engage in pre-meeting discussion.
5. Ask teachers to comment on priority rankings of items. If the proposer rates an item high and most others feel it is low, perhaps the proposer will change his rating.
6. The chairperson is encouraged to offer items following the above procedures. This offer could also be extended to other administrative and supervisory personnel and perhaps even to representatives of the student body.

As the meeting time approaches, you can summarize notes written on the display space and put them in a more formal agenda format, or you can conduct the meeting directly from the material written on the display space. If you choose the latter, use the first few minutes of the meeting to order items and to add to or delete from the list.

Guide to Building An Agenda—Structured Approach

The structured approach offers high teacher involvement but within a more established framework. In this approach, the staff assumes about half of the responsibility for agenda building. In using this approach, consider the following suggestions:

1. Provide each teacher and other interested parties (student representatives and administrators, supervisors and specialists not in your department) with agenda proposal forms to be used to propose items for consideration at department meetings. See the example.

AGENDA PROPOSAL FORM

NAME_____ DATE _____

1. What is the agenda item? Please be as specific as possible.

2. What problems underlie this agenda item? What issues does the item relate to?

3. Which of the following best applies to this item?
   _____ For information only
   _____ Status report
   _____ For discussion but not decision
   _____ Request a decision from the group
   _____ Request the group endorse a decision made elsewhere
   _____ Other, please explain

4. Estimate the amount of time needed to handle this item. _____ minutes

5. What priority do you place on this item?
   _____ high—should be considered at next meeting
   _____ medium—should be considered within three meetings
   _____ low—as time permits

6. Will you be willing to propose this item?
   _____ not applicable
   _____ yes
   _____ no

7. What materials, reports, equipment will be needed to consider this item?

8. Additional comments

2. Set a deadline for getting agenda items to you. Allow sufficient time to evaluate items, prepare an agenda schedule, and get it circulated to interested parties. If you expect people to prepare adequately for meetings, to discuss items, and to assemble materials, inform them at least three, preferably five, work days in advance.
3. Your next task is to study records of previous meetings and the Agenda Proposal Forms; summarize the latter. Consult your own schedule and examine your targets as you search for additional items. Assemble this material in a form which permits you to prepare the meeting's agenda. The agenda schedule worksheet may help you. The example allows a flex time (the difference between time available and estimated time needed) of only five minutes. This is too tight and one should consider dropping an item. Ideally you should allow ten minutes of flex time for every scheduled hour of meeting. In this case, fifteen minutes should be allowed.

AGENDA SCHEDULE WORKSHEET

MEETING DATE   3/14   MEETING TIME   2:30—4:00

ESTI-MATED TIME NEEDED MINUTES	ITEM PROPOSED BY	ITEM	PROBLEM OR ISSUE	PROBABLE ACTION REQUIRED	ORDER OF APPEAR-ANCE
5	Chairperson	Review of minutes	Continuity—accuracy	Approve, add, delete	1
5	Chairperson	Review agenda	Accuracy—new items	Approve, add, delete	2
25	John D.	Objectives	Priorities are not being set. Need help in writing objectives.	Accept subcommit-tee's suggestions	5
15	Steven A.	Organizational structure	*Evaluation of present scheduling procedure	Progress report obtain suggestions	4
10	Susan A.	Budget	Do not have all requests to complete budget priorities	Remind people—set a deadline	3
25	Ann K.	Evaluation	*Proposal to evaluate the department laboratory experiences, offerings and courses	Discussion	6
Total Time 85	Comments: Ann is sub-stituting	Comments:	Comments: *Need attachments for these items.	Comments: Push hard on getting budget requests on time.	
Time Available 90					
Flex Time 5					

4. After completing the agenda schedule worksheet you need to develop the final agenda to be circulated. The agenda might take a number of forms, but should include the following information:
   a. estimated time and probable action required for each item
   b. time and place for the meeting
   c. who, in addition to department members, will attend
   d. supplementary documents and other materials needed to support agenda items
   e. the minutes or other record of your last meeting

MEETING EVALUATION CHECKLIST

Use this checklist to evaluate each department meeting. You should do this yourself for every meeting and with the group for about one-third of your meetings. The evaluation checklist should help you plan for future meetings.

MEETING _____ DATE _____

I. Was the meeting generally productive?

_____ Yes, very productive   _____ Average   _____ No, not productive

A. Meeting was generally productive because we:
_____ did what we set out to do
_____ set challenging targets
_____ are sure of our commitment
_____ are pleased with work output
_____ solved some tough problems
_____ really learned something
_____ are now on the same wavelength
_____ resolved some disagreement
_____ improved our work relationship
_____

B. The meeting was unproductive because we:
_____ didn't do all we wanted to
_____ are not sure results will come
_____ left too many problems unresolved
_____ didn't communicate effectively
_____ did nothing new—just a rehash
_____ didn't do enough
_____ still don't see eye to eye
_____ didn't learn anything
_____ still disagree basically
_____

II. How much time did the session take? _____ minutes. Next time we need to plan _____ minutes to get the best results.

III. How was the time spent?
_____ percent looking at the past: reporting past results, reporting present work status, evaluating results or performance
_____ percent looking to the future: setting goals, ensuring results, solving problems, anticipating change, finding improvements

IV. Who did the talking?

Chairperson _____ %   Moderator _____ %   Teachers _____ %

V. *For Chairperson Only*
a. How much time was spent during the meeting in issues relating to each of your broad key results areas?

Educational _____ %   Organizational _____ %   Supervisory _____ %
Administrative _____ %   Team _____ %

b. What specific results areas were considered?

SOME NOTES ON SEATING ARRANGEMENTS

Spatial arrangements are relatively easy to influence, yet often this aspect of planning for meetings is ignored. Do arrangements make a difference? Is it important to plan arrangements which encourage one or another pattern of seating? Are some arrangements better than others in achieving a particular objective? The answer to these questions is yes, though the precise relationship between spatial and seating arrangements is not fully understood.

In the statements which follow,* some of these relationships are spelled out. Remember that the relationships are by no means perfect and can easily be confounded by a number of other concerns such as status, commitment levels, task characteristics, and group atmosphere. Consider the statements, therefore, as general guides which suggest probable but not perfect relationships.

1. One's relative position at a table has a bearing on the amount of influence he exerts in the meeting. Individuals who sit in end positions exert influence more readily than those sitting elsewhere.

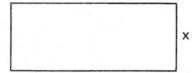

2. When two individuals are sitting on one side of a table and three on the opposite side, the two-person side is likely to contain the person who exerts the greatest influence.

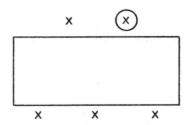

*See for example: Robert Sommer, "Small Group Ecology," *Psychological Bulletin,* Vol. 67, 1967, pp. 145–152 and Sommer, *Personal Space* (Englewood Cliffs, N. J.: Prentice-Hall, 1969). Also, L. T. Howells and S. W. Becker, "Seating Arrangements for Leadership Emergence," *Journal of Abnormal and Social Psychology,* Vol. 64, 1962, pp. 148–150.

3. The more distance which exists between two individuals sitting at a table, the less friendly and talkative each perceives the other to be.

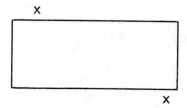

4. When one person stops speaking someone opposite rather than alongside is likely to speak next.

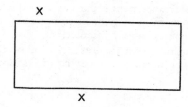

5. Persons sitting next to each other are most likely to agree and to help or cooperate with each other.

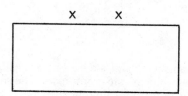

6. Persons who sit "kitty cornered" are more likely to engage in non-competitive conversations.

7. Persons who sit across from each other are most likely to engage in competitive conversations.

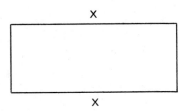

Try the triangular or circular arrangements as an alternative to the rectangular spatial arrangement. The triangular with the chairperson or moderator sitting at the apex and others generally along the base is useful for formal meetings where the dispensing of information or directions and the receiving of reports are important.

The circular arrangement is particularly suitable for problem solving and helps to shift focus from individuals to tasks and objectives. Further, this arrangement encourages open interaction.

8. The triangular arrangement focuses attention on the leader who sits at the apex and permits him to more easily control group direction and flow of interaction.

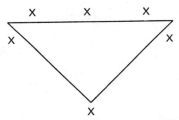

9. The circular arrangement shifts the group attention from the leader and his authority to the problems the group faces. The shift is greatly facilitated by introducing an inanimate focal point such as a blackboard or felt pen easel.

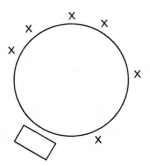

10. Sometimes the chairperson or moderator will want to open the meeting with a triangular arrangement for organizational and clarifying purposes of a routine nature; then, by joining the group, form a more circular arrangement for problem-solving activities.

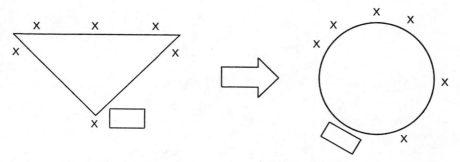

The actual spatial arrangements you make for meetings should be much more informal or irregular than the shapes suggested above. Nothing could be more stifling than entering a room where the chairs are arranged in a perfect circle or triangle. Note the informality of the triangular and circular arrangements illustrated below:

THE TRIANGULAR SPATIAL ARRANGEMENT

THE CIRCULAR SPATIAL ARRANGEMENT

Be Sensitive to Personal Space

Edward Hall* has categorized an individual's personal space into four zones: the intimate, the personal, the social and the public zones. The intimate zone for Americans is generally from skin surface to 18 inches. This zone represents a barrier within which only intimate relationships (love, comforting) are permitted and other intrusions often result in uncomfortable, defensive, or anxious feelings. On crowded elevators or in other impersonal settings persons entering this zone are seen more as objects than people.

The personal zone ranges from about 18 inches to 4 1/2 feet around a person. This is the comfortable range for most interactions which are characterized by close friendship. The social zone ranges from about 4 to 12 feet. People working together

*Edward Hall, *The Hidden Dimension* (New York: Doubleday, 1968). See also Robert Sommer, *Personal Space* (Englewood Cliffs, N.J.: Prentice-Hall, 1969).

typically maintain this kind of spacing probably working closer to 4 feet but moving more to the outside for formal and impersonal interaction. Beyond 12 feet is considered the public zone.

MEETING WITH THE PUBLIC

Occasionally, you or members of your department want or need to meet with parents or community groups. Such meetings often involve explaining new programs or teaching techniques, hearing complaints or grievances, soliciting support, or providing service. Meetings with the public (even the most routine meeting, such as "parents' night") require very special consideration and thorough planning. Generally such meetings should be kept simple, relatively informal, and candid. These characteristics hold the most promise for communicating effectively and for problem solving.

But candid, informal and simple meetings are also among the most vulnerable. A safer, but less effective strategy, is to conduct rather formal meetings structured in detail by a preconceived agenda, established by school people. Such meetings, however, tend not to be very conducive to problem solving. Use the checklist provided below to help plan for meeting with the public and to evaluate your readiness to meet.

PLANNING AND EVALUATION CHECKLIST FOR MEETING WITH PUBLIC

MEETING WITH _____ DATE _____

CHECKLIST	YES	NO	N/A	WHO IS RESPONSIBLE FOR THIS?	COMPLETED WHEN?	COMMENTS
1. Do we have goals and objectives for meeting(s)?	—	—	—	_____	_____	_____
2. Do we have the materials we need for the meeting?	—	—	—	_____	_____	_____
3. Do we have A-V aids for the meeting?	—	—	—	_____	_____	_____
4. Have we established the number of meetings?	—	—	—	_____	_____	_____
5. Have we established dates and made space arrangements?	—	—	—	_____	_____	_____
6. Has the meeting been publicized?	—	—	—	_____	_____	_____
7. Have room mothers or parent hosts been contacted?	—	—	—	_____	_____	_____
8. Has the principal's office been informed?	—	—	—	_____	_____	_____
9. Have we planned to make an accurate record of the meeting?	—	—	—	_____	_____	_____

WHICH DEPARTMENT MEMBERS WILL ATTEND THE MEETINGS?	WHO WILL ATTEND?	SPECIAL ASSIGNMENTS IF APPLICABLE
Meeting 1 (Location _____)	1. _____	_____
	2. _____	_____
	3. _____	_____
Meeting 2 (Location _____)	1. _____	_____
	2. _____	_____
	3. _____	_____

Indicate, under special assignments, who will moderate the meeting, who will initiate items, who is responsible for record-keeping, hosting, A-V presentation and any other required roles. Limit participants to three if possible in an effort to avoid establishing by sheer numbers a "we-they feeling" on either side.

EVALUATING THE HUMAN SIDE OF GROUP FUNCTIONING

In building an effective work group you are not only concerned with planning and organizing, but must also attend to the human side of group functioning. In the concepts section of this chapter we suggested that in effective work groups, the common purposes which members share are consistent with department objectives; interaction usually concerns itself with job-defined purposes and activities. There are high identity with and commitment to department objectives and task effectiveness is high. But in addition to this task emphasis we also suggested that the effective department is a psychological group and therefore members interact with each other, have a group identity, and find membership satisfying. The group is characterized by high interaction effectiveness.

In building and maintaining high interaction effectiveness among members of your department, you will need to give attention to such human conditions as morale, atmosphere, participation, styles of influence, leadership struggles, conflict, competition, and cooperation. Increasing your sensitivity to these conditions and other aspects of the groups processes can help you to spot problems early and to deal with them more effectively. Below are some observation guidelines, summarized by Philip G. Hanson, which can help you to analyze group behavior and to better understand the human side of how your department functions as a team.

What to Look for in Your Department*: Observation Guidelines

PARTICIPATION. One indication of involvement is verbal participation. Look for differences in the amount of participation among members.

1. Who are the high participators?
2. Who are the low participators?
3. Do you see any shift in participation, *e.g.,* highs become quiet; lows suddenly become talkative? Do you see any possible reason for this in the group's interaction?
4. How are the silent people treated? How is their silence interpreted? Consent? Disagreement? Disinterest? Fear?
5. Who talks to whom? Do you see any reason for this in the group's interactions?
6. Who keeps the ball rolling? Why? Do you see any reason for this in the group's interactions?

INFLUENCE. Influence and participation are not the same. Some people may speak very little, yet they capture the attention of the whole group. Others may talk a lot but are generally not listened to by other members.

*Philip G. Hanson, "What to Look for in Groups," in J. William Pfeiffer and John E. Jones (eds.), *The 1972 Annual Handbook for Group Facilitators* (LaJolla, Calif.: University Associates, 1972), pp. 21–24.

7. Which members are high in influence? That is, when they talk others seem to listen.
8. Which members are low in influence? Others do not listen to or follow them. Is there any shifting in influence? Who shifts?
9. Do you see any rivalry in the group? Is there a struggle for leadership? What effect does it have on other group members?

STYLES OF INFLUENCE. Influence can take many forms. It can be positive or negative; it can enlist the support or cooperation of others or alienate them. *How* a person attempts to influence another may be the crucial factor in determining how open or closed the other will be toward being influenced. Items 10 through 13 are suggestive of four styles that frequently emerge in groups.

10. Autocratic: Does anyone attempt to impose his will or values on other group members or try to push them to support his decisions? Who evaluates or passes judgment on other group members? Do any members block action when it is not moving the direction they desire? Who pushes to "get the group organized"?
11. Peacemaker: Who eagerly supports other group members' decisions? Does anyone consistently try to avoid conflict or unpleasant feelings from being expressed by pouring oil on the troubled waters? Is any member typically deferential toward other group members—gives them power? Do any members appear to avoid giving negative feedback, *i.e.,* who will level only when they have positive feedback to give?
12. Laissez faire: Are any group members getting attention by their apparent lack of involvement in the group? Does any group member go along with group decisions without seeming to commit himself one way or the other? Who seems to be withdrawn and uninvolved; who does not initiate activity, participates mechanically and only in response to another member's question?
13. Democratic: Does anyone try to include everyone in a group decision or discussion? Who expresses his feelings and opinions openly and directly without evaluating or judging others? Who appears to be open to feedback and criticisms from others? When feelings run high and tension mounts, which members attempt to deal with the conflict in a problem-solving way?

DECISION-MAKING PROCEDURES. Many kinds of decisions are made in groups without considering the effects of these decisions on other members. Some people try to impose their own decisions on the group, while others want all members to participate or share in the decisions that are made.

14. Does anyone make a decision and carry it out without checking with other group members? (Self-authorized) For example, he decides on the topic to be discussed and immediately begins to talk about it. What effect does this have on other group members?
15. Does the group drift from topic to topic? Who topic-jumps? Do you see any reason for this in the group's interactions?
16. Who supports other members' suggestions or decisions? Does this support result in the two members deciding the topic or activity for the group

(handclasp)? How does this affect other group members?

17. Is there any evidence of a majority pushing a decision through over other members' objections? Do they call for a vote (majority support)?

18. Is there any attempt to get all members participating in a decision (consensus)? What effect does this seem to have on the group?

19. Does anyone make any contributions which do not receive any kind of response or recognition (plop)? What effect does this have on the member?

TASK FUNCTIONS. These functions illustrate behaviors that are concerned with getting the job done, or accomplishing the task that the group has before them.

20. Does anyone ask for or make suggestions as to the best way to proceed or to tackle a problem?

21. Does anyone attempt to summarize what has been covered or what has been going on in the group?

22. Is there any giving or asking for facts, ideas, opinions, feelings, feedback, or searching for alternatives?

23. Who keeps the group on target? Who prevents topic-jumping or going off on tangents?

MAINTENANCE FUNCTIONS. These functions are important to the morale of the group. They maintain good and harmonious working relationships among the members and create a group atmosphere which enables each member to contribute maximally. They insure smooth and effective teamwork within the group.

24. Who helps others get into the discussion (gate openers)?

25. Who cuts off others or interrupts them (gate closers)?

26. How well are members getting their ideas across? Are some members preoccupied and not listening? Are there any attempts by group members to help others clarify their ideas?

27. How are ideas rejected? How do members react when their ideas are not accepted? Do members attempt to support others when they reject their ideas?

GROUP ATMOSPHERE. Something about the way a group works creates an atmosphere which in turn is revealed in a general impression. In addition, people may differ in the kind of atmosphere they like in a group. Insight can be gained into the atmosphere characteristic of a group by finding words which describe the general impressions held by group members.

28. Who seems to prefer a friendly congenial atmosphere? Is there any attempt to suppress conflict or unpleasant feelings?

29. Who seems to prefer an atmosphere of conflict and disagreement? Do any members provoke or annoy others?

30. Do people seem involved and interested? Is the atmosphere one of work, play, satisfaction, taking flight, sluggishness, etc.?

MEMBERSHIP.   A major concern for group members is the degree of acceptance or inclusion in the group. Different patterns of interaction may develop in the group which give clues to the degree and kind of membership.

31. Is there any sub-grouping? Sometimes two or three members may consistently agree and support each other or consistently disagree and oppose one another.
32. Do some people seem to be "outside" the group? Do some members seem to be "in"? How are those "outside" treated?
33. Do some members move in and out of the group, *e.g.*, lean forward or backward in their chairs or move their chairs in and out? Under what conditions do they come in or move out?

FEELINGS.   During any group discussion, feelings are frequently generated by the interactions between members. These feelings, however, are seldom talked about. Observers may have to make guesses based on tone of voice, facial expressions, gestures, and many other forms of nonverbal cues.

34. What signs of feelings do you observe in group members: anger, irritation, frustration, warmth, affection, excitement, boredom, defensiveness, competitiveness, etc.?
35. Do you see any attempts by group members to block the expression of feelings, particularly negative feelings? How is this done? Does anyone do this consistently?

NORMS.   Standards or ground rules may develop in a group that control the behavior of its members. Norms usually express the beliefs or desires of the majority of the group members as to what behaviors *should* or *should not* take place in the group. These norms may be clear to all members (explicit), known or sensed by only a few (implicit), or operating completely below the level of awareness of any group members. Some norms facilitate group progress and some hinder it.

36. Are certain areas avoided in the group (*e.g.*, sex, religion, talk about present feelings in group, discussing the leader's behavior)? Who seem to reinforce this avoidance? How do they do it?
37. Are group members overly nice or polite to each other? Are only positive feelings expressed? Do members agree with each other too readily? What happens when members disagree?
38. Do you see norms operating about participation or the kinds of questions that are allowed (*e.g.*, "If I talk, you must talk"; "If I tell my problems you have to tell your problems")? Do members feel free to probe each other about their feelings? Do questions tend to be restricted to intellectual topics or events outside of the group?

Refer to the beginning of the Concepts section of this chapter. Review the eight descriptions of departments at work. As you analyze your department using the questions provided above, estimate how often your department functions in a manner which fits each of the eight descriptions.

Problem-Solving	____ %	Mixed	____ %
Productive	____ %	Fight	____ %
Creative	____ %	Dependent	____ %
Procedural	____ %	Flight	____ %

PART THREE

THE CHAIRPERSON'S SUPERVISORY LEADERSHIP FUNCTIONS

LEADERSHIP BEHAVIOR AND DEPARTMENT EFFECTIVENESS

❧ CONCEPTS ❧

You will continue to find numerous references herein to the chairperson as a leader. In earlier chapters, it was suggested that the chairperson's leadership capabilities in education, organization, administration, and teamwork are the cornerstones of effectiveness for his department and school. Previous discussions may have built up the leadership role of chairperson to a point beyond the reach of most. This is a standard risk one runs in describing leadership. Such discussions usually conjur grandiose images of great men with vast resources of vision who make key decisions or who by their presence create excitement that dramatically affects the course of their organizations and the lives of their associates.

The great-man image is not a bad prescription for chairpersons as leaders. Indeed they should be exciting and visionary and indeed they should possess a sense of mission and purpose that transcends the everyday operation of the department and school. This theory falls apart, however, when such leadership is uniformly expected from all and, further, is expected continuously without regard to situations. Chairpersons differ in their abilities to operate as great men; situations common to the real school world often require few glamorous expressions of leadership; and in a cooperative leadership setting too many great men may result in more leadership than a situation can stand.

It is fair to say that while chairpersons are not expected to, and most are probably not capable of, operating continuously as great men, possessing a sense of mission and a depth of vision that transcend day-to-day affairs are important characteristics of leaders. However, in the remainder of this chapter the discussion will be less concerned with the chairperson's specific sense of mission and more concerned with the ways in which he behaves as a leader.

EXPRESSIONS OF LEADERSHIP[1]

By definition, leadership is different than administration in that the former involves introducing something new or helping to improve present conditions. Leadership usually involves bringing about a change in the way people think and behave and in the way the school functions. Administration refers to the maintenance, support, and service of present operations. For some people leadership comes easily and naturally. But most people in positions of leadership are not born leaders. The skills and insights needed by an effective leader can be learned through training and experience.

Once it was thought that a single best leadership style could be identified; the chairperson would need only to discover this style, learn it, and use it. Unfortunately, leadership effectiveness is much more complex, and any number of styles or approaches may be effective given the proper circumstances. Let's consider the major dimensions of leadership style and the situations which determine its effectiveness.

Leadership Dimensions

Research into leadership style in educational and non-educational settings has identified two key dimensions of leadership. Experts generally agree that leadership style is defined by 1) the extent to which the leader seems to focus on getting work done; and 2) the extent to which he seems to focus on the needs or feelings of people and his relationships with them.

In this discussion the phrase task-oriented (TO) will be used to refer to tendencies for the leader to focus on work, and relations-oriented (RO) for his tendency to focus on people in his leadership behavior. Each of these dimensions of leadership style are illustrated conceptually below in Figure 5–1.

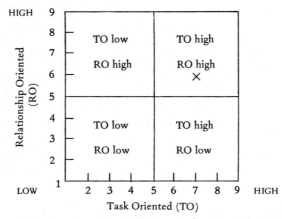

FIGURE 5-1. THE LEADERSHIP GRID. FROM T. J. SERGIOVANNI AND D. L. ELLIOTT, *EDUCATIONAL AND ORGANIZATIONAL LEADERSHIP IN ELEMENTARY SCHOOLS* (ENGLEWOOD CLIFFS, N.J.: PRENTICE-HALL, INC., 1975), p. 101.

The axis which forms the base of the grid represents the extent to which the leader's behavior shows a concern for task accomplishment (TO) with a high concern to the right and a low concern to the left. You might estimate the extent to which your leadership style shows concern for task by checking one of the numbers (1–9) on this line. The axis which forms the left side of the grid represents the extent to which the leader's behavior shows a concern for people and relationships (RO) with the top representing high concern and the bottom, low concern. Check one of the numbers on this line to estimate the extent to which you show concern for people and relationships in expressing leadership.

To find your location in the grid based on the estimates you have made find the point where lines drawn from each of the numbers you checked would intersect. For example, if you checked a 7 on the TO line and 6 on the RO line your position would be indicated by the x which appears on the grid.

The Basic Leadership Styles

This section is concerned with what each of the four quadrants of the leadership grid represent. Though there are a number of frameworks for describing leadership, W. J. Reddin's 3-D Theory of Leadership will be discussed because of its comprehensiveness, conciseness, and practicality.[2]

The lower right-hand quadrant (TO high and RO low) represents a style of leadership characterized by a good deal of drive and emphasis on work with little overt concern for the relationship dimension.

 This is called the *dedicated* leadership style and is characterized by an emphasis on organizing, initiating, directing, completing, and evaluating the work of others.

The upper left-hand quadrant (TO low and RO high) represents a style of leadership that emphasizes concern for people with little overt concern for the task dimension.

 This is called the *related* leadership style and is characterized by emphases on listening, accepting, trusting, advising, and encouraging.

The upper right-hand quadrant (TO high and RO high) represents a combination approach whereby people concerns are expressed through emphasizing meaningful work, and work concerns are emphasized by bringing together and stimulating committed groups of individuals.

 This is called the *integrated* leadership style and is characterized by an emphasis on interaction, motivation, integration, participation, and innovation.

The lower left-hand quadrant (TO low and RO low) represents a style of leadership that expresses very little concern for both dimensions. In a sense the leader removes himself from both task and people.

This is called the *separated* leadership style and is characterized by an emphasis on examining, measuring, administering, controlling, and maintaining.

The behavior indicators Reddin suggests as being associated with each of the four basic leadership styles are shown in grid four in Figure 5-2.[3]

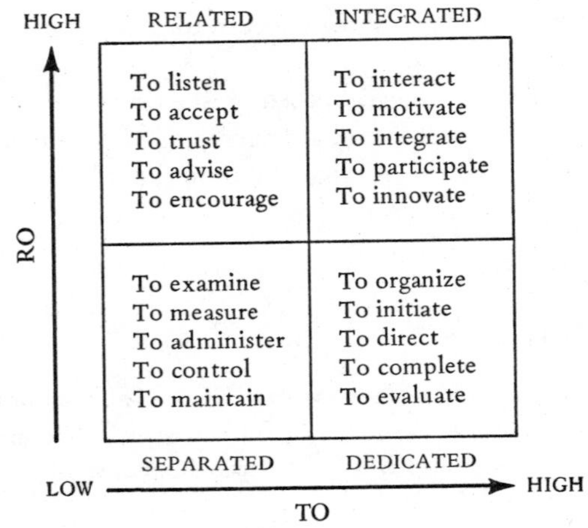

HIGH   RELATED   INTEGRATED

RELATED	INTEGRATED
To listen To accept To trust To advise To encourage	To interact To motivate To integrate To participate To innovate
To examine To measure To administer To control To maintain	To organize To initiate To direct To complete To evaluate

SEPARATED   DEDICATED

LOW ———————→ HIGH

TO

(vertical axis: RO)

FIGURE 5-2. BASIC STYLE BEHAVIOR INDICATORS. FROM W. J. REDDIN, *MANAGERIAL EFFEC-TIVENESS* (NEW YORK: McGRAW-HILL, 1970), p. 94.

Each of the four basic leadership styles is considered discrete only conceptually. In reality most chairpersons would fall on locations less clearly labelled within the leadership grid. Chairpersons probably give some attention to all or most of the twenty behavior indicators and indeed to behaviors not listed. The unique emphasis which a person gives to the indicators, especially the indicators most frequently used and most easily expressed, is what gives one a unique leadership style.

Consider, for example, a chairperson who frequently and with ease *interacts* with teachers about their work, *motivates* teachers to increase commitment and performance, *participates* with teachers in developing curricula and other decisions, *listens* to teachers' ideas and problems, and works hard building *trust* levels among department members. Of the twenty indicators these are the five most often and readily expressed. Using Reddin's 3-D theory vocabulary, his leadership style would be described as primarily integrated with the related style as a support or supplement. While one can readily describe the leadership styles of the chairperson, it is more difficult to determine if the styles he expresses are effective.

Many disagreements exist over which of the leadership styles is best. Early research in education seemed to suggest that the integrated style characterized by high TO and RO was best. Recent thought, however, assumes that effective leadership style can only be understood within the context of the leadership situation. That is, any of the four basic styles of leadership could work or not, depending upon the situation. W. J. Reddin's 3-D theory of leadership does an excellent job of illustrating the importance of situation in determining effectiveness. He assumes that related, integrated, separated, and dedicated are only four basic styles each with an effective and an ineffective equivalent depending upon the situation in which they are used. These effective and ineffective equivalents result in eight operational leadership styles as shown below.

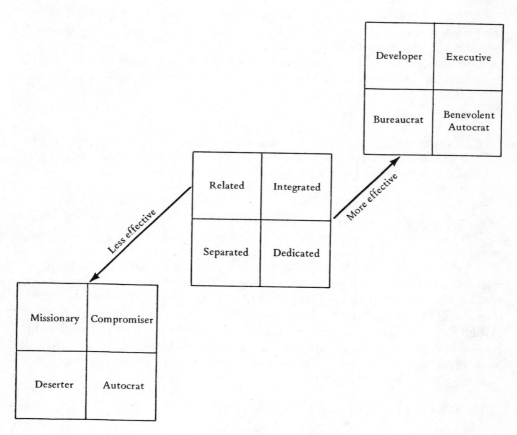

FIGURE 5-3. REDDIN'S 3-D THEORY OF LEADERSHIP. FROM W. J. REDDIN, *MANAGERIAL EFFECTIVENESS* (NEW YORK: McGRAW-HILL, 1970), p. 13.

The basic *integrated* style when displayed in an appropriate setting might lead to *compromise*, but when displayed in an appropriate setting leads to *executive* effectiveness.

As an executive the chairperson is seen as a good motivator who sets high standards, who treats teachers as individuals, and who prefers a team approach to operating the department. As a compromiser the chairperson is seen as a poor decision maker who

143

allows pressures in the situation to influence him too much, and who attempts to juggle concerns for task and relationship dimensions of his job.

The basic *related* style expressed inappropriately may be perceived as *missionary* behavior but when the situation is ripe for this style, *development* of people takes place.

As a developer the chairperson is seen as being primarily concerned with treating teachers as individuals and professionals. As a missionary the chairperson is seen as being primarily interested in harmony in the department.

If one behaves in a separated way given appropriate conditions, he is displaying an appropriate *bureaucratic* response but if his involvement in task or people or both is needed but not forthcoming, he is a *deserter*.

As a bureaucrat the chairperson is seen as being primarily interested in rules and procedures for their own sake, and as wanting to maintain and control the situation by their use. He is viewed as being conscientious. As a deserter the chairperson is seen as being uninvolved and passive.

 The *dedicated* person who is an inspirational and driving force given appropriate circumstances is seen as a *benevolent autocrat*. But when this style is displayed in inappropriate situations, he is viewed as a *repressive autocrat*.

In the first instance the chairperson is seen as knowing what he wants, and knowing how to get it without causing resentment. In the second instance he is seen as having no confidence in others, as unpleasant, and as being interested only in the immediate job.

In sum, the same style expressed in different situations may be effective or ineffective. For example, a chairperson who uses the integrated style with a teacher who is in need of personal support may be seen as compromising the person dimension by not giving exclusive attention to the needs of the individual. This same chairperson, relying exclusively on support and understanding as a teacher is searching for a task solution to his problem, may be seen as a missionary lacking in forceful leadership. This related style in the first instance, however, would have been perceived as being most effective.

Understanding Situational Leadership Variables

The situational determiners of leadership style effectiveness are difficult to identify entirely and even more difficult for the chairperson to completely read and formally catalogue as he approaches a given situation. Nevertheless, some useful generalizations can be made about situational variables and their relationship to leadership style. With a little practice one's ability to match appropriate style to situation can be improved considerably. Perhaps the three most important aspects of any situation are (a) the kinds of demands the job makes on leadership, (b) the nature and distribution of power and authority, and (c) the expectations of significant others (teachers, parents, principals) for the leader's behavior.

Compatibility between how a person does something and what he hopes to accomplish is an important determiner of effectiveness. In many respects, this compatibility often is an insurance policy since product and process in schools are often so interrelated that they defy separation. When one works with people in order to achieve human ends such as intellectual and personal self-actualization, excessively formal models which separate these dimensions are usually unworkable except for the most routine school tasks.

Generally speaking, therefore, one can assume that leadership situations in schools will seldom call for separated and dedicated styles, for in each of these cases the human dimension is neglected. This is not to suggest that occasions will not exist when low concern for people is appropriate, but only that the focus of leadership in general will be in the related and integrated quadrants.

Exceptions to this generalization occur when the job demands are such that the dedicated style which emphasizes task but not people will probably be most effective. One exception deals with routine situations where goals and objectives are uncontroversial and where the paths to reach the goal are few and clearly marked. Another exception is in situations where very favorable leader-member relationships exist. Here, members trust the leader and are willing to follow him. A third exception relates to situations characterized by excessive interpersonal tension, confusion, and stress. Short-term success in these situations can be accomplished through use of the dedicated style. This style, however, will only be the aspirin which controls the pain so that people can function adequately; the problem does not go away, nor will it stay controlled under this leadership style indefinitely. The leader's formal position in the school hierarchy is another important condition. When too much positional or hierarchical distance exists between leader and members, it is often less stressful for everyone if the leader uses a task-oriented style.

Contingency Leadership Theory

Fiedler summarizes many of these conditions in his contingency theory of leadership.[4] His research indicates that

Task-oriented leaders perform best in group situations that are either very favorable or very unfavorable to the leader. Relationship-oriented leaders perform best in group situations that are intermediate in favorableness, which is defined by the degree to which the situation enables the leader to exert his influence over the group.

Three major situational variables determine whether a given situation is favorable or unfavorable to the leader: (1) leader-member relations, which refers to the extent teachers accept, admire, and are willing to follow the chairperson because of the kind of person he is and the relationship he has developed with them; (2) task structure, the

145

extent to which the work of the department is structured, the objectives are clearly defined, and the processes available to achieve these objectives are few; (3) position power, the amount of formal authority and status of the chairperson. Elected chairpersons have less position power than appointed department heads who have hiring and firing prerogatives.

The contingency theory provides for eight leadership contexts, each defined by the situational variables shown in Figure 5–4.

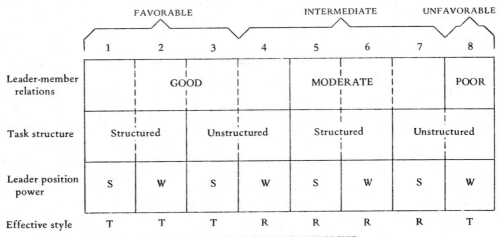

	FAVORABLE				INTERMEDIATE			UNFAVORABLE
	1	2	3	4	5	6	7	8
Leader-member relations	GOOD				MODERATE			POOR
Task structure	Structured		Unstructured		Structured		Unstructured	
Leader position power	S	W	S	W	S	W	S	W
Effective style	T	T	T	R	R	R	R	T

FIGURE 5–4. FIEDLER'S CONTINGENCY THEORY OF LEADERSHIP

Leadership contexts 1, 2, and 3 provide the leader with the most favorable opportunities for influence and Fiedler finds that task-oriented leadership is the most effective style. Leadership context 8 provides the leader with the least amount of influence and again the task or directive style is found to be effective. The remaining four contexts, according to the contingency leadership theory, seem best suited to the relationship-oriented style.

When the chairperson has the respect and good wishes of teachers and lots of formal authority to back him up, exerting influence is easy. His personal relations are such that people are willing to follow him and in addition his position power is such that people more readily yield to him the right to lead. Combine these with a structured task, as in context 1, which tends not to call for much participation anyway, and we have the perfect setting for more dedicated leadership. Contexts 2 and 3 are not quite as favorable as 1 but possess enough of the same ingredient to permit easy influence.

Contexts 4, 5, 6, and 7, on the other hand, each require the chairperson to earn the right to lead, to win the loyalty and commitment of teachers or, as in contexts 4 and 7 where tasks are unstructured, to depend upon the knowledge and abilities of others to be effective. In each case related and integrated styles are found to be more effective. Context 8 is so unfavorable that the most directive task style is recommended, at least for a short period of time. As the chairperson works to improve the situation so that it approximates context 4, for example, then his style would need to change accordingly.

The Zone of Indifference

One cannot assume that all teachers have a uniform desire to participate in school decision-making processes. When the content of decision-making is in an individual's zone of indifference, a task-oriented approach from the chairperson is appropriate. Teachers, for example, are unlikely to be interested in many administrative aspects of operating the department and probably look with pleasure at a chairperson who can regulate them in a dedicated but unobtrusive way. Teachers often resent being involved in trivial matters, serving on committees of dubious value, and sitting through long meetings on topics which do not interest them. As the zone of indifference on a particular matter decreases, however, teachers will need to be more involved and the relationship and integrated styles become more appropriate. These relationships are shown in Figure 5–5.[5]

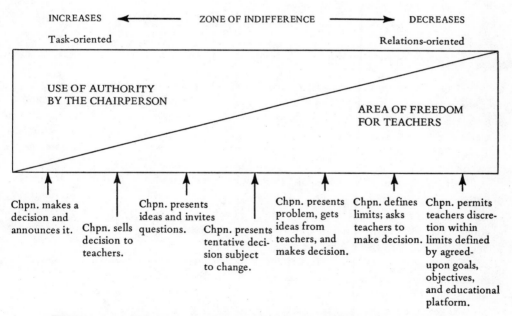

FIGURE 5–5. LEADERSHIP CONTINUUM AND ZONE OF INDIFFERENCE. ADAPTED FROM ROBERT TANNENBAUM AND WARREN SCHMIDT, "HOW TO CHOOSE A LEADERSHIP PATTERN," *HARVARD BUSINESS REVIEW,* VOL. 36, NO. 2, 1957.

A broad range of styles exists between the two extremes of task and relationship. Further, it is difficult to conceptualize leadership solely on the task and relationship continuum. For example, as one moves to the extreme right on Figure 5–5 to where the chairperson defines limits and asks teachers to make decisions and to where the chairperson permits teachers to function within limits defined by agreed-upon goals and objectives, concern for task and concern for people are both present. These are the essential characteristics of the integrated style.

Nevertheless, it seems appropriate to generalize that, first,

 as the content of decision-making moves closer to the day-by-day work of teachers and as potential changes in operation and procedure require attitudinal and behavioral changes from teachers, the zone of indifference is likely to decrease. In such cases, leadership styles which include a generous component of relationship-orientation are most likely to be effective.

Second, a relationship, similar to that appropriate for the zone of indifference concept, holds for the competence, maturity, and commitment levels of teachers. For example, the more competent teachers are, given a particular set of problems or tasks, the more appropriate are related and integrated styles. The less competent teachers are, given a set of problems and tasks, the more appropriate are the dedicated and separated styles.

Authority Relationships and Leadership Effectiveness

One important source of tension, frustration, and confusion in schools is the conflict that exists between formal authority and functional authority. Formal authority is associated with the role one occupies in an organization and is sometimes referred to as hierarchical, legal, position or office authority. This authority is defined by the schools, bureaucratic structure, and its legal system rather than by the person who occupies a given role.

Chairpersons rely on formal authority by using school rules, regulations, and policies or by "pulling rank." Formal authority is exemplified by teachers who obtain compliance from students because "the teacher says so." Youngsters here are engaged in educational activities not in pursuit of instructional, expressive and informal objectives but in obedience to the teacher's wishes.

Functional authority refers to the authority that an individual who occupies a given role or position brings to the position. His competence, ability, or expertness in functioning on the job, and his interpersonal skills in working with others within the job context (expert and referent authority) are examples of functional authority.

The dedicated style (TO high and RO low) is one that relies heavily on the formal authority which exists within the position one occupies. The chairperson has the right to decide on a change, announce it to the faculty, and implement it because he is the "boss." The separated style permits chairperson and teacher to blame the impersonal system for any inconvenience they incur as rules are enforced. Teachers like to use legal authority in disciplining students because it permits them to act "impersonally." An example of legal authority in relating to parents is when teachers blame impersonal examination test scores for a student's failures. After all, tests don't lie, so the parent often assumes, and the teacher is only doing his job in failing Johnny because the test score says so. Use of legal authority often results in helpless feelings for the person being subjected to it.

Expressions of functional authority by chairpersons usually results in their reliance on related and integrated (TO low RO high and TO high RO high) leadership styles. Successful related styles rely heavily on the interpersonal skills the individual brings to his position and successful integrated styles require substantial competence and expertness in educational matters as well as interpersonal skills. These relationships are shown in Figure 5-6.

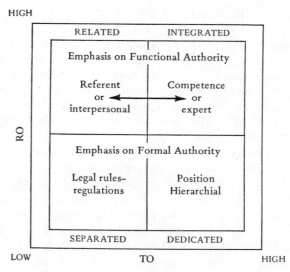

FIGURE 5-6. AUTHORITY BASES FOR THE BASIC LEADERSHIP STYLES. FROM T. J. SERGIOVANNI AND DAVID ELLIOTT, *EDUCATIONAL AND ORGANIZATIONAL LEADERSHIP IN ELEMENTARY SCHOOLS* (ENGLEWOOD CLIFFS, N.J.: PRENTICE-HALL, INC., 1975), p. 111.

One important difference between formal and functional authority is that the leader always has the former but often the subordinate has the latter. Formally, the chairperson is responsible for introducing an individualized pacing program into the department, but functionally the teachers have the understanding and ability for accomplishing this task. Chairpersons who are overly concerned about authority relationships, protocol, and status systems might be inclined to override the functional authority of teachers in order to preserve formal authority relationships, and therefore almost always assume the major leadership role.

When the chairperson finds himself in a situation where he has both formal and functional authority, he is fortunate indeed. This seems to be an ideal setting for effective use of the integrated style. When he has only formal authority, he should prepare to let the locus of leadership shift to where functional authority exists. Indeed he might use his formal authority to legitimize the functional authority which others have, by giving them ad hoc formal responsibility.

149

Substantial evidence exists that workers in educational and noneducational settings are more satisfied, work more willingly and harder when exposed to functional authority. Workers often respond indifferently to legal uses of formal authority. Position or hierarchical authority, particularly when expressed in terms of sanctions, paternalistic rewards, and punishments, evokes negative responses and results in poor performance in the long run.[6] It seems reasonable to expect that similar relationships hold for students as they are exposed to the teacher's authority in school classrooms.

Role Expectations and Leadership Effectiveness

One determiner of the chairperson's leadership effectiveness is the expectations for his performance as a leader held by important others, such as the principal and teachers. A further determiner is the extent to which these role expectations agree with each other and with how he feels he needs to behave. One need not have mirror agreement with superiors and subordinates in regard to role expectations, but reasonable agreement and mutual understanding of areas of disagreement seem to be prerequisites for leadership effectiveness.[7]

In Figure 5–2 a list of twenty style behavior indicators was presented, each grouped into one of the four basic leadership style quadrants with which it was most associated. It might be interesting to compare how you see your role as chairperson according to these indicators, with perceptions of your principal and the teachers in the department. First, pick the five indicators you use most frequently and readily. Compare these with the five you feel your principal would pick in describing what he expects from you. Next, pick the five you feel the teachers would most likely pick in describing what they expect from you. Ask the principal and teachers to pick indicators from the list.

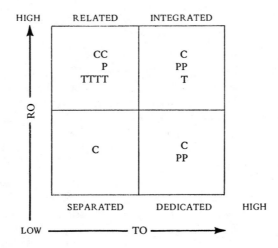

FIGURE 5-7

Using Figure 5–2, how many indicators did you pick from each of the four quadrants? Specific indicators are not as important as the quadrant from which they come. You may wish to draw a diagram similar to the example below, and plot expectations in the appropriate quadrants.

In the example above, the chairperson describes himself as using each of the four styles, somewhat with an emphasis on the related style. Such a pattern could be deliberate or could be a symptom of unsureness in the chairperson. Teachers in this example clearly expect the chairperson to behave in a related fashion, the principal on the other hand expects more dedicated and integrated behavior.

In this case, the chairperson is a victim of serious conflicting role expectations. At present neither the teachers nor the principal are apt to be pleased with his leadership, and shifting toward one set of expectations is bound to increase the displeasure of the other party. Leadership effectiveness is virtually impossible in the midst of this sort of role conflict.

 Clarifying roles and role expectations is an important aspect of leadership effectiveness.

Principals, teachers, and chairpersons together need to define what the department is to accomplish and the ways in which these objectives are best accomplished. In Chapter 4 we discussed the possibility of the department building a shared decision-making model. Such a model can serve as a useful guide to clarifying roles and expectations. Developing job descriptions more adequately based on objectives as described in Chapter 2 can also help. As department objectives, tasks, and functions are discussed and evaluated by teachers, principals, and chairpersons, the process of role clarification is taking place.

Job Demands and Leadership Effectiveness

The basic principle behind the approach to leadership described in this chapter is that leadership effectiveness is situational. The same leadership style may work in one situation but not in another. Job demands vary as department objectives and tasks change or as attention shifts from one set of problems or objectives to another. In one situation the chairperson might be more expert than teachers and in another case, they may be more expert than him.

As a general guide,[8] *if the situation involves the following job demands,*

Teachers have high expertness or unusual technical skills
Teacher identification and commitment are necessary for success
The job is arranged so that teachers can largely decide how tasks will be accomplished
It is difficult to evaluate performance outcomes precisely
Teachers need to be creative and inventive in their work

151

then the related style will be the most effective.
If the situation involves the following job demands,

The teacher's job is programmed routinely and requires the following of established procedures, curriculum formats, teaching strategies
The teacher's job is simple, easy to perform, and easy to regulate
Automatic feedback is provided so that the teacher can readily note his progress
Intellectual privacy and thinking are much more important than the teacher being actively involved in something

then the separated style will be the most effective.
If the situation involves the following job demands,

Teachers need to interact with each other in order to complete their tasks
Teachers are inderdependent; the success of one depends upon the help of others
Successful completion requires that the chairperson must interact with teachers as a group
Several solutions are possible and the number of solutions proposed and evaluated are improved by interaction among department members
Teachers can set their own pace as the department pursues its tasks

then the integrated style will be most effective.
If the situation involves the following job demands,

The chairperson knows more about the task or problems at hand than teachers
Numerous unplanned and unanticipated events are likely to occur, requiring attention from the chairperson
Teachers need frequent direction in order to complete their task
The teacher's performance is readily measurable and corrective action by the chairperson is visible and can be easily evaluated

then the dedicated style will be most effective.

SUMMARY

Two essential components in defining a particular leadership style have been described: the extent to which the principal shows concern for task (TO) and the extent to which he shows concern for people (RO). Four basic styles were identified from different expressions of these dimensions: dedicated, related, separated, and integrated. Any one of these styles can be effective or not, depending upon the nature of the leadership situation. Discussed situational variables include the nature of the work, the relationship between leader and members, the amount of stress and tension in the situation, the position power of the leader, the distribution of ability and authority among leader and members, the zone of indifference of members, role expectations of superiors and subordinates, and the unique job demands present as a result of a given problem situation or task.

ENDNOTES

1. The material in this section of Chapter 5 is based on Thomas J. Sergiovanni and David Elliott, *Educational and Organizational Leadership in Elementary Schools* (Englewood Cliffs, New Jersey: Prentice-Hall, 1975), pp. 98–116, and on Thomas J. Sergiovanni, "Leadership Behavior and Organizational Effectiveness," *Notre Dame Journal of Education,* Vol. 4, no. 1, 1973, pp. 15-24.

2. W. J. Reddin, *Managerial Effectiveness* (New York: McGraw-Hill, 1970).

3. *Ibid.*

4. Fred E. Fiedler, *A Theory of Leadership Effectiveness* (New York: McGraw-Hill, 1967).

5. Figure 5-5 is adapted from: Robert Tannenbaum and Warren Schmidt, "How to Choose a Leadership Pattern," *Harvard Business Review,* March–April, 1957, pp. 95-101.

6. See for example, Robert L. Peabody, "Perceptions of Organizational Authority: A Comparative Analysis," *Administrative Science Quarterly,* vol. 6, no. 4, 1962, and Victor Thompson, *Modern Organization* (New York: Knopf, 1961); J. R. P. French, Jr. and B. Raven, "The Bases of Social Power" in D. Cartwright and A. F. Zander (eds.), *Group Dynamics: Research and Theory,* 2nd ed. (Evanston, Illinois: Row Peterson, 1960), p. 612; Jerald D. Bachman *et al.,* "Bases of Supervisory Power: A Comparative Study in Five Organizational Settings" in Arnold S. Tannenbaum (ed.), *Control in Organizations* (New York: McGraw-Hill, 1968), p. 229, and Harvey A. Horstein *et al.,* "Influence and Satisfaction in Organizations: A Replication," *Sociology of Education,* vol. 41, no. 4, 1968, p. 389.

7. See for example, Jacob Getzels and Egon Guba, "Social Behavior and the Administrative Process," *School Review,* vol. 65, Winter, 1957, and W. J. Reddin, *op. cit.,* especially Chapter 8; Robert Kahn *et al., Organizational Stress: Studies in Role Conflict and Ambiguity* (New York: John Wiley and Sons, 1964), and Jacob Getzels, "Administration as a Social Process," in Andrew Halpin (ed.), *Administrative Theory in Education* (New York: The Macmillan Company, 1967), for helpful references in understanding role theory, role expectations, and role conflict and ambiguity.

8. Charting job demands and relating them to leadership styles is an integral part of Reddin's 3-D Theory. Reddin, *op. cit.,* pages 67–87, particularly Exhibit 7–1 which appears on page 72.

✠ CHAPTER FIVE ✠

✠ PRACTICES ✠

Two theories of leadership (task-oriented and relations-oriented) were discussed in the concepts section of this chapter. Each theory assumes that best leadership style can only be determined by a careful analysis of the leadership situation. In this practices section, you will have an opportunity to analyze situations to determine your best style. This section contains a leadership strategy planning workbook designed to help you analyze leadership situations to determine your best style; three action cases where you may select alternative solutions to a problem and receive feedback on your choices; and seven discussion cases, each focusing on a persistent problem faced by department chairpersons.

LEADERSHIP STRATEGY PLANNING WORKBOOK

Introduction

At one time it was thought that a single best leadership style could be identified. This would have certainly made things easier, for the chairperson would need only to find out what the best style is, learn it, and use it. Unfortunately, leadership effectiveness is much more complex than this and indeed any number of styles or approaches could be effective given the proper circumstances.

Since effectiveness of any leadership style depends upon its suitability to a given situation, "reading situations" is an important leadership skill. As the quarterback's effectiveness increases when his ability to read defenses increases, so will the chairperson's leadership effectiveness increase when his sensitivity to situations increases. The workbook below uses concepts and ideas from both Reddin and Fiedler's research to help analyze leadership situations.

NAME OF TEACHER OR GROUP _____   DATE_____

A. *Goals and Purposes*

   1. Do you have your goals clearly formulated? What are they?

2. Are you familiar with the problems and concerns to be considered? Do you have a feel for their history?

3. Have you thought about how the purposes of this meeting or encounter affect other department or school activities and concerns?

4. Do you have all the information you need? What information do you have and what information do you need?

B. *Analyzing the Situation*
  1. How would you describe your relationships with this person or group? To what extent do you get along? Are you trusted and seen as credible? Are you admired and respected?

     Would you describe the leader-member relationships as being primarily good _____, moderate _____, or poor _____?
  2. What are the goals and purposes sought, the jobs to be done, the problems to be solved? Could they be described as being clear and understood, easily defined and measured? Or, could they better be described as ambiguous, vague and difficult to define?

     Would you describe the goals, tasks, and problems as being primarily structured _____, or unstructured _____?
  3. What kind of authority do you bring to this situation? Do you know more about the goals, tasks, and problems than others? Do you have clear authority, accepted by others, to act in this case? Are there sufficient precedents, policies, and regulations which provide you with authority to act?

     Would you describe the authority you have (competence, position, legal or other) as being primarily strong _____, or weak _____?

C. *Decision Level 1*
     Based on the analysis so far, decide tentatively whether the situation suggests a dedicated oriented leadership style or a related oriented leadership style. Review the sections on Fiedler's contingency theory of leadership and

Reddin's 3-D theory of leadership in the concepts section of this chapter before continuing this analysis. Remember, at decision level 1 we are only trying to determine the basic style orientation, dedicated or related, that is needed. You may ultimately decide that the separated or integrated styles are better than either the related or dedicated.

Check the category in the fourth row below that best fits the situation you have described so far.

	1	2	3	4	5	6	7	8
My relationship with the group is	GOOD				MODERATE			POOR
The task structure is primarily	Structured		Unstructured		Structured		Unstructured	
The authority I have is	S	W	S	W	S	W	S	W
My situation is most like (check one box)								
The basic style orientation needed is	DEDI-CATED	DEDI-CATED	DEDI-CATED	RELAT-ED	RELAT-ED	RELAT-ED	RELAT-ED	DEDI-CATED

My first level decision is to use a _____ oriented style.

Remember that at this point you are deciding on the general leadership approach. Later you may decide to stay with your dedicated or related choice or decide to use an integrated or separated approach.

D. *Decision Level 2*

Consider other factors that may influence leadership style effectiveness. For example, what do others (teachers and the principal) expect from you as a leader, how much *time* do you have, what are your leadership *strengths* and weaknesses, and what is the *zone of indifference* of teachers given the tasks at hand? Review carefully the "Job Demands and Leadership Effectiveness" section in the first part of this chapter.

What leadership style seems most likely to be effective in this situation?

1. Moving ahead directly. Should organizing, initiating, directing, completing, and evaluating be emphasized? If so, choose the *dedicated* style.
2. Relying on existing precedents, rules, and routines. Should examining, measuring, administering, controlling, and maintaining be emphasized? If so, choose the *separated* style.
3. Developing a problem-solving partnership. Should interacting, motivating, integrating, participating, and innovating be emphasized? If so, choose the *integrated* style.

157

4. Showing high concern for the needs, views, and problems of others. Should listening, accepting, trusting, advising, and encouraging be emphasized? If so, choose the *related* style.

In this situation:
I will use the ＿＿＿＿＿ style primarily.
I will use the ＿＿＿＿＿ style as a back-up.

ACTION CASES

These three action cases allow you to make decisions about persistent problems you are likely to face as a chairperson, and to receive feedback on your choices. Each case presents a problem. Alternative courses of action are then provided. In each case, select the alternative which best describes what you would do. A discussion of each of the alternatives follows. The cases provide you with an opportunity to "test out" what you have learned about leadership styles in the concepts section of this chapter. Further, they serve as a model as to how the subsequent discussion cases might be used by chairpersons in staff development activities.

Action Case 1   Friction in the Teaching Team

You are the chairperson of a department organized into teaching teams. You notice increasing friction among the four teachers who comprise one of the teams. Several times you've noticed that this friction occurs when some teachers are not able to carry out part of their responsibilities because other teachers are not sufficiently prepared. Which statement below best describes what you would do?

1. This is a counselling situation. I would bring the teachers together, hear them out, and discuss the situation with them.   ＿＿＿＿
2. I would bring the teachers together to discuss team objectives and to clarify responsibilities each has.   ＿＿＿＿
3. I would talk separately with the teachers and tell them I expect the situation to improve.   ＿＿＿＿

DID YOU CHOOSE STATEMENT 1?   This choice is good, but not the best of the three. True, an early step in the counselling process is obtaining additional information about the situation. Bringing the group together certainly makes sense. The problem concerns relationships among team members and the group setting serves this purpose well. But by choosing this statement, you are assuming that the problem has to do primarily with personalities and feelings. You may be right, but jumping to this conclusion may be premature. Statement 1 characterizes the related leadership style discussed in the concepts section of this chapter. It is a good choice but not the best choice in this

situation.

DID YOU CHOOSE STATEMENT 2?   Of the three statements, this one offers the best strategy. This choice shares with Statement 1 a concern for relationships by bringing the group together. But this choice further assumes that the friction which characterizes relationships in the team results from aspects of the job—in this case unclear goals and ambiguous responsibilities. Bringing the team together to discuss their feelings (choice 1) without linking these feelings to aspects of the job masks the causes and treats the symptoms of friction. Clarifying responsibilities and linking them to team objectives is the first order of business. Discussing tensions and feelings is important but needs to be linked to the work of the team. Statement 2 characterizes the integrated leadership style discussed in the concepts section of this chapter.

DID YOU CHOOSE STATEMENT 3?   This is not a good choice. Dealing with individuals one at a time is not likely to result in a solution to which the team as a whole is committed. Further, visiting with individuals changes the perspective from, "We have a problem which needs to be solved," to "Someone is wrong and I am correcting this wrong." This is not a disciplinary situation yet, and may not ever be one. Statement 3 represents a poor strategy for beginning to work on this problem. This statement characterizes the dedicated leadership style discussed in the concepts section of this chapter.

Action Case 2   The New Teacher

There are ten teachers in your department. One of the teachers, Susan Smith, is new to the profession and has been on the job for about four months. Early in the semester you thought that the school had gotten an especially good teacher in Susan. She showed a lot of enthusiasm and seemed to catch on to teaching and particularly to her responsibilities in the department. Students seemed to like her and her teaching was imaginative.

In the last week you've noticed that Susan has lost much of her enthusiasm. Classes seem not to be going well and on several occasions she seemed arbitrary and detached in her handling of students. Her teaching is not bad by any means but hardly the sparkling performance you were happy to see in the first few months. Teaching seems now more like a chore for Susan. A certain dull routine has set in. You wonder if you had made an error in judgment in your earlier evaluation of Susan.

New teachers are to be formally appraised in just four weeks. This will be an important appraisal for Susan. The first formal evaluation report weighs heavily in the minds of administrators as they decide which of the new teachers are likely to be awarded tenure. You're afraid that if Susan's performance continues on its present course, you will have to rate her as being only satisfactory. Which of the statements below best describes what you would do? Check one statement.

1. I would do nothing yet but just continue my informal observations of Susan a while longer, since this change in her attitude and performance is only a recent occurrence.

2. I would talk to Susan about this apparent change in her attitude and performance.   _____

3. I would wait until after the formal evaluation period coming up soon, before talking to Susan.   _____

DID YOU CHOOSE STATEMENT 1?   If you chose this one, you selected a related leadership style as described in the concepts section of this chapter. The related style in this situation is more likely to result in missionary than developer behavior. Why is this choice appealing? It certainly gives Susan the benefit of the doubt. Perhaps she might work things out; talking with her could be interpreted as disapproval, and could result in increased tension. But this is not the best choice because as department chairperson you have the responsibility to step in and say something when you notice signs of teacher performance being less than expected.

What are the advantages of acting now rather than waiting? To begin with, quick action demonstrates your interest in Susan as a person and as a professional. You care about her and her performance. You show that you care by doing something. Often just showing interest in a teacher's performance gives him the necessary boost to get back on the track. Second, waiting could result in the situation getting worse. Susan's difficulties today could turn into disaster tomorrow. And finally, you have an obligation to the students in Susan's classes and to the other teachers in the department. Slipping performance by one teacher can have an adverse affect on the attitude and performance of the other teachers.

DID YOU CHOOSE STATEMENT 2?   There are advantages to talking to Susan now and, of the three, this choice seems best. Talking to Susan combines an interest both in her teaching performance and her personal well-being. You want and expect high-quality teaching from all of the teachers; you assume that they share this expectation; and you care enough to help when performance slips or problems arise. This combined concern characterizes the integrated leadership style discussed in the concepts section of the chapter. But the dedicated style is even more strongly suggested in this statement.

One might legitimately ask, do you have enough information or "evidence" regarding Susan's problems to act now? If the answer is no, then Statement 1 may well be a better choice than Statement 2. But assuming that you have been alert and perceptive, then enough evidence does seem to exist. You've noticed, for example, a drop in enthusiasm, classes not working out well, and problems with students. These signal that something needs to be done now.

DID YOU CHOOSE STATEMENT 3?   This strategy is implied in the many popular "truisms" available to chairpersons: "Let the system run its course," "Let sleeping dogs lie," "Most problems that you have on Friday clear up by Monday." This is a poor choice because it lets the chairperson "cop out" of a difficult situation. Letting this problem run its course shows a low concern both for the job and for people. This choice characterizes the separated leadership style discussed in the concepts section. In a sense the chairperson has deserted his leadership role.

Action Case 3   Facts and Feelings

You recently recommended a teacher in your department to be appointed an assistant principal in your school. Several days after his appointment Jeff Johnson, another teacher in your department, came to you and asked, "I am wondering why you recommended Bill for the job of assistant principal. I've been here longer than he has and I don't believe I was considered very seriously." You answer, "Jeff, I recommended Bill because I think he shows a great deal of interest and initiative in his work. He seems always to do more than what is expected of him. Also, he's got a pretty good education, has earned all the available administrative certificates and has real promise as an administrator for the future. I felt that he was the best man for the job."

Do you feel that this is a good answer? Yes _____ No _____

DID YOU CHOOSE YES?   The answer to Jeff's question seems complete. But something is missing. When a teacher asks you "why" you've done something or decided something he probably is looking for two kinds of answers—a facts answer and a feelings answer. In this case Jeff was really asking two questions. "Why was Bill recommended?" This question should and did get a facts answer. But Bill was also asking, "Why didn't I get recommended?" This question needs but did not get a feelings answer.

DID YOU CHOOSE NO?   You are correct if you picked this alternative. Jeff got all of the answers he asked for but not all of the answers he sought. It is often difficult for people to ask all of the questions they desire answered, so help them by giving answers they seek regardless of the question they ask. A situation such as this could easily be turned into a coaching opportunity. Why not discuss with Jeff his plans for the future, his strengths, and his hopes?

DISCUSSION CASES

Each of these discussion cases represents some of the kinds of problems you are likely to face as head of a department. Use the cases to familiarize yourself with these problems and to decide how you would react. In each case:

1. Start by defining the problem in its simplest terms. *You are zeroing in on the problem.*
2. Now go back the other way and examine how the problem relates to the broader array of problems, events, and activities of the school. *You are placing the problem in a broader perspective.*
3. Assemble and analyze as much pertinent data as possible. *You are trying to understand the problem.*
4. Propose tentative solutions to the problem. *You are problem-solving.*

161

5. Consider the possible impact of these solutions on the school, you as the chairperson, the other people involved, and the department's educational program. *You are analyzing consequences.*

6. Decide on the best solution available. *You are engaging in decision-making.*

7. Watch carefully the effect your decision has on each of the other steps. *You are evaluating.*

8. Be prepared to retreat from a poor solution—openly and honestly recognizing the situation for what it is. *You are growing as a person and a leader.*

9. Begin again. *You are persevering.*
   Review your decisions and course of action, paying particular attention to the styles of leadership implied (related, dedicated, separated, integrated) and to whether these styles fit the situation at hand. Use the cases as a basis for discussion with other chairpersons.*

Discussion Case 1   A Deteriorating Situation

You are the chairperson in a large science department. During a routine visit to a second-year probationary teacher's laboratory, the teaching situation deteriorates so rapidly that you consider assuming responsibility for the class.

Under what circumstances would you do this? Describe the conditions as precisely as you can. How would you relieve him? What are your actions, decisions, and recommendations?

Discussion Case 2   Chronic Lateness

As chairperson of the department of English you call meetings of the nine-teacher faculty as frequently as the need arises. Except in rare instances, each teacher has received notice of the meetings one or two days in advance of the meeting. You have had a policy of starting and stopping your meetings on time. The schedule has been arranged so that 3:00 to 4:00 on Wednesday afternoon is always open. The same three or four teachers always arrive five to ten minutes late for the meeting. When this happens, you either must wait until they all arrive, or must start the meeting and then go back and cover the material missed. In either event, significant time is lost by a majority of those present.

After the last faculty meeting, complete with late arrivals, you had brief, informal discussions with each person about the inconveniences he was visiting upon his fellow teachers. Each spoke of checking his mailbox, student conferences, reports; each was vague about his intentions of being on time for succeeding meetings. You need to have another staff meeting in three days.

What are your actions, decisions, and recommendations?

*These cases are adapted from Bill W. Brown, *Casebook on Administration and Supervision in Industrial and Technical Education* (Chicago: American Technical Society, 1970).

Discussion Case 3   A Change in Schedule

You are the division chairperson of Humanities and Fine Arts. There are twenty-two full-time teachers plus eight part-time people in your area. You have just completed an exhaustive, twelve-hour job of building the schedule for the next semester. You have taken into account possible conflicts with other disciplines, room conflicts, possible conflicts with lower-division students' classes not appearing in the same time blocks, with a reasonable balance struck between morning and afternoon classes. The only compromise you had to make involved a course with several sections being offered, so you feel very fortunate. Instructor A has come in to check with you about another matter when he spots the new schedule board. Within seconds, he has pinpointed his new assignment and, with equal speed, recommends that you make two "very small and insignificant changes" in his schedule. These changes would, of course, upset the balance you had built into the schedule and would, in fact, require extensive changes in the whole schedule.

What are your actions, decisions, and recommendations?

Discussion Case 4   Summer School Teaching

You are the teaching-department chairperson of the industrial arts department (three teachers) at a medium-sized secondary school. The need for summer teaching in your school has always been limited, although the extra pay makes such an assignment attractive. You have been rotating this assignment with yourself and one other teacher who has been with you for more than six years. The third person, who is in his final (and successful) probationary year, has once again requested summer teaching. You have already given verbal assurance to the other instructor that, in the event summer teaching is needed, his "turn" will once again be honored. The probationary teacher takes exception to your decision. The following day you receive a call from your principal asking for a conference concerning summer scheduling.

What are your actions, decisions, and recommendations?

Discussion Case 5   Snoopervision

You are the chairperson of a three-teacher department in a small high school. Your school is organized so that department leaders report directly to the principal in all matters. During lunch, the other two teachers, both of whom are non-tenured, indicate that they have a problem of some magnitude which they would like to discuss with you.

Teacher B asks if you have paid any attention to the intercom system in recent weeks. You reply that you think it is working properly—the central office can call a specific classroom or the entire building if necessary; a given instructor can reply to a question from anywhere in the classroom without raising his voice; furthermore, a teacher

163

can initiate a call to the central office by energizing a simple switch. You conclude your remarks by saying that you are sure the system is working properly. Teacher B then notes that the discriminating listener can tell when the system is on "listen," because he can hear a 60-cycle hum. Both he and teacher A believe that the principal has been using the device as a "silent-supervisory tool," hoping to gather evidence to refuse contracts to them, since they are both probationary teachers. They then ask you to investigate the situation. This might be difficult, since you also believe that this is precisely what the principal is doing; you have reason to believe that this year's departmental budget had been cut when an inadvertent remark concerning a potential surplus had been "overheard."

What are your actions, decisions, and recommendations?

Discussion Case 6   The Assistant Principal's Request

You are the chairperson of a ten-teacher social science division at a large high school. The assistant principal for instruction has required that each teacher, through the chairperson, furnish his office with a rather comprehensive course outline for each course taught in the current semester. The assistant principal's office has just called and reminded you that your division's course outlines have not yet been submitted. You are well aware of the fact that they have not been turned in since you have been holding the outlines from eight of the teachers, waiting for two to get theirs in. You call the first teacher and he promises to get them in, without fail, by Friday. The second teacher flatly refuses to comply with your request. Aside from unprintable comments, his parting shot is: "That stuff is for elementary school teachers—don't bother me with that foolishness." Both men are tenured teachers.

What are your actions, decisions, and recommendations?

Discussion Case 7   The Militant Teacher

In addition to being department chairperson of the foreign language department in your school, you also chair a group composed of all foreign language teachers and supervisors in the city school district. During a district-wide meeting Teacher A, a teacher in your school, requests time to make an announcement. The request appears to be routine until the teacher launches into a bitter diatribe against the district administration, the school board, the classroom teachers' association, and the PTA. He indicates, among other things, that anyone who supports either or all of these groups must be opposed to salary increases and better working conditions for teachers. He invites all present to come to a special meeting of the AFT that afternoon, where those who wish to can learn the purposes of the AFT, after which strike plans will be voted on.

164   What are your actions, decisions, and recommendations?

COMBINING STYLES OF LEADERSHIP

The related leadership style with its effective and ineffective expressions (developer and missionary styles) is popular with chairpersons. Chairpersons work very closely with teachers in a relatively small group setting. This intense setting increases the chairperson's sensitivity to developing and maintaining good interpersonal relations. But as important as these relationships may be, the related style *alone* is usually not sufficient. On the other hand, separated, dedicated and integrated styles which are not combined with some attention to interpersonal relations can upset the balance of good feelings so often seen important by chairpersons.

The common denominator for expressing each of these styles is attention to relationships. Consider the situations below. Each describes teachers with different temperaments.* In each case the related style is important but alone—insufficient. Which other style (dedicated, separated, or integrated) would you combine with the related? Why? Do you agree with the choices provided? Under what conditions might the choices provided in each case be wrong? Remember that choosing an effective leadership style depends upon a number of factors in addition to temperaments of teachers.

1. Mary is a "good person." She is outgoing, friendly, sociable, optimistic, energetic, industrious, emotional, excitable, nervous, distractible, talkative, adaptable, versatile, alert, cooperative. She would probably respond best to your supervision if you

   _____Are enthusiastic and optimistic.

   _____Appeal to teamwork and group spirit.

   _____Avoid giving excessive details.

   _____When necessary, counteract optimism with negative facts.

   _____Ask her to repeat important instructions.

   _____Praise or criticize directly.

   In this case, the related combined with integrated would probably be best.

2. Sally is a "worry wart." She is pessimistic, cautious, conscientious, indecisive, procrastinating, inactive, unalert. She would probably respond best to your supervision if you

   _____Encourage and show confidence in her.

   _____Offset pessimism with optimism.

   _____Help her take first step.

   _____Give assignments in small batches.

   _____Supervise closely.

   _____Praise directly; be mild in criticism.

*The description of temperaments and suggestions for supervising are adapted from Raymond O. Loen, *Manage More by Doing Less* (New York: McGraw-Hill, 1970), pp. 134–35.

In this case, the related combined with dedicated would probably be best.

3. Gerald is a "shy guy." He is sensitive, bashful, blushing, imaginative, dreaming, impractical, unapproachable, seclusive. He would probably respond best to your supervision if you

_____Express confidence in his ability.

_____Ask for his ideas.

_____Explain background of new job, but let him work out details.

_____Appeal to his imagination.

_____Insist on his being concrete.

_____Praise his work, not him.

_____Criticize mildly by stressing his good intentions, giving him an "out," and asking for his suggestions.

In this case, the related combined with separated would probably be best.

4. Phil is a "know it all." He is aggressive, driving, argumentive, intolerant, conceited, suspicious, prejudiced, close-minded, stubborn, defensive, revengeful, rationalizing. He would probably respond best to your supervision if you

_____Ask directly for his ideas and opinions.

_____Show him the credit and recognition he will get.

_____Appeal to his desire for power, prestige, and position.

_____Avoid kidding; praise directly.

_____Criticize directly but give an "out."

_____Set standards for his work.

_____Give him clean directions and expectations.

In this case, the related combined with dedicated would probably work best.

5. Betty is a "conservative." She is dependable, reserved, controlled, inhibited, perfectionistic, and conforming. She would probably respond best to your supervision if you

_____Are objective, logical, specific, matter-of-fact, and impersonal.

_____Give only required level of supervision.

_____Encourage initiative.

_____Be mild in criticism.

In this case, the related combined with separated would probably work best.

TEACHER SATISFACTION AND MOTIVATION

❦ CONCEPTS ❦

Teaching bores many teachers. It is, of course, unfair to pin this charge on teachers in general for so many are hardworking, committed, and dedicated. Nevertheless, teaching bores large numbers of teachers and their students. The zip and excitement are gone.

This chapter is concerned with the problems and challenges of motivating teachers to work. It is based on three assumptions:

1) Poorly motivated youngsters are symptoms of school, teacher, and educational program problems rather than inherent conditions in youngsters. It is probably true that some youngsters cannot be motivated within the limitations of what we presently know about youngsters and schooling. Large numbers of poorly motivated youngsters, however, are indications that the school is not performing adequately. Teacher motivation or the lack of it may be the prime trouble spot.

2) The evidence is mounting that significant changes in school effectiveness will not come about as a result of increasing salaries (merit or otherwise) of teachers, decreasing class size, introducing new teaching materials, beefing up the academic training or certification credentials of teachers, reducing the work load, introducing clerical assistants, or using performance contracts.[1] These all contribute to effectiveness but their potency cannot compare with powerful social-psychological variables such as internal commitment and motivation to work.

3) The motivated teacher must become a high priority concern of principals and chairpersons. Simply stated, quality education and effective schools are primarily a function of competent administrators, chairpersons, and teachers who are internally committed and motivated to work.

The New Turnover Problem

The seventies mark a new era in schools, of concern for job satisfaction of teachers. Where previously schools were concerned with decreasing teacher turnover or increasing retention rates, the concern now is for over-retention, teacher retrenchment, or a lack of mobility among teachers.

In the sixties teachers were hard to come by and teacher turnover was relatively high. Teachers were not quite as hesitant as they are now about moving to a neighboring school district or state in order to improve their financial condition, opportunity for promotion, job assignment, or geographic location. If a teacher found himself in an undesirable position, the solution was often easy—change jobs. Schools worked hard to compete for qualified teachers and once they were hired schools attempted to improve working conditions as a means to improve retention.

Schools are now in a period of retrenchment, of teacher surplus, of declining student enrollments, and of economic slowdown. Student enrollments are down drastically in elementary schools and are declining in secondary schools. Birthrates continue to be down and therefore this trend will probably continue for some time. Good teaching jobs are already difficult to come by and teachers will be increasingly less willing to leave once they obtain employment.

 Though some may consider low turnover a blessing, it poses problems which if not resolved can have grave consequences for the school.

Teachers who are dissatisfied with their jobs are less likely to leave. The reasons for staying are too important.

Teachers who would like to leave but can't are staying on the job for the wrong reasons.

Large numbers of such teachers can have serious adverse effects on the school and its students.

Reasons for Staying on the Job

What influences a teacher's decision to stay on the job? Some reasons for staying are listed below. As you read the list, note those items which coincide with your reasons for staying on the job and those which do not coincide. You probably can add another half dozen reasons for staying which are not included in this sample list.

1. I have the freedom and responsibility to make important decisions about my teaching and this school's educational program.
2. I don't have anything better to do and I'd probably get bored staying at home.
3. I like the feelings I get when students do well.
4. I am close to becoming vested in the retirement plan.
5. I enjoy living in my neighborhood or community.
6. My husband or wife works in the area.
7. This is a challenging job, one that requires lots of effort.

8. I like the long vacations and summer holidays. They let me spend time with my family and still hold a job.
9. I could not earn as much money elsewhere.
10. If I were to leave I might have difficulty getting a fair price for my house.
11. I've learned the ropes here and it would be too hard to learn a new job and a new system of operating.
12. I like the freedom to plan my own work.
13. I have good friends in this school.
14. I have family and relatives in the area.
15. There are lots of good ideas and practices in this school—it is an exciting place to work.

As you review the items and those that you have added, note that they tend to sort into three groups: reasons associated with the job itself, reasons associated with the conditions of work, and reasons not associated with the job.

Reasons associated with the job itself are *motivation* reasons. They relate to satisfaction derived from actual participation in the work of the school. Rewards derived from the motivation reasons are usually intrinsic. Items 1, 3, 7, 12, and 15 are examples of motivation reasons, concerned with achievement, recognition, responsibility, autonomy, and growth.

Reasons associated with the conditions of work are called *hygiene* reasons. They relate to the job context rather than the job itself. Rewards derived from the hygiene reasons are usually extrinsic. Items 4, 8, 9, 11, and 13 in our sample are examples of hygiene reasons. Hygiene reasons are concerned with work rules, facilities, preparation or break time, teaching schedules, social relationships, benefits, and salary.

Reasons not associated with the job itself or the job context are called *external* reasons. They relate to the external environment rather than the school itself. Items 2, 5, 6, 10, and 14 in our sample are examples of external reasons, concerned with outside job opportunities, community relations, financial obligation, and family ties.

It is possible for some teachers to stay on the job only for motivation reasons, some for only hygiene reasons, and others for only external reasons. Most teachers probably stay for a combination of all three reasons though differences can be expected among teachers as to which category of reasons is most important.

Figure 6–1 shows the relationship between turnover and reasons for staying for four types of teachers.[2]

The turn-offs are teachers who are dissatisfied with the opportunity their jobs provide for achievement, recognition, responsibility, and other sources of intrinsic satisfaction. Turn-offs have few motivational reasons for staying. Further, there are few hygiene or external pressures to keep them on the job. An example might be a single teacher with no present disposition for developing community ties, who has professional skills that make employment elsewhere easy. Dissatisfaction would likely result in leaving at the first available opportunity.

Teachers who are turn-offs are in a situation similar to the turn-overs except for one very important difference. They too are not intrinsically satisfied, and motivation

169

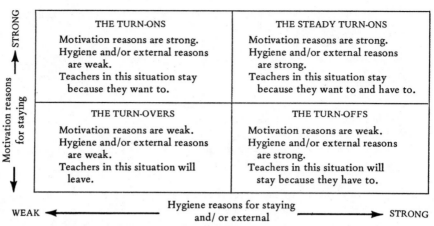

FIGURE 6-1. REASONS FOR STAYING AND TURNOVER

reasons for staying are weak but they are trapped into staying on the job because of pressures from hygiene and/or external reasons. Perhaps they feel they are too old to start over again, or are at a step in the salary schedule which makes them unattractive to other districts, or have aging parents in the area who need them, or they are locked into their jobs because of a spouse's job in the area.

Teachers who are dissatisfied but trapped into staying often take a "I'll get even" or "I'll do only what I have to" attitude. Dysfunctional union activities tend to be common in school districts with large numbers of turned-off teachers. Very few of us would want our own youngsters in classrooms of teachers who have turned off.

Often turn-offs become turn-overs when hygiene and external pressures are reduced. Having children graduate from college and move away or becoming sufficiently vested in the retirement plan are enough incentive to try a second occupation or to take a teaching job elsewhere.

The turn-ons are teachers who are highly motivated and remain on the job primarily because of the satisfactions they derive from the work itself. Turn-on teachers want to stay and are not locked in by hygiene or external reasons. They readily become turn-overs when intrinsic satisfaction ceases.

The steady turn-ons are the cadre of teachers most likely to contribute to school effectiveness over a sustained period of time. Steady turn-ons stay because of the satisfaction they derive from teaching *and* because of hygiene-external pressures. This combination of motivation, hygiene, and external reasons keeps them on the job even if satisfaction in one area temporarily declines. If a sustained decline is experienced in the motivation area, however, they most likely will become turn-offs.

Chairpersons are in a position to play an important role in keeping teachers out of the turned-off quadrant of Figure 6-1 and in helping teachers who are already there to move to one of the two turned-on quadrants.

In Chapter 1 the effective chairperson was described as working:

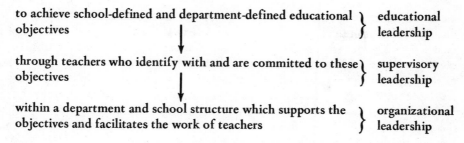

to achieve school-defined and department-defined educational } educational
objectives   } leadership

through teachers who identify with and are committed to these } supervisory
objectives   } leadership

within a department and school structure which supports the } organizational
objectives and facilitates the work of teachers   } leadership

Motivation of teachers is at the heart of supervisory leadership and may be the most important responsibility of chairpersons, for supervisory leadership is the component upon which educational and organizational leadership are built.

The objective of the remainder of this chapter is to present and help chairpersons master a theory of motivation which has direct practical value, and to help them put this theory to work.

Theories of Motivation

A basic principle in motivation theory is that people invest of themselves in work in order to obtain desired returns or rewards. Examples of investments are time, physical energy, mental energy, creativity, knowledge, skill, enthusiasm, and effort. Returns or rewards can take a variety of forms including money, respect, comfort, a sense of accomplishment, social acceptance and security. It is useful to categorize expression of investment in work as being of two types. The first type is a *participation* investment and the second a *performance* investment.[3]

The participation investment, required of all teachers, includes all that is necessary for the teacher to obtain and maintain satisfactory membership in the school: meeting classes, preparing lesson plans, obtaining satisfactory-to-good evaluations from supervisors, following school rules and regulations, attending required meetings, bearing one's fair share of committee responsibility, projecting an appropriate image to the public—in short, giving a fair day's work for a fair day's pay. Teachers not willing to make the participatory investment in work find themselves unacceptable to administrators and other teachers. On the other hand, one cannot command teachers to give more of themselves—to go beyond the participatory investment. In return for the participatory investment, teachers are provided with such benefits as salary, retirement provisions, fair supervision, good human relations, and security. In a sense, these relationships represent the traditional legal work relationship between employer and employee. Few great achievements result merely from the traditional legal work relationship. Greatness results when employers and employees exceed the limits of this relationship.

The performance investment exceeds the limits of the traditional legal work relationship. Here teachers give far more than one could reasonably expect, and in return they are provided with rewards which permit them to enjoy deep satisfaction with their work and themselves. When one speaks of motivation to work, he speaks of providing

171

incentives which evoke the performance investment from teachers. It is important to distinguish between the kinds of returns or rewards which evoke each of these investments. One does not exceed the limits of the traditional legal work relationship for more rewards of the same kind. One does not buy the second investment with more money, privileges, easier and better working conditions, and improved human relationships. These are important incentives as we shall see, but their potency is limited. Examine the motivation-hygiene theory developed by Frederick Herzberg.[4] The principles of this theory should help you to understand better participatory investments and performance investments at work, as well as why teachers stay on the job.

The Motivation-Hygiene Theory

Each paragraph below describes important features of the motivation-hygiene theory. Statements are attempts to sketch out the nature, scope, and potency of the theory. The description is then followed by an analysis of theoretical and research findings which provide the origins of the theory.

1. There are certain conditions in work which teachers expect to enjoy. If these conditions are present in sufficient quantity, teachers will perform adequately. If these conditions are not present in sufficient quantity, teachers will be dissatisfied and work performance will suffer.
2. The conditions in work which teachers expect as part of the traditional legal work relationship are called hygienic factors. Their absence results in teacher dissatisfaction and poor performance. Their presence maintains the traditional legal work relationship but does not motivate performance.
3. The factors which contribute to teachers exceeding the traditional work relationship are called motivators. The absence of motivators does not result in dissatisfaction and does not endanger the traditional work relationship.
4. Motivation factors and hygiene factors are different. Motivation to work is not a result of increasing hygienic factors.
5. Hygiene factors are associated with the conditions of work and are extrinsic in nature. Examples are money, benefits, fair supervision, and a feeling of belonging. Motivation factors are associated with work itself, and are intrinsic in nature. Examples are recognition, achievement, and increased responsibility.
6. Hygiene factors are important, for their neglect creates problems in the work environment. These problems can result in dissatisfaction and lowered performance. Taking care of the *hygiene* factors *prevents* trouble. These factors are not potent enough, however, if the goal is to motivate people to work.
7. Hygiene factors meet man's need to avoid unpleasantness and hardship. Motivation factors serve man's uniquely human need for psychological growth.
8. Satisfaction at work is not a motivator of performance *per se* but results from quality performance. Principals and chairpersons should not use satisfaction as a method of motivating teachers, but as a goal which teachers seek and which is best obtained through meaningful work.

9. Principals and chairpersons who use job satisfaction to motivate teachers are practicing human relations. This has not been proven to be an effective approach. Human relations emphasize the hygienic factors.

10. Principals and chairpersons who consider job satisfaction as a goal which teachers seek through accomplishing meaningful work and who focus on enhancing the meaning of work and the ability of teachers to accomplish this work are practicing human resource development. This has been proven to be an effective approach. Human resource development emphasizes the motivation factors.

11. True, not all teachers can be expected to respond to the motivation-hygiene theory, but most can.

In summary, the theory stipulates that people at work have two distinct sets of needs.

 One set of needs is best met by hygienic factors. In exchange for these factors, one is prepared to make the participatory investment—to give a fair day's work. If hygiene factors are neglected, dissatisfaction occurs and one's performance on the job decreases below an acceptable level.

Another set of needs is best met by the motivation factors which are not automatically part of the job but which can be built into most jobs, particularly those found in schools. In return for the motivation factors teachers are prepared to make the performance investment, to exceed the limits of the traditional legal work relationship. If the motivation factors are neglected, one does not become dissatisfied, but his performance does not exceed that typically described as a fair day's work for a fair day's pay.

Maslow's Theory of Human Needs

The psychologist Abraham Maslow[5] developed a useful framework for sorting and categorizing basic human needs such as air, water, food, protection, love, sex, respect, success, and influence. These needs are sorted into a five-level taxonomy arranged in hierarchical order of prepotency. The prepotency feature is particularly significant to the taxonomy, for it specifies that needs at the lower level of the hierarchy need to be reasonably satisfied before one is interested in needs at the next higher level.

The five need levels, according to Maslow, are physiological, security, social, esteem, and self-actualization. Figure 6–2 shows a slightly altered needs hierarchy which eliminates physiological needs and adds autonomy needs. This alteration seems appropriate in view of the fact that presently physiological needs seem guaranteed and teachers seem to express considerable interest in control and autonomy.

Figure 6–2 shows the needs hierarchy arranged in triangular form and in the form of a bar graph. To illustrate the prepotency feature, assume that a particular teacher is working at the social need level of the hierarchy. That is, his present concern is in obtaining and maintaining acceptance by other teachers. This teacher is not likely to be con-

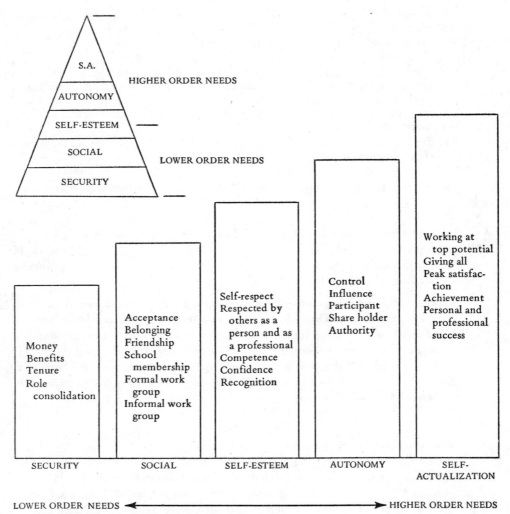

FIGURE 6-2. THE NEEDS HIERARCHY

Note: Lower order needs are associated with hygiene work needs and provide the base for identifying hygiene factors. Higher order needs are associated with motivation work needs and provide the base for identifying motivation factors. From T. J. Sergiovanni and D. Elliott, *Educational and Organizational Leadership in Elementary Schools* (Englewood Cliffs, N.J.: Prentice-Hall, Inc., 1975), p. 142.

cerned with esteem, autonomy, and self-actualization while he is working for acceptance. He will abandon his interest in acceptance, however, if security, an even lower order need, is seriously threatened. As this need becomes reasonably satiated, he then begins to focus on the next higher need, which is self-esteem.

Chairpersons need to know where teachers are with respect to the hierarchy. The level of prepotency for teachers in general and for individual teachers is important for it does not make sense to motivate at the autonomy level if teachers are insecure or to emphasize security needs when people need and seek autonomy. Chairpersons who overestimate the operating need level of teachers might "scare them off." Emphasizing responsibility and participatory decision-making with teachers who are concerned about their own capabilities can be as ineffective as underestimating operating need levels. Teachers are usually denied meaningful satisfaction at work when need levels are underestimated. One's goal may very well be to help teachers operate at the autonomy or self-actualization level but he needs to start with wherever individuals happen to be on the needs hierarchy.

Studies seem to suggest that esteem is the level of need operation of greatest concern to educators in general.[6] Figure 6–3 shows need deficiencies of secondary school teachers surveyed in Illinois. About 1,600 teachers were included in this study, all selected from thirty-six Illinois high schools of approximately 1,500 students each. Teachers were asked to indicate the extent to which each of the five needs categories were being met on the job.[7] The bars on the graph in Figure 6–3 are summaries of their responses. The taller the bar, the less need satisfaction teachers reported. These teachers reported very little dissatisfaction with their job opportunities for fulfillment of security and social needs. Largest need deficiencies were reported at the esteem level. This suggests that today's teachers are likely to work harder in exchange for rewards at the esteem level than for other rewards. Large deficiencies were also reported for autonomy and self-actualization needs, and the importance of these needs should increase as gains are made in the esteem area.

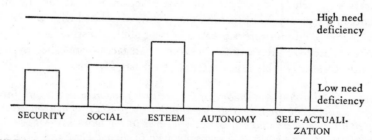

FIGURE 6-3. NEED DEFICIENCIES OF SECONDARY SCHOOL TEACHERS IN ILLINOIS

The lower-order needs of security, social acceptance, and the more material manifestation of esteem such as title and position are clearly extrinsic in nature. These are the things schools give in order to obtain the participatory investment of a fair day's work. To a certain extent, teachers take rewards of this kind for granted. After all, everyone is entitled to a decent salary, job security, a friendly work environment and job stature. One gets these by joining a school faculty, and not by hard work after employment. These needs are associated with the hygienic factors. The higher-order needs of self-concept development, feelings of competency, autonomy and deep satisfaction are needs which are best met through actual performance of work. These rewards are not taken for granted but are earned as a result of effort and successful achievement. These needs are associated with the motivation factors.

The Motivation-Hygiene Factors

The hygienic factors are those largely extrinsic in nature and associated with man's lower-order needs, and the motivation factors are largely intrinsic in nature and associated with man's higher-order needs.

Motivation-hygiene theory results from the research of Frederick Herzberg.[8] The model for his research is an interview where workers are asked to describe job events associated with satisfaction and dissatisfaction at work. The effects of these feelings and events on one's performance at work are examined. Dozens of studies have been conducted using this approach on a variety of workers, from scientists to assembly-line workers, in a number of countries.

Most studies reveal that traditional linear notions regarding satisfaction and dissatisfaction at work are in need of modification. Traditionally, it has been assumed that if a cause of dissatisfaction is identified, elimination of this cause results in job satisfaction and motivated workers. Teachers unhappy with school policies, supervision, money, and class scheduling will move to a state of satisfaction and motivation if these deficiencies are remedied. Motivation-hygiene studies largely show that this is not the case. Remedying the deficiencies which cause dissatisfaction brings a person up to a level of minimum performance which includes the absence of dissatisfaction. Satisfaction and motivation are the results of a separate set of factors. The factors associated with satisfaction but not dissatisfaction are called motivators because of their ability to stimulate performance. The factors associated with dissatisfaction but not satisfaction are called hygienic because of their ability to cause trouble if neglected. In Herzberg's words[9]:

> The motivation-hygiene theory of job attitudes began with a depth interview study of over 200 engineers and accountants representing Pittsburgh industry. These interviews probed sequences of events in the work lives of the respondents to determine the factors that were involved in their feeling exceptionally happy and, conversely, exceptionally unhappy with their jobs. From a review and an analysis of previous publications in the general area of job attitudes, a two-factor hypothesis was formulated to guide the original investigation. This hypothesis suggested that the factors involved in producing job satisfaction were separate and distinct from the factors that led to job dissatisfaction. Since separate factors needed to be considered depending on whether job satisfaction or job dissatisfaction was involved, it followed that these two feelings were not the obverse of each other. The opposite of job satisfaction would not be job dissatisfaction, but rather no job satisfaction; and similarly the opposite of job dissatisfaction is no job dissatisfaction—not job satisfaction. The statement of the concept is awkward and may appear at first to be a semantic ruse, but there is more than a play with

words when it comes to understanding the behavior of people on jobs. The fact that job satisfaction is made up of two unipolar traits is not a unique occurrence. The difficulty of establishing a zero point in psychology with the procedural necessity of using instead a bench mark (mean of a population) from which to start our measurement has led to the conception that psychological traits are bipolar. Empirical investigations, however, have cast some shadows on the assumptions of bipolarity; one timely example is a study of conformity and non-conformity, where they were shown not to be opposites, but rather two separate unipolar traits.

Achievement, recognition, work itself, responsibility, and advancement are the factors identified by Herzberg as contributing primarily to satisfaction. Their absence tends not to lead to dissatisfaction. These are the motivators—the rewards which one seeks in return for the performance investments.

Policy and administration, supervision, salary, interpersonal relationships and working conditions are the factors which Herzberg identifies as contributing primarily to dissatisfaction. These are the hygienic factors—conditions which workers expect in return for a fair day's work.

The Motivation Factors

Achievement
Recognition
Work itself
Responsibility
Advancement

 Satisfaction derived from these factors is associated with increased performance. Their absence does not lead to decreased performance but to a state characterized by a "fair day's work for a fair day's pay."

The Hygiene Factors

Salary
Growth possibilities
Interpersonal relations
Status
Technical supervision

Policy and administration
Working conditions
Job security
Personal life

 These are the dissatisfiers which lead to decreased performance if they are not present. Providing for these factors insures the "fair day's work for fair day's pay" from teachers but not much more.

177

The Motivation-Hygiene Theory and Teachers

The motivation-hygiene theory has been tested in educational settings with generally supportive results. In one study, teachers were interviewed following Herzberg's procedure to identify high and low feelings about their jobs and to collect stories which accounted for these feelings.[10] By means of content analysis the stories were examined and sorted into the sixteen Herzberg job factors. The factors were then examined to see which accounted for high feelings (the motivation set) and which accounted for low feelings (the hygiene set). The effects of these feelings on job performance were also assessed with results consistent with Herzberg's findings.

The results of this study are shown in Figure 6–4. Achievement and recognition were identified as the most potent motivators. Responsibility, although a significant motivator, appeared in only 7 percent of the events associated with satisfaction. Administrators tend not to take advantage of the motivational possibilities of responsibility in education—this factor is relatively standardized for teachers in that responsibility does not vary very much from one teacher to another. Work, itself, did not appear significantly more often as a contributor to satisfaction. Apparently, elements of the job of teaching are inherently less than satisfying. Among these are routine housekeeping, attendance, paper work, study hall, lunch duty. The negative aspects of clerk, cop, and custodial roles seem to neutralize professional teaching and guidance roles for these professionals. Poor interpersonal relations with students, inadequate supervision, unfair school policies and administrative practices, poor interpersonal relations with other teachers and with parents, and incidents in one's personal life were the job factors found to contribute significantly to dissatisfied teachers.

Herzberg found in his original study with accountants and engineers that while recognition and advancement were mentioned most often as motivators, the duration of good feelings associated with these rewards was very short. Work itself and advancement seemed to have medium effects but good feelings associated with responsibility lasted more than three times as long as achievement and recognition. Negative feelings associated with neglected hygienic factors were generally of short duration.

TEACHERS AS INDIVIDUALS. The motivation-hygiene theory provides simplified answers to complex questions. This is a bold theory which provides broad guidelines to principals and chairpersons interested in evoking the performance investment from teachers. Its boldness and its broad propositions require intelligent caution as one applies the theory to practice. For example, while the theory suggests that by and large only certain factors motivate, it would be wrong to conclude that some people are not motivated by the hygienic factors. Some individuals are indeed motivated by the hygienic factors but under ordinary circumstances they do little more than ensure the participation investment as characterized by a "fair day's work for a fair day's pay." Most healthy teachers have the capacity to respond to the principles of the motivation-hygiene theory. Further, healthy teachers who are deprived of intrinsic work satisfactions which come from the motivation factors seek these satisfactions elsewhere—at home through

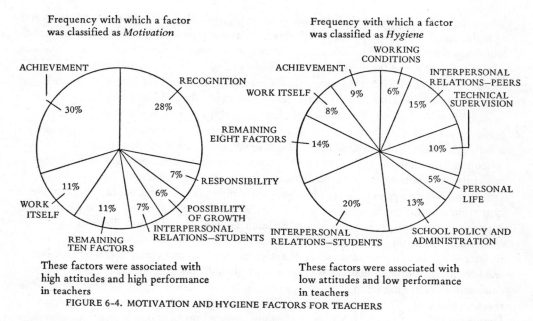

FIGURE 6-4. MOTIVATION AND HYGIENE FACTORS FOR TEACHERS

Note: Shaded areas indicate that a factor appeared more significantly as high than low on the circle to the left, and more low than high on the circle to the right. Frequency of appearance is given in percentages. From T. J. Sergiovanni and F. D. Carver, *The New School Executive: A Theory of Administration* (New York: Dodd, Mead, 1973), p. 76.

family membership, hobbies, community activity, sports. Attention to these aspects of one's life are important to all of us, but the world of work seems the natural place for professional workers to find satisfaction for their needs of esteem, competence, achievement, autonomy, and self-actualization.

Teachers who seem more interested in hygiene factors than motivation factors can be categorized as follows: (1) those who have the potential for motivation seeking but are frustrated by insensitive and closed administrative, supervisory, and organizational policies and practices; (2) those who have the potential for motivation seeking but who decide to channel this potential into other areas of their lives, and (3) those who do not have the potential for motivation seeking on or off the job. Those in the second and third groups use their jobs as a means to gain or achieve goals not related to the school.

The second group includes many teachers whose goals are a second car, a vacation house, supplementing spouse's income in order to achieve a higher standard of living, putting spouse or children through college. Men in this group often use the teaching occupation as a means to step to another job, such as coaching, counselling, or administration. These teachers are on the job for hygienic and external reasons and not motivation reasons.

The third group includes individuals who seem fixated at lower need levels. In a sense, they are obsessed with "avoiding" unpleasantness and discomfort to the point where they have not developed the ability to seek satisfaction through the motivators and at higher need levels. Many regard this obsession as a symptom of poor mental health and feel that selection procedures should be devised which will identify and filter out teachers of this type. Tenured teachers of this type will need to be heavily supervised.

Teachers who have the potential for motivation seeking but who elect to seek satisfactions of this kind outside of the school are generally good teachers who give honest labor in exchange for that which they hope to gain from the school. Extraordinary performance is lacking, however, for strong commitment to the school and its purposes is lacking. Teachers of this kind cannot be depended upon to upgrade the nation's schools substantially or to display much interest in becoming full partners in the school enterprise, unless they can become attracted to the motivation factors. Teachers interested primarily in hygienic factors but who have motivational potential can make significant contributions to the school's work if kindly but firmly supervised or when combined with motivation seekers in schools with differentiated roles and responsibilities for teachers. Hygiene teachers who have the potential for motivation seeking but who are frustrated by the school and its administration are unfortunate casualties. When we deny teachers motivation expressions, we waste not only valuable human resources but we deny school youngsters important opportunities for self-actualization. In general, hygiene teachers think of their jobs excessively (all of us are reasonably concerned with hygienic factors) in terms of salary, working conditions, supervision, status, job security, school policies, and administration and social relationships.

Job Enrichment for Teachers

Practical application of the motivation-hygiene theory in the modern high school requires that chairpersons adopt a job enrichment strategy in working with teachers.

 The purpose of job enrichment is to increase the amount of intrinsic satisfaction a teacher attains from his job.

Building intrinsic satisfaction is different than tinkering with the conditions of work in order to make things more pleasant for teachers. Intrinsic satisfaction comes from the work itself and therefore the focus of job enrichment is to increase the possibilities of teaching jobs for helping teachers become more successful and competent, in essence to derive more satisfaction from the motivation factors.

 Job enrichment should not be confused with improving the job context.

Teachers may be happy with improvements in the job context but intrinsic satisfaction and improved performance do not necessarily follow.

Understanding the relationship between satisfaction at work and improved performance is crucial to understanding how job enrichment works.

Some administrators incorrectly assume that improving teacher satisfaction and morale will improve teacher performance.

Job enrichment assumes that teachers experience improved satisfaction and morale as a result of improved performance and of additional responsibility.

These relationships are consistent with the motivation-hygiene theory where hygiene is concerned with factors related to the context of work and motivation is related to the work itself.

Examples of practices and concerns which deal with the teacher work context and with the work itself are presented in Table 6–1. Chairpersons will find it absolutely necessary to give attention to the hygienic practices in this table if they wish to avoid wholesale teacher dissatisfaction. But it is the motivation practices to which most teachers will respond with increased commitment and effort.

The development of specific job enrichment strategies for teachers in junior and senior high schools is a situational matter best done by chairpersons and teachers on the job. The possibilities and opportunities will differ, school by school. Regardless of what individual strategies are developed, they should represent attempts to load more opportunities for achievement, recognition, growth variety, interest, and responsibility into the teaching job. Some components of the teaching job where job enrichment strategies are applicable include:

1. department decision-making
2. teaching methods
3. curriculum sequence, scope, and content
4. scheduling of students
5. scheduling of instructional modules and class periods
6. goals and objectives
7. teacher and student roles and relationships
8. evaluation

Take curriculum sequence, scope, and content for example. Is the curriculum organized in a fashion which encourages teachers to teach in a mindless way with little regard for the value of material they cover or for what they are trying to accomplish? Are teachers largely direction-givers implementing a heavily prescribed curriculum and therefore making few decisions of their own? Such situations badly need enrichment. The following questions, though not inclusive, might help decide the extent to which your educational program needs enrichment:

1. Are teachers deciding what will be taught, when, and how?
2. Is the curriculum confining to teachers or does it free them to be innovative and creative?
3. Do teachers know what they are trying to accomplish and why?
4. Are schedules established and youngsters grouped by teachers for educational reasons?

181

TABLE 6-1. PRACTICES AND CONCERNS OF THE WORK CONTEXT AND WORK ITSELF FOR TEACHERS

PRACTICES AND CONCERNS THAT DEAL WITH THE TEACHERS' WORK CONTEXT		PRACTICES AND CONCERNS THAT DEAL WITH THE WORK ITSELF
Security ✓ Fairness ✓ Grievance procedure ✓ Protection from parents ✓ Protection from students Support from administration Seniority and tenure Union or association membership *Monetary* Salary schedules Retirement Sabbatical Sick leave Hospitalization Insurance Credit union Social security Annuity Mutual fund *Working Conditions* Condition of the school Office and room space Lounge space Length of work day ✓ Number of students ✓ Hall duty ✓ Study hall assignments Lunch and rest periods Parking facilities Equipment ✓ Teaching schedule	*Social* ✓ Work groups ✓ Coffee groups ✓ Social contacts ✓ Feelings of belonging and acceptance ✓ Professional groups *Status* ✓ Job definition Job title ✓ Classroom size and location Equipment ✓ Student type ✓ Class load Grade level Privileges *Supervision* ✓ Recruitment ✓ Selection ✓ Assignment ✓ Orientation ✓ In-service program ✓ Evaluation programs Work rules ✓ Communication channels ✓ Committee work	*Achievement, Responsibility* Delegation of authority ✓ Participation ✓ Involvement Planning ✓ Goal-setting ✓ Freedom to act ✓ Visibility ✓ Accountability ✓ Creative expression Promotion *Recognition, Personal and* *Professional Growth* Merit increases Differentiated responsibility ✓ Leadership role ✓ Community responsibility ✓ Publications ✓ Innovations Supervisory responsibility ✓ Problem-solving ✓ Aptitudes utilized

From T. J. Sergiovanni and F. D. Carver, *The New School Executive: A Theory of Administration* (New York: Dodd, Mead, 1973), p. 111. Granted many of the practices and concerns are beyond the reach of direct influence of chairpersons. Items checked seem more within their province than others

5. Are teachers free to deviate from schedules for good educational reasons?
6. Is curriculum standardization avoided for teachers and for students?
7. Is the teacher more accountable for achieving agreed-upon goals and objectives than for teaching the curriculum or operating his classroom in a given way?
8. Do teachers have some budget control and responsibility for their areas?
9. Can teachers team together if they wish?

10. Are teachers free to choose their own curriculum materials within budget constraints?[11]

In the next section a job enrichment worksheet is provided. Its intent is to provide an opportunity to brainstorm about job enrichment in an attempt to accumulate as many suggestions as possible. Job enrichment suggestions should be generated for each of the motivation categories. One example under each category is provided to help get the process started.

Job Enrichment Worksheet

Your task is to develop a list of ways in which the job of teaching can be enriched. The purpose of enrichment is to increase the amount of intrinsic satisfaction one derives from work. Enrichment can take place by modifying the job and by modifying one's job relationships with others. Why should chairpersons be interested in job enrichment? As intrinsic meanings and satisfactions are built into jobs, teachers will work harder to obtain their rewards. The result: greater satisfaction for teachers *and* improved performance for the school.

How can the job of teaching be enriched to provide teachers with more opportunities for:

1. *Achievement—success*
   EXAMPLE:
   General—Encourage teachers to try new ideas
   Specific—Provide psychological support and expert help to teachers to ensure success when they try out new ideas

2. *Recognition for quality work and good ideas*
   EXAMPLE:
   General—Provide opportunities for teachers to share ideas
   Specific—Encourage teachers out of isolation, to work together in teams, to combine classes, to plan units of study together across classes

3. *Personal and career advancement and growth*
   EXAMPLE:
   General—Help teachers to develop professional targets and goals
   Specific—Develop an individualized staff development program where each teacher, with the chairperson's help, develops a plan for his own self-improvement

4. *Experiencing important, interesting, and meaningful work*
   EXAMPLE:
   General—Provide teachers with opportunities to make more decisions about what they teach
   Specific—Encourage English teachers to develop their own reading lists of books they think are most appropriate for the objectives they have and for the youngsters they have

183

5. *Enjoying more responsibility*
EXAMPLE:
General—involve teachers directly in decisions relating to educational program
Specific—develop a shared decision-making model in the department

Successful job enrichment strategies assume that the curriculum is largely in the minds and hearts of teachers; rely heavily on decentralized decision-making; hold teachers accountable for living up to and working toward agreed-upon goals and objectives (with teachers provided considerable autonomy for deciding how); and rely on flexible teaching and curricular arrangements.

Most comments in this chapter, from discussion of why teachers stay on the job, through motivation theories, to job enrichment, apply also to students. They, too, need to stay on the job as students for the right reasons, must be provided with motivation factors, and need to be subjected to the principles of job enrichment.

ENDNOTES

1. Frederick Mosteller and Daniel P. Moynihan (eds.), *On Equality of Educational Opportunity: Papers Deriving from the Harvard University Faculty Seminar on the Coleman Report* (New York: Random House, 1972).

2. Adapted from Vincent S. Flowers and Charles L. Hughes, "Why Employees Stay," *Harvard Business Review*, Vol. 51, No. 4, 1973, pp. 49–60. Conversations and correspondence with Charles L. Hughes were very helpful in developing this section of Chapter 6.

3. The discussion of theories of motivation, the motivation-hygiene theory, and Maslow's theory of human needs, follows section of Chapter 10, "Motivating Teachers to Work," in Thomas J. Sergiovanni and David Elliott, *Educational and Organizational Leadership in Elementary Schools* (Englewood Cliffs, N. J.: Prentice-Hall, 1975).

4. Frederick Herzberg, Bernard Mausner, and Barbara Snyderman, *The Motivation to Work* (New York: John Wiley and Sons, 1959); Frederick Herzberg, *Work and the Nature of Man* (New York: World, 1966).

5. Abraham Maslow, *Motivation and Productivity* (New York: Harper and Brothers, 1954).

6. Francis M. Trusty and Thomas J. Sergiovanni, "Perceived Need Deficiencies of Teachers and Administrators: A Proposal for Restricting Teacher Roles," *Educational Administration Quarterly*, Vol. 2, Autumn 1966, pp. 165–180; and Fred D. Carver and Thomas J. Sergiovanni, "Complexity, Adaptability and Job Satisfaction in High Schools: On Axiomatic Theory Applied," *Journal of Educational Administration*, Vol. 9, No. 1, 1971, pp. 10–31.

7. Respondents completed a thirteen-item need deficiency questionnaire modeled after each of five categories of Maslow's need hierarchy. The instrument assessed on a seven-point scale the amount of need fulfillment available as well as the amount needed

for each category. The difference between actual and desired need fulfillment was computed and labeled a "perceived need deficiency." Mean differences used to construct Figure 6–3 were security .67, social .89, esteem 1.45, autonomy 1.25, self-actualization 1.34.

8. Herzberg *et al., op. cit.,* 1959.

9. Frederick Herzberg, "The Motivation-Hygiene Concept and Problems of Manpower," *Personnel Administration,* Vol. 27, No. 1, 1964, p. 3.

10. Thomas J. Sergiovanni, "Factors Which Affect Satisfaction and Dissatisfaction of Teachers," *The Journal of Educational Administration,* Vol. 5, No. 1, 1976, pp. 66–82.

11. Thomas J. Sergiovanni, "From Human Relations to Human Resources Supervision." In T. J. Sergiovanni (ed.), *Beyond Human Relations: Professional Supervision for Professional Teachers* (Washington, D.C.: Association for Supervision and Curriculum Development, 1976).

☙ CHAPTER SIX ☙

☙ PRACTICES ☙

Suggestions for maintaining and improving satisfaction and motivation of teachers in the department are woven throughout each concepts and practices section. Virtually all of the activities of department chairpersons can influence satisfaction and motivation. Department organization, staff meetings, communication channels, scheduling classes and assigning teachers, staff development activities, supervisory support systems, educational program concerns and teacher evaluation are examples of such chairperson activities. Refer to Table 6–1 in the concepts section of this chapter for an itemized list of additional practices and concerns. Further, parts of Chapter 2, Section 1, dealing with "criteria for worthwhile action" and "the social sciences as a basis for action," suggest more specifically the interrelationship between teacher satisfaction and motivation and most chairperson responsibilities in junior and senior high schools.

It is possible, nevertheless, to identify some chairperson responsibilities which seem to have separate and significant implications for teacher satisfaction and motivation. Two of these responsibilities are the art of identifying, recruiting, and selecting teachers likely to be not only competent in a technical sense, but also highly motivated and committed to their jobs, and orienting these teachers properly to the department and school.

Selection and orientation get the prime attention in the second section of this chapter. Attention is also given to identifying motivation-hygiene tendencies of teachers and to helping chairpersons plan and evaluate strategies for increasing teacher motivation. Understanding of the motivation-hygiene theory in particular, and human motivation in general, as discussed in the concepts section, is presumed as we proceed.

Included in this section are:

Suggestions for selecting staff
What should be appraised
Suggestions for reviewing applicants' credentials
A guide for interviewing teachers
Chairperson's interview checklist
Sample interview form
Sample selection form
Interview questions which help get at motivation to work
Suggestions for orienting new teachers

SELECTING STAFF

Common weaknesses in selecting staff tend to be characterized by proceeding almost entirely on an intuitive basis without clear understanding of what one seeks in a candidate, or where procedures exist, developing and articulating them in a fashion which enhances descriptions of candidates without directly helping evaluation. An effective selection procedure is one which proceeds with full knowledge of job requirements, critical selection areas and required competencies associated with the job in question. It is for this reason that chairpersons typically play a key role in the selection procedures and that involvement of other teachers in the department is usually critical.

Certainly central office personnel have much to contribute to the selection process and though often at a disadvantage in evaluating a candidate in some critical selection areas, they may be in a better position to evaluate in other areas. The selection process should be seen as a team effort which involves concerned individuals at a number of levels in the school.

New staff are not being added at the same rate as in the past. School populations are stabilizing and declining. Teacher turnover is becoming less common and teachers, once hired, are inclined to stay employed in the same school for a long time. This makes the selection process perhaps more important now than at any other time in the history of American education. The young teacher you hire is likely to stay on the job for the next two or three decades. Keep this in mind as you plan and implement your selection procedures.

What Should Be Appraised?

The decision to select a teacher for your department should be based on an assessment of five critical areas. Before a teacher is considered he should show at least minimum competence in each area and outstanding competence in some. The critical selection areas are:

Technical:
1. The extent to which the candidate *can do* the job: his *ability*
2. The extent to which the candidate *will do* the job: his *achievement* potential

Human:
3. The extent to which the candidate can *relate* successfully with adults: his *social effectiveness.*
4. The extent to which the candidate can *understand,* relate to and be a model for students: his *student sensitivity.*

Professional:
5. The extent to which the candidate is likely to continue to grow and *develop* as a person and professional: his *will grow* potential.

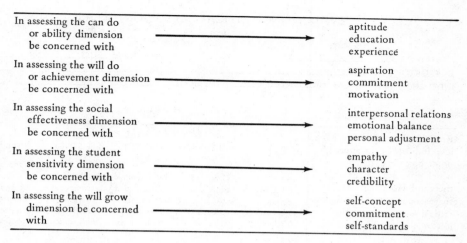

In assessing the can do or ability dimension be concerned with	aptitude education experience
In assessing the will do or achievement dimension be concerned with	aspiration commitment motivation
In assessing the social effectiveness dimension be concerned with	interpersonal relations emotional balance personal adjustment
In assessing the student sensitivity dimension be concerned with	empathy character credibility
In assessing the will grow dimension be concerned with	self-concept commitment self-standards

It is not intended that each of the critical areas be treated equally. Some candidates may have such overriding strengths in one category that they tend to offset minimum strengths in another. For example, a candidate may show high potential in the will grow and achievement areas which compensate for present minimum strength in the ability area. Further, some teaching jobs may be defined so that working with or relating to other adults does little to enhance effectiveness. That being the case, social effectiveness may be considered much less important than other critical dimensions.

An example of a summary form for recording observations in each of the critical selection areas appears below. Such a form can be used to gather evaluations from a number of people and as a basis for discussing each critical area as evidenced in several aspects of the selection procedure.

EVALUATING CRITICAL SELECTION AREAS

CANDIDATE _____   POSITION _____
EVALUATOR _____   DATE _____
INFERENCES MADE FROM: CREDENTIALS _____   INTERVIEW _____   OTHER _____

CRITICAL SELECTION AREAS

Review the factors listed below. Indicate in the appropriate box the extent to which your assessment of this candidate in each factor suggests competence in each critical selection area. Use low, medium or high ratings.	ABILITY	ACHIEVEMENT	SOCIAL EFFECT	STUDENT SENSITIVITY	WILL GROW
	Ability to be an effective teacher	Drive and motivation to be an effective teacher	Interpersonal skills needed to relate effectively with others	Epathy, understanding, and character to work effectively with students	Interest in long-range growth and development as a person and professional
Early experiences with family and school					
Educational background					
Non-educational work experience					
Educational work experience					
Current interests and life style					
Self-evaluation					

Comments:

REVIEWING APPLICANTS' CREDENTIALS

Announcements of teaching openings in most departments are likely to elicit a large number of applications. Some preliminary screening will take place at the central office level; nevertheless, many credentials will find themselves on the chairperson's desk. From there, only a handful of the most qualified will be invited to interview for the position. Teachers are often involved in the interviewing process and should also be involved in the second-level screening of applicants, which occurs in the department. Teachers may be asked to review credentials and vote up or down on them regarding which shall be invited for interviews but a better procedure is to ask teachers to comment on strengths and weaknesses discovered in the credentials. Commenting requires that credentials be analyzed and provides data to help the chairperson and principal decide on who to invite for interviews.

FORM FOR REVIEWING CREDENTIALS

_____   _____
APPLICANT'S NAME   POSITION SOUGHT

TEACHING FIELDS: 1. _____ 2. _____ 3. _____

    The attached folder contains the credentials of an applicant for a teaching position. Please review the information and pass the folder to another on the routing list just as soon as possible. In the space provided, give your opinion concerning the advisability of considering this applicant for the position.

ROUTE TO: COMMENTS ON STRENGTHS AND WEAKNESSES

_____   _____

TEACHER A   _____

                                    _____

_____   _____

TEACHER B   _____

                                    _____

_____   _____

DEPARTMENT CHAIRPERSON   _____

                                    _____

_____   _____

OTHER   _____

                                    _____

NOTE The last person to review these credentials should return them to the chairperson's office. If an interview is scheduled, the credentials will again be made available for reference during the interview. The chairperson is to forward the review to the principal with a recommendation as follows:

      Strong prospect for interview _____   Comments:
      Average prospect for interview_____
      Weak prospect for interview_____

      Date forwarded to principal _____
                                      Action taken:
      Date forwarded to chairperson_____

A GUIDE TO INTERVIEWING TEACHERS

Interviewing is a technique used to obtain ideas, attitudes, feelings, and other information from another person. Often the purpose of the interview is to make a decision or to diagnose a need and it is assumed that this purpose is enhanced as information is obtained. Many meetings which are intended to be interviews become something else because of misunderstandings regarding interviewer and interviewee roles. In order to obtain the information he needs, the interviewer needs to provide some direction and to facilitate the interviewee's sharing of his thoughts and ideas. But it is the thoughts and ideas of the interviewee which should dominate the meeting. The following suggestions may help you to interview prospective teachers:

1. *Listen to the candidate in a patient, friendly, but critical manner.* Your job is to listen to what the person has to say. The quickest way to stop a person from expressing himself is by interrupting him. But listening is not enough, you need to understand what the person is saying. From time to time try to summarize what the person has said and ask if this is what he means. Let him know you understand his thoughts, positions, or ideas.

2. *Avoid displaying any kind of authority.* Your intent is to free the person to talk and the more equal he feels the better able he will be to speak fully and candidly. Avoid hiding behind a desk. Avoid other symbols of your authority.

3. *Do not give advice or make judgments about what the person says.* If a person describes a problem he had in disciplining students on an occasion, don't tell him what he should have done. If he shows a distrust for administration, don't admonish him. In the first case, ask "How did you work this problem out?"; and in the second, "Why do you feel this way?". The intent is to get the person to speak more fully and therefore to increase your understanding, and not to correct or advise.

4. *Avoid arguing with the person.* If you are able to get the person to talk about important educational issues, values, and beliefs you will obtain a great deal of information to help make a better decision. At the same time, you run the risk of disagreeing with the person. Your job is not to tell him what you think and argue with him but to understand how he thinks and why.

5. *Limit what you say* in the interview to questions and comments which help the person talk, which relieve him of anxieties, and which praise him for sharing his views.

6. It may be appropriate at the *end* of the interview to *invite the person to interview you* about your beliefs and those of the department and about other aspects of the school which interest him. Avoid beginning in this fashion, however, because your views are likely to influence his comments.

It is often useful to plan specific questions which you wish to ask the candidate and wish to have standard for all candidates as a basis of comparison. An example of a list of questions with a simple rating scale for each is provided below. This checklist contains thirteen questions, probably too many unless they form the basis for the whole interview. The questions are intentionally general and serve to invite the person to express his views.

Questions of the yes-no or other concise answer variety are admittedly easier to summarize and rate but yield less information and lend themselves more to eliciting socially-accepted responses rather than actual feelings.

CHAIRPERSON'S INTERVIEW CHECKLIST

APPLICANT_____   SCALE: 5 = EXCELLENT
POSITION_____   1 = POOR

QUESTION ASKED	I CONSIDERED THE RESPONSE TO BE:				
1. Why did you want to become a teacher?	1	2	3	4	5
2. What are your beliefs about the significance of education?	1	2	3	4	5
3. What do you enjoy most about teaching?	1	2	3	4	5
4. How can you get students excited about learning?	1	2	3	4	5
5. What are your sources of ideas?	1	2	3	4	5
6. What new ideas would you like to initiate in your classroom when you start teaching?	1	2	3	4	5
7. How do you want your students to view you?	1	2	3	4	5
8. Do you know a person who is a good listener? Please describe this person as a listener.	1	2	3	4	5
9. How can you tell when you are doing a good job of listening?	1	2	3	4	5
10. What do you do when a supervisor criticizes a teaching technique you are using?	1	2	3	4	5
11. A teacher tells you that a student said your class was boring. What would you do?	1	2	3	4	5
12. What are your personal goals and aspirations?	1	2	3	4	5
13. What help from supervisors will you need to do your best work as a teacher?	1	2	3	4	5

SAMPLE INTERVIEW SUMMARY FORM

This sample interview form includes definitions of its terms and clues as to where in the credentials or how in the interview you might obtain information needed to make assessments. In using the form, provide enough narrative information so that you adequately communicate information about the candidate and your interpretation of this information. Use direct quotes when appropriate but indicate the extent to which you feel certain or uncertain about what the candidate said. Under personal characteristics, three rating scales are provided. These are designed to supplement the narrative portion of your summary. If you feel it important to comment and elaborate rather than rate, indicate that on the summary sheet and use the back side for your comments.

In making your judgments, pay close attention to the definitions of terms provided and to the guidelines, but consider other factors if they are important. If everyone is working from the same list of definitions and considerations, it may be wise to indicate on the back side other factors you considered.

When summarizing assets and liabilities do so with reference to the five critical selection areas mentioned under Selecting Staff (pp. 188–90): can do or ability, will do or achievement, social effectiveness, student sensitivity, and will grow potential. Review the critical selection areas, identifying the best things you can say about the candidate. Use this analysis for summarizing the assets. Repeat the procedure with the worst things and summarize the liabilities.

When preparing the overall summary, you need now to relate the assets and liabilities in each critical selection area to the demands and needs of the particular position in question. This is followed by a final assessment in the form of an overall rating. A rating of three should mean that you assess this candidate to be currently or potentially equal to the average faculty member in your department or school.

SAMPLE INTERVIEW SUMMARY RATING FORM*

NAME _____ DATE _____ AGE _____
JOB CONSIDERED FOR _____ INTERVIEWER _____

EARLY HOME LIFE

EDUCATION AND TRAINING	FAVORABLE			UNFAVORABLE	
	1	2	3	4	5

WORK EXPERIENCE	FAVORABLE			UNFAVORABLE	
	1	2	3	4	5

CURRENT OFF-THE-JOB LIFE

PERSONAL CHARACTERISTICS

ABILITIES AND SKILLS (1–5)

( ) Mental ability (test scores?)   ( ) Communications skills
( ) Mental flexibility   ( ) Practical judgment
( ) Incisiveness   ( ) Ability to plan, organize, and
                                             follow up

MOTIVATION AND INTERESTS (1–5)

( ) Willingness to work hard, self-discipline   ( ) Interest in people
( ) Initiative on job   ( ) Breadth of interests
( ) Drive to improve self and get ahead   ( ) Realism of goals and aspirations

PERSONALITY AND SOCIAL EFFECTIVENESS (1–5)

( ) Self-confidence   ( ) Team worker
( ) Personal adjustment   ( ) Social effectiveness and
( ) Character   persuasive skills
                           ( ) Leadership and supervisory skills

ASSETS	LIABILITIES

*From: Theodore Hariton, *Interview! The Executive's Guide to Selecting the Right Personnel* (New York: Hastings House, 1970), p. 93–98.

OVERALL SUMMARY

OVERALL RATING	FAVORABLE			UNFAVORABLE	
	1	2	3	4	5

Definition of Terms Used on Rating Form

General Mental Ability: ability to learn, reason, and cope with complex problems.

Consider: Scores on psychological tests, school performance (level of grades, complexity of subject matter, and academic standards of school), complexity of work assignments, nature of reading habits, ability to cope with depth questions in interview.

Mental Flexibility: ability to change mental set from one situation to another, to handle diversified tasks, to be receptive to new ideas.

Consider: Broad curriculum in school, broad work assignments requiring changes in mental set, open-mindedness, range of off-the-job interests, efforts to develop self, personal adjustment.

Incisiveness: ability to cut through to the heart of a problem with a minimum of distractions.

Consider: Crispness of answers during interview, clarity of reasons why behind actions, amount of irrelevant detail, time required to make a point, depth of thinking.

Communications Skills: effectiveness in expressing oneself clearly in speech and in writing.

Consider: Vocabulary range, grammar, clarity, level of concepts presented, performance in verbal subjects in school, experience in writing and public speaking on and off the job, reading habits.

Practical Judgment: ability to apply talents in making sound decisions, especially regarding education, work, and personal life.

Consider: Reasons behind choice of school and major, relevance of schooling to vocational career, reasons for taking and leaving jobs, job accomplishments, financial stability, balance between on-the-job and off-the-job life.

Ability to Plan, Organize and Follow-Up: ability to direct not only one's own work, but also the work of others.

Consider: Extent of administrative responsibilities in school or on job, utilization of time, attention to details, meeting of deadlines, need for closure, ability to see big picture, organization of own presentation in interview.

Willingness to Work Hard, Self-Discipline: application to the job beyond minimum requirements without control and direction from superiors.

Consider: Amount of part-time and summer work as a youngster and in school, grades in school in relation to intelligence, energy level as indicated by number of activities in which engaged, health, hours of work, performance when on own.

Initiative on Job: effort to expand job scope and suggest or try new approaches.

Consider: Performance in unstructured situations, self-starting tendencies, competitiveness, level of aspirations, desire for independence, drive to achieve.

Desire to Improve Self and Get Ahead: continuation of self-development program for purposes of furthering vocational career.

Consider: Self-insight, reaction to criticism, attitude toward schooling (past, present and future), nature of outside activities, level of aspirations, willingness to extend self or make job moves to get ahead.

Interest in People: enjoyment of contact with people both on and off the job.

Consider: Extent of activities with other people beyond that which is required by the job, motivation for engaging in people activities (help others versus opportunism), history of solitary versus group activities.

Breadth of Interests: varied activities and broad perspective—intellectual, social, political, physical.

Consider: Time devoted to job versus off-the-job interests, range of reading habits and general fund of knowledge, pursuits which contribute to physical and mental hygiene, participation in family activities.

Realism of Goals and Aspirations: career objectives in line with talents and record of accomplishment—neither too high nor too low.

Consider: Record of accomplishment and anticipated accomplishments in future, rewards to date and expected rewards, demands of future job in relation to qualifications, plan of self-development and job progression to attain goals.

Self-Confidence: belief in self and willingness to act on the basis of this belief.

Consider: Realism of self-image, how seen by others, extent of confidence (as individual contributor versus leader), willingness to take risks, own up to shortcomings and make decisions.

Personal Adjustment: relatively free from emotional problems; mature and realistic outlook toward life.

Consider: One-sided or balanced life, objectivity of judgment, adaptability to new situations, reaction to strain and pressure, presence or absence of symptoms

199

produced by anxiety and tension, history of good or poor relationships with people, criticalness versus acceptance of people, sense of humor.

Character: honesty in dealings with people on and off the job; high moral and ethical standards.

Consider: Candor in describing self in interview, spontaneity and consistency of responses, willingness to discuss difficulties and shortcomings, concern for others.

Team Worker: work cooperatively toward attainment of common objective; contribute to the effort but not as a star.

Consider: Give-and-take relationships with others (home, school, job, elsewhere), adaptation to military service, willingness to accept authority, size of ego, concern for others as well as for self.

Social Effectiveness and Persuasive Skills: effectiveness in inter-personal relations—superiors, peers, subordinates, clients, public; not merely being "nice."

Consider: Extent of public contact activities, social mobility (ability to deal with people at different socio-economic levels), behavior during interview including sensitivity to the interviewer as a person, appearance.

Leadership and Supervisory Skills: effectiveness in directing activities of others.

Consider: Experience in leading others (school, service, job, community), willingness to delegate, sensitivity to the interplay in group situations, forcefulness and tough-mindedness, command presence, sphere of influence.

Examples of Narrative Comments

1. *Early Home Life:* Fred Fisk is the older of two children, has a sister who is currently enrolled in a pharmacy program at Penn State. Fred's father is a graduate of Lehigh University and has owned and operated a small independent carpet sales and service store. The store has had its highs and lows and though opportunities have existed for expansion, Fred's father seems to prefer a smaller, safer, more manageable enterprise. Fred's father's relationship with his family has not been close because of the demanding hours the business has required. Fred said that he depended on his mother almost entirely as a child. When she was not responsive or busy with his younger sister, he had no one to turn to. He reports spending a lot of time alone as a child. This early home environment may have contributed to what I sense to be a withdrawn and personally insecure pattern in Fred. This view is supported by the vague career goals Fred describes and by what I judge to be a resentment toward people in positions of authority.

2. *Education and Training:* Fred took an academic program in a high school of 500 students. He describes his high school experience as being "boring" but seemed not to know why. He said he wasn't much interested in school and didn't do well

until his mother transferred him to a Catholic high school in the next town. It was tougher there, he reports, particularly with regard to discipline, and his grades improved markedly. He went to Penn State and majored in literature. At the end of the first year he switched to business administration. He dropped out after two years (with a C average) and entered the army for two years active duty and a reserve commitment. He then entered Mansfield State Teachers College as a transfer junior. He reports being indifferent to the social climate at Mansfield. He managed a strong B average at graduation. Grades in his more practical education courses are lower than those in his academic program. However, he earned an A in his educational practicum experience. In his words, "My cooperating teacher was real tough with me and the kids. I liked that and felt as long as I knew what she expected, and that she encouraged me when I did what she expected, that I could do a good job. I did a good job too and I really enjoyed that experience."

SAMPLE SELECTION SUMMARY FORM

This section contains a sample selection summary form which could be useful in situations where a large number of people are involved in the selection process, thus making it necessary to "survey" opinions in order to reach some decision. This summary form does not ask for detailed information but rather provides for ratings of items which permit the use of simple descriptive statistics (mean, range, deviation) to summarize assessments of a candidate.

SELECTION SUMMARY FORM

APPLICANT _____ POSITION _____

RATER _____ DATE _____

Area 1   Credentials

FACTORS	RATING				
1. Overall undergraduate college	1	2	3	4	5
2. Overall graduate college	1	2	3	4	5
3. Major	1	2	3	4	5
4. Minor	1	2	3	4	5
5. Previous work experience	1	2	3	4	5
6. Student teaching	1	2	3	4	5
7. Membership in professional organization	1	2	3	4	5
8. Participates in in-service workshops	1	2	3	4	5

Area 2   Interview

FACTORS	RATING*				
9. Philosophy complementary to department's educational program platform	1	2	3	4	5
10. Awareness of modern teaching techniques	1	2	3	4	5
11. Creative and innovative abilities	1	2	3	4	5
12. Willing to improve	1	2	3	4	5
13. Willing to accept additional responsibilities	1	2	3	4	5
14. Willingness to become involved in school's total program	1	2	3	4	5
15. Appearance	1	2	3	4	5
16. Personality	1	2	3	4	5
17. Communicativeness	1	2	3	4	5
18. Open-minded	1	2	3	4	5
19. Willingness to share and cooperate	1	2	3	4	5

Comments:

Overall Recommendation   1   2   3   4   5

*Note: A rating of three means you view the candidate to be on par potentially or actually with the average teacher in the department or school.

INTERVIEW QUESTIONS THAT HELP GET AT MOTIVATION TO WORK

The portion of the interview which is designed to get at motivation to work is an important supplement to other portions attempting to determine teaching competency and educational philosophy. Review the concepts section of this chapter, particularly discussions of the Motivation-Hygiene Theory. It is critical that you understand the theory thoroughly before using this interview format. Motivation factors refer to the job itself and consequent satisfaction which one earns. A teacher who shows a high concern for motivation factors is said to be intrinsically motivated.

Hygiene factors refer to the conditions of work. Most teachers have some concerns for conditions of work but those with high concern with these factors exclusive of the motivation factors are said to be extrinsically motivated. The attitude and performance of intrinsically and extrinsically motivated teachers vary greatly and, while much can be done to increase intrinsic interest after a person is on the job, efforts should be made during the job interview to determine those likely to be more intrinsically motivated. Consider the following interviewing suggestions:

1. Begin by focusing on previous work experience.
    "I notice in your folder that you have had some previous jobs. Tell me
        something about your work experiences."
Allow the person to elaborate until he can recall previous jobs. Ask the follow-
    ing questions:
    "Take one of the jobs as an example and recall a time when you *felt excep-
        tionally good* on that job. Now tell me what happened."
Your objective is to get the person to talk about those aspects of his job and
    those events which occurred in his job which he found very satisfying.
    Remember, these are clues to what this person is likely to find satisfying if
    hired as a teacher in your department.
Try to get this person to recall a specific period of time or sequence of events
    when he felt exceptionally good. You are now ready to explore these
    events factually until you think you understand the incident that made him
    feel good. Ask such questions as:
    "What was going on at this time?"
    "What happened then?"
    "What did you do next?"
    "What reasons did he give you?"
Now shift your questions less to ascertain facts of the events but more the
    values, attitudes, motivations, and beliefs of the candidate. You are trying
    to find out why the events made him feel good. Ask such questions as:
    "What was there about this situation that made you feel good?"
    "Why did this make you feel exceptionally good?"
    "I think I understand what made you feel good, but tell me in your own
        words why this pleased you."

2. Repeat the cycle outlined above but this time focus on the candidate's experi-

203

ences in college. This setting often evokes incidents and events which readily reveal one's intrinsic and extrinsic tendencies.

3. Summary Question.

"Suppose you accepted a teaching position in a school district somewhere. After four years, you have a chance for a job with another school district. What is the one factor that would influence your decision most?"

ORIENTING NEW TEACHERS

Much of the initial and formal responsibility for orienting new teachers to the school and district will be assumed by building and central office administrators. By the first day of school the new teacher probably has attended an orientation meeting, been provided with a teacher's manual, received a letter of welcome from the Superintendent, been called upon by community agencies such as "welcome wagon," and has received a packet of information from the local Chamber of Commerce. No question about it, all these are useful in helping the new teacher learn about and become a part of the community and school. If your school or district does not follow these practices, you should take the lead in establishing some of them.

But such practices only represent the beginning of an effective orientation program. The critical phase of the program begins once the person is on the job and continues until that teacher reaches a point of professional confidence and competence to function independently and effectively. This phase will take at least a year even for the most promising newcomers. More likely, this phase will continue into the second and maybe even the third year.

Perhaps one of the greatest tragedies in our field is our reluctance to differentiate among teachers. Ours is perhaps the only profession or craft where beginners have identical responsibilities and tasks as seasoned, competent veterans. A successful orientation program treats the beginner differently because it does not assume that he is ready, in terms of competence, confidence or familiarity, to assume full responsibilities as an independent professional.

The success of this critical phase of the orientation program depends almost entirely on the chairperson's leadership. There are three main thrusts to this critical phase:

 providing the beginner with minimum expectations held by the school and by the department

providing the beginner with personal and job security

ensuring that the teacher's career in the department and school is characterized by early success

1. With respect to minimum expectations, new teachers need to have a relatively clear understanding of what is expected of them and the earlier this is accomplished the better. Certainly this includes the standard items such as critical policies, controls, and

resources, but they should also understand school objectives and philosophy, and the department's educational program platform. Read the chapters on educational leadership, particularly Chapter 9, for an elaboration of educational program platform. The beginner might well be assigned a relatively light independent teaching load and make up the difference by interning in a course taught by an outstanding veteran teacher. Supervision should be heavy in the early weeks to help the teacher become acquainted with critical role expectations. This is in contrast to the generally-accepted practice of deliberately leaving beginners alone until they find themselves.

2. Beginners have needs for personal and job security which differ markedly from those of more experienced teachers. The beginning teacher often worries about discipline and student control, being liked and accepted by students and by other teachers. The beginner is often particularly fearful of parents and is concerned about his own adequacy, about subject matter adequacy and about being evaluated.

Frances Fuller has identified three important phases through which beginning teachers move in becoming polished professionals.* These phases have critical application for your orientation program as well as for your development of subsequent supervisory and staff development plans.

Phase 1. This is the "where do I stand?" phase in which the new teacher explores the parameters of his role as a teacher and his relationship with important others such as teachers, chairperson, and students. Often this involves testing his authority with these groups in an attempt to define limits. He wants to know what he can do and can't do; what you expect of him and what others expect of him; how much authority he has and doesn't have, and answers to similar questions which help him define his relationships and position in the school.

Phase 2. This is the "how adequate am I?" phase. Typically the new teacher is unsure of himself and wonders if he knows the subject matter well enough, if he can answer tough questions from bright kids, if he can adequately communicate about department affairs with other teachers, if he can handle a tough discipline situation, if he can survive supervisory visits. His unsureness focuses most often on discipline, acceptance as a colleague and friend by others, subject matter content knowledge, and evaluation.

In phases 1 and 2 the teacher's focus is on self. As the questions of "where do I stand?" and "how adequate am I?" become settled, he then begins to look outward and shows a concern for building professional competencies and for participating more effectively in the department's educational program.

Phase 3. This is the "professional-awareness" phase, marked by a shift in emphasis from self-survival and adequacy to the job of teaching. As the shift continues, the teacher is increasingly concerned with such professional problems as improving understanding, student achievement, planning, specifying objectives, the psychology of learning, individualizing instruction and developing and improving educational programs.

The phases resemble in a sense the motivation-hygiene theory discussed in the concepts section of this chapter. Before the beginning teacher is able to focus adequately on the professional problems relating to his work and on professional growth and im-

---

*Frances F. Fuller, "Concerns of Teachers: A Developmental Conceptualization," *American Educational Research Journal*, Vol. 6, No. 2, 1969, p. 207.

provement, he needs to settle the two prior questions of standing and adequacy. Some teachers reach the professional-awareness phase after only a month or two on the job, but others take several years, and unfortunately some never get beyond the first two concerns. Close supervision in the early weeks, directed at helping the teacher to work through the first two phases, greatly accelerates the process.

3. With respect to ensuring early success, new teachers are likely to be affected by their early experiences. If left to sink or swim, they often abandon many of the newly learned ideas, beliefs, and techniques of the trade and resort to those which more effectively ensure their survival and control—often at great costs to the intellectual stimulation and self-realization of students. Early childhood educators have long known the principle that early successes in learning typically establish a pattern of success in students and early failures a pattern of failure. This principle applies as well to teachers at work—early success as a teacher has much to do with determining the kind of teacher one will be and early failures, though later reversible with considerable effort, are similarly potent. Ensuring early success is an important goal of orientation efforts of chairpersons.

Suggested Orientation Practices

1. Send a welcoming letter to the new teacher soon after the appointment. Include in this letter any material you feel will be helpful, such as a description of department courses, an educational platform statement, and department and school policies.
2. As soon as available, send the newcomer an exact schedule of classes, clearly confirming what courses or classes he will teach. Ask the new teacher to begin sketching out plans as to how he intends to tackle the courses. Tell him that late in the summer you will visit with him about his plans and together firm up lesson plans for the first two weeks. Mark your calendar and remember to call him a week or so before school starts.
3. Send the new teacher materials and books normally used in his classes, and a list of other material available in the school.
4. In assigning classes schedule a reduced load for the new teacher (at least one less class but optimally assign only a half-load) and make up the difference by having the teacher intern with an outstanding veteran teacher. This suggestion will unquestionably cost the school money and therefore may well be met with resistance by administrators. But over the long haul, this investment should yield returns which cannot be as economically purchased through future supervision and staff development. In essence, argue that it will prove less costly to prevent poor starts and early mistakes, through a first-year combination of independent teaching and internship experience, than to correct deficiencies in the future.
5. If an internship program is not now possible, keep working on it, but in the meantime provide the beginner with a sponsorship arrangement (buddy system) with an experienced teacher.
6. In making assignments to the new teacher, provide the best possible conditions. Provide the best room, the most complete materials, the best classes, and the best books. Be sure to screen the list of students assigned to his classes to

ensure that he is not accidentally or intentionally loaded with problem students. Being a new teacher is not the time to be treated equally.

7. Set up opportunities for the new teacher in your department to meet with other new teachers. Such a meeting could quickly evolve into a mutual support group where new teachers can discuss problems, share ideas, and help each other.

8. Start from the very beginning to become a natural part of the new teacher's work day. Become a common, concerned, and helpful supervisory fixture to the teacher. The new teacher should come quickly to realize that in your department, supervision is not something special done formally by appointment but part of the everyday life of the department.

9. Introduce the new teacher to each of the teacher organization building representatives. They will want to do some orienting of their own.

FACILITATING CHANGE

✿ CONCEPTS ✿

Some tend to shy away from talking directly about change, change roles and change strategies in schools. To many, change implies manipulation and chairpersons are reluctant to be cast in this light. Further, discussion of change roles and strategies is seen as threatening to many teachers, and chairpersons wish to avoid evoking anxiety and resistance.

This tendency to avoid discussing change has resulted in the popularization of a number of soft code words for change. Self-renewal programs, organizational development, professional growth plans and staff development activities are examples of such code words. Teachers are not engaged in change programs directly but in workshops at teacher centers, in educational program evaluation, and in target-setting programs. These are all examples of important developments but it is important to recognize each of them for what they are—planned change efforts. Each requires that the chairperson know and understand the process of change and be able to function as a direct change agent or as a change facilitator.

 The chairperson assumes the direct change agent role when he works directly to bring about changes. *Change is his goal and his task.* This role is more effective in some situations than in others.

The chairperson assumes the change facilitator role when he helps others to bring about change. *Change is his goal but not his task.* The facilitator is concerned with developing an environment supportive of change and with helping teachers become agents of change. This role is more effective in some situations than in others.

Change effectiveness is increased as one's ability to match roles with situations increases.

Though we speak of the direct change agent role and the change facilitator role as being separate and discrete, in practice they appear together in an assortment of combinations. Our reference, therefore, is to a tendency toward one role or another rather than to roles in absolute or pure form.

THE DIRECT CHANGE AGENT ROLE

A guide to deciding when a chairperson should tend more toward the direct change agent role or more toward the change facilitator role is the level of acceptance required from teachers in order for proposed changes to occur successfully. Reddin's change-acceptance scale can be helpful in determining this level.[1] He suggests that the acceptance of change can be seen as moving along a scale from 0 to 8, from sabotage to commitment.

0   sabotage
1   slowdowns
2   protests
3   apathy
4   indifference
5   acceptance
6   support
7   cooperation
8   commitment

Changes which need teacher acceptance at levels 6, 7, and 8 require that the chairperson tend toward the facilitator role. His emphasis is on helping teachers become the agents of change and on building an environment which nurtures change.

Not all changes require teacher acceptance at levels 6, 7, and 8. Indeed many changes can happen successfully with teacher indifference or apathy, even with mild grumbling or protest. Under these conditions the direct change agent role is probably preferred and certainly efficient.

The sabotage and slowdown levels of acceptance cause special problems for chairpersons. If one anticipates these levels of acceptance, he should consider shifting away from the direct change role toward the facilitator role or abandoning or postponing the proposed change.

The closer the chairperson moves toward behaving as a direct change agent, the lower the level of acceptance he can expect from teachers.

The closer the chairperson moves toward behaving as a change facilitator, the higher the level of acceptance he can expect from teachers.

If the minimum level of acceptance for successful implementation of the proposed change is 2, 3, 4, or 5, then the chairperson should assume more of a direct change agent role.

If the minimum level of acceptance for successful implementation of the proposed change is 6, 7, or 8, then the chairperson should assume more of a change facilitator role.

Chairpersons are more familiar with how the direct change agent role works than the facilitator role. Chapter 5 describes some aspects of this role in its discussion of the dedicated leadership style. First, the role requires that chairpersons have sufficient formal and/or functional *authority* to act. Next, the chairperson needs to plan thoroughly *what* is to be changed, and *why* it will be changed. Third, a change *strategy* needs to be developed which includes an estimate of the level of acceptance expected from teachers and an analysis of forces for and against change. This step is discussed in detail later in this chapter. Finally, a conscientious *communication* program needs to accompany every aspect of the change process, from inception to implementation. Unknowns build anxieties and contribute to misunderstandings and rumors. When the proposed change involves new learnings for teachers or new ways of operating, a *support* system needs to be made available to them. Authority, planning, strategy building, communicating, and providing support—these are key activities associated with successful implementation of the direct change agent role.

The focus in the remainder of this chapter will be on the less familiar, but more important change facilitator role for chairperson. This is the "long way" to bring about change in schools, an approach very expensive in time, money, and human talent and energy. But implementation of change based on internal commitment is the expected outcome and often (but not always) is worth the price. Using the long way when it is not necessary is a waste of human and material resources and may irritate teachers. Some changes are simply not worth the involvement; other changes are of little concern, and still others require specialized or technical knowledge for meaningful involvement.

As an example, teachers are generally disinterested in many of the routine and managerial aspects of running the department and school. Often the solutions to such problems are routine, the problems are of little interest to teachers, or active participation requires special knowledge or skills which teachers do not have or want. Further, these changes can be made without internal commitment of teachers.

WORKING AS A CHANGE FACILITATOR

Like it or not, chairpersons will find that most situations they face force them to operate more as a change facilitator than as a direct agent of change. For many changes mere teacher acceptance—even cooperation—will not guarantee success.

Sizer describes schools as being labor intensive. Schools are primarily holding companies for people, and not so much structures in and of themselves. The typical school budget allocates 80 percent to human resources—teachers. Change in education usually means change in teachers. Buildings, schedules, materials, curriculum formats, and other changes should not be ignored but need to be considered with relationship to change in teachers. In Sizer's words, "Any theory of school reform must start with teachers: they control the system. Subtle matters—their self-esteem, pride, loyalty, commitment—are crucial."[2]

In the final analysis, what matters is what the teacher decides to do day by day with students in the classroom, and this daily encounter needs to be the focus of change.

If change efforts fail to reach this daily encounter, they can be described as *structural changes* but not *internalized changes*.[3]

The high school has wide experience with structural change. Team teaching, modular scheduling, differentiated staffing, packaged teaching materials and open campus plans are examples of structural changes. Such changes often seem widespread to the casual observer. But, for those who experience the high school carefully it seems that though structural arrangements of the classroom and school may have changed dramatically, teachers and administrators have not. They may still see students the same way; they may still be working under the same assumptions; and for all intensive purposes their behavior and their effect on students may vary little from previous modes. Schools have been fairly successful in implementing structural changes in high schools but not internalized changes and as a consequence, little has been gained in the process. Internalized changes, on the other hand, have the capacity to reach the school where it counts—in what teachers believe and how they behave.

This discussion of the change facilitator role is based on the work of Chris Argyris and his development of a theory of intervention.[4] Argyris identifies three basic requirements for successful intervention activity; these requirements become the primary task of the change facilitator. In his words[5]:

> *One condition which seems so basic as to be defined axiomatic is the generation of* valid information. *Without valid information it would be difficult for the client to learn and for the interventionist to help.*
>
> *A second condition almost as basic flows from our assumption that intervention activity, no matter what its substantive interest and objectives, should be so designed and executed that the client system maintains its discreteness and autonomy. Thus* free, *informed choice is also a necessary process in effective intervention activity.*
>
> *Finally, if the client system is assumed to be ongoing (that is, existing over time), the clients require strengthening to maintain their autonomy not only vis-à-vis the interventionist but also vis-à-vis other systems. This means that their commitment to learning and change has to be more than temporary. It has to be so strong that it can be transferred to relationships other than those with the interventionist and can do so (eventually) without the help of the interventionist. The third basic process for an intervention activity is therefore the client's internal commitment to the choices made.*
>
> *In summary, valid information, free choice, and internal commitment are considered integral parts of any intervention activity, no matter what the substantive objectives are (for example, developing a management performance evaluation scheme, reducing intergroup rivalries, increasing the degree of trust among individuals, redesigning budgetary systems, or redesigning work). These three processes are called the primary intervention tasks.*

The role of an outsider who intervenes in an ongoing system in order to facilitate change awareness, and perhaps change itself, is somewhat different from that of chairpersons who are members of the system. Nevertheless, valid information, free and informed choice and internal commitment are key concerns as one works to bring about change. The task is admittedly more difficult in some respects for an insider because he is a known quantity. A history of attitudes and behavior often exists, which could result in teachers and chairpersons holding mutually rigid and often defensive perceptions of each other. Initially generating valid information can be a challenging experience. Another difference between the outside interventionist and the chairperson is that valid information, free and informed choice, and internal commitment need to be viewed as part of the total culture of the school rather than as intervention steps. They are really dynamic dimensions which interact continuously with each other. That is, valid information leads to free and informed choice which increases the validity and quantity of information, both of which result in internal commitment. Internal commitment in turn helps generate valid information and so the cycle continues.

GENERATING VALID AND USEFUL INFORMATION

Valid and useful information is fundamental to understanding and dealing with problems which teachers and schools face. Such information helps to describe the parts of problems, feelings associated with these problems, and how these parts and feelings relate to each other and to other parts of the total classroom, department, or school. Having reasonably accurate and nonevaluative information about what is going on is valid information. Objectives we value and goals and purposes which we have in mind are further examples of valid information. A comparison of this real and ideal information often provides us with a third set of valid information—descriptions of where we are and where we would like to be.

Usually valid and useful information consists of facts, hard data, and other forms of cognitive information. We have been expert at generating such rational information. Such information, however, is not enough, because the major problems facing schools are people problems. Many teachers, for example, seem well aware of the importance of individualizing instruction for students but may resist continuous progress approaches or informal approaches to education because of fear they will lose control of a group of students engaged in learning at different rates or engaged in different activities. Or perhaps they are worried about failing in this new approach, or are concerned about what others in the school would think of the noise level in their classrooms or of the room becoming cluttered and a little messy.

Often the most important valid information which needs to be generated deals with feelings, assumptions, fears, values, defenses and worries which each of us has to some degree. One important block to generating valid information is the tendency for people working in formal organizations to engage in role playing. The major roles are those of teacher, principal, chairperson, and student. The problem with role playing in schools is that one often behaves more like an actor than himself—his behavior becomes inauthentic. A teacher may behave as he feels he needs to behave in order to preserve the teacher's role, rather than in a way which seems most suited for the learning encounter at hand.

Teachers are supposed to know the answer; therefore, we must not place ourselves in positions where students can find out how little we know. Teachers hide behind role faces from other teachers, from chairpersons, and from principals. Chairpersons and principals are often guilty of role playing in their interaction with teachers. The more emphasis a school places on status, position, authority, hierarchy, role rights and prerogatives, rules and regulations, channels and procedures, the more likely human behavior approximates a certain artificiality we describe as role playing. That is, the reason for behavior is the preservation of the role system rather than to help the school respond more humanly and to achieve its educational objectives.

Generating valid information is a long and difficult task. This effort is often facilitated by obtaining outside help from a professional interventionist. In any event, valid information requires a commitment from the chairperson to be open and frank about his opinions and feelings in a way that helps others to be open and frank. This is quite different from being "honest," that is, saying exactly what you think regardless of the situation and of how other people feel. The chairperson will probably need to take the initiative in generating valid information and as small successes begin to accumulate, valid information will become the responsibility of everyone. Valid information can be judged by the extent to which people are giving nonevaluative feedback, are expressing their own feelings and permitting others to express ideas, feelings and values, are showing openness to new ideas, feelings, and values and are experimenting and taking risks with new ideas and values.[6]

Free and Informed Choice

Free choice within the context we describe is not simply the right to choose or not to choose without the benefit of valid information, but free and informed choice. That results from having examined a problem from its cognitive and affective dimensions, then freely choosing a course of action or nonaction.[7]

> *A choice is free to the extent the members can make their selection for a course of action with minimal internal defensiveness; can define the path (or paths) by which the intended consequence is to be achieved; can relate the choice to their central needs; and can build into their choices a realistic and challenging level of aspiration. Free choice therefore implies that the members are able to explore as many alternatives as they consider significant and select those that are central to their needs.*
>
> *Why must the choice be related to the central needs and why must the level of aspiration be realistic and challenging? May people not choose freely unrealistic or unchallenging objectives? Yes, they may do so in the short run, but not for long if they still want to have free and informed choice. A freely chosen course of action means that the action must be based on an accurate analysis of the situation and not on the biases or defenses of the decision-makers. We know, from the level of aspiration studies, that choices which are too high or too low, which are too difficult or not difficult enough will tend to lead to psychological failure. Psychological failure will lead to increased defensiveness, increased failure, and decreased self-acceptance on the part of the members experiencing the failure. These conditions, in turn, will tend to lead to distorted perceptions by the members making the choices. Moreover, the defensive members may unintentionally create a cli-*

mate where the members of surrounding and interrelated systems will tend to provide carefully censored information. Choices made under these conditions are neither informed nor free.

Some teachers may wish to give up responsibility for free and informed choice— the burden of free and informed choice may be too much for them. They may want others to make decisions for them. If forced into choosing freely, they may choose no change or try to please those in authority by accepting the changes being advocated. It is important to remember that accepting a change and internalizing a change are not always the same. When one accepts a change he may be only adopting the manifestations of change; when he internalizes a change, it becomes incorporated into his value system and behavior. Free and informed choice does not come easy for people who have little experience in accepting responsibility. Indeed chairpersons may need to help teachers, and teachers may need to help each other to feel comfortable with exercising free and informed choice.

Obviously, free and informed choice cannot be practiced constantly and in all school decisions. As has been suggested, internal commitment may not be necessary for some changes. Often teachers may not have the appropriate background or interest to meet the informational requirement to make a free and informed choice. Certain school functions which teachers consider strictly administrative such as bus scheduling, maintenance problems, purchasing routines and the like, may be examples.

Internal Commitment

Internal commitment results from free and informed choice and may be the most important contributor to school effectiveness. As part of the discussion in Chapter 2 of action variables, human effects variables, and school success variables, the importance of the school's human organization was described. In a sense, this human organization mediates or absorbs the effects of the school's organizational structure, management system, manifestations of administrative behavior such as leadership styles, distribution of power, status and authority, planning procedures, communication systems and decision-making philosophy. It was observed that these school management inputs did not have a very strong direct effect on the extent to which a school was successful.[8] Rather it is the effect of these variables on teachers and students which seems to be the essential link to school effectiveness. Internal commitment is basic to this link.[9]

Internal commitment means the course of action or choice that has been internalized by each member so that he experiences a high degree of ownership and has a feeling of responsibility about the choice and its implications. Internal commitment means that the individual has reached the point where he is acting on the choice because it fulfills his own needs and sense of responsibility, as well as those of the system.

The individual who is internally committed is acting primarily under the influence of his own forces and not induced forces. The individual (or any unity) feels a minimal degree of dependence upon others for the action. It implies that he has obtained and processed valid information and that he has made an informed and free choice. Under these conditions there is a high probability that the individual's commitment will remain strong over time (even with reduction of external rewards) or under stress, or when the course of action is challenged by others. It also implies that the individual is continually open to reexamination of his position because he believes in taking action based upon valid information.

BUILDING A CHANGE STRATEGY

In this section we describe a practical approach to: 1) estimating the expected level of teacher acceptance of a proposed change; 2) analyzing the driving and restraining forces which act upon the proposed change; and 3) using the estimates and analysis in building a change strategy.

The change strategy model we present can apply both to the direct change role and the facilitator change role. In the first instance the proposed change is likely to be more solution-oriented, the chairperson is likely to have more authority, and the minimum level of acceptance needed from teachers is likely to be relatively low. In the second instance the proposed change is likely to be more problem-oriented with solutions to come from teachers, the chairperson has less authority, and the minimum level of acceptance needed is relatively high.

Resistance to Change

Let's begin with some assumptions about resistance to change:

 Teachers usually do not resist changes in teaching method, school organization, educational technology and curriculum development, and implementation as such. What they resist are changes in the human relationships which usually accompany these more structural and technical changes.

Change strategies which rely primarily or exclusively on rationality may be effective in bringing about technical and structural changes but only rarely result in committed behavioral changes in people.

Change strategies which rely primarily or exclusively on power and "authority" bases (administrative ruling or decision and political manipulation) may also be effective in bringing about technical and structural changes but only rarely result in committed behavioral changes in people.

Committed behavioral change in people is a necessary ingredient for successful and sustained implementation of an educational change.[10]

When teachers resist change, confusion often exists over what they mean when they say they are resisting. Change problems are not primarily related to rationality but to people's feelings. Rationality refers to the extent to which a change is well-conceived educationally and implemented according to a logical plan. Change strategies which rely exclusively on rationality are typically not successful. Lionberger suggests the steps toward structural and technical change are developing: *awareness* to a new idea, product, or practice; *interest* by seeking information about the idea to determine its usefulness; *evaluation* by weighing and sifting information and evidence in the light of existing school conditions; *trial* whereby ideas are tried out and evaluated; and *adoption* or incorporating the practice into the operation of the school.[11] Structural and technical changes, however, are only part of the problem; successful implementation relies on social change—change in human relationships which typically accompany technical change.

The problem is not one of choosing between rational authority or human bases for change, but one of developing a planning strategy which includes each. Obviously, changes need to make educational sense by increasing our effectiveness as we pursue goals; changes need to be legitimized and incorporated into the structure of the school; and changes need to be accepted by those who will be responsible for sustained implementation.

One's first reaction to a proposed change is, "How will this affect me?" For example, the prospect of family team teaching or a new pattern of organization such as nongraded, school within a school or middle school, raises a teacher's questions, not for the educational efficacy of the idea but:

"How will my relationship with the students change?"
"How will my view of myself change?"
"How will my authority and influence change?"
"How will the amount of work I do change?"
"How will my relationship with teachers, parents, and administration change?"
"Will I be more or less successful as a teacher?"
"Who will be the team leader or master teacher?"

All of these concerns are legitimate and deserve answering. Unless the first set of concerns, the human concerns, are adequately resolved, answers to these educational questions or job concerns will only raise new questions and skepticism about the proposed change. Healthy people naturally are concerned with how changes will affect them, their work, and relations with others, and one is hampered in evaluating the educational worth of a change when troubled with these human concerns.

W. J. Reddin has conveniently grouped ways in which people are affected by change at work. These appear as questions which compose a change-reaction checklist as shown in Table 7–1.

The Reddin list needs to be modified or extended given specific situations; it is only representative of concerns teachers might express. Each item on the list could represent a reason why teachers might be attracted to a change (driving force) or why teachers might resist change (restraining force).

In building a change strategy chairpersons can use this or a similar list to predict reactions from teachers to a proposed change. Further by cataloging and charting which

TABLE 7-1. REDDIN'S CHANGE-REACTION CHECKLIST

Self	(S–1)	How will my advancement possibilities change?
	(S–2)	How will my salary change?
	(S–3)	How will my future with this company change?
	(S–4)	How will my view of myself change?
	(S–5)	How will my formal authority change?
	(S–6)	How will my informal influence change?
	(S–7)	How will my view of my prior values change?
	(S–8)	How will my ability to predict the future change?
	(S–9)	How will my status change?
Work	(W–1)	How will the amount of work I do change?
	(W–2)	How will my interest in the work change?
	(W–3)	How will the importance of my work change?
	(W–4)	How will the challenge of the work change?
	(W–5)	How will the work pressures change?
	(W–6)	How will the skill demands on me change?
	(W–7)	How will my physical surroundings change?
	(W–8)	How will my hours of work change?
Others	(O–1)	How will my relationships with my coworkers change?
	(O–2)	How will my relationships with my superiors change?
	(O–3)	How will my relationships with my subordinates change?
	(O–4)	How will what my family thinks of me change?

From W. J. Reddin, *Managerial Effectiveness* (New York: McGraw-Hill Company, 1970), p. 163.

of the items represent driving forces and which represent restraining forces a change-reaction diagram based on force field analysis can be constructed. (An example of how to build and use a change-reaction diagram is presented in the practices section of this chapter.) Force field analysis is a method advocated by the distinguished psychologist Kurt Lewin as a means to understanding and planning for change.[12] It assumes that change takes place when an imbalance occurs between the sum of driving forces and the sum of restraining forces. This imbalance unfreezes the present pattern or equilibrium which exists in the situation. When driving forces become strong enough to overcome restraining forces, change takes place. When restraining forces are sufficiently reduced or weakened, change takes place.

The View from Practice

Warren Bennis, a social scientist with a long interest in organizational change, in 1967 accepted a key administrative post at the State University of New York at Buffalo. Bennis was to play an important role in Buffalo's planned transformation from a sleepy university to a progressive Berkeley of the East. Bennis' attempts to effect dramatic changes at Buffalo are described in a 1972 *Psychology Today* article.[13] His candid report admits to large-scale failure to pull off the planned transformation. We summarize here his ways to avoid major mistakes in making changes.

218

Recruit with scrupulous honesty

Principals and chairpersons often promise more than they can deliver to new recruits to the faculty. When new faculty members are recruited, particularly for innovative programs, a tendency exists to paint an unrealistic picture of how wonderful everything will be. This may be tough to deliver and can result in resentment and disappointment.

 Guard against the crazies

Take great care to distinguish between those teachers who are interested in innovation as a means to better deliver educational services to students, and those who are attracted to anything different only because it is different, or who are against anything already established simply because it is established.

 Build support among like-minded people, whether or not you recruited them.

Innovation often is accompanied by a tendency to divide faculties into insiders and the outsiders. The insiders participate in developing or become part of the change and the outsiders are left out. Often leaders feel compelled to bring in their own people as a way to ensure proper identity with the change; consequently, they tend to ignore those already on the job. Further, a tendency exists to rely on newer and younger teachers with some writing off of the old ones. Adding new blood can help, but successful changes are likely to be more dependent upon recirculating the old blood.

 Plan for change from a solid conceptual base—have a clear-cut understanding of how to change as well as what to change.

Knowing what you want to accomplish and why you want to accomplish it is not enough. Goals are not the same as programs. You need a clear notion of what the change will look like in practice and a plan for bringing about change.

 Don't settle for rhetorical change.

A plan sketched out on paper, even a plan which results in altering structures and arrangements, is not enough. Change takes place in the minds and hearts of people and is manifested in changes in their behavior.

Don't allow those who are opposed to change to appropriate such basic issues as academic standards.

The public and often teachers readily discredit change efforts viewed as being too permissive or as falling down on academic standards. While open-oriented educational arrangements may be designed to help youngsters learn to make choices for which they are accountable and to assume more responsibility for their education, they can be seen as "letting kids do what they want." Individualized programs are attempts to raise academic standards but since not everyone does the same thing they can be seen as standards-dropping changes. If proponents of these changes first used arguments of teaching self-discipline and responsibility and of raising academic standards, the opponents would have been deprived of very powerful weapons. Symbols and images are crucial and change arguments need to identify and capture those important to teachers and community. The antiwar movement of the sixties lost much when advocates abused the American flag while the "hard hats" gained much by using the flag as a symbol for their position.

 ### Know the territory

Understand the culture of the school and community, and the culture's language system and symbols in bringing about change. A solid communication program which articulates the changes in the language of the people (not the language of professional education) should be part of the change strategy.

 ### Appreciate environmental factors

Overcrowding, inadequate or poorly-designed facilities can take their toll on proposed changes. Individualized programs, learning centers, team teaching, mini-schools, independent study, open space are not solely dependent upon environmental factors but they can make a difference.

 ### Allow time to consolidate gains

A common failing of change programs is the tendency to move so fast that the necessary girdings of change are not sufficiently developed. A successful school is one which adapts to external stimuli: it changes, but it also maintains itself internally; it consolidates and incorporates its changes. Imagine building a dock out in a lake. If you extend the dock out too far without the necessary support posts, it will collapse.

 ### Remember that change is most successful when those who are affected are involved in the planning.

This point has been argued in this book several times. Bennis notes, "This is a platitude of planning theory, and it is as true as it is trite. Nothing makes persons as resistant to new ideas or approaches as the feeling that change is being imposed upon them." He continues, "People resist change, even of a kind they basically agree with, if they are not significantly involved in the planning. A clumsier, slower, but more egalitarian approach to changing . . . would have resulted in more permanent reform."

CHANGE ETHICS

Chairpersons often feel uncomfortable when asked to assume the direct change agent role or the change facilitator role. Further, discussion of change and tips on overcoming resistance to change and on building change strategies imply, for many, manipulation. Educational change does raise important value questions. We believe that the change role for chairpersons is inescapable. Sometimes change behavior is questionable, but certain ethical principles can be developed to guide change behavior.

James MacDonald, for example, accepts the change role for supervisors provided that they work within the framework of fundamental principles relating to democratic change ethics and to the dignity and worth of those who are the targets of change. He notes:

1. Teaching is a complex integration of behaviors and single behavior chains cannot profitably be grafted onto the teacher's behavioral system.
2. It is morally wrong to set out to change teacher behavior unless the change sought has been rationally selected by the teacher from among a range of known alternatives.
3. Learning is an individual matter and how something is learned is determined primarily by the internal structure of needs, perceptions, readiness, motivations, of the individual—not by the external conditions of an outside person desiring change.[14]

Kenneth Benne proposes a set of norms which can be used to develop acceptable working guidelines for chairpersons to ensure that their change behavior is acceptable.[15]

1. The engineering of change and the meeting of pressures on a group or organization toward change must be collaborative.
2. The engineering of change must be educational for the participants.
3. The engineering of change must be experimental.
4. The engineering of change must be task-oriented, that is, controlled by the requirements of the problem confronted and its effective solution, rather than oriented to the maintenance or extension of the prestige or power of those who originate contributions.

Collaboration suggests that chairpersons and teachers form a change partnership with each being aware of the intentions of the others. Change intents are honest and straightforward. Teachers, for example, don't have to endure being "buttered up" today for the announced change tomorrow. *Educational* suggests that chairpersons will try to help teachers become more familiar with the process of problem solving and changing so that they are less dependent upon them. Giving a teacher a solution is not as educational as helping a teacher muddle through a problem. *Experimental* implies that changes will not be implemented for keeps but tentatively until they prove their worth or until a better

221

solution comes along. *Task-oriented* refers to the chairperson's primary motive for change. The chairperson has job-related objectives in mind first and his own success and self-interest second. If he fosters change to get attention from superiors, to improve his standing or influence, he violates ethical principles. He may indeed be interested in these benefits and entitled to them but his primary motives are job-oriented.

ENDNOTES

1. W. J. Reddin, *Managerial Effectiveness* (New York: McGraw-Hill, 1970), p. 166.

2. Theodore Sizer, "Educational Reform: Speculations from Retrospection," *Notre Dame Journal of Education,* Vol. 4, No. 1, 1973, p. 52.

3. See for example, Thomas J. Sergiovanni, "Synergistic Evaluation," *Teachers College Record,* Vol. 75, No. 4, 1974, pp. 546–47. Charters and Jones make a similar distinction in W. W. Charters and John E. Jones, "On the Risk of Appraising Non-Events in Program Evaluation," *Educational Researcher* (Washington, D.C.: American Educational Research Association, Nov., 1973), p. 6.

4. Particularly important to this discussion is Chris Argyris, *Intervention Theory and Method: A Behavioral Science View* (Reading, Mass.: Addison-Wesley Publishing Co., 1970). See also his *Integrating the Individual and the Organization* (New York: John Wiley, 1964), and *Organization and Innovation* (Homewood, Ill.: Irwin, 1965). The discussion and application of Argyris' work follow closely portions of a similar discussion which appears in Thomas J. Sergiovanni and David Elliott, *Educational and Organizational Leadership in Elementary Schools* (Englewood Cliffs, N.J.: Prentice-Hall, 1975). Chapter 9.

5. Argyris, *Intervention Theory and Method,* pp. 16–17.

6. *Ibid.,* p. 66.

7. *Ibid.,* pp. 19–20.

8. The importance of the people variables, the human organization, or the school's socio-psychological life are coming to be understood as being even more significant as determiners of success than even their strongest advocates have realized. The now famous Coleman report (The Equal Educational Opportunity Survey), conducted in 1966, showed that conventional school inputs such as bigger and better buildings, smaller class size, graduate credits earned by teachers and more money in the form of per pupil expenditure, merit pay and salary increases were not convincingly related to school output such as student achievement. Recent reanalysis of the Coleman data by Moynihan and his associates suggests that inputs of this kind are linked even less directly to school output. School effectiveness seems less dependent upon resources of this kind and more dependent upon intrinsically motivated and committed teachers.

9. Argyris, *Intervention Theory and Method,* p. 20.

10. See for example Paul R. Lawrence, "How to Deal with Resistance to Change," *Harvard Business Review,* Vol. 52, No. 3, May–June, 1954, pp. 49–57. For a detailed discussion of rational, empirical, legal and authority approaches to change see Robert Chin and Kenneth D. Benne, "General Strategies for Effecting Changes in Human Systems," in Warren G. Bennis, Kenneth D. Benne and Robert Chin (eds.), *The Planning of Change,* 2nd edition (New York: Holt, Rinehart and Winston, 1969), pp. 32–60.

11. Herbert Lionberger, *Adoption of New Ideas and Practices* (Ames: Iowa State University Press, 1960), pp. 3–4.

12. Kurt Lewin, *Field Theory in Social Science* (New York: Harper and Row, Publishers, 1951).

13. Warren Bennis, "The Sociology of Institutions or Who Sank the Yellow Submarine?" *Psychology Today,* Vol. 6, No. 6, 1972, pp. 112–122.

14. James B. MacDonald, "Helping Teachers Change," in James Raths and Robert R. Leeper (eds.), *The Supervisor: Agent for Change in Teaching,* The Association for Supervision and Curriculum Development, Washington, D.C., 1966, p. 3.

15. Kenneth D. Benne, "Democratic Ethics and Social Engineering," *Progressive Education,* Vol. 27, No. 7, 1949, p. 204.

✠ CHAPTER SEVEN ✠

✠ PRACTICES ✠

This section contains a practical approach to planning for change and to building a change strategy. A "Planning for Change Worksheet" is provided to help you apply this approach to your change problems. A case, "Changing the Curriculum at Southside" with discussion, is included to give you an opportunity to analyze a change attempt that failed and to propose alternate change strategies.

This section includes:

Framework and procedure for building a change strategy
Change-reaction diagram
Planning for Change Worksheet
The Go, No-Go Decision
Change-acceptance Scale Decisions
Case Study: "Changing the Curriculum at Southside"
Working to Implement Change from Below

BUILDING A CHANGE STRATEGY

First, you are presented with a framework and set of procedures for building a change strategy. Second, you are given a worksheet for building change strategies.

Assume that the cadre of chairpersons and the principal of a junior high school are exploring alternatives to the present method of organizing the school. One alternative considered is grouping students across grades and grouping teachers across departments into teaching teams to form several minischools within the larger junior high school.

The following steps outline how a change-reaction diagram should be constructed to better understand the driving and restraining forces which are likely to exist if this change is proposed to teachers.

1. Examine each item on Reddin's change-reaction checklist which appears in the concepts section of this chapter (or one developed to fit your circumstances), marking those which are likely to increase acceptance of the change with a (+); those likely to increase resistance to the change with a (−).
2. From this list select the five most important driving forces and the five most important restraining forces. The analysis will be concerned only with these ten major forces.

3. Each of the five driving forces must now be weighted to indicate their relative importance. Take ten points and distribute them among the five forces in a way which reflects their importance. If all are equally important, assign each two points. You might choose a 4, 2, 2, 1, 1, or 3, 2, 3, 2, 0, or any other combination providing that the total number of points assigned is ten.

4. Repeat step three for the five restraining forces.

5. Each of the five driving forces must now be rated in accordance with the chairperson's or school's ability to influence the reaction of teachers. Forces which can be increased in attractiveness to teachers would be given a "high influence" rating. Forces which cannot be increased very much or at all in attractiveness to teachers should be given a "low influence" rating. Rate each of the driving forces as high, medium or low influence.

6. Each restraining force must now be rated similarly. Restraining forces which can easily be reduced or eliminated by the school or chairpersons would be given a "high influence" rating. Restraining forces which cannot be reduced very much and indeed which often must be accepted unchanged are given a "low influence" rating. Rate each of the restraining forces as high, medium, or low influence.

Each of the five driving forces and the five restraining forces should now have two scores: an importance weight and an influence rating. Using the example of forming teaching teams to operate as relatively autonomous minischools within the larger school, let us assume that five key driving forces are identified: S-4, S-5, S-9, W-3, and W-4. Chairpersons see the new arrangements as being attractive to teachers because they will be afforded increased status and prestige, their images as autonomous professionals will increase, their control over future events will increase and they will have greater opportunities to engage in more important and challenging work. The five key restraining forces identified are S-1, S-8, W-1, W-8, and O-1. Some teachers, for example, might be concerned about not being chosen team or unit teacher, thus lessening their chances of moving into administration. Others find the ambiguities about their future roles as team members uncomfortable. Further, a general concern might exist about the difficulty of work that their plan will require. Not knowing how teams will be formulated and who will work with whom is another major restraining force anticipated.

For the purposes of our example, each of the forces is weighted and rated as follows:

		IMPORTANCE WEIGHT	INFLUENCE RATING
Driving Forces			
S-4	How will my view of myself change?	1	Low
S-5	How will my formal authority change?	3	High
S-9	How will my status change?	2	Medium
W-3	How will the importance of my work change?	2	High
W-4	How will the challenge of the work change?	2	High

Restraining Forces

S–1	How will my advancement possibilities change?	2	Low
S–8	How will my ability to predict the future change?	1	Medium
W–1	How will the amount of work I do change?	3	High
W–8	How will my hours of work change?	3	High
O–1	How will my relationship with my coworkers change?	1	Medium

Each force and its respective weight and rating are used to construct a change-reaction diagram which appears below based on force field analysis. Each of the ten arrows on the driving-forces side and on the restraining-forces side represents points distributed to reflect relative weights of the forces. Formal authority (S–5) was given an importance weight of three points relative to the other driving forces and therefore is represented by three arrows. Two arrows for less advancement (S–1) on the restraining side show its assigned weight of two points.

CHANGE–REACTION DIAGRAM

DRIVING FORCES

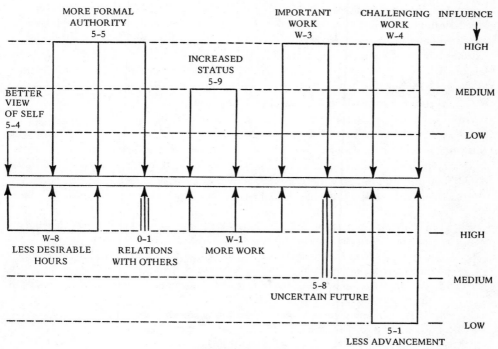

FIGURE 7-1. CHANGE-REACTION DIAGRAM

227

The amount of influence which chairpersons estimate they have over expanding each of the driving forces or reducing the restraining forces is represented by the height of the arrows. Formal authority (S–5) is not only an important driving force accounting for three of ten arrows but because the chairperson can readily expand the attractiveness of this force, it is rated high in influence. Its influence power is represented by the length of the arrow. The more important and powerful forces exert more pressure down on the restraining forces. The scale is reversed for restraining forces with those more readily influenced represented by shorter lines. They exert less pressure upward to hold back the driving forces.

The change-reaction diagram is a tool to be used by chairpersons in systematically analyzing driving and restraining forces. The diagram can also be used in 1) predicting the probable level of acceptance of teachers; 2) in determining whether a "go" or "no go" decision should be made; and 3) in planning specific strategies of change which enhance the driving forces and decrease the restraining forces.

In this change example, the change-reaction diagram shows that the driving forces overwhelmingly outweigh the restraining forces. The level of acceptance from teachers is estimated to be in the 6, 7, or 8 range with cooperation and commitment likely. Refer to the concepts section of this chapter for a discussion and display of change acceptance levels. The change strategy would probably include an emphasis on showing teachers that less desirable work (W–8) and more work (W–1) are over-estimated or, in comparison to expected benefits, worth the price to pay. Not much emphasis will be given to the less-advancement (S–1) question since the influence level is perceived to be low. More challenging work (W–4), more important work (W–3) and more formal authority (S–5) are likely to be the benefits highlighted as the change process proceeds.

If the change-reaction diagram shows a pattern opposite to that which we illustrate (that is, if restraining forces heavily outweigh driving forces), then we are faced with two alternatives: 1) abandoning the change or postponing moving forward at this time; or 2) forcing the changes by using legal or coercive authority as driving forces. In this case, the level of acceptance from teachers is likely to be relatively low and indeed could be manifested in apathy, protest, slowdown or even sabotage.

Keep in mind the following guidelines:

1. Change takes place when an imbalance occurs between the sum of driving forces and the sum of restraining forces with the driving forces favored.
2. Strategies for change include increasing the driving forces and/or decreasing the restraining forces in order to create this imbalance.
3. An overwhelming imbalance in favor of the driving forces is likely to result in high acceptance of change from teachers.
4. If an imbalance in favor of the restraining forces exists, change can be forced by adding to the driving forces, formal or coercive authority. In this case acceptance from teachers is likely to be low and on occasion could result in protest, slowdown, and sabotage.

PLANNING FOR CHANGE WORKSHEET

NAME OF INDIVIDUAL OR GROUP_____ DATE _____

A. State briefly the proposed change. Be as specific as you can recognizing the actual proposal or solution might be different than your present thinking as staff is involved.

B. Indicate what problems are to be solved or what objectives are to be met by this proposed change. Steps A and B, problems and tentative solutions comprise the educational side of planning for change.

C. Now focus on the human side of planning for change. What are likely to be the benefits to teachers who will be involved in and affected by the change? How might the proposed change positively affect the teachers, their work, and their relationships with others? Refer to Reddin's change-reaction checklist in the concepts section of this chapter for ideas. These are the driving forces. List the five main potential benefits below:

DRIVING FORCES	IMPORTANCE RATING	INFLUENCE RATING
1.		
2.		
3.		
4.		
5.		

D. What are likely to be considered by teachers as drawbacks or disadvantages? These are the restraining forces. List the five main potential drawbacks below:

RESTRAINING FORCES	IMPORTANCE RATING	INFLUENCE RATING
1.		
2.		
3.		
4.		
5.		

E. Next to each driving force listed above, place a number from one to ten that indicates the estimated importance of the force to teachers. Repeat the procedure for the five restraining forces. In each case the sum of ratings cannot exceed ten.

F. Next to each driving force and restraining force listed above, indicate the amount of influence you have in increasing or decreasing its effect on teachers. Rate each force low, medium, or high.

229

G. Use the outline below to construct your change-reaction diagram.

DRIVING FORCES

INFLUENCE

↓

- — — HIGH

- — — MEDIUM

- — — LOW

↓ ↓ ↓ ↓ ↓ ↓ ↓ ↓ ↓ ↓

↑ ↑ ↑ ↑ ↑ ↑ ↑ ↑ ↑ ↑

- — HIGH

- — MEDIUM

- — LOW

RESTRAINING FORCES

THE GO, NO-GO DECISION

How overpowering must the driving forces be to suggest that change efforts are likely to be successful? The word successful makes this a hard question to answer. Change takes place when an imbalance exists in favor of the driving forces. Whether this change will be effective or not depends upon two factors.

1. Strength of the driving forces in comparison with restraining forces.
2. Level of acceptance required from teachers for successful implementation.

Early in this chapter the change-acceptance scale was presented and discussed. Use the scale in making the decisions below:

REDDIN'S CHANGE-ACCEPTANCE SCALE

0 sabotage
1 slowdown
2 protest
3 apathy
4 indifference
5 acceptance
6 support
7 cooperation
8 commitment

1. Estimate the level of acceptance needed from teachers in order for the change to be implemented successfully.
   Estimated acceptance level needed is_____.
2. Review your change-reaction diagram. Considering the needed acceptance level, is the imbalance in favor of the driving forces sufficient? Remember the higher the required acceptance level, the greater must be the imbalance.
3. Decide whether this is a go or no-go decision. Go_____ No_____

If you decide to proceed with the change, use the driving and restraining forces identified in your analysis to help determine your change strategy. Your analysis should suggest what forces are of sufficient importance to be considered and which forces can realistically be influenced.

CHANGING THE CURRICULUM AT SOUTHSIDE

Suggestions for analyzing and using cases are provided in the practices section of Chapter 5. Several short cases are presented in that chapter as illustrations of persistent problems facing chairpersons. Here a longer case is provided for your analysis. Cases may be studied from a variety of perspectives. In the following case, for example, one can learn much from analyzing the school's informal organization and the principal's relationship to this organization. The analysis could also focus on school structure and organization or perhaps on communication channels, or the use of power and influence. It is useful to decide beforehand on the basis of one's analysis. Case analysis is complex and this procedure simplifies the task.

Use this case to analyze the change process from inception to planning, structuring and implementing. Notice not only the principal's actions but also where department chairpersons do and could fit in to this process. Further, use the materials and ideas associated with Reddin's 3–D Theory of Leadership presented in Chapter 5 to analyze the leadership style and strategy of the principal.

The Case*

The story relates the struggle of a determined principal to produce curriculum change in his school. The flow of information and ideas and the use of communication channels are depicted in this process. The swirl of inharmonious values, representing the new and the old, stability and change, are shown. The powerful effect of informal organization upon change is also delineated. Since the desired curriculum change was not successfully consummated, a question is raised of why it was a failure. To answer this question, one is led to a careful assessment of Bell's philosophy and leadership techniques. Such an assessment should lead one to an involvement with issues which are common to many administrative situations.

Ted Bell was just beginning his seventh year as principal of the Southside School. Large in physical stature, Bell was a middle-aged man who had devoted most of his life to education. His experience had been at various levels in large and small districts and in urban and rural areas. Before he became principal at Southside, he had been an assistant superintendent in a large city school. Active in many organizations, both state and local, Bell was regarded by many colleagues as an outstanding educational leader. A professor of curriculum in a neighboring university described him as "one of the best-informed high school principals on curriculum in the metropolitan area."

Southside High School, which Bell headed, was more than 35 years old and housed approximately 2500 students in grades 10, 11, and 12. It was one of five large high schools in a western city of more than 300,000 people. Located in one of the more "respectable" areas of the city, it drew most of its students from the middle socioeconomic class. For many years its patrons were almost entirely middle-class. With a recent influx in population, however, a substantial number of students of lower socioeconomic origin had entered the school. Although they constituted less than a third of the total enrollment, their influx had created various problems for the administrators and teachers at Southside.

Southside's curriculum was strongly influenced by upper middle-class values, a situation which resulted in considerable emphasis on academic achievement. Each year

---

*This case is abridged from Jack Culbertson, Paul Jacobson, and Theodore Reller, *Administrative Relationships: A Casebook* (Englewood Cliffs, N.J.: Prentice-Hall, Inc., © 1960), pp. 346–366. Reprinted by permission of Prentice-Hall, Inc.

school officials consistently announced that a relatively large proportion of the graduating students had received scholarships to numerous universities throughout the country, including some of the oldest, finest, and best established.

More recently, under Bell's leadership, the school was seeking a more diversified curriculum. Efforts had been made to provide various kinds of curriculum offerings for students of varying levels of ability. Shortly after Bell came to Southside, he made changes in the counseling system, including the adoption of a homeroom organization. When the issue was first raised, teachers were very much opposed to this change and voted it down. Several months later, after further discussions, an affirmative vote resulted. Even after the vote, many of the teachers did not believe that the idea was practicable or desirable, and they continued to complain. Five years later, however, it was generally accepted that the homeroom organization for counseling was a marked improvement in Southside's educational system.

The preceding year, one of the teachers had suggested to Principal Bell the idea of forming a special class for gifted students. Bell saw in this another way of diversifying the curriculum and gave his full support to the teacher. Therefore, the teacher had initiated and conducted a class for 30 students who, in the opinion of their counselors, were highly gifted. The content of the course was classical literature and philosophy.

In considering other curriculum alternatives, Principal Bell had recently made a decision to try to initiate a schedule that would allow teachers to have one of their classes for a full half-day each Tuesday afternoon. One purpose of such a schedule was to allow field trips to supplement the more abstract textbook learnings.

He saw in such half-day excursions advantages for educating the students who were not as capable as others. In his own words, he believed "that the traditional academic curriculum could not meet the needs of students with the low levels of ability." He strongly believed that a high school should develop a program that would allow all students to develop their potentialities.

In addition, he believed that a better relationship between teachers and students could be obtained through the plan. By spending an entire half-day with students, he believed the teachers could gain a better understanding of the strengths and needs of students. He was keenly aware of the large size of the Southside High School and was concerned that the teacher-student relationships might be overly impersonal. Bell's decision was also influenced by the successful experience which two other eastern schools had reported.

In Principal Bell's desire to put the half-day schedule into effect, a question that confronted him early was how to initiate the change. With approximately 100 teachers to reach, Bell was sharply aware of communication problems. He knew that the formal and informal systems of interaction would be important elements in instituting the change.

Southside's Formal Organization

Southside High School had a line-and-staff organization. Directly responsible to the principal were two vice-principals. Bell was responsible to an assistant superintendent in charge of curriculum, and the latter reported to the superintendent of schools. When

Bell came to Southside, department heads were largely responsible for the supervision and evaluation of teachers. Shortly after Bell's arrival he assumed the responsibility for evaluating and supervising teachers. Department-head duties then were to pass on information from the administration to teachers, to take care of texts, to be in charge of tests, to have department meetings, and to give information to counselors. When this shift was made, Bell also suggested that department heads might rotate annually and be elected by teachers. This proved to be an unpopular idea and nothing came of it.

When Bell first came, a large proportion of the teachers were middle-aged or older. According to some of the teachers, Bell had in recent years sought to bring in younger teachers with liberal points of view who spoke their mind on educational issues. It was also reported that a part of the difficulty which Bell had incurred in instituting changes in the past was due to the fact that many of the teachers were older and more conservative in outlook.

At Southside High School there were various channels of communication which could be utilized in introducing educational change. The faculty meeting, which convened once monthly, was one means of administrator-teacher communication. Another means involved department heads, the principal, and two vice-principals and was called the *instructional council.* Meeting once weekly, this group discussed procedures and policies pertinent to curriculum.

Still another communication system which most teachers considered important was the suggestion committee. This committee was composed of the principal, two vice-principals, and three elected representatives of the teachers. The representatives were chosen each semester from among the teachers who had free second periods, since this was the time at which weekly meetings were scheduled. All teachers were encouraged to report suggestions, complaints, or questions orally to members of the committee, or to write their ideas anonymously and place them in the boxes of the teacher-representatives. It was generally understood that no names would be mentioned in the meetings of the suggestion committee.

Department meetings were held once every six weeks. At these meetings curriculum matters directly pertinent to departments were discussed and clerical and procedural matters were also handled. Central-office supervisors were available for the various departments in the high school. However, they visited the school infrequently, and most curriculum changes were brought about through committees representing the various city high schools. The assistant superintendent in charge of curriculum, as well as the central-office staff, encouraged local initiative in the different junior and senior high schools.

Southside's Informal Organization

Southside also had its informal communication systems. About 60 per cent of the teachers belonged to clearly defined informal groups whose operations could be easily observed. For various reasons the remaining 40 per cent of the teachers were not attached to any of these defined groups. Several reasons for this were suggested by different representatives of the informal groups.

First, a number of teachers had outside interests, such as family relationships, and they were not interested in developing attachments at school. These persons were interested in coming to school, doing their work, and leaving as soon as possible. Other persons had not become closely attached because they had not been in the school long enough. Often a person taught for as much as a year before he joined a group or before a group accepted him. A third reason why teachers did not establish informal relationships was an innate shyness on their part. As one teacher said, "Some teachers may come to the cafeteria, but they are too timid to associate or form close relations with other teachers." Still another reason was suggested by one teacher, who said, "We cannot get along with some of these teachers, and frankly I don't see how the students can get along with them either." Finally, some teachers did not attach themselves to particular informal groupings even though they were well known and no doubt would have been accepted by different groups. Some of the outstanding leaders in the school would fall into this category, including both teachers and department heads. They interacted informally with a large number of people in the school but were not clearly attached to any one informal group.

There were five informal groups that were clearly defined at the Southside School. They could be labeled as follows: the small, opposing group, the large social group, the men's group, the cafeteria group, and the women's group.

The small opposing group was composed of older persons, and the chief cohesive element which held them together appeared to be their educational philosophy. This philosophy was described in various ways, but the main theme, as one person put it, was that, "Strict academic pursuit is the function of education."

Most members of the school staff viewed the small, opposing group as generally resisting the policies of the administration when the latter wished to effect change. In general, members were very critical of Principal Bell and his manner of school administration. Jim Newton, one of the leaders in the small, opposing group, stated, "The main problem around here is the attitude of Bell. He does not want to listen to what we have to say, and he feels very intense and does not want to take criticism."

Another member of this group called the faculty meeting "a vestigial remain of school administration," and was also critical of the suggestion committee when he stated, "I don't think it is successful so far as the teachers are concerned. The real purpose, I believe, is to give the principal a chance to get his ideas across to us, rather than for us to get our ideas across to him."

Also important in the interpersonal dynamics of the school was the large social group made up of approximately forty teachers. The binding element in this group appeared to be social fellowship, since persons of different ages and somewhat different outlooks were associated with one another. As more than one person stated, "We enjoy being together." Periodically, the members had parties outside of school hours, but they apparently were not all able to meet together at the school. Parts of the group did meet at lunch periods and at free periods during the day. They were generally much more liberal in their outlook than the small, opposing group and were also more friendly toward Principal Bell. There were many persons in this group who supported Principal Bell ardently and spoke words of high praise for him. The following description is typical of how a number of persons in the large social group viewed Principal Bell: "Bell is the greatest of

235

the great. He is a regular fellow who does not throw his weight around. I have worked under several principals and most of them are pretentious and act as if authority gives them special privileges, but you can talk to Bell and tell him a good story the same as you can to anybody. Bell is not a vindictive person, and he is tolerant of other points of view. He operates in a democratic way."

Teachers were more conscious of the large social group and the small, opposing group than they were of other informal bodies in the school. It was also well known that there was considerable organizational rivalry between these two groups. One person in the large social group stated, "We have two groups that are important here. One group we call the senior conservatives, and the other is the liberal element in the school. The senior conservatives say what they want to do, but we defend what we believe is right, too. So the two groups often disagree and oppose one another on school issues."

The third group, the cafeteria group, was composed of eight of the younger teachers in the school. Most of them did not have tenure, as they had been at the school only a year or two. They held common perceptions, among which the following was expressed: "I find Bell very hard to approach and to talk to. I always feel that he leaves me in my place and rapport is not established."

Other persons in the organization had ways of explaining this lack of rapport. For example, a teacher of long tenure stated, "Mr. Bell is basically a shy man. If he meets a person in the hall, he may not give a warm greeting, or on other occasions he may be wrapped up in educational ideas or plans and not notice a person who is passing by. Some people interpret this differently from others. Those who would not ordinarily feel free to visit the office interpret this to mean that Principal Bell would not welcome them."

The men's group was a small aggregation that had lunch daily with one another in the men teachers' room. According to one of the members, the group did not see itself as taking part in developing or opposing policy, except that policies and procedures were often discussed during lunch time and opinions were formed through this process.

The women's group closely followed the lines of the physical education department, but included one other person. This assemblage also met periodically outside school hours away from the school environment. Generally its members were more concerned with policy which dealt directly with affairs in their own department, and they were not seriously concerned with policies affecting the entire school.

Initiating the Half-Day Schedule: The First Attempt

In introducing the proposed half-day schedule, Principal Bell had to decide where to initiate the idea. After discussing the matter with his vice-principals, a decision was made to discuss the half-day schedule with the instructional council.

Since the department heads would have some responsibility for carrying out the program, this move seemed desirable to Bell; also, he always found the council a good place to test ideas. With a few exceptions, Principal Bell saw his department-head members as effective leaders. Two of the department heads he saw somewhat differently, since they seldom initiated ideas and, worse, as far as he was concerned, frequently did not comply with ideas that were suggested to them. Generally speaking, the department heads were very loyal to Principal Bell and had closer relationships in general than did the other teachers. One department head, for example, stated: "Bell is quite different from his predecessor. His predecessor would close the door when he was busy and did not want to be bothered, but Bell always asks people in if they come outside his office. He met considerable opposition when he first came to the school seven years ago, but he does not give up easily and continues to try to get his ideas into practice. He is not only a good administrator, but he is also an educator."

Another department head made the following statement: "When Bell came here, the school was actually being run by the dean of girls because the principal in charge at that time was afraid to make decisions. There were also strong cliques in the school, and they were extremely unfriendly to one another. That was not good, and I believe one reason why the situation came about was that we did not have a strong principal. Everybody has his say here now, but you know who is running the school, for Bell is very decisive. I am sure there are people here whose ideas Bell especially respects, but they do not run the school. I believe he judges ideas on whether they are important, whether they can be used for the good of the majority, and whether most of the people want them."

Principal Bell chose one of the regular weekly meetings of the instructional council to present his idea. He explained how the half-day schedule might work. Each Tuesday afternoon would be set aside for the schedule. On the first Tuesday, the regularly scheduled nine o'clock class would have the half-day period. The next week, the ten o'clock class would be scheduled; the following week, the eleven o'clock class; and so on.

The reasons for adopting the schedule were also set forth. First, it would allow the teachers to take excursions to use community resources as learning experiences. For example, the journalism teacher might wish to take his class to see a print shop or a newspaper press. The half-day schedule would also allow teachers who did not take excursions to spend a half-day with one class. The theory behind this proposal was that teachers would have a better opportunity to become acquainted with their students and, as a consequence, could do a better teaching job.

The instructional council was generally favorable to trying the idea, although they raised several problems that had to do with scheduling, with students who might not wish to go on excursions, and with the extra burden that detailed planning might place upon the teachers. Most of the opposition was voiced against the frequency of the schedule, and it was finally agreed that the half-day schedule should be held once every two weeks instead of once weekly.

Bell's next step was to present the half-day schedule to the teachers. This he chose to do with small groups of teachers. His procedure was to ask all of those teachers who had a free first period to meet in the council room. After talking with these teachers, he met those with second periods free, and so on throughout the day. During these sessions the principal presented the idea of the half-day schedule and told the teachers why he believed it would be good to put this into practice at Southside. There was also an opportunity for raising questions and pointing up problems pertinent to the proposed idea. Bell thought the method which he used was a good technique for communicating with teachers because the groups were small, and questions could be raised. He saw this as one of the most effective ways of changing teacher opinion and gaining support for school policy.

Teachers reacted to this experience in different ways. One of the teachers who was a leader in the large social group described the meeting as follows: "I felt the discussions were very superior because all of the teachers could be involved. The group was small enough so all the members could participate, and the atmosphere was conducive to persons' giving their opinions. Of course, there was the problem of the senior conservatives being a part of the group. As it happened, our group was made up mostly of senior conservatives, so we had a hard time getting going."

Olden, one of the leaders of the small opposing group, had a different view: "This meeting did not serve any purpose other than that of the administration. We were indoctrinated into the administration's way of thinking so we would go along willingly, rather than resentfully. Not only were we brain-washed by Bell, but at the same time it was hard on teachers who are already overworked and who do not have the energy or time for such things."

In spite of such opposing views, the use of the small group meetings gave Principal Bell an opportunity to learn about the sentiments of his teachers and to know something about how sentiment was divided on the issue at stake.

In initiating policy changes, he described his usual procedures as follows: "The ideas are sometimes initiated in faculty meetings, but they are almost always taken up in the instructional council so that we can iron out the bugs. Then in important changes we usually discuss the problem with the teachers in small groups. If after such discussions I decide that opinion is closely divided on the issue at hand, I postpone the problem, and a process of education is involved. This may last a year or more. If there seems to be a clear majority of sentiment for an issue or a proposal at stake, then we put the proposal to a vote of the faculty."

Principal Bell was aware that sentiment about the half-day schedule was closely divided. He knew that such a proposal was clearly opposed to the philosophy of persons in the small opposing group and of others in the school. There were others who hesitated because of the problems involved in scheduling and carrying through the program. However, he judged that the sentiment was in favor of the half-day schedule, so he decided to put the issue to a faculty vote. When the votes were counted, a majority of the teachers voted against the half-day proposal. Therefore, Principal Bell did not make further plans immediately to put the schedule into effect. He announced the vote to the faculty, which was only slightly in favor of not adopting the half-day schedule, and he indicated that he hoped that they would reconsider the issue in the future, and that eventually it would be possible to adopt a half-day program at Southside.

Initiating the Half-Day Schedule: The Second Attempt

During the following year, Principal Bell did not abandon the idea of instituting a half-day program. His action supported the view that many persons held toward him, namely, that he did not give up easily. Wherever the opportunity presented itself, he attempted to persuade the teachers to his point of view. For example, when someone complained about persons who were taken from their classes to go on excursions, he would point out that the absence would not be necessary with the half-day schedule. Or, when teachers spoke of the individual differences in their classes, Bell pointed out the advantages of field trips in that slower students could have more concrete learning experiences.

After almost a year of this "process of education," Bell decided to put the half-day schedule to a faculty vote for a second time. Even though they were expanding the grade club program at the same time, he judged that there was enough faculty support to get a majority of votes approving the half-day schedule. Therefore, arrangements were made and the votes were cast. When the votes were tallied, there was a clear majority in favor of instituting the half-day program.

The increased favorable opinion for the half-day schedule was attributed to at least two factors. First, according to a number of the teachers, they had come to understand the half-day schedule better and could see its advantages from the standpoint of their own classroom teaching. Second, a number of people voted positively because of their loyalty to Principal Bell. As the following quotation would indicate, some members changed their minds partially out of respect for him and perhaps partially in order to please him.

> At this school the principal tries to get teachers to enter into policy decisions. For instance, if some policy comes up, he will announce it in faculty meetings, and sometimes 90 per cent of the teachers may not like the idea. Then we discuss it later on, and then maybe only 75 per cent of the teachers don't like the idea. He talks to us some more and then maybe 60 per cent are opposed to the idea. At that point you say, "Why not? Let's give him a chance to try out this idea."

Since the vote was taken near the end of the fall semester, the plan was to begin the half-day program at the beginning of the second semester. During the second week of the second semester, the first half-day schedule was instituted.

It did not take many weeks to reveal that all was not going smoothly with the new program. Some of the problems were revealed in informal conversations of teachers. A Latin teacher had this to say, "This program might be all right for some teachers, but it certainly is not appropriate for my class. How can I take a class of students who are studying Latin on a half-day field trip? There is no place in this community that would be suitable for a visit, and I don't like the idea of spending an entire half-day with the same class here at school."

Another teacher found it difficult to hold the same class for an entire half-day and to plan effective learning experiences, as the following statement made during the lunch period shows: "If you are going to have a whole half-day class, you have to have a varied plan. I am not able to introduce enough variety into the teaching situation to make it very successful. Besides, my students are slow learners, and they are hard enough to interest even for one period. I don't think the idea is very practical."

Objections were also raised about how the trips were planned. As one teacher said, "We do not have the time to make pre-visits, and this is important if these excursions are really going to be successful. Also, when we get back to the classroom, we do not have time to follow up on the excursions, because then we must begin thinking about what we are going to do two weeks hence."

Keeping up with the administrative procedures proved to be a burden for some teachers, as the following quotation shows: "There is so much record-keeping in this new schedule. Every student must pay fifty cents for transportation, for instance, and we have to keep a record of this. If we make a mistake, we are responsible for it. This is just another burden in an already long and hard day."

The feature of the program which perhaps caused the most widespread concern among teachers was that some of the teachers came in for extra supervision. Since all of the students in the classes did not always take part in the excursions and could not be compelled to do so, someone had to supervise those who remained behind. Sometimes this fell to teachers who remained at school with their regular classes, but on some occasions, teachers who had the half-day period schedule free lost the period, since they were assigned to supervise students who remained. This aroused negative feelings among teachers, not only because they felt that it was unfair, but also because they were under the impression that the administration had assured them that such a condition was not likely to occur when the half-day schedule went into effect. Although there was considerable clamor about this problem from the inception of the half-day program, it was never satisfactorily solved. A department head almost a year after the program's beginning described its manner of treatment as follows: "We first brought up the problem in the department meeting last fall. The problem was then passed on to the suggestion committee. Nothing happened except that the matter was pushed back to the department heads, who were supposed to solve it. I finally divided the period between two teachers, so they did not lose all of their period. In a way we were left holding the bag. The day that I made this decision, Principal Bell was sick, I believe. At least he was not at school."

Thus, various objections about the half-day program were raised by different groups in the school. Even though the large social group had generally supported the half-day program by their vote, some members began to express reservation about its value. The small opposing group, of course, had objected to the program from the beginning. Olden described the origin of the idea as follows: "What happens around here is that the principal identifies the success of the school with himself. Bell got this idea of the half-day program somewhere in New England. Since there had never been such a thing tried in the West, he wanted to make a success out of it. That is the reason it was started. A problem in education is that administrators go around and get their ideas from administrators, and they should, of course, get more of them from teachers."

Many teachers retained favorable attitudes toward the new program. However, dissatisfaction in general mounted. More and more notes raising objections to the half-day schedule were written to the suggestion committee. Even some of the more loyal followers of Bell began to raise questions. Notes such as the following were received: "I feel that it is too much of a drain on us to carry on this half-day schedule. We are keeping books all the time, and when one excursion stops we have to start getting ready for the next one. It is such a taxing job supervising these students when they are on trips, and I don't think my arteries are going to stand it. There are many other teachers who are also objecting."

As the objections to the half-day program were heaped one upon the other, Principal Bell realized that some action had to be taken. About halfway through the semester, he decided to put the half-day schedule to another vote. Since it was not easy for him to think of giving up the half-day schedule, he decided to propose a vote on two temporizing alternatives. The choice given to faculty members was to vote on whether the half-day program would be continued for the remainder of the semester, or whether it would be dropped and taken up again at the beginning of the next year. Principal Bell made this proposal for two reasons. First, he believed that if the program were postponed until the fall, he and his staff would have an opportunity to iron out some "bugs" in the project. Because he had had to devote a great deal of time to another project that had been going on during the year, he felt that he had not had adequate time for the half-day schedule. He believed that the next year would allow him to give more care and attention to the half-day schedule. A second reason for the postponement was that he disliked the idea of giving up the half-day schedule because, in his own words, "It is very difficult to get such an extensive program started again after you have once given it up."

Having made his decision, Principal Bell announced his proposal at a faculty meeting and promised that the ballots would be available within a few days.

Keeping his promise, Principal Bell had ballots distributed at the beginning of the next week. A large number of teachers participated in the voting, and when the tally was made it was clear that a marked majority of the teachers favored abandoning the half-day schedule for the rest of the semester, with the understanding that it would be continued again the next fall. Although there was some dissatisfaction with the alternatives proposed for the ballot, there was considerable relief among many faculty members in that the half-day program was to be abandoned at least for a few months.

As could be expected, members of the small opposing group were not at all happy with the manner in which the problem was solved. Their attitude was reflected somewhat in the words of Olden as follows: "We don't like to feel that things are being crammed down our throats, but it seems to us that the vote was worded in such a way that you lost whichever way you voted. This is a Russian tactic. I don't know how the ballots got that way, whether they were rigged or not, but they sure seemed that way." That this attitude prevailed among members of the small opposing group was evident to most of the faculty when it became known that Newton had sent an anonymous note to the suggestion committee which set forth in very strong language the feelings which his group harbored. One of the notes attacked the principal in a personal way and spoke rather derisively of the "Russian ballot." Since there was always a written record of the complaints which came to the suggestion committee, and since this written record was distributed among teachers, everyone learned of this note to Principal Bell and it was broadcast rapidly throughout the school. When it became widely known that the note had been written by Newton, considerable sentiment developed both pro and con. Members of the small opposing group generally looked upon this event with considerable glee, while many members in the large social group expressed strong feelings against Newton and argued that Principal Bell did not deserve such harsh words. It was proposed informally that those who wrote letters to the suggestion committee should be divested of their anonymity, and in the future everyone writing notes should sign his name. However, no real action on this issue eventuated.

241

Faculty members who generally supported Bell looked upon the balloting much more favorably. Many of them appreciated Bell's solution because they felt that their principal had yielded in his own plans and in the process was showing consideration for members of his faculty. Thus, in their own perceptions, Principal Bell was behaving democratically, which, of course, contrasted strongly with the opposite views held by members of the small opposing group.

There were others in the school who perceived Principal Bell's solution as astute administration. In the words of a representative of the cafeteria group, "Bell was very shrewd in the way he handled this problem. We voted on whether to discontinue the program until next fall, or whether not to discontinue it. We did not vote on whether to discontinue it for all time. Bell's excuse was that the program had not been tried sufficiently. In other words, he raised the question of how we could know the real value of the half-day schedule until enough evidence had been collected in order to make a good judgment about it."

Initiating the Half-Day Schedule: The Third Attempt

When school opened in the fall, Principal Bell was determined to make a success of the half-day schedule. He felt that the activity program was well established, and that he could now devote most of his time to the half-day program. He still strongly believed in the value of this program, and he thought that, for the good of the students at Southside, it was worth special efforts to make it successful.

Returning with renewed energy, many teachers also undertook the task with new hope. During the first weeks of the semester, more excursions than ever were taken into the surrounding community. On one day, for example, 357 students went to a local theatre to see the movie "Julius Caesar." On any Tuesday afternoon a number of large yellow buses lined one after the other could be observed in front of the Southside School ready to take the students on field trips.

However, a listener to the school's informal communication system would soon conclude that the old dissatisfaction with the half-day program had not disappeared. Problems of preparing for a half-day's teaching with one class, of finding desirable places to go for learning excursions, of burdensome record-keeping, and of responsibility for supervising students all weighed upon teachers. Finally, the old issue of teachers' losing free periods by having to supervise students who remained behind caused considerable concern among the teachers in Southside. Notes about the problem were written to the suggestion committee, but nothing constructive was done about the problem. As a member of the suggestion committee said, when a fellow teacher inquired about the solution of this problem: "We discussed it in the meeting, this morning, but it was not solved, and I don't think that it can be solved."

Some of the persons who had been most loyal to Principal Bell were no longer able to support the program's continuation. It was with some satisfaction that Olden reported one day to the small opposing group that he had heard that one of the department heads who was one of Bell's loyal supporters had gone to Bell directly and informed him of the widespread sentiment against the recent curriculum innovation. Another loyal supporter of Principal Bell remarked to some teachers, one day in the cafeteria, that she believed the half-day schedule was not feasible. In her own words, "It is like so many things in education. It sounds very good in theory, but it does not work well in practice."

As dissatisfaction mounted for the third time, Principal Bell decided that the faculty should again vote. He proposed that a vote be taken at the end of the semester, as this would give them adequate time to judge its worth, and that at that time the faculty should vote as to whether they wished to drop the half-day schedule or whether they wished to continue. In the meantime, arrangements were made to study the program's results through an opinionaire survey of all the faculty members.

A committee was appointed to develop an instrument which could be used for gathering opinions and findings about the half-day program. Having gathered the information, the committee gave a written report to the faculty near the end of the semester.

A few days later, a vote was cast. When the vote was tallied, Principal Bell announced at a faculty meeting that the schedule innovation, which they had tried to make succeed, would be dropped because a substantial majority had voted against it. Once more he stated that he hoped they would be able to try out the half-day program once again sometime in the future.

The next day there was considerable informal talk about the dropping of the half-day schedule. Teachers were generally expressing satisfaction that they did not have to continue with the program. Olden and the members of the small opposing group seemed especially happy that they had finally won out in achieving the objective for which they had worked. Olden thought that the victory was clear-cut: "Principal Bell, you will notice, did not announce the number of votes yesterday at the faculty meeting. There was a good reason for this, because the vote was unanimously in favor of doing away with the half-day schedule."

Other faculty members, on the other hand, expressed the idea that Principal Bell had reported the vote accurately and that only a substantial majority was in favor of abandoning the half-day program. Some teachers expressed regret that the schedule was abandoned because, as one person said, "Even though it was tough for an algebra teacher or a world history teacher, it worked fine for me as a biology teacher."

During the middle of the next semester, Principal Bell reported that more teachers than ever were taking their students into the community. In his own words, "There have been more requests for excursions this semester than ever before, and I perhaps get a devilish pleasure from it. This means, no doubt, that in the future a new plan will have to be derived for meeting this problem. Even though we took a beating in the voting, the half-day program has caused some teachers to change their methods of teaching."

Questions

1. To what extent did Bell conduct an analysis of the change problem? Did he have a strategy or plan in mind?
2. What were the driving and restraining forces effecting change in this case? To what extent was Bell aware of these forces?

3. What level of acceptance from teachers did Bell need in order to insure mean-ingful adoption of the proposed change? Was estimating acceptance-level part of Bell's change strategy?
4. What role did department chairpersons have in Bell's attempt to change the curriculum?
5. How could department chairpersons have been better used?

Suggested Activity

Use the "Planning for Change Worksheet" presented earlier in this section, and the "Leadership Strategy Planning Workbook" presented in the Practices section of Chapter 5 to conduct a leadership and change analysis for this case. Have several chairpersons conduct analyses separately and spend an in-service afternoon or a chairperson's meeting or two comparing and discussing responses.

Discussion

Bell has important qualities and strengths as an administrator and supervisor. He is concerned about the school's educational program and is not shy about exercising educa-tional leadership. His ideas about curriculum and learning are progressive and well-rea-soned. Most admirably, he finds the time and personal resources to keep abreast of educa-tional program matters and to exercise educational leadership.

But something is wrong at Southside and with Bell's perspective on leadership. Successful implementation of the proposed change indeed requires that Bell be a strong educational leader but also that he be a strong supervisory and team leader. Successful change requires that *one not only know what is worth changing but how to manage the change situation.*

Bell does not have a plan for change and has not conducted a careful analysis of the forces affecting change. He assumes that one need only be concerned with the educa-tional advantages of a proposed change and that reason will prevail. But those affected by changes in schools react to change in human ways. If Bell was as concerned with feelings as he was with facts, he might have proceeded differently. Further, Bell seems unable to differentiate between "structural" and "internalized" changes. He operates mostly at the structural level, working to implement his proposals rather than at the internalized level by seeking identity and commitment to the proposals.

Bell's leadership style seems clearly "dedicated" with tendencies to "compro-mise" this emphasis with the "related" style. His dedication shows in his excessive focus on the *solution* to a curriculum problem rather than to the problem itself. Bell wants *his* program implemented according to the schedules and plans *he* devises. But his solution might not be the only solution or even the best solution to the problem. What kind of style is needed in this case?

If we assume that acceptance level and achieving internalized change are impor-tant requisites to successful change then the integrated style seems best. But using the integrated style may well mean that Bell must retreat from his particular solution and focus more specifically on the problem itself. He now is in a position of trying to "sell" *his* plan—a tough way to get the needed commitment. What he needs is a faculty solution—one with wide ownership—to the curriculum problem with which he is concerned.

WORKING TO IMPLEMENT CHANGE FROM BELOW*

Most of those who will want to use this book will not be in positions of power or authority with respect to the system they want to change. Nevertheless, it is possible to be effective working from within and from below. A few special points are in order for change agents in this situation.

First of all, diagram the organization as a system. What are its goals, norms, key subsystems, and key people?

Second, with your diagram in hand or in mind, look for allies and potential allies. If you have a concern, the chances are that many others silently or vocally share your concern. Some of these allies will be insiders like yourself but some will be outsiders, community members, and others who can become part of a *team* working together.

Third, build your own "expert power." Know your "innovation" inside and out, its strengths, and its weaknesses; know what evaluations have been done; what objections might be raised by administrators, teachers, and students, and have answers ready for these objections.

Fourth, *be persistent* if you know you have a good case. Many studies have shown that successful change agents try harder and keep on trying. Your advantage over the outside expert consultant is that you are there and you won't go away.

Fifth, if you have an adversary (usually someone over you or further up the hierarchy than you are), analyze the situation from his point of view. Total up the pros and cons from his vantage point. This exercise should help you to understand how he might be won over or bypassed. It may even show you something about your innovation that should be changed.

Sixth, develop a sense of timing and act strategically; wait for the opportune moment and don't confront the opposition impulsively but only when there are other forces working in your favor.

Last, but not least, be prepared to let others share the credit. People feel rewarded if they feel they have done something for themselves; if the change is identified as "yours," they may not be so enthusiastic. This may be especially important for administrators who are concerned about maintaining their leadership image.

---

*From Ronald G. Havelock, *The Change Agent's Guide to Innovation in Education* (Englewood Cliffs, N.J.: Educational Technology Publishers, 1973), p. xi.

PART FOUR

THE CHAIRPERSON'S ADMINISTRATIVE LEADERSHIP FUNCTIONS

ADMINISTRATIVE LEADERSHIP AND DEPARTMENT MANAGEMENT

🐚 CONCEPTS 🐚

One tends to downgrade the management aspects of leadership roles in education. Often management concerns are seen as separate from—even opposed to—supervisory and educational leadership responsibilities. Indeed, many define leadership as that behavior which initiates *new* structures, procedures, goals, and programs. Administration and management on the other hand are considered to be behaviors of those who operate within *existing* organizational structures, procedures, goals, and programs.[1] If one accepts this dichotomy he then needs to make a clean choice between being an administrator and therefore associated with the status quo, or being a leader who is change-oriented.

On paper the choice is easy for the latter designation is much more pleasing to one's self-concept. But the realities of the job, particularly that of chairperson in a junior or senior high school, awaken one to the realization that a large portion of time will be spent in doing and maintaining. The typical chairperson is responsible for a certain number of teachers. He executes this responsibility by supervising, evaluating, providing a system of coordination and communication, and by providing adequate material resources and organizational support. This requires him to plan, schedule, keep records, develop operating procedures, and control events. These, in turn, require *not* the separation of administration and leadership as they are often defined, but the integration of the two.

The chairperson's administrative leadership responsibilities are the focus of this chapter.

 Administrative leadership is not and should not be a substitute for educational, organizational, and supervisory leadership but rather is a foundation for and facilitator of these responsibilities.

That being the case, one leadership focus is not inherently better than another but rather should be considered as an interdependent component of one's total leadership responsibilities.

Sometimes educational leadership thrusts fail because of administrative support shortcomings. Sometimes administrative leadership thrusts are faulty because they are not linked to educational goals and purposes.

Leadership effectiveness in the chairperson role usually depends upon the successful integration of a number of different leadership emphases.

COMPONENTS OF ADMINISTRATIVE LEADERSHIP

The essential components of administrative leadership are internal *maintenance* of the department and *planning* for future events. As planning is extended, adequate support needs to be constructed at key pressure points. A collapse, often the fate of educational innovators who ignore maintenance demands, can hardly be equated with effective leadership, but moving forward with attention to adequate support systems can.

ORGANIZATIONAL REQUIREMENTS FOR YOUR DEPARTMENT

The sociologist Talcott Parsons identifies four basic needs or effectiveness requirements[2] for any organized social systems such as the school or department within a school:

1. The need for the social system to *adapt* to its external environment.
2. The need for the social system to *achieve* its goals.
3. The need for the social system to *integrate* its subparts and for the social system itself to be integrated into the larger organizational system.
4. The need for the social system to cultivate and *maintain* value patterns over time.

Chris Argyris proposes two critical requirements for organized social systems to remain effective over time—that they maintain themselves internally and that they be externally adaptive.[3] Internal maintenance corresponds to requirements three and four proposed by Parsons and being externally adaptive corresponds to requirements one and two.

These effectiveness requirements for social systems, such as the junior or senior high school department, are considered in each chapter of this book. Review any chapter and notice a concern for getting work done and targets met; for changing, improving and developing; for coordinating and integrating; and for the maintenance of climate, concern for individuals, and the development of a supportive group. Administrative leadership contributes to each of these effectiveness requirements and again each chapter reflects a concern for systematic planning and the building of an adequate maintenance system to introduce reasonable control, reliability and efficiency. The purposes of control, reliability, and efficiency decisions and actions (the maintenance system) are to program routine behavior, thus freeing people to give attention to more important matters; to set standards of excellence; and, to coordinate interdependent activities of department members. A procedure for handling attendance records is an example of the first; establishing a request form for considering new courses is an example of the second; and developing a system of sharing and communicating is an example of the third.

THE PLANNING SIDE OF ADMINISTRATIVE LEADERSHIP

Planning is an important but often overlooked aspect of leadership effectiveness. Why is planning often overlooked? Chairpersons often plead that they don't have the time for planning and that most planning strategies are not only time-consuming but too complex and demanding. Their observations are largely true. Time is short and planning models do tend to be cumbersome. In this section you are shown an approach to planning which is not demanding in time, is simple to understand, learn and use, and which can increase effectiveness. While this approach is greatly enhanced by a commitment to planning at all levels of the school, it is nevertheless independent. That is, one chairperson can use this approach even though others in the school do not. The essential parts of this planning process are:

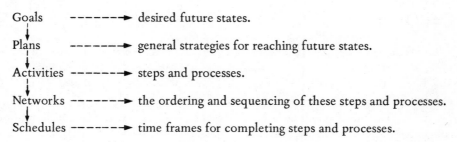

Goals ------> desired future states.

Plans ------> general strategies for reaching future states.

Activities ------> steps and processes.

Networks ------> the ordering and sequencing of these steps and processes.

Schedules ------> time frames for completing steps and processes.

Leaders are concerned with defining alternative futures and planning ways in which these alternative futures might be realized. True, leaders have other responsibilities and duties but this one is inescapable and *success here distinguishes great leaders from ordinary ones.* (For a review of alternative futures, setting goals and targets, and analyzing key results areas, see Chapter 2.) But knowing what you want to accomplish and planning only generally to reach goals and targets is usually not enough. The leader needs then to move beyond these steps to defining activities, developing networks, and constructing schedules. These are steps in the planning process.

Plans are the means to move from a present state to some future state.

It will not always be possible to plan in great detail how to reach a future state. This is particularly true where one of several alternative futures might be acceptable. Some systematic planning is necessary, although plans should be flexible and should be revised as unanticipated but perhaps more desirable objectives or future states are discovered.

Activities are things, processes or steps a chairperson does, as the designated leader, in an effort to reach a future state.

A chairperson, for example, might decide he needs to announce a meeting, assign responsibilities, authorize certain actions, collect certain information and verify results in order to move from a present to future state.

DEVELOPING AN ACTIVITY NETWORK

When the activities in his plan number eight or more, the chairperson will find it useful to develop an activity network.

A network is the ordering and numbering of activities, which comprise one's plan, in sequence, showing what needs to be done and when.

This ordering and numbering can be done by developing a network flow chart as follows:

1 ------→ 2 ------→ 3 ------→ 4 ------→ 5 ------→ 6

This example shows that each activity must be completed in sequence before proceeding to the next activity. Sometimes the activities can be arranged in a more complex but useful fashion. Consider the following networks which appear in Figure 8-1 for example.

In example 1, activities 1, 2, and 3 can be worked on simultaneously but must be completed before the chairperson can continue on to activity 4. Four, 5, and 6 are then handled one at a time, in sequence. Example 2 shows that activities 1 and 2 can be worked on simultaneously and then when completed, the chairperson can move on to simultaneous work on steps 3 and 4 and finally, continuing on to steps 5 and 6. Example 4 is a more efficient network because the project is completed within three time frames rather than four. Developing activities into networks helps the chairperson not only to understand and organize his activities but perhaps discover more efficient ways of reaching goals.

In deciding on the sequencing of activities consider the following questions:

1. Does it make more sense in this instance to work backwards from your goal in sequencing steps or toward your goal? Usually, but not always, working backwards is more effective.
2. Which activities must be completed before others?

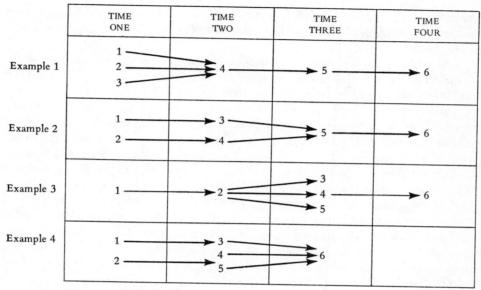

FIGURE 8-1. NETWORK EXAMPLES

3. Which activities can be worked on at the same time?
4. Which activities are time bound? That is, are there dates and deadlines which must be met for the completion of any one activity?
5. Which activities must be done by the same person?
6. Which activities can be grouped together?

DEVELOPING A SCHEDULE

Scheduling is a critical part of the planning process. Some chairpersons are conscientious in planning the "whats" and "hows" but tend to slight the "whens." You can tell if you are slighting the scheduling aspect of planning if (a) you find yourself short of time when you begin an activity; (b) you use a calendar as your only scheduling device; (c) you schedule only one week at a time; (d) you are unable to combine a number of activities on the same schedule; or (e) you find that your planned activities are out of sequence with the plans of co-workers.

Being short of time is often a symptom of not planning in blocks of time large enough for the task. Remember that the most scarce resource you have is time. Your objective is to plan and keep control of about 30 percent of your time for activities of your choosing. (Review, for example, the section on Guidelines for Setting Priorities and Managing Time which appears in the Practices section of Chapter 2). Thirty percent is not that much and it dissipates rapidly if allocated in bits and pieces. Therefore, large, continuous, uninterrupted blocks of time need to be built into your schedule. Set aside every third day, every third half-day, or perhaps one-third of each day for engaging in activities of your choosing.

Most chairpersons rely almost exclusively on the calendar as a means of scheduling time. Valuable as a calendar may be, it is still difficult to show what needs to be accomplished concurrently one week from another over a span of months or over the year.

A more sophisticated use of the calendar is the Gantt schedule (named after Henry L. Gantt, an early figure in the scientific management movement) which shows on a calendar, but in graphic form, which activities must be accomplished concurrently and linearly in relation to the total time available. Color can be used to code activity bars by goals and objectives. Further, by varying the length of the bar the importance of the activity compared to others can be shown.

For purposes of illustration, let us assume that a chairperson sets three priority tasks for himself. He plans to introduce an individualized staff development program for the tenured teachers in the department; to introduce a program of group supervision for the non-tenured teachers; and to evaluate the department's student learning resource center which was established last year as an option to regularly scheduled department classes. These activities are charted on a Gantt schedule, Figure 8-2.

The Gantt schedule permits the chairperson to review at a glance a projection of time and tasks for a period of several months and to readily see what needs to be accomplished during any given time period. In early November, for example, top priority must go to beginning the target-setting sessions for tenured teachers, to beginning the evaluation of the learning resource center and to completing the planning and developing phase of the group supervision project for non-tenured teachers. The evaluation and group super-

FIRST PRIORITY	SEPTEMBER	OCTOBER	NOVEMBER	DECEMBER	JANUARY	FEBRUARY
1. Individualized Staff Development Program for Tenured Teachers						
A. Planning, Developing and Information Phase	▓	▓				
B. Target-Setting Sessions			▓	▓	▓	
C. Individual Conferences				▓	▓	▓
D. Group Sharing and Evaluation					▓	
2. Evaluate the Departments Learning Resource Center			▓	▓	▓	▓
3. Group Supervision Program for Non-Tenured Teachers						
A. Planning and Developing Meetings	▓	▓				
B. Group Evaluation Sessions		▓	▓			▓
C. Classroom Visits				▓	▓	

FIGURE 8-2. A GANTT SCHEDULE

vision projects are earmarked to receive continuous attention during their time periods but as the end of the month approaches, emphasis in the staff development project shifts from target setting to individual conferences.

 The Gantt schedule should be developed as a primary scheduling device for chairpersons. This should not replace the more familiar writing of events and appointments on your daily calendar. Both can be kept. Further, major activities which span several weeks or months on the Gantt schedule should then be selected for network scheduling.

Network scheduling offers still another alternative to chairpersons. Basically, this is a process which facilitates an organized attack on a project by breaking up and charting the events which must be completed in order for the project to be completed. Usually starting in reverse direction (that is, with the project's completion), one identifies each activity which must be accomplished. These activities are then arranged in a sequence as shown in Figure 8–1, to develop a graphic flow chart to show how the various parts of the project depend upon each other and how certain activities must be finished before others are started.

 Networks become schedules when specific time frames are added. Scheduling means putting dates and deadlines on activities which are part of one's plan.

The example of networks shown in Figure 8–1 can be converted to network schedules by adding dates and deadlines as shown in Figure 8–3. Network scheduling is actually a combination of Gantt scheduling and the network technique.

Time frames could of course be in hours, days, or weeks depending on the type and scope of the project under consideration. Further, it is not intended that the Gantt network format be necessarily numbers keyed to activities and arrows showing sequences. To simplify matters, the arrows are eliminated from example three and actual activities are written into the schedule in example four. The most useful schedule will be that which is simple and easy to use. One might well start the scheduling process with numbers and arrows as shown in examples one and two but his working schedule should look more like example four.

Often the general time frames shown in the Gantt type network will not be easy to predict or will not provide sufficient detail for adequate planning. It may be necessary therefore to make more precise estimates of time required to complete various activities which comprise the schedule. Consider the following example. A chairperson is asked to give an oral report on a special program to a combined meeting of the board of education and citizens' advisory committee. He decides to develop a network of the activities involved and to determine the timing of these activities. He identifies and orders the following activities:

1. Develop report objectives.
2. Interview teachers involved in the program.
3. Review evaluation reports.

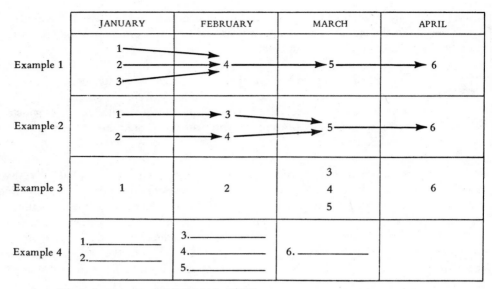

FIGURE 8-3. NETWORK SCHEDULING: GANTT

4. Write the report in the form of an oral presentation.
5. Have illustrations drawn.
6. Make transparencies.
7. Have report typed.
8. Rehearse report.
9. Give report.

He then draws the following network to show relationships between activities and the order in which they must be accomplished.

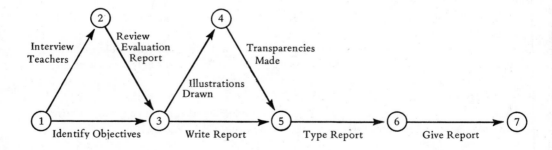

His network reveals that he must first identify objectives of his report, then write it, have it typed and finally give it. During the identification stage, he can simultaneously interview teachers involved in the program and study evaluation reports. These activities must be completed before he writes the report. During the writing stage, he can have illustrations and transparencies prepared. These activities must be completed before the report can be typed.

ESTIMATING TIME REQUIREMENTS

The next questions which face the chairperson are "When should I begin this project?" and "How much time will each activity take?" He needs to estimate the time required for each activity and for the completion of the entire project. Further, how much leeway exists between each activity? Is it important to stay on schedule? Must each new activity begin immediately after the previous activity? These questions can be answered in part by the following procedures:

1. Determine the earliest possible time required for completion of each activity. This should be an *optimistic* estimate which assumes maximum conditions and that everything will go right. Let's refer to this optimistic time estimate as T_1.
2. Determine the normal amount of time required for each activity. This should be an estimate based on the chairperson's experience with similar activities, his knowledge of other work demands and circumstances which could affect this project. This estimate should suggest the *most likely* time that would be needed if the activity were repeated a number of times. Let's refer to this *most likely* time estimate as T_2.
3. Determine the maximum amount of time required for each activity. This should be a *pessimistic* estimate which assumes the activity would be carried out under difficult circumstances. Let's refer to this *pessimistic* time estimate as T_3.
4. To determine the *expected* time (T_e) for each activity in your network schedule, use the following formula:

$$T_e = \frac{T_1 + 4T_2 + T_3}{6}$$

Consider the network schedule example used for preparing the school board-citizens' advisory committee report. In this case, however, each activity includes optimistic (T_1), most likely (T_2), and pessimistic estimates (T_3) for completion.

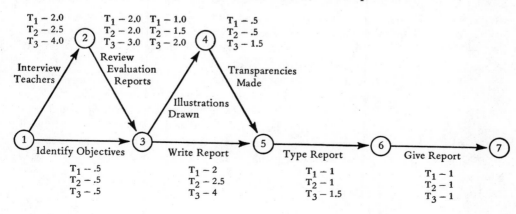

In this example the total optimistic time for completion of the project is four days for activities one through three, two days for activities three through five and two days for activities six and seven for a total of eight days. These estimates assume that the interviewing, evaluating, and objectives activities will occur simultaneously as will the writing of the report, drawing illustrations and having transparencies made. Following the same procedure, the most likely time for completion is eight and one-half days and the most pessimistic time is thirteen and one-half days. Starting time for this project should be based on careful consideration of this pessimistic time. If the consequences of not completing on time are great, then this pessimistic estimate should determine starting time. Using the formula above, we can now compute expected time for each activity and for completion of the project. Expected time estimates are shown below.

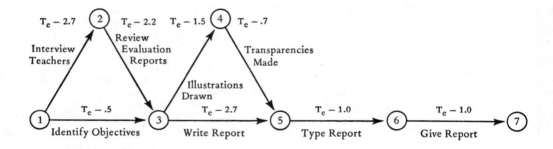

COMMON PITFALLS IN PLANNING

Planning should be viewed as a tool which can help the chairperson be more effective. Planning can help accomplish targets which are associated with key results areas or targets associated with trivia. Even planning linked to effectiveness areas and important targets guarantees nothing. Planning can help, but it needs to be used in combination with other tools of leadership such as those suggested in chapters dealing with supervisory leadership. One's knowledge of and ability to work effectively with change, motivation and department climate are examples. The point is, planning knowhow is an important supplement to *but not a substitute for* other competencies the chairperson needs.

Two other pitfalls in planning are a tendency to overlook the needs and concerns of people affected by the plans, and a tendency to overplan and thus become subservient to one's plans. These pitfalls are summarized below:

1. *People are often overlooked.* We have talked about the "whats," "hows," and "whens" of planning. Now it is time to talk about the "whos," the involvement of people. Since most plans either require that something be done to or by people, and since more often than not successful implementation requires that people accept, identify with, and be committed to your plan, it becomes important that they be involved as much as practical in the planning process. If your plans require the support of superordinates or of groups or agencies which interact with your school, then they too will need to be involved in the planning process.

2. *Sometimes we overplan.* As guidelines, plans make sense but overplanning often results in a rigid and impersonal planning system. Plans often project an unnecessary image of infallibility, when, indeed, planning which involves people in human organizations is filled with uncertainty. Human behavior in organizations is more characterized by circular than linear response. Mary Parker Follett made this important distinction many years ago[4]:

> There is circular *as well as* linear *response, and the exposition of that is, I think, the most interesting contribution of contemporary psychology to the social sciences. A good example of circular response is a game of tennis. A serves. The way B returns the ball depends partly on the way it was served to him. A's next play will depend on his own original serve plus the return of B, and so on and so on. . . . We must remember that whenever we act we have always "started something," behavior precipitates behavior in others. Every employer should remember this. One of the managers in a factory expressed it to me thus: "I am in command of a situation until I behave; when I act I have lost control of the situation." This does not mean that we should not act! It is, however, something to which it is very important that we give full consideration.*

It is because life in organizations such as schools is more circular than linear that overplanning and overcommitment to one's plans need to be avoided. A good plan provides direction but is also flexible. If flexibility is lost, the chairperson can become subordinate to his plans. If this is the case, then he might be better off with no plan at all.

ADDITIONAL ADMINISTRATIVE RESPONSIBILITIES

Three additional responsibilities which are particularly demanding on the chairperson are: administering the department budget, scheduling classes, and maintaining a department communication system. By no means are the chairperson's responsibilities in these areas independent or complete. Budget parameters, requirements, and constraints are determined elsewhere. Schedules need to fit into the larger scheduling network. Much of the content of a department communication system comes from outside sources. As chairpersons execute these responsibilities, degrees of freedom are limited. Often chairpersons take a fatalistic view of their responsibilities because of imposed limitations. But within these limitations exists sufficient space for leadership which can appreciably increase department effectiveness.

Budgeting

Sometimes departments are allocated sums of money after submitting budget requests to the principal's office, but the more common pattern is for departments to be allocated sums of money based largely on a formula involving numbers of students, classes and teachers. This amount is generally augmented for unusual and non-recurring

259

expenditures. Ideally, budgets should be based on targets and educational program needs. Actually, department allocations are based primarily on funds available.

How can one best use available funds? Chairpersons should be concerned with two budgets—a planning budget and an operational budget. The planning budget should be based on the very best educational practice and should meet optimal professional standards. This budget should be clearly linked to the department's goals and educational platform (see Chapter 10). The operational budget, which is constructed from the planning budget, should be based on the funds actually available. The planning budget serves as a blueprint for developing an operational budget which is linked as much as possible to the department's goals and targets. A planning budget can provide a well-conceived and influential basis from which a chairperson might successfully argue for additional resources, and can help him to develop his operational budget in a way which uses his resources to gain optimum advantage for the department's educational program.

If a school is presently using a Planning Programming Budgeting System (PPBS) then the chairperson has available a means for developing goal and program priorities and for linking resources and expenditures to these goals and priorities. If a school or system-wide PPBS is not available, then the chairperson should develop a local or a department means to make this link.

Every item in the budget should be coded to either department objectives or educational platform dimensions (again, see Chapter 10). Further, each actual expenditure should also be coded. At the very least, resources and expenditures should be coded by courses offered in the department, but coding by goals or goals and courses is preferable.

The largest operational cost in the educational program is of course the salaries of professionals. A complete system of accounting for links between expenditures and department objectives and programs includes estimates of staff costs. A simple way in which such an estimate might be made is to have teachers keep a log of time spent each week on each department objective or platform statement for each course they teach.

 A minimum system of accounting for department resources is keeping track of expenditures by courses offered in the department. This enables the chairperson to know the costs of each department course.

A better system of accounting for department resources is keeping track of expenditures by department goals and/or educational platform dimensions. This enables the chairperson to know not only the costs of each course but goals pursued in all courses.

The best system of accounting is to combine actual dollars expended in each course and the goals pursued with the amount of time teachers spend working on each goal. This system reflects percentages of teacher salaries expended in pursuit of each goal.

Careful planning of how resources will be used and careful accounting for expenditures by courses and/or department goals become critically important as real resources become stable. Chairpersons cannot expect much increase in real resources (those over and above normal salary increments and inflation increases) in their department budgets. Resources for new programs, new thrusts, new ideas are not likely to be added on to the budget as readily as they were at one time. The pattern of the future is likely to be characterized by new programs, goals, and courses supported *within existing* budget allocations. This will require that chairpersons face up to decreasing present programs, goals, and courses as new ones are added. For this to be done intelligently, an accounting system which links programs to expenditures will need to be available to provide an adequate data base for decision-making.

Scheduling Classes

The grand scheduling design for a particular school will likely be decided by administrations elsewhere and represents the parameters within which the chairperson must work. Except for special organizational and scheduling plans (school within a school or computer-generated daily or weekly schedules) the chairperson's independent responsibility is to implement the schedule by assigning classes and teachers. He is usually provided with a set of directions which vary in detail depending upon the complexity of the school's scheduling program. Below is an example of fairly complex scheduling directions for a school which combines three eight-period shifts (within the school day's ten class periods) with some tracking of students.

Scheduling is an important activity because it is influential in structuring and defining a school's educational program. Innovation and curriculum improvements are often operationally defined as changes in the school's schedule, as was illustrated in the case, "Changing the Curriculum at Southside" which appeared in Chapter 7. Department chairpersons should assume key roles in developing, evaluating, and changing the school's scheduling pattern and are primarily responsible for listing classes and assigning teachers within the existing schedule. The chairperson should work closely with the administration in identifying courses and other activities to be offered, determining the number of sections to be offered per grade level, and assigning teachers to specific classes.

In identifying courses and activities and in determining the number of sections to be offered the chairperson will need to consider: what courses are required to complete a specific major, what courses are required for graduation, what courses are prerequisites for other courses, and what courses are elective. The chairperson will need to consult general school requirements, seek the advice and judgment of teachers in the department, and conduct periodic surveys of student interests in determining answers to these questions.

An effort should be made to spread department classes throughout the school day equitably. Consult records of class schedules for the last five years and plan to rotate classes each year so that each has a chance to meet at preferred times. Avoid assigning more than a fair share of seventh-grade or freshman-level classes, or classes of students in a particular track, at the end of the day.

Assigning teachers to classes can be tricky. Teachers have strong preferences as to the time of day, the level of students and the particular courses they want to teach and

GENERAL INFORMATION FOR DEPARTMENT CHAIRPERSONS

I. *Teacher Schedules*—Teachers will be assigned to one of the three eight-period shifts diagrammed below:

DAILY CLASS PERIODS and HOURLY SCHEDULES										
PERIODS	1	2	3	4	5	6	7	8	9	10
Hourly Schedule	7:30 to 8:18	8:23 to 9:11	9:16 to 10:04	10:09 to 10:57	11:02 to 11:50	11:55 to 12:43	12:48 to 1:36	1:41 to 2:29	2:34 to 3:22	3:27 to 4:15
Shift 1	← 5-1/2 Assignments →								☒	☒
Shift 2	☒	← 5-1/2 Assignments →								☒
Shift 3	☒	☒	← 5-1/2 Assignments →							

Teachers' schedules will include:

(1) 5-1/2 periods of assignments all year or a combination of 5 assignments one semester and 6 the other for an average of 5-1/2.

(2) 1-1/2 periods of conference each semester or 1 period one semester and 2 periods the other semester for an average of 1-1/2.

(3) 1 lunch period.

(4) Teachers are eligible for 5 class assignments.

(5) Teacher shift assignments will be set to accommodate the 10-period day.

Department chairpersons are to establish a tentative department schedule including course, room, period and shift assignments. Final decisions on teacher shift assignments and the period assignments of classes remain with the scheduler. Use last year's departmental schedule as a guide in preparing a tentative schedule for this year. Reserve periods 1 and 2 primarily for Junior-Senior level courses and attempt to assign only Freshmen-Sophomore courses to periods 9 and 10.

II. *Lunch periods*—Lunch periods are planned for periods 4, 5, 6, and 7.

III. Instructional Council will meet period 3.

IV. *Singleton Courses*—Singleton courses in your department can be assigned to the same periods as last year. Conflicts will require additional adjustments.

V. *Assignment of Students to Special Tracking*—Department chairpersons will receive course counts and listings of students registering for their courses about March 25. Tracking lists are to be submitted no later than April 16th. Tracking lists must include (1) last and first names of students, (2) year of graduation, (3) alpha order by "class year" or "all school." Return sectioning information on the *computer printout course lists* if possible. O.O., D.E., D.O., C.W.T., Music lists, etc., are to be complete as of April 16th.

VI. A 2nd tally count will be made during the last week of April. This tally run will include your student tracking assignments. Listings of students will be returned to department chairpersons May 7.

Course tallies and conflict identification will also be received as output. Firm class projections can be made at that time. Build your tentative department schedule.

VII. *Fifth Subjects*—Both juniors and seniors are eligible for fifth subject enrollment.

VIII. *Cancellation of Course Offerings*—Cancellation of low enrollment sections will be made by the scheduler and are based on the March and April registration counts. Cancellation of courses will be discussed with department chairpersons. Suggestions as to possible alternative courses for students in these cancelled courses may be submitted. The scheduler will provide counselors with the lists of students requiring changes due to cancelled courses.

IX. *Scheduling Time Table for next year:*

March 25	Course counts and listings of students registered in each course delivered to departments.
March 17-April 4	Meetings with department chairpersons.
March 20-April 4	Determine next year's departmental staff requirements.
March 25-April 16	Determine sectioning. Deadline for turning in tracking lists, music lists, is April 16.
Late April	Departments receive 2nd Tally of course counts and course lists including tracking.
May 16	Department Chairpersons submit tentative teacher schedules.
May 26	Athletic Department submits students to be placed on athletic shifts (Deadline).

are quick to show their displeasure at other assignments. In assigning teachers take into account competencies and interests of teachers and needs of students. That crackerjack teacher who wants only to teach senior elective courses is needed by freshmen in the introductory course too. Avoid the tendency to assign new or weak teachers to first-year classes.

Teachers should be consulted about their preferences; these should be honored if department and student needs will not be compromised. Teachers' understanding will increase as their participation in the process increases. Have teachers write requests for a particular assignment. If possible, limit assignments to two general preparations per day. Take into account not only official requirements such as college preparation or past experience in teaching a particular course but also hobbies, informally achieved competencies, and interests of teachers. Often the latter strengths result in an intellectually rich and interesting course experience for students.

COMMUNICATING AND INFORMATION MANAGEMENT

The department chairperson is responsible for developing and articulating a communications system which:

Conveys to department members information from the school's administration
Reports back to the administration on department activities
Facilitates interaction among members of the department
Facilitates interaction with other departments
Provides for communications interfaces with the public

Much has been written about the social-psychological aspects of communications in formal organizations such as secondary schools.[5] Chairpersons who are considering a communication are reminded that they should be concerned with the *purpose* of the communication; the *channels* or networks which will be used to convey the communication; the *medium* or method of transmission; the *content* of the communication including information, facts, attitudes, feelings, and values to be transmitted; and the intended recipient. Many of the suggestions for communicating are summarized below.

1. Clarify your ideas before preparing the communication. Systematically analyze the ideas to be communicated and anticipate the reactions of those who will receive the communication and those affected by it.
2. Try to identify the actual purpose of the communication. Sometimes the reason will be apparent but other times more covert. What do you really want to accomplish? Do you want to obtain information, encourage someone, reprimand someone, initiate an action, change attitudes, stimulate thought? Target your actual purpose and set the tone of your communication accordingly. Be above board. Make it easy for the reader to know what you intend.
3. Consider the general environment and setting before communicating. Consider for example timing, whether you should communicate privately or publicly, custom and past practice for communicating and expectations which others have for you.
4. Consult with others on occasion before communicating. You may be communicating about a sensitive problem and the counsel of your principal or teachers might help. Often others can provide insights that had not occurred to you or an objective stance which you are unable to bring.
5. Try to gear your communications in a fashion which receivers find helpful and valuable. Take into account their perspective, feelings, and interests. Showing that you understand another point of view or problem improves receptivity to your ideas.
6. Try not to communicate between the lines or convey hidden messages. These are often found in the general tone of your message and in the words you choose.
7. Look forward. Emphasize tomorrow as well as today. Communications most often respond to today's problems. Try to move beyond today to suggest new directions and goals.

ENDNOTES

1. See for example James Lipham, "Leadership and Administration," 1964 Yearbook of the National Society for the Study of Education, *Behavioral Science and Educa-*

tional Administration (Chicago, 1965), pp. 119–141; and James K. Hemphill, "Administration as Problem Solving," Andrew Halpin (ed.), *Administrative Theory in Education* (Chicago: Midwest Administrative Center, University of Chicago, 1958), p. 98.

2. Talcott Parsons, *Structure and Process in Modern Societies* (Glencoe, Illinois: Free Press, 1960), pp. 16–96.

3. Chris Argyris, *Personality and Organization* (New York: Harper & Row, 1957).

4. Mary Parker Follett, "The Psychological Foundations: Constructive Conflict," Henry C. Metcalf (ed.), *Scientific Foundation of Business Administration* (Baltimore: Williams and Wilkins, 1926).

5. See for example Jack R. Gibb, "Communication and Productivity," *Personnel Administration,* Vol. 27, No. 1, 1964; Lloyd McCleary, "Communications in Large Secondary Schools—A Nationwide Study of Practices and Problems," *The Bulletin,* National Association of Secondary School Principals, Vol. 52, No. 325, 1968; Jack Culbertson *et al., Administrative Relationships: A Casebook* (Englewood Cliffs, N.J.: Prentice-Hall, Inc., 1960), pp. 380–384.

❧ CHAPTER EIGHT ❧

❧ PRACTICES ❧

This section contains suggestions, models, and ideas to help you plan more effectively. Included are:

Suggestions for developing a calendar of deadlines
Suggestions for developing a Gantt schedule
Suggestions for developing a network schedule
A network schedule planning sheet
A procedure for linking expenditures to goals: a simple accountability program
Suggestions for writing memos, letters, and reports.

DEVELOPING A CALENDAR OF DEADLINES

Many secondary schools issue a district-wide calendar of deadlines. If your district follows this practice, your task is easy. Refer to this calendar and extract those deadlines which apply to you. If not, carefully review other documents and memos, directives from your principal, and last year's calendar, searching out activities required of you and deadlines. Be sure also to keep track of to whom reports are submitted. Prepare a tentative calendar of your deadlines, as is illustrated below. Check with appropriate administrators to confirm dates, routing procedures, and other details. The calendar below is organized by category. You might want to organize your calendar by due dates.

SAMPLE CALENDAR OF DEADLINES—CHAIRPERSONS

CATEGORY	ACTIVITY	DUE DATE	SUBMIT TO	COMMENTS
Curriculum	1. File requests for new courses, experimental courses.	Dec. 1	Curriculum council	needed for predicting student registration and
Instructional Materials	1. File notification of textbooks to be changed next year w/recommendations.	Sept. 14	Appropriate district coordinator	for proper procedures, forms, see policies and procedures handbook

CATEGORY	ACTIVITY	DUE DATE	SUBMIT TO	COMMENTS
Staff Evaluation	1. 1st evaluation, 2nd year teachers	Nov. 8	Principal	End of 1st quarter
	2. 1st evaluation of all teachers new to district	Nov. 26	Principal	60 school days after 1st day of school
	3. 2nd evaluation of all 2nd year teachers	Feb. 3	Principal	
	4. 2nd evaluation of all teachers new to district	Feb. 3	Principal	
	5. Write up tenure recommendations for all 2nd year teachers for Bd. of Education	Mar. 3	Principal	—use form provided for this purpose
	6. 3rd evaluation of all 2nd year teachers	Apr. 11	Principal	End of 3rd quarter
	7. 3rd evaluation of all teachers new to district	Apr. 11	Principal	End of 3rd quarter
	8. Evaluation of tenure teachers	June 13	Principal	Use appropriate dist. evaluation instrum. one evaluation per year
Expenditures	1. File requests for bldg. alterations for next year	Jan. 15	Asst. Principal	Submit four copies
	2. File requests for bldg. equip. for next year	Jan. 15	Asst. Principal	Submit four copies
	3. Cutoff date for ordering educational equipment	Feb. 3	Asst. Principal	Submit two copies
	4. Cutoff date for ordering educational supplies	Apr. 1	Asst. Principal	Submit two copies
Additional Deadlines	1.			
	2.			
	3.			

DEVELOPING A GANTT SCHEDULE

A calendar of deadlines can easily be converted into a more useful planning tool by estimating start-up time for each activity in order to meet each deadline, and then by casting this information into a Gantt schedule format. Refer to pp. 254–57 for a discussion of Gantt scheduling. This simple graphic procedure permits the chairperson to view activities which must be accomplished concurrently and linearly in relation to specific time frames and the total time available. Gantt schedules may take different forms, one of which is illustrated below. This schedule was developed by a chairperson of a thirteen-teacher department in a large suburban high school. In this example:

only activities which are linked to deadlines or which are routinely scheduled are included.
activities scheduled are divided into three broad areas of responsibility (administration, supervision, and teaching) and color-coded as entered into the schedule.

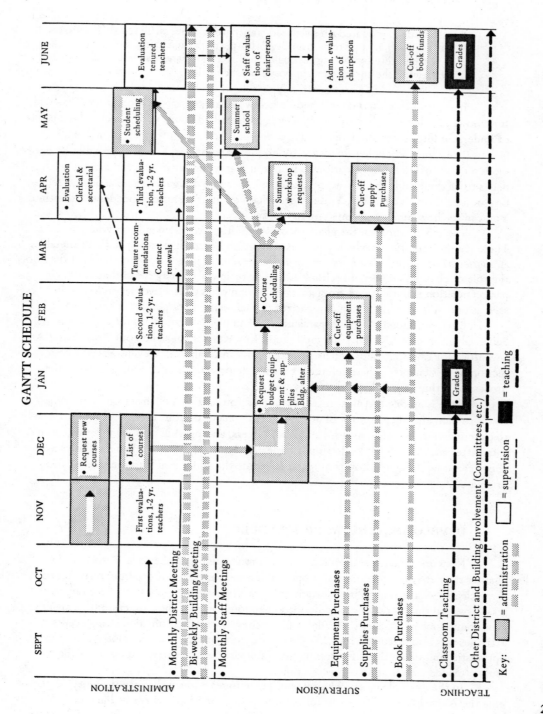

GANTT SCHEDULE

Key:

▦ = administration

☐ = teaching

■ = supervision

269

the schedule is prepared on overhead transparency sheets. Three sheets are used, one for each area of responsibility. This permits the chairperson to view each area separately by leafing through the three transparent sheets or all together by viewing the sheets superimposed on each other.

In reproducing this Gantt schedule below, all areas appear on one page. You will find, however, that using transparency sheets as described above adds a useful dimension of understanding as you prepare a similar schedule.

The Gantt schedule provided is by no means complete, but as is, provides an enormous amount of useful information to help you plan your activities. You can see what needs to be done and when. You can decide what can be delegated to an assistant, secretary or aide if one is available. You can see what activities are interdependent with others. You can see how much flex time you have left.

The information on the chart focuses on fairly fixed demands on your time. These are the activities in which you must engage and according to a specified timetable. *Activities of this type should not consume more than 70 percent of your time.* If they do, the role of chairperson in your school should be reviewed. It may mean that the chairperson position is not defined from an examination of key effectiveness areas and not seen as one of leadership which emphasizes the achieving of targets.

Review Chapters 1 and 2, particularly "Sample Competencies for Chairpersons: Self-Evaluation Checklist" in Chapter 1; and "Key Results Areas in Your Role" and "An Inventory for Charting Department Effectiveness" in Chapter 2. Review also the concepts section of this chapter. These references should help you and your principal begin the process of rethinking and reevaluating your role.

Time is among the most scarce resources you have as a chairperson. Your objective is to plan and keep control of *at least* thirty percent of your time. This permits you to examine your key effectiveness areas, set targets, and provide ways to meet these targets. After all, this is what leadership is basically about. The Gantt schedule illustrated above can now show you how you might schedule the additional activities which you originate.

DEVELOPING A NETWORK SCHEDULE

Network schedules often look more complicated than they are. Earlier in this chapter the network schedule was proposed as a simple means of ordering activities to show clearly what needs to be done and in what order as one moves toward a target. It was suggested that network schedules become more useful if they are cast into a specific time frame such as a Gantt schedule. A more complex method of calendaring events and activities was also discussed (pp. 257–58). Here the planner states the most pessimistic, optimistic, and likely times for completion of a particular activity and by using the formula provided arrives at an estimated time.

In the example below, chairperson Janet Jones is given the responsibility of planning the Annual County Institute for Administrators and Supervisors in the county's schools. Janet decides to develop a network schedule cast against a Gantt schedule as her planning mechanism. She elects a time frame of one week for calendaring various activities which need to be completed to arrange for the Institute. She could have chosen a less standard and more specific method of estimating time but she wants to avoid becoming involved in a very complicated planning procedure.

Janet notes that the Institute is scheduled for December 1. She needs to determine what activities and events must take place, in what order, and when in order for the project to begin on time. She starts with the opening of the conference on December 1 and begins *backwards* from this point thinking of steps and activities which must be accomplished. She notes that final arrangements need to be made, a reception planned, participants identified and assigned to various Institute sessions, educational materials ordered, announcement of the Institute distributed, materials selected, announcements developed, Institute sessions scheduled, speakers obtained, space arrangements made.

Janet systematizes her thoughts by filling out the "Network Schedule Planning Sheet."

Janet first records the activities in the order in which they must be completed. Activities that can be worked on simultaneously are grouped together. She then estimates the time required for completion of each activity or group of activities. With this knowledge, she is able to go to a calendar and establish actual dates for beginning and completing activities. Her next step is to determine who will be responsible for completing each activity. Time frames should be discussed with that person and Janet's figures may well be altered as a result. Any special comments or helpful notes are made under the comments heading. The next step is to assign each activity a network number and by noting time frames (in this case one or two weeks) develop a network schedule as illustrated below:

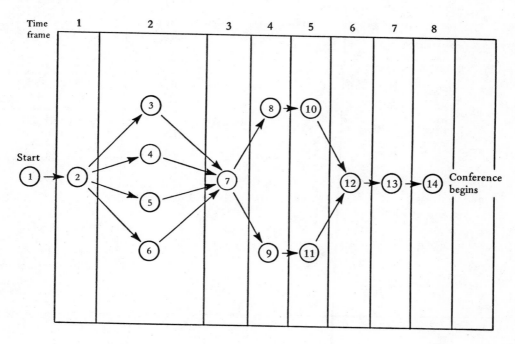

NETWORK SCHEDULE PLANNING SHEET

PROJECT TITLE _County Teacher Evaluation Workshop_ DATE _Sept. 22_
TARGETS, OBJECTIVES _Annual County Institute: create_ PROJECT DEADLINE _Dec. 1_
awareness of new practices (i.e., clinical supervision) DIRECTOR _Janet Jones_

TIME FRAMES	ACTIVITIES	NETWORK NUMBERS	EST. TIME	CALENDAR TIME	PERSON RESPONSIBLE	COMMENTS
	Start up	1	Deadline is Sept. 29	Dec. 1, 9 weeks allowed for planning. Start up time is Sept. 29. Thanksgiving holiday not counted.		
1	Plan program	2	1 wk.	Sept. 29-Oct. 3	Jones	Do this in committee.
2	Make space arrangements	3	2 wks.	Oct. 6-Oct. 17	Peterson (3,4,6) and Jones (5)	Can be worked on at same time.
	Layout announcements	4				Note: *two* week time frame.
	Obtain speakers	5				
	Develop mailing lists	6				
3	Develop work shop sessions	7	1 wk.	Oct. 20-Oct. 24	Jones	Do this in committee.
4	Select materials	8	1 wk.	Oct. 27-Oct. 31	Jones (8)	
	Have announcements printed and distributed	9			Peterson (9)	
5	Order materials	10	1 wk.	Nov. 3-Nov. 7	Peterson	Kanihu to call speakers, let them know numbers of potential participants and how assigned.
	Review participants and assign to sessions	11			Kanihu	
6	Plan reception	12	1 wk.	Nov. 10-Nov. 14	Peterson	
7	Make final arrangements	13	1 wk.	Nov. 17-Nov. 21	Jones	
8	Conference begins	14		Dec. 1	Jones	Note: wk. of Nov. 24 omitted because of Thanksgiving holiday. Use for emergencies if necessary.

Janet's network schedule summarizes the activities which must be accomplished and when, at a glance. She and others will, of course, consult her planning sheet for additional details. Try developing a network schedule to help plan a project for which you have responsibility.

SUGGESTIONS FOR LINKING EXPENDITURES TO GOALS: A SIMPLE ACCOUNTABILITY PROGRAM

The linking of resources and expenditures to department goals has been discussed (pp. 259–61). It was suggested that a minimal accounting procedure be developed which keeps track of expenditures by courses. A better system is one which keeps track of expenditures by goals or educational platform dimensions as well as by courses. The best system is one which, in addition to the above, accounts for percentage of time teachers spend working on various goals.

This information can be used to determine if department priorities are being reflected in actual expenditures and in how teachers spend their time. Further, areas can be identified where *too much* as well as not enough financial and time resources are being spent. Moreover, this information provides a data base for defending this year's budget allocation and in obtaining next year's allocation. Teachers benefit by focusing deliberately on goals, being careful in planning expenditures and planning deliberately how they will use their time and effort.

Two sample forms are provided below. Form A provides a means for actual dollar expenditures and items or services purchased by each course offered in the department and goals pursued within that course. The chairperson will need to maintain one such form for each course. He should ask teachers who requisition materials or otherwise request expenditures to indicate the course or courses for which the expenditures are intended. Further, teachers should indicate initially the department goals for which the expenditures are intended. This estimate can be corrected at the end of the year by recalling actual use. Admittedly, this is a difficult step, for often expenditures span several goals. Such an accounting system is intended to provide only a general indication of expenditures.

Form B provides a means for teachers to estimate the time they spend on each department goal for each course they teach. The teacher keeps this time log for a period of days or weeks and periodically gives it to the department office for summarizing. Teachers are asked to spend some time each week (perhaps as a way of planning for the next week) reviewing carefully the week's plans and actual events which occurred in each course. On the basis of this review, the teacher estimates for each course the amount of time spent in and outside of class on each department goal.

FORM A: DOLLAR EXPENDITURES FOR DEPARTMENT GOALS BY COURSE

DEPARTMENT__English_____

COURSE _____

DEPARTMENT GOALS	ACTUAL EXPENDITURES					
	GENERAL SUPPLIES ACCT #		TEXTBOOKS ACCT #		AUDIO/VISUAL ACCT #	
	ITEM	COST	ITEM	COST	ITEM	COST
1. The department should strive for equality of educational opportunity by providing experiences geared to the needs and strengths of each student—taking into account his level of understanding and capitalizing on his unique talents, abilities and interests.						
2. The department should provide opportunities in every area of its program for students to achieve excellence.						
3. The department should provide opportunities for students to acquire the basic skills of reading, writing, speaking, listening.						
4. The department should provide opportunities through which students can learn how to learn and how to think critically in order to cope with a world of change.						
5. The department should provide opportunities for inventiveness, originality, creativity, and self-expression.						
6. The department should provide opportunities for students to be involved in aesthetic experiences as creators, participants, and observers.						
7. The department should provide opportunities for all students to acquire knowledge, skills, and attitudes that will serve them both in the world of work and in the creative use of their leisure time.						
8. The department should foster feelings of adequacy and self-worth and a sense of belonging to the school community on the part of everyone associated with the schools.						

ADMINISTRATIVE LEADERSHIP AND DEPARTMENT MANAGEMENT: PRACTICES

FORM A: DOLLAR EXPENDITURES FOR DEPARTMENT GOALS BY COURSE

SCHOOL YEAR _____

INSTRUCTOR _____

ACTUAL EXPENDITURES					
CAPITAL OUTLAY ACCT #	MAINT/REPAIRS ACCT #	FIELD TRIPS ACCT #	OTHER CATEGORIES (SPECIFY)	TOTAL $ PER GOAL	COMMENTS
ITEM COST	ITEM COST	ITEM COST	ITEM COST		
				Total	
				Total	
				Total	
				Total	
				Total	
				Total	
				Total	
				Total	

FORM A: DOLLAR EXPENDITURES FOR DEPARTMENT GOALS BY COURSE (*continued*)

DEPARTMENT _English_

COURSE_____

DEPARTMENT GOALS	GENERAL SUPPLIES ACCT #		TEXTBOOKS ACCT #		AUDIO/VISUAL ACCT #	
	ITEM	COST	ITEM	COST	ITEM	COST
9. The department should provide an environ-ment in which students can understand, appreciate, and respect individual and cultural differences.						
10. The department should help students to understand the relationship of the individual to society. It should help students to develop a sense of values, to develop self-direction and to understand and practice the rights and responsibilities of democracy.						
Total expenditures in each category						

FORM A: DOLLAR EXPENDITURES FOR DEPARTMENT GOALS BY COURSE (*continued*)

SCHOOL YEAR _____

INSTRUCTOR _____

ACTUAL EXPENDITURES					
CAPITAL OUTLAY ACCT #	MAINT/REPAIRS ACCT #	FIELD TRIPS ACCT #	OTHER CATEGORIES (SPECIFY)	TOTAL $ PER GOAL	COMMENTS
ITEM COST	ITEM COST	ITEM COST	ITEM COST		
				Total	
				Total	
				Total	

FORM B: ESTIMATES OF TIME SPENT ON GOALS BY COURSE

DEPARTMENT English   TIME PERIOD Jan. & Feb.

COURSE _____   INSTRUCTOR _____

DEPART-MENT GOALS	PERCENTAGE OF TIME								COMPUTE EIGHT WK. PERCENTAGE	
GOAL #	WK 1	WK 2	WK 3	WK 4	WK 5	WK 6	WK 7	WK 8	TOTAL	COMMENTS
1										
2										
3										
4										
5										
6										
7										
8										
9										
10										
Totals	100	100	100	100	100	100	100	100		

SUGGESTIONS FOR WRITING MEMOS, LETTERS, AND REPORTS

It is said that armies march on their stomachs and large organizations crawl in a sea of paperwork. Schools must share in this indictment. Still, it is not always possible to communicate face-to-face and often some record needs to be made so that events and activities will be available for wide circulation and for future reference. Chairpersons frequently will be asked to prepare reports. Occasionally it might be useful for all administrators to keep a log for a week of memos, letters and reports written along with reasons for preparing these documents. An analysis of the logs during an in-service workshop might provide useful information regarding uses and abuses and might suggest more effective written communication procedures.

Memos can be an efficient way to communicate. A good memo is concise and specific. Try to limit memos to only one topic. If you must exceed the one-topic limit, clearly indicate at the beginning of the memo the topics of concern. Then rank topics in order of importance and treat them one at a time. Remember, *memos do not provide for two-way communications.* If you need feedback or desire discussion, avoid using a memo and communicate by informal conference, small gathering, or formal meeting.

Writing letters is another common method of communicating, particularly with individuals, groups, and agencies outside the school. Letters become the legal property of the person to whom they are sent and that person has wide latitude in using the letter as he sees fit. For this reason, be particularly careful with what you write and how. Poor grammar, misspellings, and other errors in your letter can be embarrassing. Avoid this by having someone routinely check letters before they are sent. Chairpersons are particularly vulnerable when answering complaints, questions of policy, and other sensitive issues by letter. In these cases, it is best to have your letter reviewed by your principal or another appropriate administrator. Consider the following suggestions as you write letters:

Have only one purpose in mind per letter. What actions do you want the reader to take?

State the essence of your letter in the first sentence. You can elaborate and give reasons later.

Write as you would talk to this person, using active verbs and avoiding trite and formal expressions.

Use personal pronouns and names.

Avoid big words or multi-syllable words. Use one syllable words about two-thirds of the time.

Avoid long sentences. Limit sentences to about fifteen words.

Try to keep your letter no more than one page in length.

Be conscious of appearance. Your margins, indentions, captions, style of typing, quality of typewriter and paper all help the reader form an impression of you.

Send copies of the letter selectively. Avoid distributing copies widely—it could embarrass the person to whom the letter is addressed and it tends to turn your letter into just another memo. Avoid sending copies to one's superior unless it is a letter of praise.

Writing Reports

Modern junior and senior high schools are decentralized, with chairpersons and teachers assuming considerable responsibility for decisions. Principals and other administrators, however, remain accountable for the actions of chairpersons. This accountability makes it important for them to know what is going on and to exercise reasonable control over and reasonable evaluation of chairpersons' activities. Further, principals and other administrators are dependent upon the advice and counsel of chairpersons. One way in which administrators exercise reasonable control and obtain the advice of chairpersons is by asking for reports of various activities or reports which investigate an area and provide recommendations. When preparing a report, consider the following suggestions:

1. Provide a standard for comparing your ideas or activities. Do this by linking your report to school and department intents. Try to make your report results-oriented.

2. Focus your report on important trends and significant exceptions to the ordinary. Hold the routine to a minimum. Assume that the administrator asking for your report is aware of day-by-day activity. Give attention to the critical areas of your responsibility.

3. Be timely in making your report. A prompt report insures that pertinent information will be available for action.

4. Keep your report simple. Try not to cover everything. Avoid overkill. The person receiving your report ought not to have to work to find out what's important. Summarize data instead of providing lengthy tables of raw numbers. Don't discourage the reader with excessive length.

5. Write your report clearly, so it will be understood. Assume that your report must be understood by someone of average intelligence who is not familiar with professional education.

6. Link your report to other reports and activities. Help the reader to review what you say within the larger framework of the school's information system.

7. Focus on the future. Look forward more than backward. Emphasize directions, predictions, trends, goals, and growth rather than just providing historical data.

PART FIVE

THE CHAIRPERSON'S EDUCATIONAL LEADERSHIP FUNCTIONS

EDUCATIONAL PROGRAM LEADERSHIP

CONCEPTS

The intent of Part 5 is to help chairpersons

 See their roles less as instructional leaders in a provincial sense concerned only with narrow subject matter areas than as educational leaders with a healthy stake in the school's total educational program.

View educational program as a curriculum, not only with aims, content, and evaluation, but with a supporting educational platform housed in a context for learning.

Understand how the subtle aspects of a school's educational program—the exchange of teacher-student influence in classrooms for example—may be as important as what content is taught.

This is a critical juncture in our discussion of the chairperson and his leadership roles; here is where the crux of effectiveness is determined. Organizational, administrative, supervisory, and team expression of leadership in schools can only be justified as vehicles which nurture and develop an intellectually sound and humane educational setting and program for students. In a sense, therefore, expressions of educational leadership are substantive while other expressions of leadership are contextual. Ideally, educational leadership legitimizes and justifies the chairperson role; other leadership supports and facilitates the educational.

This section will focus more broadly on educational program rather than on the more limited concept of curriculum. Educational program includes patterns of school and classroom organization for instruction, teaching strategies, assumptions and objectives, and the school's overall set of beliefs, philosophy, or sense of mission, as well as the curriculum. Curriculum refers specifically to the educational experiences and encounters associated with the content and subject matter of the various disciplines and teaching areas. Curriculum theorists generally view educational experiences and encounters across the disciplines in an integrative pattern, but in practice curriculum has come to mean the subject matter taught in a course.

Further, patterns of school and classroom organization for instruction and teaching strategies are often viewed separately from curriculum. The concept of educational programs represents a broader system of interacting forces of which the subject taught is only a part. Our discussion will assume chairperson competencies with a particular subject matter area and with the literature of that area. We will focus on the broader concepts and ideas that encompass the array of subject matter, and on which of these to develop.

TRADITIONAL CONCEPTIONS OF PROGRAM AND CURRICULUM

The curriculum theorist Ralph Tyler identifies three major decision points in developing curriculum: the selection of specific objectives, the identification and ordering of learning experiences intended to achieve these objectives, and the evaluation of effects to determine the extent to which objectives have been achieved.[1] Presumably, if learning objectives are not satisfactorily achieved the evaluation phase becomes the basis for revising learning experiences and subject matter formats. This conception of program and curriculum provides us with direction and knowledge as to why we engage in certain educational activities, a vast improvement over coverage of content because it is in the textbook, course outline, or syllabus.

Many junior and senior high schools tend to operate from a very vague knowledge transmission model of schooling. Barth describes such a model as follows[2]:

> The transmission of knowledge model posits existence of an accumulated body of knowledge (K), usually encoded in written language. It is stored from Plato to nuclear physics, in the Library of Congress. The proper business of education is to transmit as much of this knowledge as possible to students. The proper function of students is to assimilate as much of this knowledge as possible as efficiently as possible and to display its possession upon demand of school authorities. A student is judged (evaluated) according to how much K he has acquired, how fast, and how able he is to demonstrate this acquisition.

Chairpersons are generally familiar with problems associated with this knowledge transmission model. What knowledge is worth teaching, for example, is taken for granted by teachers who tend to teach in this way. Why selected knowledge is being taught is a question often lost in the haste of teaching the knowledge itself. The result is often anti-intellectual and trivial teaching which is of dubious value to teacher or student. But this is often the stuff that youngsters must learn and upon which they are graded. This stuff becomes the basis of who is successful and who is a failure in the eyes of the school.

The Tyler rationale has great appeal because its emphasis is on goal focus. By asking the question, "What knowledge is most worth knowing?" this approach attacks the drift into trivial teaching. Further, the approach is relatively simple and easy to understand.

In this approach, objectives need to be defined which help focus on what knowledge is worth knowing; learning experiences and subject matter formats need to be developed to meet these objectives; and evaluation must occur.

Objectives do not just appear but originate, according to Tyler, from studies of society and its needs, studies of learners and their needs and learning styles, and concepts, content, and ideas considered important by specialists in the subject matter areas. These objectives are then filtered through accepted principles of learning and the school's particular philosophy or point of view. This filtering is intended to cull out potentially inconsistent, unimportant, or unsound objectives. Schematically the Tyler framework for educational program development appears in Figure 9–1.

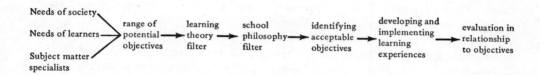

FIGURE 9–1. TYLER TYPE FRAMEWORK FOR CURRICULUM DEVELOPMENT

The Tyler model has been adopted extensively[3] and is now the dominant conceptualization of educational program development.

 Granting its virtues of simplicity and goal focus, the Tyler approach is inadequate to describe how program and curriculum emerge and develop, how one works to change program and curriculum, and how evaluation takes place.

AN EXPANDED VIEW OF PROGRAM AND CURRICULUM

Program and curriculum decision-making is not as rational or objective a process as one might think. Curriculum workers and chairpersons tend not to start with objectives when engaged in planning and development, nor do they bring to the decision-making process total objectivity or rationality. If you reflect for a moment on your own experience, it is probable that teachers, chairpersons, and principals bring to decision-making a rather extensive set of agendas—perhaps somewhat hidden but real nevertheless. It is useful to think of these agendas as educational platforms, comprising what people stand for, what they believe in, and what they hope to accomplish. Platforms represent something to stand on, from which one may make rational decisions.[4]

What each person believes is true and desirable comprises the educational platform that he brings to educational decision-making.

An individual's platform is composed of his assumptions, theories, beliefs, and desires that form the basis for his decisions.

An educational program platform consists of the assumptions, theories, and aims that underlie and give direction and meaning to that program.

In each case many aspects of educational platform are known but other aspects are unknown or latent. Often disagreement exists between what teachers and faculties claim to be their platform and the platforms which are inferred from actual teacher behavior and from analysis of the educational program in action.

Helping to construct a teacher's working educational platform (his *theory in use*) by making inferences from his actual teaching behavior and contrasting this with the teacher's espoused platform is a major principle underlying clinical approaches to supervision.[5] This "dilemma surfacing" strategy will receive extensive examination in Chapter 11, Supervision and Evaluation of Teachers.

The concept of educational platform has important implications for curriculum development and change. Too often the emphasis has been on changing aims and objectives, the instructional strategies and subject matter formats associated with aims without sufficient regard for the implicit assumptions and theories of teachers.

 In practice the curriculum exists more in the minds and hearts of teachers than in aims, objectives, textbooks or curriculum guidelines.

Curriculum change has tended to focus on the *structural* aspects of the curriculum: the materials used, the subject matter, and the organization and design of educational activities. Important as these are, they must be accompanied by corresponding changes in educational platforms of people.

ADDITIONAL CONCEPTS FOR VIEWING EDUCATIONAL PROGRAM

To this point it has been suggested that assumptions, theories and intents, as manifested in educational platforms, substantially influence decisions made by teachers and chairpersons regarding educational program and classroom activity. It has further been suggested that while some aspects of one's educational program are known and espoused, other aspects are unknown and must be inferred from classroom activity. How one might identify and construct otherwise unknown aspects of educational program will be suggested in Chapter 11.

Known or unknown, educational platform provides a more realistic basis for understanding and making a variety of decisions (including selecting, organizing and evaluating curriculum content) than does the rational Tyler-modeled framework.

 Educational platform assumptions, theories, and intents are manifested in *patterns of classroom influence* and in the general environment or *context for learning*.

Patterns of classroom influence refers to the extent teachers and students influence classroom goals and objectives, curriculum decision-making, and instructional activities.

Context for learning refers to the environment in which learning activities take place. Context includes emphasis given to intrinsic and extrinsic motivation, personal and culturally defined meanings, and interpersonal setting.

Students often learn as much from how classrooms are organized and structured, methods of instruction, and other aspects of the educational context as they do from the context of the curriculum itself. Educational leadership requires that in addition to subjects, patterns of influence and contexts for learning become proper agenda items in planning, curriculum development, teaching and evaluation.

Patterns of Classroom Influence

One important way in which classrooms can be described is on the basis of the type and amount of student influence and teacher influence. That is, to what extent is the teacher free to influence and contribute to establishing classroom goals and objectives, to making important curriculum decisions, to deciding instructional activities and to regulating, controlling and scheduling classroom events? Similarly, to what extent are students free to influence the character and life of classrooms?

Junior and senior high school classrooms vary considerably in the nature and distribution of influence. In some classrooms teachers are very influential in deciding goals

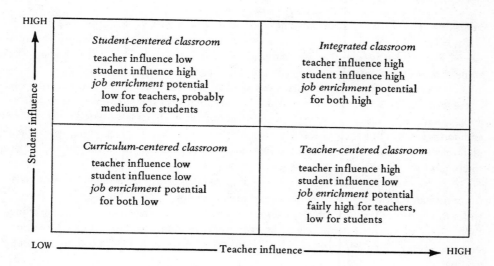

FIGURE 9-2. PATTERNS OF CLASSROOM INFLUENCE. FROM THOMAS J. SERGIOVANNI, "HUMAN RESOURCES SUPERVISION," IN T. J. SERGIOVANNI, ED., *PROFESSIONAL SUPERVISION FOR PROFESSIONAL TEACHERS* (WASHINGTON, D.C.: ASCD, 1975), p. 25.

and objectives, what will be studied, how and when. Such teachers may very well have the students' interest at heart and indeed often demonstrate this by flexible and creative teaching but it is understood that students will have little to say about such decisions. In other classrooms, teachers function mechanically as they implement a curriculum with which they have little identity or understanding. Here neither teacher nor student assumes responsibility for goal selection and curriculum decision-making. In a few classrooms, teachers and students exercise major influence as they participate together in goal and objective development and in curriculum decision-making. In an occasional classroom one may find that the teacher exercises virtually no influence, having abdicated the responsibility for goal selection and curriculum decision-making entirely to students.

Several relationships are illustrated in Figure 9–2. The abscissa represents the extent to which teachers are able to influence classroom practices. The ordinate represents the extent to which students are able to influence classroom practice. Each quadrant represents a general type of classroom defined by its pattern of influence. Very few classrooms would fall neatly into one quadrant; nevertheless classrooms tend toward one or another of these basic types.[6]

Teacher-Centered Classrooms

Teacher-centered classrooms are characterized by high teacher influence and low student influence. Large numbers of junior and senior high school classrooms are characterized by teachers who assume strong leadership functions which include planning objectives and goals, strategies, programs, activities, and policies; organizing methods, materials, equipment, and students; teaching through instructing, mediating, communicating, and developing; and controlling by measuring, evaluating, correcting, rewarding, and punishing. The choice of materials, methods, and approaches, within approved limitations, is largely up to the teacher, not textbook writers, curriculum developers, or supervisors. The teacher is free to adjust materials and methods according to his perception of student needs providing that specified content areas are covered.

Leadership functions are often assumed by dedicated teachers who have the best interest of students at heart but who feel that they know best what students need. In good teacher-centered classrooms, and there are many, students are treated with kindness and consideration but their classroom roles are limited primarily to responding to teacher planning, organizing, and leading by doing the instructional programs and then submitting to controls which measure effectiveness.

Often teachers need to engage in selling, persuading, convincing, appealing, and other human relations skills in order to get serious commitment from students. Sometimes this is too difficult or time-consuming and the teacher falls back on horse-trading—"When you are finished with the assignment, you may take a game from the shelf and play quietly at your desk" or "Tomorrow we will have a test and this assignment will help you pass."

Job enrichment opportunities in the teacher-centered classroom are good for teachers.[7] Influencing classroom practices increases opportunities for teachers to experience achievement, recognition, responsibility, and intrinsically interesting and meaningful work. One can describe successful teacher-centered teachers as being fairly well motivated to work for students and the school.

Students, however, often do not get to be "part of the action." Decisions are made for them and their roles are clearly defined as passive responders. Job enrichment for students is on the low side and building proper intrinsic motivation and commitment can often be a problem.

Student-Centered Classrooms

Student-centered classrooms are characterized by fairly high student influence and low teacher influence. In classrooms of this type the teacher rarely, if at all, exercises leadership. Responsibility for learning is abdicated completely to students. Classrooms such as these are usually part of educational experiments and are rarely found in regular schools. Some consider schools and classrooms associated with this quadrant to offer an attractive approach to education, but this approach is in our view limited by the passive role assigned to the teacher. Generally, job enrichment opportunities for teachers are low in this setting and though higher for students, are not fully realized.

The Curriculum-Centered Classroom

The least satisfactory approach to schooling is represented by the curriculum-centered quadrant and is characterized by low teacher *and* low student influence. Classrooms of this type represent a nonleadership approach which characterizes a large percentage of our junior and senior high schools. Here the controlling force is in the textbook, the highly structured and sequenced curriculum and other materials which for the most part determine class and school goals and objectives, and decide pacing, sequencing, and scope of instruction. Teachers and students need only follow directions.

In classrooms of this type teacher and students have abdicated all rights and responsibilities to impersonal experts, as manifested in textbooks, overly structured curriculum and other devices which rigidly program how teachers and students are to behave, and the nature of activities with which they will be engaged. Teachers who operate deep into their quadrant have deserted their classrooms by not providing leadership and have become mere followers and givers of directions.

The question is not simply one of texts, materials, and curriculum but one of control. Do teachers use texts, materials, and curriculum guides as means to achieve individual and school goals or are these ends in themselves? This question is not merely academic but one of survival of teaching as a profession as opposed to merely an occupation. There will always be teachers, but the number of professionals in teaching may decrease as more and more classrooms drift into this quadrant. Curriculum-centered classrooms simplify or make easy the "job of teaching" but impede the job of keeping control of students, for the typical student response is likely to be indifference, apathy, protest, and slowdown. Soon teachers respond similarly. True, some teachers, because of limited potential in commitment or competence, may prefer curriculum-centered classrooms, but most would prefer a richer environment.

Integrated Classrooms

In classroom types previously discussed, conflict is often assumed between student initiative and self-actualization, and the academic goals, cultural and societal demands to which the school must respond. In the student-centered classroom, one sides with the student and in the teacher-centered classroom, one sides with societal demands as perceived by the teacher and school. In the curriculum-centered classroom both sides of this alleged conflict are suppressed in favor of the wisdom of impersonal experts.

In integrated classrooms no conflict is assumed between student initiative and academic goals. Indeed the two are seen to be interdependent with students finding rich personal meanings only through engaging in worthwhile educational experiences. Further, the difference between intellectual enrichment and merely going through the motion of schooling is the initiative, excitement, commitment and meaning which the student brings to any learning encounter.

In integrated classrooms, teachers and students assume major responsibility for planning, organizing, and controlling the learning environment with chairpersons providing leadership which supports this effort. Since teacher and student involvement in setting goals and in planning work are high, identification and commitment to work are more assured. These in turn are likely to result in high performance by teachers and students. This is the setting which makes most accessible the motivation factors of achievement, recognition, work itself, responsibility, and personal growth for both teachers and students.

The question of teacher-student influence is more potent than it at first seems. The pattern of influence sets the tone for how instruction will take place and what instruction will take place. These are issues which chairpersons should raise and issues which need to be considered by teachers in program planning, teaching, and evaluation. Assumptions, theories and intents as they relate to patterns of classroom influence are an important part of one's educational platform.

THE HUMAN CONTEXT FOR LEARNING

Knowledge is the commodity of exchange in the educational enterprise and teachers with a depth of understanding of their respective and related academic areas are an essential ingredient to the success of that enterprise. Indeed the difference between the amount of intellectual activity found in a school or department and its opposite, trivial teaching, is often the caliber of training and depth of understanding which teachers have in the substance of their teaching areas. But it takes more than quality academic training and depth of understanding to produce an intellectual activity. It takes keen involvement and interaction of students with the knowledge being offered.

Intellectual activity requires the interaction of knowledge with personal qualities which students bring to this knowledge.

No knowledge in itself will affect student behavior over time until that student has discovered the personal meanings for him inherent in that knowledge.

Knowledge begins to have personal meanings to an individual and modifies his intellectual and behavioral outlook as he interacts with that knowledge. Teachers interested in promoting intellectual activity and in affecting student behavior cannot assume that their responsibility ends with excellence in the presentation of knowledge alone, but must further assume responsibility for developing a human context for learning which promotes keen involvement of students.

Human context for learning can be defined by three critical dimensions, motivation, meaning and setting.[8]

 Motivation dimension refers to the extent students are *intrinsically* or *extrinsically* involved in the learning activity.

Meaning refers to the extent students are expected to derive from the learning activity meanings and insights which are *personal,* or which are decided beforehand by the teacher as being *culturally* important.

Setting refers to the pattern of *interpersonal* organization and interaction involved. Are students working as a group, as individuals, or in pairs?

Intrinsic and Extrinsic Motivation

Why someone does something is an important indication of his quality of life and his personal maturity. If one's life consists largely of trying to *become* something or someone striving for success, reaching the next milestone, acquiring the next thing, or getting to the next step, without sufficient attention to being able to enjoy who he is, where is is, and the job of living for its own sake, he may miss the whole point of life. Nor is a sole emphasis on being enough in our interdependent and complex world; too many others are dependent upon what we become. Being and becoming need not conflict, though they often do. Becoming in and of itself, however, represents a shallow view of life.[9]

Being is differentiated from becoming by the end intended. Being behavior or activity seeks no end outside of itself. It is satisfaction intrinsic to the knowledge or activity that is important. Becoming behavior or activity on the other hand is instrumental. The focus is on solving a problem, answering a question or gaining a specific objective in order to obtain some reward external to the problem, question or objective.

Educational words which come close to describing being and becoming are *intrinsic* and *extrinsic.* Is a teacher, for example, motivating students to learn primarily because they will get something from him in return? (Examples would include passing a test, getting a grade, being able to move to the next step in a learning sequence or hierarchy, winning our approval, obtaining more free time, and avoiding homework.) Does he encourage students only to engage in learnings and activities which youngsters find intrinsically meaningful and satisfying? Or, does he attempt a balance between the two motivations for learning?

Personal and Culturally Defined Meanings

Personal meanings are those which students bring to and freely extract from learning encounters. They act as filters through which all learnings are processed. As a result, outcomes from learning encounters are usually different for each student.[10] The outcomes teachers hold for students in a given lesson or as a result of a given learning experience, are examples of specific culturally defined learnings. Generally, schools, communities, nations and societies hold a set of expectations in regard to what knowledge is worth knowing. This knowledge comprises the core of culturally-defined meanings to which the school is obligated to give some attention. It is doubtful, however, if culturally defined meanings can ever be fully understood and appreciated by focusing on them at the expense of personal meanings.

Literature, for example, often becomes an exercise for demonstrating comprehension, understanding structure, or answering prepared questions about what is read. What a particular novel, story or play means to a student, how it affects his values, feelings, thoughts, and behavior tends not to have an important place in the curriculum. The social science report on comparing rural and urban living might be judged on the student's ability to demonstrate acquaintance with economic, sociological, geographical, and ecological facts rather than on his perceptiveness as a human being, on his interpretation of social science principles, or on reminiscence based on spending summers on a relative's farm.

In geology class, the emphasis might be on identifying, testing, classifying, and sorting rocks and minerals. No place exists for the student who is awed by the beauty of rock formations, the complexity of rock samples, or by the metaphysical question about how or why all of this came to be. What a student learns incidentally about navigation may be of little consequence to the teacher who assigns grades on the basis of weekly mastery tests on the more skill-oriented forms of mathematics or computation. Examples abound in all of the instructional areas of the junior and senior high school educational programs.

Combs criticizes the neglect of personal meanings in schools when he states: "In our zeal to be scientific and objective, we have sometimes taught students that personal meanings are things you leave at the schoolhouse door. Sometimes, I fear, in our desire to help people learn, we have said to the . . . student, 'Alice, I am not interested in what you think or what you believe. What are the facts?' As a consequence, we may have taught . . . students that personal meanings have no place in the classroom, which is another way of saying that school is concerned only with things that do not matter! If learning, however, is a discovery of personal meaning, then the facts with which we must be concerned are the beliefs, feelings, understandings, convictions, doubts, fears, likes, and dislikes of the pupil—these personal ways of perceiving himself and the world he lives in."[11]

It is the interaction of gaining new information and discovering personal meaning which results in intellectual activity. As Nyberg argues, learning is a "product of two functions: acquiring information and, more importantly, discovering and developing *personal meaning*. It's the interaction of the two for the learner which results in a behavioral change. Learning=Information+Personal Meaning →Behavioral Change."[12]

A second dimension in defining and mapping the human context for learning is the extent to which personal meanings and culturally defined meanings or combinations of the two are being emphasized. This dimension can be combined with the first so that one learning environment might emphasize personal meanings with intrinsic motivation, another personal meanings with extrinsic motivation, a third culturally-defined meaning with intrinsic motivation, and still another with culturally-defined meanings and extrinsic motivation.

INTERPERSONAL SETTING. Conversation, two individuals working together, one person helping another, expressions of friendship between two people, are among the most natural modes of interpersonal relationships for adults. Indeed growth in these areas is a sign of personal maturity. Further, it is at the center of marriage, of the family, of our social activities, and has become an important part of our work culture. In real life, bridges and cities are built, the air will be cleaned and cancer will be conquered as a result of people working and sharing together in pursuit of these problems. Teamwork has largely replaced the pattern of individuals working alone and indeed in competition with others to solve man's problems. Schools, however, continue their emphasis on learning contexts composed of interpersonal settings which pit one person against another. Conversation, working together, the helping relationship and expressions of friendship seem sometimes at best tolerated and more often frowned upon. Two students enjoying conversation or helping each other with their school work are likely to be admonished for "talking" or for "copying" another's work.[13]

> *Group activities and discussions contribute to the person's ability to relate to others, to share in group goals, and to surrender selfish attitudes and values for the benefit of the group. Sometimes, however, group participation in school activities can be made a fetish. Conversation with another person can usually be carried on at a deeper level than discussion in a group and can lead to the formation of the stronger ties of friendship. And there are times when it is good for the person to be alone, to work alone, to simply get away from all the talk and think things over on his own. This third dimension of human growth can be represented as a continuum moving from individual activity to conversation and activity with a friend to discussion and activity in a group.*

One is tempted to identify the group as the most common interpersonal setting for instruction in junior and senior high schools. Students are indeed grouped in classrooms but more often than not this setting qualifies only as the presence of a physical group. As we have suggested in Chapter 4, physical groups should not be confused with psychological groups or effective work groups. If the class is only a physical group then

293

instruction is probably taking place on a one-to-one basis and the setting—though standard for all students—is actually individual. The teacher lectures to all as one. The teacher asks a question and one person answers. True group settings require a certain climate, group identification, identification with the task at hand, and horizontal patterns of interaction among students. Again, the reader is referred to Chapter 4.

Junior and senior high schools need to arrange learning experiences in each of the three settings—students working alone, working closely with another and functioning as members of effective work groups. Interpersonal setting adds a third dimension to defining the context for learning.

EXAMPLES OF LEARNING CONTEXTS

Motivation, meaning, and interpersonal setting are the concepts which can be used to plan, develop, and evaluate learning contexts. Combination of the three dimensions provides us with a number of contexts, some of which are illustrated graphically in Figure 9–3.

		1	2	3	4	LEAST COMMON 5	6	MOST COMMON 7	8	9	10	etc.
Meaning	Personal (P)			✓	✓	✓	✓			✓		
	Culturally Defined (C)	✓	✓					✓	✓	✓		
Motivation	Intrinsic (IN)	✓	✓			✓	✓			✓		
	Extrinsic (E)			✓	✓			✓	✓	✓		
Interpersonal Setting	Individual (I)		✓	✓		✓		✓		✓		
	Friendship (F)	Permutations using friendship not shown.								✓		
	Group (G)	✓			✓		✓		✓	✓		
LEARNING CONTEXT		1	2	3	4	5	6	7	8	9	10	etc.
		C IN G	C IN I	P E I	P E G	P IN I	P IN G	C E I	C E G			

FIGURE 9-3. EXAMPLES OF LEARNING CONTEXTS

Learning context 1, for example, is characterized by an emphasis on culturally-defined meanings, intrinsic motivation and group setting. Context 2 is similar to context 1 except for interpersonal setting, which is individual.

Our experience suggests that the vast majority (perhaps exceeding 80 percent) of junior and senior high school classroom learning environments can be classified as contexts 7 and 8. Here the emphasis is on culturally-defined meanings, extrinsic motivation, and either individual or group settings. Would this be true of your department and other departments in your school? Contexts 5 and 6 on the other hand, characterized by personal meanings, intrinsic motivation, and either individual or group settings, would be least common. The paired relationship or friendship setting seems virtually outlawed in so many secondary schools that we fail to show it in combination with others in our sample of contexts. The neglect of the friendship setting is indeed an unfortunate circumstance.

All contexts for learning are important and each must be planned for, developed and evaluated. Teacher and chairperson should not completely replace one setting with another but must plan for balance among each.

 Too much emphasis is given in junior and senior high school classrooms to learning contexts 7 and 8, not enough emphasis is given to contexts 5 and 6, and little emphasis is given to the friendship setting.

All of the contexts are important and should be reflected in the implementation of education program but better balance is needed among the contexts.

A sound evaluation program will not ignore the context for learning, as difficult as it may be to pin down. Chairpersons and teachers will need to rely on observation, professional judgments, shared discussion, and consensus agreements as evaluation tools. Attempts should be made to establish hard information where possible (by visiting with students, by observations and conferences among teachers and between teachers and the chairperson) about the kinds of contexts developed and patterns of contexts used in a given classroom or department over a period of time.

ENDNOTES

1. Ralph Tyler, *Basic Principles of Curriculum and Instruction* (Chicago: University of Chicago Press, 1947).

2. Roland Barth, *Open Education and the American School* (New York: Schocken Books, 1974), p. 61.

3. See, for example, Hilda Taba, *Curriculum Development: Theory and Practice* (New York: Harcourt, Brace and World, 1962), and John Goodlad *et al., Curriculum: Decisions and Data Sources* (Waltham, Mass.: Blaisdell Publishing, 1972).

4. See, for example, Decker F. Walker, "A Naturalistic Model for Curriculum Development," *School Review,* Vol. 80, no. 1, 1971, pp. 51–65. Walker proposes a naturalistic model of curriculum as one more realistic than Tyler's linear model. He identifies five components of platform: conceptions, theories, aims, images, and procedures.

5. Chris Argyris and Donald Schon, *Theory in Practice: Increasing Professional Effectiveness* (San Francisco: Jossey-Bass, 1974).

6. Our discussion of each of the classroom types follows that which appears in Thomas J. Sergiovanni, "Human Resources Supervision," T. J. Sergiovanni, ed., *Professional Supervision for Professional Teachers* (Washington, D.C.: ASCD, 1975), and Chapter 5, "Teacher-Student Influence in Instructional Organization," in T. J. Sergiovanni and David Elliott, *Educational and Organizational Leadership in Elementary Schools* (Englewood Cliffs, N.J.: Prentice-Hall, 1975).

7. See our discussion of job enrichment in Chapter 6.

8. This discussion of learning contexts is abbreviated from Starratt's "Design for a Human Curriculum," which is Chapter 13 of Thomas J. Sergiovanni and Robert A. Starratt, *Emerging Patterns of Supervision: Human Perspectives* (New York: McGraw-Hill, 1971). Starratt's discussion is much more extensive and includes a number of examples of different learning contexts in secondary schools.

9. See, for example, Abraham H. Maslow, "Some Basic Propositions of a Growth and Self-Actualization Psychology," in Arthur Combs (ed.), *Perceiving, Behaving, Becoming,* Association for Supervision and Curriculum Development, National Education Association, Washington, D.C., 1962, p. 41.

10. See, for example, James MacDonald, "An Image of Man: The Learner Himself," in Ronald C. Doll (ed.), *Individualizing Instruction,* Association for Supervision and Curriculum Development, National Education Association, Washington, D.C., 1964, p. 39.

11. Arthur W. Combs, "Personality Theory and Its Implications of Curriculum Development," in Alexander Frazier (ed.), *Learning More About Learning,* Association for Supervision and Curriculum Development, National Education Association, Washington, D.C., p. 11.

12. David Nyberg, *Tough and Tender Learning* (New York: National Press Books, 1971), p. 127. See also Arthur Combs, *Educational Accountability Beyond Behavioral Objectives, op. cit.,* p. 39.

13. Sergiovanni and Starratt, *op. cit.,* p. 249.

∛ CHAPTER NINE ∛

∛ PRACTICES ∛

The purpose of this practices section is to help you and the teachers in your department focus on questions of educational program leadership. A number of cases and discussion pieces are included. You can use them to help focus attention and to raise issues. Change in one's perspective regarding educational program is difficult to achieve. Certainly creating awareness is an important early step in the change process. Sections of Chapter 1 dealing with clinical supervision and of Chapter 7 dealing with change provide more specific suggestions beyond the awareness level treated here. Additional practical help in developing an educational platform and in working with objectives are provided in the next chapter. This section contains:

A checklist and suggestions on "How to Focus Staff Attention on Educational Program"
Two case studies, students' views of their lives in school
A discussion of student alienation
A personal-meaning checklist for analyzing classroom activities
A futures forecasting exercise to be used in program planning
"Subject Matter: Stuff to Teach or Stuff to Teach With?"
Providing Leadership in Unit and Lesson Planning

HOW TO FOCUS STAFF ATTENTION ON EDUCATIONAL PROGRAM

Checklist and suggestions

	YES	NO
1. Has your department defined the goals of its educational program? If not:	___	___

   a) carefully review the concepts and practices sections of the next chapter for ideas on how to develop department goals.

   b) have teachers review lesson plans, teaching encounters, homework assignments and evaluation procedures each week to determine what department goals have been attained and the emphasis given to each goal.

2. Has your department developed a set of agreements, a list of worthwhile activities, or similar statements which comprise the department's educational platform? _____ _____

   a) Carefully review the discussion of educational platform which appears in the concepts section of this chapter. Review the sample set of agreements provided in Chapter 11. With this list as an example, find out where you and other department members stand with reference to what you value and what you believe about how students learn, the nature of knowledge, how you should be teaching. Use this discussion as a basis for developing an educational platform for your department.

   b) Have teachers review lesson plans, teaching encounters, homework assignments, discipline procedures and other aspects of classroom activity on a weekly basis to determine consistency with the department's educational platform. See Figure 11–3 for an example of a Teacher's Log which could be kept to record emphasis given in teaching to each platform dimension.

3. Do you have and maintain an educational program resource center for the department? If not: _____ _____

   a) Establish a center in an area easily accessible to department faculty. Remember that the closer the center is to teachers the more likely it is to be used. School-wide centers are not as effective as department centers, and district-wide centers are generally not used extensively by teachers.

   b) Stock the resource center with periodicals, reference books, and other professional materials. Only thought-provoking materials of high quality should be included, but remember that the materials should also be readable and practical. Locate teaching aids, simulation materials, films and records in the center. Include with these materials an envelope which contains information on who used the materials and when, and a brief comment or two on how useful the materials were found to be. The next potential user then can check with other users if he or she requires further information.

   c) Establish a set of files in the resource center where unit outlines, teacher plans, tests, assignments, ditto sheets, and other teaching materials developed and used by faculty are deposited. Teachers should indicate on these materials objectives sought and link to the department's educational platform, how the materials were used, and reactions of students to the materials.

   d) Either as part of c) above or separately, establish a file of units taught in each of the courses and programs of the department. Specific tips, ideas, articles and other materials appropriate to each of these units of study could be deposited in the file by teachers, and perhaps even by students, as they are discovered.

4. Do you duplicate and circulate articles and other materials you discover which might be of interest to a particular person in the department as a whole? If not:

   a) Begin circulating materials selectively. Be sure that materials you circulate are important, readable and likely to be applicable to the teacher's work.

   b) Occasionally circulate materials or articles which are intended to create awareness, to evoke an unsettling feeling and to stimulate critical thinking about the events programs and activities of the department. Try circulating the cases provided in this section, for example. Be careful not to overuse these materials. You do not want to sermonize nor do you want to be arbitrarily critical. All you want to do is create awareness, and stimulate thought.

   c) Send copies of your materials regularly to other department chairpersons and ask them to respond similarly.

   d) Summarize or outline articles you circulate, or use a marker for highlighting important passages. Teachers are busy and efforts to summarize increase the likelihood that materials will get attention.

5. Do you keep a record of conferences attended and provide a systematic means of sharing ideas learned from conferences? If not:

   a) Keep a record in the resource center of who attended what conference, when, where, and of conference themes or programs.

   b) Ask those attending conferences to prepare a brief summary of conference events and a short evaluation statement.

   c) Provide an opportunity during department meetings for sharing conference experiences.

6. Are instructional materials and teaching aids selected cooperatively with teachers and with reference to the department's goals and educational platform? If not:

   a) Circulate catalogues and get suggestions from teachers as to what might be ordered as a general addition to the resource center or for a particular class use.

   b) Have teachers specify how such materials might be used to meet department goals, educational platform specifications.

7. Do department members exchange ideas concerning curriculum and teaching on a regular basis and do they help each other with teaching problems they face? If not:

   a) Provide time in department meetings; for teachers, in rotation, to describe what they are presently working on in class, to share successes and to discuss problems.

   b) Arrange for each teacher to spend some time each month (perhaps a half day) in the classroom of another teacher working as an assistant. If substitutes cannot be arranged to cover classes of visiting assistants, take the class yourself or combine the class with that of another teacher not involved at the moment in visitation. If large group instruction at that time is not educationally sound—use these large group settings to get student evaluations of the department's program.

CASE STUDIES

Each of these case studies is critical of the present structure and functioning of secondary school classrooms. The cases are provided as examples of materials which chairpersons can use to help teachers critically examine classroom and department functioning. Both cases describe the reactions of junior high students to their schools. The case of Patty Wirth as told in "My Views of School" is real. These are the words of a thirteen-year-old, eighth-grader describing her views of life in a midwest suburban junior high school. The case of the poor scholar was written by an adult who used this method to raise serious questions about the relationship between educational programs and student needs and interests.

Case 1 My Views of School*

First of all, to look at me you'd never think I would write anything protesting anything. I look and am middle-class, sheltered, etc., etc., etc. But the main reason I think I am (was?) so oblivious of big issues is because of schools. I am in seventh grade, go to an ultra-"good," modern, junior high school in the suburbs. The teachers there, and the ones at the last year of elementary school, talk about how sad it is that kids today don't have any consciousness of people in the inner city living in slums—but as I said before, it's mostly because of the teachers that I am that way. Not once in school have I had any discussions concerning the draft, Black Panthers, or any controversial issue. Excepting, of course, the stuff I had on drugs—but then I had no opinion to express whatsoever.

I don't have an opinion on anything. I'm being more and more controlled, and I'm not learning anything. I remember a feeling I had in the first grade—like a sponge soaking up knowledge that I'd always be able to use: reading, writing, etc. I haven't had that feeling once this year. It's just taking down what the teacher says, memorizing it, taking the test—and promptly forgetting everything. I'm not getting any impressions, experiences, I'm not interested. For example, sometimes when we are reading page 307 in class I feel like jumping up and saying, "Who is really interested in this? Who thinks this is fascinating?"

I "learn" stuff, how to write morpheme strings, how to conjugate Spanish verbs, but will I ever use these when I'm older? There is a pattern: I learn morpheme strings, not necessarily because they'll help later in life, but because how else could I pass to eighth grade? In eighth grade I'll "learn" equally useless stuff so I'll pass to ninth grade, tenth grade, eleventh grade—if I can just make it to

*This case is excerpted from Patty Wirth, "My Ideal School Wouldn't Be a School," *Teachers College Record*, Vol. 72, No. 1, 1970, pp. 57–59.

college! In college I'll study so I can get some well-paying job, marry some clean-cut guy, and settle down in a house in the suburbs. And anyone who breaks the pattern is looked down upon and given a weird name like—hippie.

I'm getting in a rut, and I'm not having any new experiences. And if I would say this to a teacher, he would probably smile gently, cross his arms, and say, "I understand your point, but I'm sorry, you're wrong." Or, "But if you don't get an education. . ." and the unspoken part of the sentence is, "You won't be like us."

Everything is narrowing down. In first grade we were encouraged to write stories and read them to the class, and we continued to be encouraged through fourth grade. Then in fifth grade there wasn't really enough time for that, it became less important, and there was more textbook material, more homework. In sixth grade we were introduced to the facts that one-sentence paragraphs were out, and all paragraphs should be about the same length. (God!) But I was saved by "creative writing" where I could still express myself without fear of making (horrors!) a grammatical error. Now in seventh grade the creativity has been dropped out almost entirely. Several people I know who have finished school say that subjects they really liked before junior high, high school, etc., they hated after their "education" because they weren't free to expand on their ideas.

Another thing which I think is wrong with my (the?) school(s) is the textbooks. We have to cover the material we have to cover the material we have to cover the material! I carry a mental picture around of one of my teachers pulling my class through a waist-deep ocean of mud—which in reality is pp. 327–331, Nos. 1–5—saying "Onward, children! We must make it by Tuesday!"

Another example of this: One of my teachers saying to us, "C'mon, if we can just get through these last two pages, I'll let you do something fun for the rest of the period." And then there is the teacher who says, "Good afternoon, class. Open your books and turn to page sixty-six. John, would you care to read for us?" Am I learning anything from that?

I mentioned before the lack of discussions. I have never had one discussion in which I was really involved. There is no free exchange, no real communicating. It's just to have the teacher say, "And what do you think?" We all obediently raise our hands. "Johnnie?" And the kid meekly states his answer which is always right or wrong, never just an opinion.

The kids in the schools are one big inconspicuous blob. On the first day of school our principal warned us, "Don't dress in clothes that attract unusual attention or that are conspicuous in any way." And that's the whole thing. Fit into the pattern, the Establishment, or you'll be an outcast, you'll be looked down upon.

Maybe I seem really hostile. But maybe that's because I am. I disagree so completely with everything the school says, and yet I can't disagree. If I would mutter "Oh, Jesus!" when the teacher mentioned hippies, pot, or campuses, there would be a shocked silence; and the teacher would proceed to bawl me out.

I don't want to be controlled. I can feel myself being squashed. Very few of my teachers ever seem to say anything spontaneously. The ground we will cover has already been mapped out. I can't really break away though. Cute clothes and money are too important to me. But I really don't want to be the middle-class-y type of person. I'm kind of two people right now and I don't like being that way. But the reason I have this big conflict is mainly because of the schools.

DISCUSSION. Melvin Seeman in his classic article "On the Meaning of Alienation" identifies five critical components which characterize alienation. Cast in reference to students in schools, they are as follows:

Powerlessness. The students' perception that he is not able to determine or control events which affect him in the school.

Meaninglessness. The students' perception that what he is asked or required to do in school does not relate to future outcomes he sees as important.

Misfeasance. A feeling which a student has that the only way to get ahead in school or to beat the system is through some improper activity such as manipulation, deceit, trickery, or cheating.

Futility. The student has a low regard for the goals, activities, or behaviors valued and championed by the school and its staff.

Self-Estrangement. The student participates in school activities primarily in exchange for extrinsic or materialistic rewards (grades, favored assignments, good recommendations for college, to make the team) rather than rewards derived from the act of participation itself (intellectual excitement, personal satisfaction, fun).

Teachers and students are interdependent participants in the educational enterprise. They need each other. If one "cops out" or "turns off," the other can't get the job done.

You are likely to find that most teachers in your department are interested in their work and want to provide students with rich intellectual experiences. Further, they want youngsters to grow in human qualities—in their ability to accept responsibility, to share with others. Students have the potential to be eager learners and bring with them past experiences, insights, feelings and knowledge. But the intents of teachers and potential of youngsters are not likely to be realized unless students (and teachers too—see, for example Chapter 6) have some stake in what is going on, some control over decisions which affect them, and some identity with school goals. Having a stake in the educational enterprise can begin in your department when teachers help students to become more active shareholders in classroom and department activities.

Does considering a student a shareholder mean giving him equal power over what will be taught, by whom, and when? No. It is not realistic to assume that students will be equal or majority shareholders but they should be accorded reasonable influence in classroom activities and department affairs.*

Patty Wirth's views may well be extreme but to what extent would they be shared by students taking courses and programs in your department?

Do you and other teachers in your department collect reactions to teaching from students on a regular basis?

Are these reactions shared and discussed with students?

Case 2 *The Poor Scholar's Soliloquy†*

No I'm not very good in school. This is my second year in the seventh grade and I'm bigger and taller than the other kids. They like me all right, though, even if I

---

*Some suggestions as to how to involve students can be found in Chapters 4 and 6 (Motivational Activities, and Providing for Individual Differences) of Kenneth Hoover's *The Professional Teacher's Handbook: A Guide for Improving Instruction in Today's Middle and Secondary Schools,* 2nd ed. (Boston: Allyn and Bacon, Inc. 1976).

†Stephen M. Corey, "The Poor Scholar's Soliloquy," *Childhood Education,* Vol. 20, No. 1, 1944, pp. 219-20.

don't say much in the schoolroom, because outside I can tell them how to do a lot of things. They tag me around and that sort of makes up for what goes on in school.

I don't know why the teachers don't like me. They never have very much. Seems like they don't think you know anything unless they can name the book it comes out of. I've got a lot of books in my own room at home—books like Popular Science Mechanical Encyclopedia, *and the Sears' and Ward's catalogues, but I don't very often just sit down and read them through like they make us do in school. I use my books when I want to find something out, like whenever Mom buys anything secondhand I look it up in Sears' or Ward's first and tell her if she's getting stung or not. I can use the index in a hurry to find the things I want.*

In school, though, we've got to learn whatever is in the book and I just can't memorize the stuff. Last year I stayed after school every night for two weeks trying to learn the names of the Presidents. Of course I knew some of them like Washington and Jefferson and Lincoln, but there must have been thirty altogether and I never did get them straight.

I'm not too sorry though because the kids who learned the Presidents had to turn right around and learn all the Vice Presidents. I am taking the seventh grade over but our teacher this year isn't so interested in the names of the Presidents. She has us trying to learn the names of all the great American inventors.

KIDS SEEMED INTERESTED

I guess I just can't remember names in history. Anyway, this year I've been trying to learn about trucks because my uncle owns three and he says I can drive one when I'm sixteen. I already know the horsepower and number of forward and backward speeds of twenty-six American trucks, some of them Diesels, and I can spot each make a long way off. It's funny how that Diesel works. I started to tell my teacher about it last Wednesday in science class when the pump we were using to make a vacuum in a bell jar got hot, but she said she didn't see what a Diesel engine had to do with our experiment on air pressure so I just kept still. The kids seemed interested though. I took four of them around to my uncle's garage after school and we saw the mechanic, Gus, tearing a big truck Diesel down. Boy, does he know his stuff!

I'm not very good in geography either. They call it economic geography this year. We've been studying the imports and exports of Chile all week but I couldn't tell you what they are. Maybe the reason is I had to miss school yesterday because my uncle took me and his big trailer truck down state about two hundred miles and we brought almost ten tons of stock to the Chicago market.

He had told me where we were going and I had to figure out the highways to take and also the mileage. He didn't do anything but drive and turn where I told him to. Was that fun! I sat with a map in my lap and told him to turn south or southeast or some other direction. We made seven stops and drove over five hundred miles round trip. I'm figuring now what his oil cost and also the wear and tear on the truck—he calls it depreciation—so we'll know how much we made.

I even write out all the bills and send letters to the farmers about what their pigs and beef cattle brought at the stockyards. I only made three mistakes in 17 letters last time, my aunt said—all commas. She's been through high school and reads them over. I wish I could write school themes that way. The last one I had to write was on, "What a Daffodil Thinks of Spring," and I just couldn't get going.

I don't do very well in school in arithmetic either. Seems I just can't keep my mind on the problems. We had one the other day like this:

If a 57 foot telephone pole falls across a cement highway so that 17 3/6 feet extend from one side and 14 9/17 feet from the other, how wide is the highway?

That seemed to me like an awfully silly way to get the width of a highway. I didn't even try to answer it because it didn't say whether the pole had fallen straight across or not.

NOT GETTING ANY YOUNGER

Even in shop I don't get very good grades. All of us kids made a broom holder and a bookend this term and mine were sloppy. I just couldn't get interested. Mom doesn't use a broom anymore with her new vacuum cleaner and all our books are in a book case with glass doors in the parlor. Anyway, I wanted to make an end gate for my uncle's trailer but the shop teacher said that meant using metal and wood both and I'd have to learn how to work with wood first. I didn't see why but I kept still and made a tie rack at school and the tail gate after school at my uncle's garage. He said I saved him $10.

Civics is hard for me, too. I've been staying after school trying to learn the "Articles of Confederation" for almost a week because the teacher said we couldn't be good citizens unless we did. I really tried, because I want to be a good citizen. I did hate to stay after school, though, because a bunch of us boys from the south end of town have been cleaning up the old lot across from Taylor's Machine Shop to make a playground out of it for the little kids from the Methodist home. I made the jungle gym from old pipe and the guys made me Grand Mogul to keep the playground going. We raised enough money collecting scrap this month to build a wire fence clear around the lot.

Dad says I can quit school when I'm fifteen and I'm sort of anxious to because there are a lot of things I want to learn how to do and as my uncle says, I'm not getting any younger.

Student Alienation

This is the story about a young man in seventh grade who doesn't fit the curriculum he is expected to follow but who is likely to be a success in any event. Who should decide what is worth learning? Are the "things" that the "poor scholar" is learning of less value than the "things" that comprise the curriculum? This is admittedly a difficult question which cannot be answered by taking sides. What the schools see as important, the culturally-defined meanings in the language of the concepts section of this chapter, are often valid and useful. But youngsters, too, bring to school rich personal meanings which need to be recognized and appreciated. Further, it is often through these personal meanings that the knowledgable teacher is able to achieve his objectives.

Have each teacher in the department keep track of the extent to which he emphasizes personal and culturally-defined meanings for a week. Use the checklist provided. Summarize teacher responses to the checklist and use them as a basis for department discussions. Remember to brief them beforehand on the differences between personal and culturally-defined meanings. Duplicate parts of the concepts section of this chapter if that will help. Passing out copies of "The Poor Scholar's Soliloquy" case will also help. Assure teachers that they are not being evaluated in a summative sense.

In discussing checklist responses, pay particular attention to the nature of the educational activity in question. In the example given, the activity for 3/16, Planning a Field Trip, seems much more suitable for emphasizing student meanings than the activity for 3/15, Defining Terms. Look for patterns over a period of time. That is, to what extent are student meanings emphasized over fifteen classes?

Personal Meaning Checklist

To what extent did my goals, questions, assignments and evaluation emphasize learnings and meanings judged important by me, the text, or the curriculum, as opposed to learnings and meanings judged important by students?

Directions: For each category of classroom activity estimate the *percentage* of concern exhibited for personal (student) meanings and for culturally defined (teacher) meanings.

Date		3/14	3/15	3/16	3/17
Class		Sc. 10	Sc. 10	Sc. 10	
Activity		Rock Testing	Defining Terms	Planning Field Trip	
My goals and plans	Student	15%	0%	70%	
	Teacher	85	100	30	
Questions I asked	Student	0	5	50	
	Teacher	100	95	50	
Assignments I gave	Student	100	0	60	
	Teacher	90	100	40	
My evaluation emphasis	Student	15	5	60	
	Teacher	85	95	40	
Teacher Meanings		40/360	10/380	240/160	
Totals in percent		89%	98%	66%	

THE FUTURE AS A BASIS FOR PROGRAM PLANNING

An accepted purpose of education is to prepare students for adult roles in our society. Certainly many aspects of schooling can and should be justified on the basis of their intrinsic value to individuals, but an important task for the schools is preparing tomorrow's adults, able to function in and improve our society. Educators have become increasingly interested in predicting the future as a means for planning better educational programs. Futures research has become widely used by policymakers at all levels of government and public service as well as in business. A number of public and private agencies, states in the United States, and Provinces in Canada have developed forecasts of alternative futures and implications of these forecasts for educational planning.

A Choice of Futures

Forecasts of futures are developed after a careful and systematic study of social structures and social problems (marriage, religion, work, family health care, race relations, mental illness, crime, drug use), value systems (ascending and declining), population trends, economic development, and technology. These forces are studied and implications of the forces are predicated on individuals, society, and the organizations and institutions which comprise that society. An example of such a forecast with implications appears below. The forecast assumes that we (North Americans in general and Albertans in particular) are presently ending the first phase of an industrialized society. Two alternative futures are forecast: a Second-Phase Industrial Society and a Person-Centered Society. We do not have complete control over the future but most forecasters assume that man can indeed shape aspects of his future. For educators engaged in program planning, forecasts of alternative futures suggest demands which society will make and purposes for the schools as we prepare people for society; and they suggest ways in which our present plans and activities can affect the future.

What Future for Your Department?

Examine each of the characteristics and implications contained in the two forecasts provided below. Do you line up clearly in favor of one forecast or the other? Would the choices you make depend upon the particular characteristic in question?

Share "A Choice of Futures" with members of your department. Using the "What Future for Our Department?" checklist, ask teachers to indicate futures they personally favor and characteristics of futures they believe are reflected in their teaching and in the department's programs. What agreement and disagreement exists among members of the department? Do department goals, educational platform dimensions, and classroom activities coincide with these agreements? If you do not have agreement on department goals and educational platform, use this discussion as a basis for starting this important task.
Share your thoughts about alternative futures with other department chairpersons.

A CHOICE OF FUTURES

TWO ALTERNATIVE FUTURES; THEIR CHARACTERISTICS AND IMPLICATIONS

FEATURES	CHARACTERISTICS	
	SECOND-PHASE INDUSTRIAL SOCIETY	PERSON-CENTERED SOCIETY
1. Central Values and Goals	Dominance of economic values which lead to goals such as continuing expansion of goods, increased consumption which subordinates individual needs to the requirements of industry and technology	Dominance of person-centered values which emphasize the goals of individual fulfillment and subordination of industrial system to human needs
2. Economic Activity	High level of economic growth — distribution of goods and services based on price system	High level of economic growth — distribution based on human needs and provision of economic security
3. Technology	High level of technology which is used to further requirements of industry	High level of technology which is influenced and directed by human and global needs
4. Decision-Making Structures	Concentration of power in a highly professional and intellectual elite which form a network linking all major agencies and organizations in society	Emphasis on participation with more sharing of power and decision-making among different levels in society
5. Work and Leisure	Maintenance of the distinction between work and leisure with more leisure for all except those in important technical and managerial positions	More leisure time and a blurring of distinctions between work. leisure, and education
6. Education	Continued segregation of the education system from the mainstream of society	Centrality of education in society as it becomes a lifelong process and as the occupation of the student becomes a valid one
	Strong reliance on behavior control and behavior-shaping approaches to education	Utilization of new approaches to education which emphasize the development of self-learning skills in the person and creation of conditions which foster spontaneous learning
	Acquisition of specific vocational skills, continuation of the importance of grading and provision of credentials	More diversity in educational pursuits together with less emphasis on grading, credentials
7. Social Problems	Continuation of current problems of alienation, social unrest and conflict between groups in society	Increased efforts to solve social problems and greater response to human needs will lead to a decrease in social problems
8. Law Enforcement	Increased control over overt expressions of social unrest and conflict accompanied by widespread resistance to law enforcement in society.	More equal and humane treatment of citizens by law enforcement agencies will help decrease social tensions.
9. The Individual		
Governing values	Self-control and self-discipline Self-advancement	Self-discovery and self-expression Service to others

From *A Choice of Futures.* Report of the Commission on Educational Planning (Alberta, Canada: Department of Education, Edmonton, 1972), pp. 31 and 32.

| FOUNDATIONS | IMPLICATIONS | |
	SECOND-PHASE INDUSTRIAL SOCIETY	PERSON-CENTERED SOCIETY
	Conformity	Individualism
	Puritanism	Sensualism
	Emphasis on narrow interests	Emphasis on wide interests
	Endurance of stress	Capacity for joy
Life goals	Acquirement	Self-fulfillment
10. Society		
Values underlying the structure of society	Hierarchical structure and authoritarian relationships	Flexible structures that promote equal relationships
	Work orientation	Leisure orientation
	Independence	Interdependence
Values governing the conduct of activity	Competition	Cooperation
	Education for work	Education for living
	Authoritarian decision-making	Participation-involvement
Values governing the external relations of society	Parochialism	Global village concept
Dominant goals	Economic and technological advance	Humanism, fulfillment of the individual
Time perspective	Tradition oriented	Future-oriented experimentation
11. Formal Organizations		
Goals	Separate	Linked
Values underlying organizational structure	Bureaucratic forms	Flexible forms
Values governing organizational relations	Competitive relations	Collaborative relations
Organizational strategies	Responsive to crisis	Anticipative of crisis
	Specific measures	Comprehensive measures
	Requiring consent	Requiring participation
	Short planning horizon	Long planning horizon
	Standardized administration	Innovative administration
	Separate services	Coordinated services
Values regarding resources	Resources regarded as owned exclusively	Resources regarded also as belonging to society

WHAT FUTURE FOR OUR DEPARTMENT?

CHARACTER- ISTICS AND IMPLICATIONS	THIS IS THE FUTURE I PERSONALLY FAVOR			THIS IS THE FUTURE OUR EDUCATIONAL PROGRAM EMPHASIZES			MY TEACHING PREPARES STUDENTS FOR THIS FUTURE		
	INDUS- TRIAL II	PERSON	COMBI- NATION	INDUS- TRIAL II	PERSON	COMBI- NATION	INDUS- TRIAL II	PERSON	COMBI- NATION
1. Central Values and Goals									
2. Econom- ic Activ- ity									
3. Technol- ogy									
4. Decision- Making									
5. Work and Leisure									
6. Educa- tion									
7. Social Prob- lems									
8. Law En- force- ment									
9. Individ- ual									
10. Society									
11. Formal Organiza- tion									
Total									

Subject Matter: Stuff to Teach or Stuff to Teach With?

Department chairperson, cabinet and curriculum council meetings getting you down? Liven one up by circulating the statement below.* Ask each chairperson or other committee member to bring a portfolio containing the *last* test or quiz given by each teacher in their department. Examine the tests to determine if the emphasis is on subject matter as stuff to teach or stuff to teach with. Try the same thing in your own department meetings or on an Institute day. Use weekly plan books as well as classroom tests. See Chapter 12, Supervision and Evaluation of Teachers, especially the section on clinical supervision for additional help in using this technique.

> *There are always two views of subject matter that we include in the curriculum. The common one is that content is stuff to teach, to "put across." If you have this view, then you ask yourself a perfectly reasonable question: "What is the best content?" Or, if you want to get fancier, you adopt a pretentious tone and ask the fancier version, "What knowledge is of most worth?" Then, when you've decided what to teach, you mobilize technique to put it across; and then you test to see whether you did put it across (and you do the testing as quickly as you can, before the students forget it, because down in your heart you know they're going to forget it).*
> *Now the second view is that content is chiefly stuff to teach* with, *not just stuff to teach. If that's your view then you decide on some fundamental purposes you want to achieve. Then you start scouting around to pick out some content and experiences that look as if they might (with some kids anyway) produce that kind of side effect; and you choose your methodology that way, too, with one eye always on the long-run effects.* *

Providing Leadership in Unit and Lesson Planning

How can the chairperson keep the curriculum, through its texts and other teaching materials, from literally taking over major decision-making about what is learned and how instruction will take place? How can the chairperson guard against the teacher shifting from a professional educational decision-maker to a mere follower of directions or implementer of decisions made by textbook writers? These issues were discussed with reference to ultra-rational curriculum models and to patterns of influence in classrooms. It was pointed out, for example, that in many junior and senior high school classrooms teachers tend to function mechanically as they implement a curriculum with which they have little identity. Teachers must be active in classroom decision-making; one way in which their influence can increase is through proper planning of units and lessons.

"Helping Teachers Plan Units and Lessons," is excerpted from Hoover's handbook for secondary school teachers. Use the materials as a basis for discussion with the department faculty and as a general model for their development of unit and lesson plans.

*Fred T. Wilhelms, "Design of the Curriculum," in J. Galen Saylor and Joshua L. Smith, eds., *Removing Barriers to Humaneness in the High School* (Washington, D.C.: Association for Supervision and Curriculum Development), 1971.

HELPING TEACHERS PLAN UNITS AND LESSONS*

Planning, like map making, enables one to predict the future course of events. In essence, a plan is a blueprint—a plan of action. As any traveler knows, the best-laid plans sometimes go awry. Sometimes unforeseen circumstances even prevent one from beginning a well-planned journey; other times, conditions while on the trip may cause one to alter his plans drastically. More often, however, a well-planned journey is altered in *minor* ways for those unpredictable "side trips" which may seem desirable from close range.

Likewise, teachers must plan classroom experiences. They must plan the scope and sequence of courses, the content within courses, the units to be taught, the activities to be employed, and the tests to be given. While few teachers would deny the necessity of planning, there is some controversy with respect to the scope and nature of planning. Indeed, methods specialists themselves differ relative to the essential scope of planning. Some seem to feel that unit planning renders lesson planning almost unnecessary. Others stress the importance of lesson plans while minimizing the value of unit plans. While the planning needs of teachers will vary markedly, there is considerable justification for *both* unit and lesson planning.

THE YEARLY PLAN

The process of planning begins when a teacher sets out to determine what major ideas or dimensions will be emphasized during the year. All available textbooks in the area, curriculum guides, and course-of-study aids should be surveyed for this purpose. Although each teacher often prepares his own yearly plan, increased emphasis is being given to joint participation by all members of a department. This promotes appropriate integration of related courses and enables teachers of the same course to develop desirable commonalities. At the same time it leaves each instructor free to develop various aspects of the course in his own way.

Oddly enough, some teachers have limited their preparation for yearly planning to a single selected textbook. Such a practice, in effect, makes both teacher and students slaves to a single frame of reference. Textbook units, chapters and topics, accordingly, are studied in a chapter-by-chapter and page-by-page manner. It must be emphasized that a textbook, at its best, merely provides all learners with one comprehensive source of information. Since textbooks are designed to fulfill the needs of as many people as possible, they usually contain some materials which will be of marginal value to individual instructors. As each textbook writer tends to emphasize certain aspects over others, it behooves the teacher to survey as many such sources as possible for the purpose of ascertaining what aspects *he* will emphasize.

How Are Major Course Concepts Identified?

Concepts exist at different levels. The most abstract level, for instructional purposes, is identification of several broad ideas (concepts) which should be developed during the course. At this point they will be broad and suggestive only. There may be as many as a dozen of these. It is usually desirable to state them as complete thoughts. To illustrate from a course in general business:

1. Production standards in the United States make this nation the distribution center of the world.
2. Retail markets in the United States are consumer-oriented.

*From Kenneth H. Hoover, *The Professional Teacher's Handbook: A Guide for Improving Instruction in Today's Middle and Secondary Schools,* 2nd ed. (Boston: Allyn and Bacon, Inc., 1976), pp. I-34–46.

3. Selling is a joint process of communication between buyer and seller.

After several tentative course concepts have been stated, they are revised and reworked until six or eight basic ideas remain. (Some teachers prefer to incorporate course concepts into course objectives. This step is not essential, however.)

Frequently a need for two or more units may be developed from a single major concept. This suggests the need for more specific concepts. Eventually there usually will be a unit for each major concept. Appropriate unit titles, based upon the illustrated concepts in a general business course, follow:

1. The United States: Distribution Center of the World
2. The Consumer Determines the Market
3. Sales Promotion and Advertising

After major unit titles have been tentatively established, an approximate time schedule for each unit is established. This will reflect relative degrees of emphasis to be given to each unit. It may be that time limitations will necessitate basic changes. Sometimes certain proposed units must be deleted. Units are seldom less than three or more than six weeks long.

How Are Major Course Purposes Developed with Students?

After major units have been selected, the teacher is in a position to develop for students an overview of the major aspects of the course. Purpose of this experience is to give students an opportunity to develop a series of expectations relative to the course. Basic purposes, at their level of understanding, are offered. Students, in turn, are provided an opportunity to ask questions and to offer suggestions. The effect of such an experience is that of creating initial interest in the experiences which are to follow.

Such an introductory statement may be handled as a lecture-discussion experience. With a little added imagination, however, an atmosphere of eager anticipation may be established. Almost any instructional method or technique may be a useful means of attracting students to the particular course of study. There is an abundance of instructional media available for such purposes.

At least one class period should be devoted to this activity. A course introduction can be found in the unit plan that follows at the end of this section.

THE TEACHING UNIT

The teaching unit is designed to center the work of the class around meaningful wholes or patterns and to make the work of different days focus on a central theme until some degree of unified learning is attained. *The basic elements of a teaching unit consist of a group of related concepts, unified for instructional purposes.*

The process is essentially one of combining related ideas into some intellectual pattern. It provides opportunities for critical thinking, generalization and application of ideas to many situations.

Unit titles, as illustrated in the yearly plan, do not usually correspond to textbook units. In order to make instruction attractive to boys and girls, a teaching unit most appropriately focuses upon a central, practical idea or theme. Although some English teachers would attempt to structure a unit around Julius Caesar, for example, youngsters would likely be more attracted to a unit dealing with "ambition." Such a unit, of course, would focus upon Julius Caesar as an avenue to realizing the major objectives.* Instead of

*John B. Chase, Jr., and James L. Howard, "Changing Concepts of Unit Teaching," *The High School Journal* 47, no. 4 (February, 1964): 180-7.

studying evolution, a science teacher might construct a unit around the concept of "change." The idea of evolution would become one dimension of a much more comprehensive theme. Such a unit concept approaches what Jerome Bruner has termed the basic structure of knowledge.*

Implicit in unit planning are three different phases: initiating activities, developing activities, culminating activities. The first phase of unit planning is similar to the steps in yearly planning. Unit planning is necessarily more restricted and specific than the latter. In all cases, however, the process must be consistent with, and fit into, the overall framework established in the yearly plan.

What Purpose Does the Content Outline Serve?

As an aid in developing a series of cohesive experiences, a content outline of each unit should be developed. Various aspects of the unit can be readily developed if basic content is clearly delineated in either detailed or topical fashion. Basic textbooks serve a most useful purpose in this phase of unit planning.

The content outline must be detailed enough to indicate points of emphasis, yet brief enough to be useful in the derivation of major unit concepts. The content outline which appears in the illustrated unit is rather brief. In a subject such as history or political science a more elaborate outline would be appropriate.

How Are Major Unit Concepts Identified?

Using the unit outline as a broad frame of reference, the teacher develops from six to ten unit concepts. They are most appropriately expressed as complete thoughts. In essence, they are to become the structural foundations of the unit. If properly developed, concepts have high retention and transfer value. Although based upon content, they must possess generalizability. *Thus they are most appropriately phrased as generalizations suggesting current life applications.*

The illustration which follows is based upon a unit in general business, Sales Promotion and Advertising.

1. Customer satisfaction is the most important product.
2. Customer needs are the prompters for purchasing decisions.
3. Advertising can be an effective means of preselling products.

In many subject areas it is relatively easy to meet the criterion of current life application. In a few subject areas, however, this is a rather complicated, but nevertheless essential, task. In history, for example, a two-step process seems necessary. First, one must identify the major ideas of the unit; then he must expand them into generalizations that are viable today. Without the second step, history teaching is likely to remain the dry and generally useless process of memorizing names, dates, and places.

To illustrate from a unit in United States history on World War I (*To Make the World Safe for Democracy*):

1. *Major unit idea*—Wilson's mistakes due to the peace treaty caused his unpopularity at home.
2. *Major unit concept*—Ill-advised public expression (e.g., riots, etc., against Wilson) can adversely affect statesmanship.

It is seen from the foregoing that each major unit concept is derived from an idea which is specific to a given era of history. Many of the concepts will occur again and again

---

*Jerome Bruner, *The Process of Education* (Cambridge, Mass.: Harvard University Press, 1961), pp. 17–18.

as the student studies other history units. In this way the learner can become aware of the repetition of diplomatic errors. New concepts, of course, also will be emphasized in each subsequent unit.

In other subject fields the task of concept identification is often complicated by textbook organization. In American literature, for example, textbook content may be organized around the broad themes of literary forms, historical themes, and the like. A historical theme on colonial America, for example, offers the reader numerous selections, each with its own story theme. The teacher's task, again, is two-fold in nature. First, he must identify major unit concepts (e.g., major threads of thought which occur repeatedly); then he must identify the particular selections which can be used in teaching each given concept.

How Are Instructional Goals and Behavioral Outcomes Derived from Unit Concepts?

Based upon unit concepts, appropriate unit goals with their accompanying outcomes are developed. Unit goals provide a necessary transition from what the teacher views as the ends of instruction to statements of pupil behaviors necessary for and indicative of the desired learnings. Frequently each unit goal will embody a different unit concept, but sometimes two or more *may* be embodied within a single goal. Indeed there are usually more concepts than goals.

Instructional outcomes may apply to *minimum essentials objectives,* or they may be applied to *developmental objectives*. If they are of the minimum essentials variety, the specific conditions and expected level of performance must be specified. If, however, outcomes are developmental in nature, this degree of specificity is not appropriate. In academic courses the latter is emphasized. Accordingly, the illustration which follows is *developmental* in nature.

Concept: Customer needs are the prompters for purchasing decisions.

Instructional Goal and Accompanying Behavioral Outcomes: After this unit the student
  should have furthered his understanding of the role of basic human motives and
  wants in selling, as evidenced by:
  A. His ability to apply appropriate psychological principles in simulation games.
  B. His interpretation of sales resistance evident in sociodrama.

It should be noted that the named behavioral outcomes are complex, calling for a whole *class* of responses. They do suggest, however, specific methods and techniques which would represent appropriate *means* of goal achievement. Lesson outcomes are much more specific than unit outcomes.

How Are Learning Experiences Evolved from Anticipated Behavioral Outcomes?

As indicated in the foregoing, each behavioral outcome suggests one or more methods or techniques which will contribute to goal achievement. Both a simulation game and a sociodrama were suggested in the illustration. At this point the teacher identifies the specific methods problems to be developed. To illustrate:

1. *Simulation Game:* "People, U.S.A."
2. *Sociodrama*
    Problem: How does a customer feel when he is pressured into buying a
      product?
    Broad Situation: Mary wants to buy a gift for her husband's birthday. Jim is
      a salesman in a department store.

The act of preplanning some of the activities does not mean that the teacher must assume the role of taskmaster. Students may actively participate in the planning of class activities, but this does not replace the need for a certain number of preplanned activities *suggested* by the teacher. As in the sample unit, different pupils often will be involved in different activities; thus provision for individual differences may become a reality. For beginning teachers it may be necessary to make a special point of this in the unit plan.

How Is Goal Achievement Assessed?

Although unit evaluation is not a preinstructional activity, it is foreshadowed during preinstructional planning. Indeed, a unit plan may be rendered ineffective if students anticipate being asked to recall specific facts while the teacher focuses his planning around specific unit concepts. Measurement and evaluation must be consistent with unit goals and anticipated behavioral outcomes. As indicated in the previous chapter, behaviors which are appropriate as learning activities are usually not adequate for evaluating learning. They do provide sound bases, however, for development of the needed evaluational experiences. For example, the case analysis activity (cited as one of the learning activities) should help students identify pertinent facts, feelings, and relationships associated with selling. Thus test items based on another case might well be utilized for these purposes.

Essentially, activities of the unit are designed to provide *practice* essential to achievement of identified behavioral outcomes. This practice will tend to be *identical* to terminal assessment experiences when minimum essentials objectives are involved (e.g., a minimum level of typing). When developmental objectives are involved, the unit experiences usually will not be identical; rather they will be analogous or similar. A case analysis, for example, will not necessarily be followed with another case analysis as terminal assessment activity. Since the case method is designed to emphasize human emotion in a conflict situation, any test item which emphasizes such a situation would be appropriate.

How Are Major Unit Purposes Developed with Students?

As with yearly planning, it seems desirable to assist students in gaining an overall perspective of the unit. Major objectives and some of the anticipated unit activities should be discussed with students. This not only creates a state of learning readiness, but it can provide valuable feedback from students. A teaching unit is *not* preplanned for the purpose of prescribing all aspects of the learning experience; rather it is designed as a basis for further planning with students. Modifications must be expected.

The unit introduction essentially entails setting realistic expectations with students. While it is *most inappropriate* to identify specific unit concepts for students, it is appropriate to impress upon them the nature of the concept approach to teaching and learning. (After a unit or two has been completed, this activity may need no further reinforcement.) By following this with suggestions for activities which should promote goal achievement, the student at least begins to see the need for various unit activities and assignments.

LESSON PLANNING

A lesson plan is an expanded portion of a unit plan. It represents a more or less detailed analysis of a particular *activity* described in the unit plan. For example, one of the unit activities is called *class discussion*. While the problem title was stated in the unit plan, no indication was given as to *how* the problem would be developed. In discussing a *problem of policy*, careful planning is essential. The lesson plan serves such a purpose.

The essentials of a lesson plan are somewhat similar to the important elements of a unit plan. Although forms and styles differ markedly from one teacher to another, a lesson plan usually contains a goal, lesson introduction (approach), lesson development, and lesson generalizations. Depending on the nature of the lesson, it also may include a list of materials needed, provision for individual differences, and an assignment.

The common elements of lesson planning erroneously suggest a more or less standard routine. While it is true that most plans will be structured around the common elements described, significant differences will be observed within this framework. Different teaching methods often are designed for different instructional purposes; they involve different sequences. Thus lesson plans must be modified accordingly. Sample lesson plans, prepared for the purposes of illustrating each of the major teaching methods, appear in the respective methods chapters. A comparison of some of these plans is recommended. The particular style of lesson planning illustrated in this book is suggestive only.

What Role Does the Unit Concept Play in Lesson Planning?

Each lesson plan is based upon a *unit* outcome, deemed essential for achievement of a *unit* concept. Thus back of every lesson plan is a concept. Two or more lessons may be essential to ensure the attainment of a single concept. It is desirable to restate the concept prior to development of a lesson plan. Although some feel that in certain contexts the concept may be stated for student guidance, most authorities apparently feel that students should be guided inductively toward concept achievement.

By restating the unit concept with each lesson plan, subsequent aspects of planning are simplified. Furthermore, one tends to focus upon one and only one major idea during the lesson.

How Are Lesson Goals and Outcomes Evolved from the Unit Concept?

From each unit concept the teacher must decide what major goal domain must be emphasized, for example, cognitive, affective, or psychomotor. It may be that two or even all three of these should receive emphasis. Usually there will be a different lesson for each major goal domain to be emphasized. Sometimes, however, more than one domain may be stressed in a single lesson. This applies especially to certain inquiry methods which, in effect, involve several unified lessons.

By way of illustration, unit concept 3 from the illustrated unit is reproduced along with unit goal II.

Unit concept: Advertising can be an effective means of preselling products.

Unit goal: After this unit the student should have furthered his understanding of the relationship between impulse buying and advertising, as evidenced by:
1. His ability to test hypotheses of impulse buying in a class discussion.
2. His ability to apply appropriate advertising principles in role-played situations.

Unit outcome 1 suggests class discussion and the cognitive domain (although the affective domain can be stressed in certain types of discussion). Using the unit concept as a guide, then a lesson goal with appropriate lesson outcomes can be derived. To illustrate: After this lesson the student should have furthered his understanding of the importance of impulse buying, as evidenced by (1) the questions he asks during the discussion, (2) his ability to offer and/or evaluate hypotheses posed during the discussion, (3) his ability to derive generalizations from the discussion.

It will be noted that the specific learning outcomes represent behaviors which can be expected during a problem-solving discussion experience.

How Is the Lesson Problem Developed?

Every major instructional method is based upon a problem. With the exception of the lecture method, instructional methods problems usually involve some form of policy problem. The above illustration, for example, calls for a discussion problem. One example might be, "What can we as marketers do to stimulate buying?"

Since the processes of reflection demand a constant referral back to the basic problem, it is usually placed on the chalkboard. In this way, it functions as an effective guide for the learning experience. An inappropriately worded problem usually results in an ineffective lesson.

What Is the Function of the Lesson Approach?

Every lesson must be so designed as to capture student interest at the outset. This may range from two or three introductory questions in a class discussion to a five- or ten-minute demonstration in a science discovery-type lesson. Whatever technique is employed the purpose is essentially that of preparing the learner for subsequent class activities.

The lesson approach is comparable to the course and unit introductions except that it applies to a specific lesson. Caution must be exercised or the activity may be overextended. It, in effect, merely sets the stage for learning.

What Are the Essentials of the Lesson Development?

Major activities of the lesson are incorporated in this phase of a lesson plan. Subdivisions of the lesson development will vary with the particular method to be used. The teacher must first identify the different aspects of the reflective process germane to the particular method involved. He then writes out points, questions, and/or comments deemed essential in the instructional process. In class discussion, for example, this may consist of only two or three key questions in each area to be explored. At this point the reader will want to study the illustrated lesson plans provided in the methods chapters.

The sequence of key questions (or events) is extremely important in achieving lesson objectives. Essentially, questions serve a dual role. They focus on the content being discussed and on the cognitive processes as well. Instructional processes which foster critical thinking must be sequenced. The first sequence of questions pertains to analysis of the problem. These, in turn, are followed with key questions which pertain to the higher levels of cognition, analysis, and synthesis of hypotheses or proposed solutions. Finally, some attention is given to the highest level of cognition (evalatuion).

How Is the Lesson Culminated?

The culminating portion of a lesson is often neglected or rushed. This is particularly unfortunate, since it is at this point that students are expected to derive concepts or generalizations. The culmination of almost every lesson should involve students in the derivation of generalizations, based on the current lesson experiences. The lesson generalizations are collectively equal to the basic unit concept upon which the lesson rests. Thus any one lesson generalization cannot be identical to the basic unit concept upon which the lesson rests.

Lesson generalizations should be derived by students. Some authorities insist that they be written out by students. In many instances students will verbally derive lesson generalizations which are written for all to see. Students are expected to record them in their notes, however.

Basic unit concepts, contrary to lesson concepts or generalizations, are derived by teachers as they plan for instruction. Concepts, at the unit level, are sometimes inductively derived by students as a *culminating* unit activity. As an aid in teaching, the instructor usually writes out one or two anticipated lesson generalizations in his lesson plan. They are to be used as an instructional guide only. To illustrate from the cited lesson problem:

1. Buying is associated with personal status.
2. Quality products sell themselves through satisfied customers.

VALUES

Unit planning provides a basic course structure around which specific class activities can be organized.

Through careful unit planning, the teacher is able to integrate the basic course concepts and those of related areas into various teaching experiences.

Unit planning enables the teacher to provide adequate balance between various dimensions of a course. By taking a long-range look he is able to develop essential priorities in advance of actual classroom experiences.

The unit plan seems to be the best technique yet developed to enable a teacher to break away from traditional textbook teaching.

Emphasis upon behavioral outcomes in both unit and lesson planning tends to result in a more meaningful series of learning experiences.

LIMITATIONS AND PROBLEMS

A teacher may become a "slave" to his plans. This is a special hazard for those who prefer detailed lesson plans.

Excessive planning may promote an authoritarian class situation. This factor may become apparent when the changing needs of students are largely disregarded.

Unless adequate caution is exercised, lesson plans may become a mere outline of textbook materials. If practical lesson goals, along with specific behavioral outcomes, are developed *as a basis for* class activities, this need not be a hazard.

Thorough planning takes time—more time, in fact, than is available to some first-year teachers. Furthermore, it is usually impractical to construct lesson plans more than three or four days in advance of the experience. (By making substantial use of marginal notes a teacher may use effective plans as a basis for subsequent planning.)

ILLUSTRATIONS

I. A unit plan is illustrated on pp. A–1-6 of the Hoover book from which this material is excerpted. Lesson plans are provided in each of the chapters dealing with instructional methods, in the Hoover book.

II. Useful in history classes. The following illustration depicts the two-step process of changing unit concepts of historical events into concepts with viable and current life applications. Instructional goals are derived from the latter.

This illustration is based upon a unit in United States history called, *World War I: To Make the World Safe for Democracy.*

Content Ideas (specific to a given unit)	Major Unit Concepts (generalized understandings)
1. The assassination of Franz Ferdinand of Austria was the "kick off point" that led to war.	1. Insignificant events often lead to unforgettable disaster.
2. Wilson's personal belief that democracy could save all mankind greatly affected the United States and its involvement in World War I.	2. The misleading notion that "Democracy can save all mankind" originated with Woodrow Wilson.
3. America's entrance into World War I was related to her isolationist policy.	3. Isolation and lack of communication whether it be between nations or individuals, lead to inevitable conflicts.
4. Wilson's idea of peace without victory was impractical.	4. Peace without victory may set the stage for later conflict.
5. Germany's submarine warfare influenced our decision to enter the war on the side of the Allies.	5. Aggression (e.g., submarine warfare during World War I) tends to widen gaps between peoples.
6. The United States was solidly united due to the war effort.	6. A common cause (e.g., the U.S. during World War I) tends to unite peoples.
7. Bitter feelings of the Allies toward the Central Powers made peace terms very demanding.	7. Bitter feelings toward individuals and nations (e.g., the Allies toward the Central Powers following World War I) make peaceful relationships difficult to establish and maintain.
8. The Big Four's acceptance of the League of Nations necessitated compromise which led to its ultimate demise.	8. Unwanted compromise (e.g., the League of Nations) tends to lessen the effectiveness of peace-keeping organizations and treaties.
9. Wilson's stance on the peace treaty led to his unpopularity at home.	9. Ill-advised public expression (e.g., riots, etc., against Wilson) can adversely affect statesmanship.
10. High reparations and other demands assessed against the defeated countries contributed to the depression of 1929.	10. Misuse of power by the victor (e.g., reparation demands of the Central Powers following World War I) may adversely affect inter-group relations for many generations.

It is seen from the foregoing that each of the major United States history concepts is derived from an idea which is specific to a given era of history. Many of the named concepts will occur again and again as the student studies other history units. In this way the learner can become aware of the repetition of diplomatic erros. New Concepts, of course, also will be emphasized in each subsequent unit.

III. Useful in literature classes. Illustrated below is the two-step process of identifying major unit ideas (concepts) and then organizing content selections which tend to develop each idea. The Illustrated unit in American literature is entitled "Colonial America: Birth of a New Culture."

Concept: The conditions of the time influence the nature of literary contributions.
Illustrated by: *Of Plymouth Plantation*
The Prologue
The Author to Her Book
The Preface
Upon a Spider Catching a Fly
Sinners in the Hands of an Angry God
Diary of Samuel Sewall
The History of the Dividing Line
From the Journal of John Woolman
Letters from an American Farmer

Concept: Puritan ideals have had and still have an influence on our social system.
Illustrated by: *The Prologue*
The Author to Her Book
The Preface
Upon a Spider Catching a Fly
Sinners in the Hands of an Angry God
Diary of Samuel Sewall

Concept: Reaching worthwhile goals involves hardships and struggles.
Illustrated by: *Of Plymouth Plantation*
The History of the Dividing Line
From the Journal of John Woolman
Letters from an American Farmer

Concept: Freedom embodies responsibility and interdependence of man.
Illustrated by: *Of Plymouth Plantation*
Sinners in the Hands of an Angry God
The History of the Dividing Line
From the Journal of John Woolman
Letters from an American Farmer

Concept: Realities of life are not always consistent with ideals.
Illustrated by: *Sinners in the Hands of an Angry God*
Diary of Samuel Sewall
The History of the Dividing Line
From the Journal of John Woolman
Letters from an American Farmer

Concept: If ultimate ideals are to be achieved, one's perception of reality must change.
Illustrated by: *Of Plymouth Plantation*
Sinners in the Hands of an Angry God
Diary of Samuel Sewall
The History of the Dividing Line
From the Journal of John Woolman
Letters from an American Farmer

GOALS, OBJECTIVES, AND EDUCATIONAL PROGRAM EVALUATION

ॐ CONCEPTS ॐ

Schools are pressured to be accountable and to concern themselves increasingly with purposes, goals and objectives. As educational leaders, chairpersons should be concerned with what is desirable and whether we are accomplishing it; focusing on goals, objectives and evaluations is one important way to show this concern. Concern for objectives is welcome but abuses which need to be checked exist in the objectives movement now embracing education.

 Emphasizing goals and objectives is important but the objectives movement has followers whose enthusiasm, though well-intended, is often manifested dogmatically and results in unanticipated negative consequences.

Problems with Evaluation

Popular conceptions of evaluation assume that a statement of purpose accompanied by *clearly defined objectives stated in the form of measurable student behaviors* is a necessary first step in the evaluation process. Evidence is then accumulated from which judgments are made to determine how well the objectives have been accomplished. This view represents an appropriate procedure in many instances but as an exclusive view of evaluation seems unnecessarily tidy and rigid: Indeed this simplistic view of evaluation has resulted in a number of fundamental problems including:

 Substituting precision for accuracy. This is a tendency to select, fit or force objectives, activities, and events to be evaluated into forms which match available precise evaluation procedures. The methods and procedures of evaluation tend to determine what will be evaluated.

Honoring ends over means. This is a tendency to focus on evaluating prespecified student behaviors, thus slighting what the teacher does, the context or environment for learning, and unanticipated learning outcomes.

Erosion of professional confidence. This is a tendency toward a growing loss of confidence in teachers and chairpersons in their own abilities to make judgments, to assess, to evaluate. Tests and measurements are becoming substitutes for, rather than supplements to, professional observation and judgments.

Accuracy and Precision in Evaluation

Collecting objective evidence to determine the extent to which objectives are being met sometimes places emphasis in the wrong place. When this occurs, one risks trading accuracy for precision.

 Accuracy refers to the importance or value of an educational activity or goal.

Precision refers to the scientific rigor with which the educational activity or goal can be pursued and measured.

A fairly accurate set of objectives relating to a unit on family life in a social science or literature class might include:

> Helping students understand that families everywhere fulfill similar functions although ways of living differ among societies.
> Helping students to compare, understand, and appreciate how their own family does or could function and their roles in this functioning.
> Helping students to be better family members when their roles change from child to adult and to understand the adult roles of husband, wife, and parent.

Most would grant the importance of these objectives but they leave much to be desired in ease of evaluation. They are accurate but not very precise. More precise objectives dealing with the same topic might include:

> List the various roles "father" plays in three named cultures.
> Given a list of ten family functions, identify five common across the three named cultures, three which are dissimilar and two which are not appropriate.
> Identify the main characters and family order they assume in three short stories. Match the character with the correct role and both with the correct story.

This group of objectives is more precise than the first group but less accurate. Students could, and many do, study for and pass a test constructed to determine if objectives have been met without really understanding much about family life, what it means to them, and how they might function in present and future family roles.

Often the most precise objectives have the least to do with intellectual and humane activity for students. Consider the following examples from a variety of topics:

The student will be able to label the body parts of a frog.

The student will be able to define the following trigonometric function: Sine (e.g., an acute angle in a right triangle is the ratio of the side opposite the angle to the hypotenuse), cosine, tangent, cotangent, secant, and cosecant.

The student will be able to define a *personal-liberty law* (a state law prohibiting compliance with the Fugitive Slave Act).

The student will be able to list five foods eaten by Indians living in Southern Mexico in the 16th century.

The student will be able to identify the protagonist in the play *Feathertop*.

Relationships between accuracy and precision are illustrated in grid form in Figure 10–1.

Precision + Accuracy − 1	Precision + Accuracy + 2
Precision − Accuracy − 3	Precision − Accuracy + 4

(ordinate: Precision — LOW to HIGH; abscissa: LOW — Accuracy — HIGH)

FIGURE 10-1. ACCURACY AND PRECISION IN EVALUATION

The four quadrants of the grid are formed by comparing the emphasis given to accuracy and precision in evaluation. The abscissa of the grid represents the extent to which accuracy is emphasized (from low to high) and the ordinate represents the emphasis given to precision.

 Quadrant two represents situations characterized by high accuracy and high precision. The events, activities and objectives being evaluated are important in their intellectual potency and in their humanistic substance. Further, the evaluation methods and procedures are efficient and readily implemented. This is the ideal setting for evaluation.

Quadrant four represents situations characterized by high accuracy but low precision. The events, activities and objectives being evaluated are important in their intellectual potency and in their humanistic substance. However, the evaluation methods and procedures are not efficient, but are subjective and difficult to implement.

323

Quadrant one represents situations characterized by low accuracy but high precision. Evaluation methods and procedures are efficient and readily implemented but events, activities, and objectives being evaluated are unimportant—often they are trivial, anti-intellectual and lacking in humanistic substance.

Quadrant three represents situations characterized by low accuracy and low precision. Inefficient evaluation procedures are used to evaluate unimportant objectives and activities.

Chairpersons and departments should always be involved in educational settings characterized by the pursuit of important objectives, activities, and events (quadrants 2 or 4) with whatever instructional and evaluation tools available. Sometimes the tools will be precise but at other times they will be ambiguous. Often one relies on judgment, consensus, and hunch in making assessments. Objective and rational methods of instruction and evaluation have much to contribute to the work of educators, but intoxicating as the aura of science is, our field is more similar to craft than scientific activity. The lure of science often results in instructional and evaluation activity suggested in quadrant one—precise methods and measurements of activities and objectives of dubious value. This is the plight of the cowboy who played in a crooked poker game because it was the only one in town.

An Expanded View of Objectives

Most educators agree on the need for goal focus and on the importance of objectives. Controversy exists, however, over what is a legitimate objective and how it should be stated. Behavioral objectives advocates often fight the battle on one extreme, insisting that all objectives be predetermined and stated in the form of measurable expected student outcomes. Those opposed to behavioral objectives insist that no place exists for such objectives in education and that when objectives are used, they should be general or derived incidentally from learning experiences.

Both sides to this argument are right and wrong. Behavioral objectives (henceforth referred to as instructional objectives) are worthwhile and important in some situations and obstructing and often comical in others. Many situations lend themselves to general or to incidentally derived objectives but in some situations their use is inefficient and irresponsible. Objectives should be viewed as coming in varieties, each type a tool which, when properly used, can help chairpersons and teachers develop more effective learning experiences. Four types of objectives are described below[1]:

 Instructional objectives. Outcomes and solutions are provided and specified in the form of student behavior. Expected student behavior is specified in advance of the learning encounter or teacher activity.

Expressive objectives. Outcomes of an educational encounter or activity. The encounter or activity was not designed to lead to any specific objective but to a range of objectives not determined beforehand. Evaluation involves looking back to assess what value occurred from the encounter or activity. Most any worthwhile objective discovered is acceptable.

Middle-range objectives. These do not define the outcomes or solutions expected from youngsters beforehand but rather the problems with which the student will deal. The student is not free to come up with any worthwhile solution but one which meets the specification of the problems under study.

Informal objectives. Focus less deliberately on content and concepts *per se* and more deliberately on process. Informal objectives usually accompany other objectives.

INSTRUCTIONAL OBJECTIVES. Instructional objectives are concerned with the student and behavior expected of him. The objectives do not speak to what the teacher does, the methods used or the nature of the educational encounter directly. Such objectives are intended to define measurable outcomes in order to facilitate direct evaluation. Used properly, such objectives can help teachers select learning experiences, materials and educational settings which will best lead students to the desired behavior. Examples of such objectives include:

> Given a graph showing the GNP of common market and noncommon market western countries, the student will be able to interpret the data by answering specific questions which involve the use of the graph.
> The student will be able to measure his height, weight, arm length, finger span, foot size, and leg stretch to the nearest metric unit.
> The student will be able to match the name of each planet with number of moons, rank in distance from the sun, rank in size, pull of gravity, and probable atmospheric composition.
> Given a diagram of a frog (grasshopper, eye, ear, geographic feature, battlefield, water pump) the student will label prespecified parts.
> The student is able to define condensation, evaporation, precipitation, and transpiration.

Chairpersons often complain that teachers' instructional objectives overly emphasize identification and description skills at the knowledge-recall-comprehension level of the hierarchy of educational objectives, and not enough emphasis is paid to objectives of application, analysis, synthesis, and evaluation of knowledge, Further, instructional objectives tend not to emphasize affective learning. Part of the problem may be that these higher-order objectives are simply not getting the emphasis they deserve generally in the high school educational program. More advanced kinds of learning, however, lend themselves less well to the rigor of being predetermined for each learner and the rigor of being behaviorally stated and organized.

Starratt raises some additional issues in using instructional objectives exclusively[2]:

(1) Does the specification of behavioral objectives and the learning experiences leading to their acquisition imply that every student can and must behave in ex-

325

actly the same way in order to validate the objectives? Further, does it imply that the only way to achieve the objectives is by progressing through such and such a series of preordained learning experiences? If the answer to both questions is affirmative, without any qualification, then we have simply substituted one kind of dogmatism for another. Any talk about respecting individual differences becomes ridiculous, for even if students are allowed to progress at their own individual rates of learning, they must move toward the same fixed goal. (2) Do educators have the absolute, unchallengable right, based on an assumption of competence, to require that their students will achieve certain objectives rather than other objectives?

Much merit exists in using instructional objectives. Indeed their use becomes more important where inferior teaching exists for improvements can be expected from fairly close supervision based on such objectives. *But too rigid or exclusive use of instructional objectives can stifle superior teaching.* Chairpersons can work through these issues by viewing instructional objectives as only one kind, where successful use depends upon balance of emphasis with other kinds of objectives.

EXPRESSIVE OBJECTIVES. The use of expressive objectives requires that chairpersons and teachers focus less on specific expected outcomes from students and more on the arrangement of potent, high-quality educational encounters or activities which will stimulate the emergence of a number of worthy outcomes.[3]

Expressive objectives differ considerably from instructional objectives. An expressive objective does not specify the behavior the student is to acquire after having engaged in one or more learning activities. An expressive objective describes an educational encounter; it identifies a situation in which children are at work, a problem with which they are to cope, a task they are to engage in—but it does not specify the form of that encounter, situation, problem, or task they are to learn. An expressive objective provides both the teacher and the student with an invitation to explore, defer, or focus on issues that are of peculiar interest or import to the inquirer.

Examples of expressive objectives might be:

To arrange for students to participate in a mock trial.
To have students interview shoppers exiting from the supermarket about their opinions on the freedom of assembly, redress of grievances, and right to bear arms provision of the Bill of Rights.

In each case the emphasis is not on what the student will specifically learn but on developing and arranging a learning encounter. A number of important outcomes can result from students conducting a mock trial. Differentiating fact from conjecture, learning roles and functions of those involved in the judicial process, evaluating the rules of operation of the court system, preparing oral and written arguments, analyzing evidence, experiencing first-hand how one's values affect one's opinion, and analyzing the content and issues of the court case—all are rich with potential learning outcomes for students. The expressive objective is any worthwhile outcome of the trial activity planned by the teacher or together by teacher and students. The trial activity is not designed to lead the student to a prespecified goal or predetermined form of behavior but to forms of thinking, feeling, and behaving that are of his own choice.

Expressive objectives permit students to engage in learning encounters and activities on an equal footing. The teacher assumes a major role in deciding and arranging the learning setting but the student has the option of responding to this setting in many ways. Objectives emerge as a result of the educational encounter. The task of the evaluator is to look back to evaluate what happened to the student.

MIDDLE-RANGE OBJECTIVES. Middle-range objectives provide more freedom than instructional objectives for students to determine what will be learned, but less freedom than expressive objectives. In instructional objectives the solution is provided. In expressive objectives, the setting is provided and the student discovers his own solution from a range of possibilities. In middle-range objectives, the problem is provided along with specification for the solution. The student then discovers his solution not from a wide range but from a range which conforms to the specifications. Examples of middle-range objectives include:

> Using data from an actuarial table of life expectancy for individuals in selected occupational groups, develop a series of visual aids which explain the data. The visuals you develop should be understood by average fifth grade students without the assistance of accompanying verbal or oral text. In other words the visuals should be so labelled and keyed that they are self-explanatory to this group.

> Designing an outdoor fort or play house which meets the following specifications:
> 1. Costs less than $40.
> 2. Can be built by 10- to 12-year-olds.
> 3. Requires only hand tools.
> 4. Is at least two feet off the ground.
> 5. Is safe to play in.

> Developing a set of plans, construction instructions, and materials list to accompany your design.

In each case the student is provided with a problem to solve and is free to develop any solution to the problem which meets the specification. "What the teacher looks for in evaluating achievement is not a preconceived fit between a known objective and a known solution but an appraisal, after inquiry of the relative merit of solution to the objective formulated."[4]

INFORMAL OBJECTIVES. Informal objectives differ from the others in that they focus less deliberately on content and concepts than on processes. Informal objectives include the development of personal meanings, intrinsic satisfaction, joy in learning, interpersonal competencies, and love of self found in the affective domain of objectives as well as more cognitively-oriented process goals such as exploring, feeling, sensing, comparing, sorting, clarifying, and creating. Informal objectives add the necessary balance of how something is learned to what is learned.

The content learned by comparing and categorizing various types of mental illness for example, may be important but the processes of comparing and categorizing are important in their own right. The output of a social science group report on the geography of world poverty is important but so are informal learnings which occur as students work in groups—leadership, value clarification, cooperation, group process skills. Teachers and chairpersons need to plan educational experiences and curriculum formats with high informal objectives, and to evaluate informal happenings.

Developing Balanced Objectives

The extent to which each of the four types of objectives is provided in the curriculum and the emphasis given to each in instruction are fundamental questions in evaluating the school's educational program, texts, and materials and the work of teachers in the classroom. Chairpersons and teachers should work to assess the extent to which a balanced emphasis on instructional, expressive, middle-range and informal objectives is reflected in:

homework assignments
study hall assignments
lab and work-book assignments
teacher plan books
the choice of teaching materials
daily teaching activity
work-study programs
teacher made tests
commercially prepared tests
grade book scores, test records, report card marks

A careful analysis of the present distribution of emphasis among objective types is a first step for change. As a department works to achieve a more balanced distribution, it enriches the intellectual potency and humanistic substance of the school's educational program.

Developing Potent Learning Experiences

A further characteristic of an intellectually sound and humane educational program is the potency level of learning experiences:

 Potency of learning experiences refers to the conceptual level at which knowledge is addressed and the ability of the knowledge to generate new understanding and uses.

One useful tool for assessing the potency level of educational experiences is by comparing objectives and activities being pursued with levels of a taxonomy of educational objectives. The taxonomy of cognitive objectives described in this chapter is a classification scheme, developed by Benjamin Bloom and his associates, which identifies, lists, and sorts objectives into six general categories.[5] The categories are arranged in hierarchial fashion. Each category is assumed to involve cognitive behavior which is more complex and potent than the previous category.

The categories identified by Bloom and his associates are as follows[6]:

Knowledge	Analysis
Comprehension	Synthesis
Application	Evaluation

Objectives and activities at the *knowledge* level require students to *recall*:

Bits of specific information such as the main export of Brazil.
Specific facts such as names, dates, and places
Chronological sequence
Accepted conventions such as the parts of speech
Trends and sequences such as causes of the civil war
Classification systems such as the taxonomy of educational objectives
Criteria such as the essential moves in a breast stroke
Steps such as what to do before turning the ignition key in driver's education
Principles such as the atmospheric conditions needed to induce precipitation
Theories such as alternate explanations for why the universe is expanding

 Action words associated with the knowledge level include listing, knowing, recalling, selecting, defining, distinguishing, memorizing, labelling, naming, identifying, recognizing, and matching.

Within the knowledge category, some levels are more important than others. Recalling the names and dates of Roman emperors or classical musicians seems not as potent an example as recalling principles and theories. The emphasis, however, is still on recalling knowledge and students are not asked to understand, use, apply, integrate, or evaluate this knowledge.

 Knowledge-level objectives and activities involve remembering and recalling.

Some knowledge is worth remembering and recalling for its own sake. Generally, however, knowledge recall is not an end in itself but a means to other ends.

Schools which unduly emphasize the knowledge level see knowledge and subject matter as something to teach. Educational programs in such schools tend to be more mechanical than purposeful and intellectual.

Schools which emphasize the more potent levels of the taxonomy of educational

329

objectives see knowledge as something to use to achieve other objectives. Educational programs in such schools tend to be relatively purposeful and intellectual.

Most objectives and activities pursued in junior and senior high schools probably could be classified at the knowledge level. The way to check this is not by relying on what people claim as their intents but by observing their actions and those of their students. A further clue can be found in the tests and examinations which are given to students.

Objectives and activities at the *comprehensive* level require students to *understand:*

By translating (or paraphrasing) knowledge from one form to another without altering meaning.

By interpreting knowledge so that it is recorded, rearranged and seen from a different perspective.

By extending knowledge to the point where corollaries, trends, and effects are extracted.

Action words associated with the comprehension level include translating, interpreting, extending, rearranging, restating, explaining, inferring, transforming, summarizing, and commenting.

Comprehensive is a low level of intellectual activity, more potent than merely recalling knowledge but not as potent as using, analyzing, synthesizing, and evaluating.

About 80 percent of the cognitive objectives and activities engaged in by junior and senior high students can be categorized in either the knowledge of comprehension levels, knowledge receiving more attention than comprehension.

Objectives and activities at the *application* level require students to *relate* abstract understandings such as concepts, to concrete problems.

Action words associated with the application level include applying, generalizing, dramatizing, organizing, solving, using, restructuring, classifying, choosing, and transferring.

In applications the emphasis is on using conceptual knowledge and understanding to solve problems which are fairly concrete.

Objectives and activities at the *analysis* level require students to *analyze* (recognize, distinguish, discover):

Parts which contribute to a whole
Unstated assumptions
Facts from hypotheses
Relationships between hypotheses and assumptions
Interrelationships among ideas

Action words associated with the analysis level include comparing, categorizing, analyzing, diagramming, discriminating, differentiating, subdividing, and deducing.

Analysis is an attempt to clarify communication and ideas, to understand how they are organized, the assumptions upon which they rest, and how they manage to convey meaning. Logic, induction and deduction, and formal reasoning are examples of analysis.

Objectives and activities at the *synthesis* level require students to integrate and combine elements and parts to *create* a new whole. Synthesis includes:

Combining ideas to form a new pattern structure
Developing proposals and plans
Creating new forms of expression through writing, art, drama
Discovering and making generalizations
Developing theories

 Action words associated with the synthesis level include originating, developing, modifying, creating, formulating, planning, composing, designing, and constructing.

Objectives and activities at the *evaluation* level require students to make *judgments* about:

The value of ideas, theories, methods, materials
The adequacy of criteria in evaluation
The appropriateness of criteria in evaluating
The accuracy of communications and ideas

 Action words associated with the evaluation level include judging, appraising, evaluating, weighing, considering, concluding, rating, and criticizing.

Evaluation is also concerned with the comparison of major generalizations, theories and ideas of one source, discipline or culture with those of others.

The root work in evaluation is *value*. This suggests a close link between the more intellectual levels of this cognitive hierarchy of educational objectives and more affective concerns such as values and belief system. The important characteristics which differentiate intellectually-oriented educational programs from their counterparts, potency of learning experiences and personal meanings which students bring to and take from learning experiences, were described earlier. In a sense, personal meanings represents the integration of cognitive and affective dimensions to learning. Intellectual experiences of high quality will not be in abundance without concern for and integration of affective as well as cognitive learning.

331

As an extension of the original work in developing a taxonomy of educational objectives for the cognitive domain Krathwohl and his associates developed a taxonomy for the affective domain.[7] The five major categories of their taxonomy are presented below with each level assumed to involve affective behavior which is more complex and potent that the previous category.[8]

Receiving
Responding
Valuing
Organizing
Characterizing

Objectives and activities at the receiving level require that students develop *awareness* of and *sensitivity* to the less obvious aspects of their environment. Sounds in the street, tolerance in taste, acceptance of difference in people, aesthetic qualities in design and architecture, rhythm in poetry, and mood in drama are examples. To know that this phenomena exists, is all that is required; one is not asked to like or dislike, accept, or reject, or to respond. Receiving is a low level of affective learning because it relies primarily on describing what is, rather than reacting to what is. Learning about the intentions of a musician, author, or artist are examples. Students may be asked to explain the views of Thoreau and to be aware of examples of his views being manifested in their everyday lives. But unless the student responds in some way by examining and altering his views, beliefs and behavior as a result of his encounter with Thoreau, he is in a sense dealing cognitively with affective ideas.

 Action words associated with the receiving level include listening, asking, accepting, choosing, and attending.

Objectives and activities at the *responding* level imply *action* on the part of students. The student is sufficiently motivated so that not only is he aware but he does something about it. He may be aware of what tolerance means and respond by becoming more tolerant. He may be aware of the complexity and power of Russian novels and respond by reading them for pleasure.

 Action words associated with the responding level include telling, reciting, acclaiming, approving, helping, and volunteering

Affective objectives and activities are usually neglected parts of the school's educational program

When they are attended to, usually the level of learning can be described as receiving and to a lesser extent responding

Objectives and activities at the *valuing* level require that the student assess his

beliefs with regard to certain ideas and issues. Valuing implies acceptance and rejection against some standard internal to the learner. This internal standard is composed of important assumptions and beliefs which give rise to consistent and stable behavior. As assumptions and beliefs become more manifest and understood, values are developed and internalized.

 Action words associated with the valuing level include supporting, sharing, joining, appreciating, and choosing.

Objectives and activities at the *organization* level require that students *systemize* values so that as a group they have more relevance and meaning than when considered individually. Organizing values into a system, determining their interrelationship and interdependencies and arranging them by similarity and importance are examples of organization level activities.

 Action words associated with the organization level include formulating, relating, defining, and defending.

The highest level of objectives and learning experiences in the affective domain taxonomy is called *characterization*. At this level it is assumed that students have begun the process of developing and internalizing assumptions and beliefs and that a value system is emerging. Activities at this level help to refine the value system by modifying, evaluating, testing, revising, verifying, and reaffirming beliefs in the light of new evidence. Further, the refinement of this value system helps students to develop a personal code of behavior, set of ethics, and philosophy of life. How shallow and insignificant many knowledge-level and receiving-level objectives and activities seem, when compared with objectives and learning activities drawn from this category.

Facts, Concepts, and Values

The 1966 publication *Values in Teaching* by Louis Raths, Merril Harmin and Sidney Simon[9] provides chairpersons with still another useful system for generating, categorizing, and evaluating educational experiences. This book and subsequent works by Simon and his associates have focused attention on the need for values clarification and values level teaching.

Simon refers to three levels of teaching: the facts level, the concepts level, and the values level—each level necessary and important but presently emphasized in most schools in such a way that the concepts level ranks as a poor second and the values level is at best a neglected stepchild.

Simon and Harmin provide examples of each of the three levels of teaching facts, concepts, and values, as follows:

Information which stays merely at the level of filling in the holes of a crossword puzzle, or name-dropping at a suburban cocktail party, is information which we

333

really do not need. So much of schooling is at this facts-for-facts level. There is a second level, a higher level, engagingly presented by Bruner, and this is called the concepts level. We believe that there is still a higher level, a level which makes use of facts and concepts, but which goes well beyond them in the direction of penetrating a student's life. This we call the values level.

Let us look at an example to make this point. Take the favorite social studies topic, "The United States Constitution." We can teach this at the facts level, the concepts level, or the values level.

FACTS LEVEL:
1. Information about where and when the Constitution was drawn up.
2. Who was involved and which colonies wanted what in it.
3. Information about how it differed from the Articles of Confederation.
4. Data on what was in the preamble and perhaps asking the class to memorize it.
5. A list of the first ten amendments and why they were called the Bill of Rights.
6. The order in which the colonies ratified the document.

The above items should be fairly familiar facts to most of us, although we have probably forgotten the specifics. At one time this topic was presented to us in an organized manner, each fact building upon fact. Unfortunately, it was difficult to remember then and it still is hard to retain. It was of interest to only a few students and of little use even to them in any relevant search for values which might enlighten living in today's world.

Thus, many teachers, encouraged by Bruner and his followers, tried to teach the Constitution at the concepts level.

CONCEPTS LEVEL:
1. Our Constitution as a landmark in the evolving concept of democratic forms of government.
2. The concept of "compromise" and how it operated in reconciling the economic forces of the period.
3. The motives of the signers and the constituencies all representatives are obligated to serve.
4. The social injustices which the Bill of Rights attempted to correct.
5. The concept of amendment and how it has operated in state legislatures and in Congress.
6. The Constitution today as seen in the actions of the Supreme Court and the American Civil Liberties Union, Etc.

The above "subject matter" will be seen as the basis for good teaching. It attempts to build relationships between random facts and to pull together generalizations supported by data. Many educators would be proud to have this kind of teaching going on in their schools, but we would argue that this approach is simply not good enough for these complex times. Let us look now at the values level, that third level to which subject matter needs to be lifted.

334

VALUES LEVEL:

1. What rights and guarantees do you have in your family? Who serves as the Supreme Court in disputes?
2. Have you ever written a letter to the editor of a newspaper or magazine?
3. Many student governments are really token governments controlled by the "mother country," i.e., the administration. Is this true in your school? What can you do about it? If not you, who should do it?
4. Should the editorial board of your school newspaper have the final say about what is printed in it? How do you reconcile the fact that the community will judge the school, a tax supported institution, by what is printed in the school paper?
5. When was the last time you signed a petition? Have you ever been the person to draw one up? What did the last sign you carried on a picket line say?
6. Where do you stand on wire tapping, financial aid to parochial schools, censorship of pornographic magazines, or the right of a barber to decide if he wants to cut a black person's hair?

This kind of teaching is not for the fainthearted. It often hits at the guts, but if we are to see the school as more than a place from which we issue the press release each spring which tells which colleges our students made, then we must do more teaching at this third level, this values level.

The authors do not intend that values-level teaching replace fact and concept levels. Indeed values-level teaching is based on facts and concepts. But the most significant educational experience is that which touches a person's self awareness, personal meanings and beliefs in such a fashion that the experience changes his outlook on life and his behavior in life. Values-level teaching adds this human-personal dimension to the teaching of facts and concepts.

Using Taxonomies

A humane and intellectually oriented educational program is one which:

 Recognizes the importance of affective objectives and learning activities and plans deliberately for their inclusion throughout the curriculum.

Insures that planning and teaching efforts give prime attention to the valuing, organization, and characterization levels of the affective domain taxonomy.

Does not ignore knowledge and comprehension levels of the cognitive domain taxonomy, but recognizes that mediocre teaching and learning results from *overemphasizing* these levels.

Recognizes that knowledge is not merely stuff to teach but stuff to teach with and therefore gives prime attention to applications, analysis, synthesis, and evaluation-level objectives.

335

Plans deliberately for educational experiences at the fact, concept *and* value levels of teaching.

Taxonomies can be useful in evaluating one's educational platform, in building curriculum, in planning teaching and learning activities, and building tests and examinations. Further, by sorting present actions into levels of a taxonomy, one can infer the *actual* level of objectives being pursued. The actual level can then be compared with intended levels.

Teachers may want to keep track of the amount of time they and their students spend on cognitive versus affective objectives and on levels within each of these domains. This can be done by keeping daily logs, examining lesson plans and tests, collecting and analyzing assignments and tests given to students, and keeping track of the kinds of questions teachers ask and types of interactions which take place in class.

Secondary school teachers often tend to focus on their subject matter content in such a way that it becomes an end in itself—stuff to teach. Chairpersons as instructional leaders often support this tendency but as educational leaders they must work against it.

To this point mechanical and trivial teaching have been cited as characteristics which work against developing humane, intellectually-oriented schools. We have suggested that goal focus and careful planning can help avoid such teaching. But goals and objectives are only one part of educational platforms which teachers and others bring to the arena of educational decision-making. Communicating accurately about educational programs requires that one give attention also to the less explicit but perhaps more important assumptions and theories from which objectives emerge.

A Comprehensive View of Evaluation

A comprehensive view of educational program planning, developing, implementing and evaluating would include attention to the following:

- educational platforms of individual teachers, departments, and the school as a whole. A platform is composed of important assumptions, theories, and objectives
- assumptions which refer to what is possible and comprise the beliefs which exist about accepted truths with reference to knowledge, learning and students. Beliefs of this type form the boundaries of educational decision-making
- theories, which refer to what is true and assumptions about the relationships among beliefs about knowledge, learning and students. Beliefs of this type form the basis for developing instructional strategies, classroom influence patterns, and learning contexts
- aims, which refer to what is desirable. Beliefs of this type form the basis for developing educational aims and objectives
- objectives, which come in a variety of shapes and forms each suitable in some situations but not in others
- instructional objectives, which specify in advance expected outcomes and solutions in the form of fairly measurable or observable student behavior

- expressive objectives, which are outcomes of an educational activity or encounter not designed to lead to specific objectives or solutions
- middle-range objectives, which do not define outcomes or solutions beforehand but are outcomes which meet specification of a particular problem or activity under study
- informal objectives, which focus less deliberately on content and concepts *per se* than on process
- patterns of influence as defined by the quality and quantity of influence which teachers and students exhibit in classroom decision-making
- learning contexts as defined by the character of motivation, meaning, and interpersonal setting which exists in the learning environment
- the potency of learning experiences to ensure that a reasonable distribution exists among the levels of the cognitive and affective hierarchies

Evaluation in education is much more demanding and complex than the simple paradigms of stating objectives, measuring output, and comparing the difference between our intents and observations. Flattering as it may be to many who think of education as a science with fail-proof evaluation technology at its disposal, the field is not so sufficiently advanced as to permit value-free ultra-rational and highly objective evaluation methods to dominate. Education compares favorably to medicine in this regard. Science and technology as a supplement to professional insight, perceptiveness, and judgment are the tools of the trade. The key word is *supplement to* and not *substitute for* professional judgment.

ENDNOTES

1. For a discussion of instructional objectives, see W. James Popham and Eva L. Baker, *Establishing Instructional Goals* (Englewood Cliffs, N. J.: Prentice-Hall, 1970) and John D. McNeil, *Toward More Accountable Teachers* (New York: Holt, Rinehart and Winston, 1971). For a discussion of expressive and middle-range objectives see Elliot Eisner, "Instructional Expressive Objectives: Their Formulation and Use in Curriculum," *AERA Monograph Series in Curriculum Evaluation: Instructional Objectives.* Robert Stake, ed. (Chicago: Rand-McNally, 1967), and Eisner, "Emerging Models for Educational Evaluation," *School Review,* Vol. 80, No. 4, 1972, pp. 573–589. Eisner refers to middle-range objectives as "Type III objectives."

2. Thomas J. Sergiovanni and Robert J. Starratt, *Emerging Patterns of Supervision Human Perspectives* (New York: McGraw-Hill, 1971), p. 230.

3. Eisner, "Instructional Expressive Objectives," p. 15.

4. Eisner, "Emerging Models," p. 582.

5. Benjamin S. Bloom (ed.), Max Englehart, Edward Furst, Walker Hill, and David Krathwohl, *A Taxonomy of Educational Objectives: Handbook I the Cognitive Domain* (New York: Longman, Green), 1956.

6. *Ibid.,* p. 201.

7. David R. Krathwohl, Benjamin Bloom, and Bertram Masia, *A Taxonomy of Educational Objectives: Handbook II, the Affective Domain* (New York: McKay and Company, 1964).

8. *Ibid.*

9. Louis Raths, Merrill Harmin, and Sidney Simon, *Values and Teaching* (Columbus, Ohio: E. Merrill, 1966).

10. Sidney Simon and Merrill Harmin, "Subject Matter with a Focus on Values," *Educational Leadership*, Vol. 26, No. 1, October, 1968. For further examples of fact, concept and value level teaching in a number of subject matter areas see Sidney Simon and Howard Kirschenbaum (eds.), *Readings in Values Clarification* (Minneapolis: Winston Press, 1973).

☙ CHAPTER TEN ❧

☙ PRACTICES ❧

Perhaps the most demanding responsibility of the chairperson is that which focuses on teacher and program evaluation. Because evaluation is so demanding, often the most simplistic images of evaluation have an irresistible appeal to the chairperson. What could be more efficient than filling out an evaluation form? And in program evaluation, what could be more simple, yet seemingly scientific, than specifying detailed measurable objectives, collecting data, and comparing intents and outcomes?

Simplicity and precision, as was discussed in the concepts section, are treasures but should not be honored over appropriateness. Educators' work is complex and often unpredictable. It should not be simplified to fit an evaluation model. Simplifying often results in disregarding or slighting the most important issues, concepts, and objectives. Evaluation strategies should be designed to fit the task at hand and this often means that relatively imprecise techniques must be used.

In this section the major focus is on evaluating aspects of the department's education program rather than specific classroom activities (treated in the next chapter). Included below are:

General statement of goals
Evaluating educational materials
Textbook evaluation form
Supplementary materials evaluation form
Evaluating your department's program
An example of an evaluation of an English department
Evaluating cognitive level of classroom activities
Self-evaluation form for estimating cognitive level

A GENERAL STATEMENT OF GOALS

This statement of goals,* for the secondary school which sets high standards for student self-realization, can serve as a model and as a basis for discussion as you define

*By Robert J. Starratt, from T. J. Sergiovanni and R. J. Starratt, *Emerging Patterns of Supervision* (New York: McGraw-Hill, 1971), pp. 270-273.

your department's goals and program platform. The statement combines general goals with specific indicators for making curricular-instructional decisions. These goals show high concern for human values, personal meanings, individual self-realization and other aspects of what could be considered "humanistic education" without compromising tough intellectual standards of inquiry and scholarship.

Review the content of the goals. Do they suggest to you the essential characteristics of the author's educational platform? To what extent are the statements compatible with your department's educational platform? How would you revise this statement to make it more compatible with your department's platform?

General Goals for the Secondary School

1. The student is free from fear:
   a. of himself
   b. of the unknown
   c. of authority
   d. of insecurity
   e. of commitment and risk
2. The student is free from ignorance:
   a. about himself
   b. about the functioning of present society
   c. about history
   d. about natural phenomena
   e. about the demands of interpersonal relationships
   f. about the methods of inquiry and communication
3. The student is therefore free to explore his world, to respond to it appropriately, and to participate in its struggles and joys.
4. The student is therefore free to communicate by means of language, ritual, and other art forms.
5. The student is free to organize his values and to commit himself to a hierarchy of values.
6. The student is free to accept the limitations of his freedom by both social and natural causes.

These overarching goals, however, require further specification if they are to provide clear and forceful direction to the curricular-instructional program. To propose freedom as a central objective of schooling does not mean doing whatever seems appealing at the moment. Any artist will testify that freedom to express oneself in an art medium requires mastery of its techniques, gained by immersing oneself in the medium in order to manage over it. This ability to *use* the medium to express subtle shades of meaning and to interpret the phenomena of experience demands hours of work.

It is necessary, therefore, to describe those skills and understandings which the student must master to achieve the freedoms described in our general goals. Once again, these more specific objectives will be described as student learnings and competencies.

These will be described at the *completion* of his secondary education, thus providing objectives which can be broken down into segmented patterns of growth for students at various age levels. This specific description of the goals of the curricular-instructional program should lend itself readily to measurement of goal achievement, but notice that they are still general, allowing the student the elbow room necessary to personalize these learnings.

SPECIFIC GOALS OF THE CURRICULAR-INSTRUCTION PROGRAM

1. The student is able to use the symbolic tools of thinking, communicating, and inquiring.
    a. He has mastered the basic methods of logic, as can be shown by his ability to reason consistently in oral debate, to analyze critically newspaper editorials and political speeches, to draw inferences from general statements, and to construct valid generalizations from individual instances.
    b. He has mastered the English language—a mastery which will be shown by his ability to use it orally and in writing according to accepted standards of usage and style and his ability to read and to interpret what he reads according to accepted performance criteria.
    c. He has mastered the basic symbolic systems of mathematics, the natural sciences, and the social sciences. This mastery will be indicated by his knowledge of central concepts, of essential operations and functions, and of unifying theories, as well as by his ability to perform basic laboratory operations.
    d. He has mastered the elementary forms of artistic expression. This mastery will be indicated by his ability to use the techniques of the art form (such as his use of color, symmetry, and perspective in painting, his use of verbal imagery and metaphors in poetry, his ability to interpret the personality of the character whose part he plays in drama, and so forth). Mastery in the arts would also involve knowledge of evaluative principles so that the student could both enjoy and make an informed appraisal of the work of art. It also involves familiarity with a variety of past and present works of art in literature, painting, music, drama, and sculpture.
2. He is able to systematize and interpret basic facts of the physical world and their interrelationships by means of conceptual structures. This ability would be indicated by his interpretation and analysis of health problems, conservation problems, new scientific accomplishments such as the space program, the use of thermonuclear energy, and so forth.
3. He is able to organize information into patterns of past cultural development. He would indicate such competence by his ability to explain central ideas and images which permeated all aspects of cultural eras such as classical Greek and Roman cultures, medieval culture, the Renaissance, and others, to locate the roots of many current social problems in past historical movements, to interpret the international scene against the backdrop of past international power struggles, and to identify at least some of the complex elements in such struggles, pointing out similarities and the unique character of different power confrontations.
4. He is able to understand and use the methods of regulating the social order. This goal refers to the student's understanding of the basic principles of our

national, state, and local economy, of basic laws and why they were instituted, or political power and how it is used, and of democratic political action through voting, organizing lobbying groups, organizing grass-roots political action groups, and so forth. Such understanding and use of the methods of regulating the social order can be evaluated through simulated case studies or through molar problem solving which requires the student to draw upon a variety of understandings in order to interpret the demands of the situation and to make decisions which he can justify.

5. He is able to integrate and defend his values from a basic philosophic, ethical-religious, and aesthetic stance. He will manifest competence in this area by his ability to make decisions in matters of conflict or in matters requiring evaluative judgment. The student does not necessarily have to be put in an actual conflict situation, but through exposure to hypothetical or simulated conflict situations he can indicate the consistency and reasonableness of his decisions and judgments.

EVALUATING EDUCATIONAL MATERIALS

Evaluating and selecting educational materials is an important responsibility. This is not a job for you to do directly but rather a process for you to facilitate. Staff involvement is important in the evaluation and selection process. The effectiveness of even the most well-conceived set of educational materials is endangered if users are not committed to the materials.

Evaluation and selection of materials should take place within your department's educational platform. An early step in the process is identifying this platform (see Chapter 9), the general goals of the department, and the more specific goals for each course or other experience provided to students.

After faculty members have reviewed materials in light of goals and platform dimensions they need to share and discuss observations with others at a special department meeting. Holding a special meeting elevates the importance of materials selection and review, and helps ensure that staff members come properly prepared. Remember, the purpose of these discussions is to review and select materials which will best help achieve your goals and enhance your department's educational platform. This is not an occasion for various people to make "sales pitches" for a particular set of materials.

Two forms are provided* to help you evaluate educational materials. The first form is designed for text and supplementary book review, and the second for nonbook materials. In each case review carefully criteria used to determine the value of materials. You may need to modify the criteria somewhat or add to the list to suit the special needs of your department.

*Each form is adapted from *Handbook for Department Leadership in Social Studies.* Social Studies Development Center, Indiana University, Bloomington, Indiana.

342

TEXTBOOK EVALUATION FORM

SUBJECT _____

TITLE OF BOOK _____

COPYRIGHT DATE _____ AUTHOR(S)_____

PUBLISHER _____

AVAILABLE IN (PLEASE CHECK) HARDBOUND _____ PAPERBACK _____ BOTH _____

EVALUATOR _____

Directions: Read each question slowly and thoroughly. To answer a question make an "X" on the left-hand scale over the number indicating your evaluation of the material. There is another scale to the right of the question. This scale allows you to grade the questions' value. Place an "X" by the side of the word which indicates your evaluation of the question.

SAMPLE:

| 0 | 1 | 2 | 3 | 4 | 5 | 6 |

NO OR LITTLE EXTENT   TO SOME EXTENT   GREAT EXTENT

To what extent does the title indicate the content of the book?

QUESTION IS:
___ 0. Unimportant
___ 1. Relatively unimportant
___ 2. Moderately important
___ 3. Important
___ 4. Extremely important

A. OBJECTIVES:

| 0 | 1 | 2 | 3 | 4 | 5 | 6 |

NO OR LITTLE EXTENT   TO SOME EXTENT   GREAT EXTENT

1. To what extent are objectives stated?

QUESTION IS:
___ 0. Unimportant
___ 1. Relatively Unimportant
___ 2. Moderately Important
___ 3. Important
___ 4. Extremely Important

| 0 | 1 | 2 | 3 | 4 | 5 | 6 |

NO OR LITTLE EXTENT   TO SOME EXTENT   GREAT EXTENT

2. To what extent do the objectives require students to use higher cognitive skills (analysis, synthesis, etc.)?

QUESTION IS:
___ 0. Unimportant
___ 1. Relatively Unimportant
___ 2. Moderately Important
___ 3. Important
___ 4. Extremely Important

| 0 | 1 | 2 | 3 | 4 | 5 | 6 |

NO OR LITTLE EXTENT   TO SOME EXTENT   GREAT EXTENT

3. To what extent do the objectives of the text compliment the goals and objectives of your course?

QUESTION IS:
___ 0. Unimportant
___ 1. Relatively Unimportant
___ 2. Moderately Important
___ 3. Important
___ 4. Extremely Important

343

B. CONTENT:

```
/ / / / / / /
0   1   2   3   4   5   6
NO OR       TO SOME     GREAT
LITTLE      EXTENT      EXTENT
EXTENT
```

4. Is the text narrative based or activity based?

QUESTION IS:
— 0. Unimportant
— 1. Relatively Unimportant
— 2. Moderately Important
— 3. Important
— 4. Extremely Important

```
/ / / / / / /
0   1   2   3   4   5   6
NO OR       TO SOME     GREAT
LITTLE      EXTENT      EXTENT
EXTENT
```

5. How is subject matter developed?

QUESTION IS:
— 0. Unimportant
— 1. Relatively Unimportant
— 2. Moderately Important
— 3. Important
— 4. Extremely Important

```
/ / / / / / /
0   1   2   3   4   5   6
NO OR       TO SOME     GREAT
LITTLE      EXTENT      EXTENT
EXTENT
```

6. To what extent do the materials focus on the major concepts and/or ideas of the theme or category being evaluated?

QUESTION IS:
— 0. Unimportant
— 1. Relatively Unimportant
— 2. Moderately Important
— 3. Important
— 4. Extremely Important

```
/ / / / / / /
0   1   2   3   4   5   6
NO OR       TO SOME     GREAT
LITTLE      EXTENT      EXTENT
EXTENT
```

7. To what extent is the subject matter geared to the interests, abilities, and needs of the students using the material?

QUESTION IS:
— 0. Unimportant
— 1. Relatively Unimportant
— 2. Moderately Important
— 3. Important
— 4. Extremely Important

```
/ / / / / / /
0   1   2   3   4   5   6
NO OR       TO SOME     GREAT
LITTLE      EXTENT      EXTENT
EXTENT
```

8. To what extent does the content of the text-book (both pictorial and written) reflect the pluralistic, multi-ethnic nature of our society, past and present?

QUESTION IS:
— 0. Unimportant
— 1. Relatively Unimportant
— 2. Moderately Important
— 3. Important
— 4. Extremely Important

```
/ / / / / / /
0   1   2   3   4   5   6
NO OR       TO SOME     GREAT
LITTLE      EXTENT      EXTENT
EXTENT
```

9. To what extent does the material depict both male and female members of various groups in society in situations which exhibit them un-biasedly in a wide variety of roles?

QUESTION IS:
— 0. Unimportant
— 1. Relatively Unimportant
— 2. Moderately Important
— 3. Important
— 4. Extremely Important

```
/ / / / / / /
0   1   2   3   4   5   6
NO OR       TO SOME     GREAT
LITTLE      EXTENT      EXTENT
EXTENT
```

10. To what extent is the role of various religious and socio-economic groups, past and present, accurately and fairly presented?

QUESTION IS:
— 0. Unimportant
— 1. Relatively Unimportant
— 2. Moderately Important
— 3. Important
— 4. Extremely Important

L__L__/__/__/__/__L
0   1   2   3   4   5   6
NO OR   TO SOME   GREAT
LITTLE   EXTENT   EXTENT
EXTENT

11. To what extent would the book tend to encourage a positive self-image for students of all ethnic and socio-economic groups?

QUESTION IS:
__0. Unimportant
__1. Relatively Unimportant
__2. Moderately Important
__3. Important
__4. Extremely Important

L__L__/__/__/__/__L
0   1   2   3   4   5   6
NO OR   TO SOME   GREAT
LITTLE   EXTENT   EXTENT
EXTENT

12. To what extent does the program develop accurate con-cepts and generalizations?

QUESTION IS:
__0. Unimportant
__1. Relatively Unimportant
__2. Moderately Important
__3. Important
__4. Extremely Important

L__L__/__/__/__/__L
0   1   2   3   4   5   6
NO OR   TO SOME   GREAT
LITTLE   EXTENT   EXTENT
EXTENT

13. To what extent are historical, social, scientific or other events based on the latest evidence and on social data?

QUESTION IS:
__0. Unimportant
__1. Relatively Unimportant
__2. Moderately Important
__3. Important
__4. Extremely Important

L__L__/__/__/__/__L
0   1   2   3   4   5   6
NO OR   TO SOME   GREAT
LITTLE   EXTENT   EXTENT
EXTENT

14. To what extent does the book tend to raise open questions and present issues?

QUESTION IS:
__0. Unimportant
__1. Relatively Unimportant
__2. Moderately Important
__3. Important
__4. Extremely Important

L__L__/__/__/__/__L
0   1   2   3   4   5   6
NO OR   TO SOME   GREAT
LITTLE   EXTENT   EXTENT
EXTENT

15. To what extent does the material analyze inter-group tension and con-flict frankly, objectively, and with emphasis upon resolving our social problems?

QUESTION IS:
__0. Unimportant
__1. Relatively Unimportant
__2. Moderately Important
__3. Important
__4. Extremely Important

L__L__/__/__/__/__L
0   1   2   3   4   5   6
NO OR   TO SOME   GREAT
LITTLE   EXTENT   EXTENT
EXTENT

16. To what extent is the legitimacy of a variety of lifestyles acknowledged?

QUESTION IS:
__0. Unimportant
__1. Relatively Unimportant
__2. Moderately Important
__3. Important
__4. Extremely Important

L__L__/__/__/__/__L
0   1   2   3   4   5   6
NO OR   TO SOME   GREAT
LITTLE   EXTENT   EXTENT
EXTENT

17. To what extent does the material necessitate the use of supplementary instructional media (films, simulation/games, filmstrips, tapes, etc.)?

QUESTION IS:
__0. Unimportant
__1. Relatively Unimportant
__2. Moderately Important
__3. Important
__4. Extremely Important

/ / / / / / /
0 1 2 3 4 5 6
NO OR   TO SOME   GREAT
LITTLE   EXTENT   EXTENT
EXTENT

18. To what extent does the language of the material accommodate the range of abilities and backgrounds of the students most likely to be using it?

QUESTION IS:

___0. Unimportant
___1. Relatively Unimportant
___2. Moderately Important
___3. Important
___4. Extremely Important

C. ORGANIZATION:

/ / / / / / /
0 1 2 3 4 5 6
NO OR   TO SOME   GREAT
LITTLE   EXTENT   EXTENT
EXTENT

19. Is the material published in a single volume or as a multi-volumed set?

QUESTION IS:

___0. Unimportant
___1. Relatively Unimportant
___2. Moderately Important
___3. Important
___4. Extremely Important

/ / / / / / /
0 1 2 3 4 5 6
NO OR   TO SOME   GREAT
LITTLE   EXTENT   EXTENT
EXTENT

20. Are lessons developed independently or in a series?

QUESTION IS:

___0. Unimportant
___1. Relatively Unimportant
___2. Moderately Important
___3. Important
___4. Extremely Important

/ / / / / / /
0 1 2 3 4 5 6
NO OR   TO SOME   GREAT
LITTLE   EXTENT   EXTENT
EXTENT

21. To what extent can the teacher depart from the sequence of material prescribed by the author(s) without impairing its effectiveness?

QUESTION IS:

___0. Unimportant
___1. Relatively Unimportant
___2. Moderately Important
___3. Important
___4. Extremely Important

/ / / / / / /
0 1 2 3 4 5 6
NO OR   TO SOME   GREAT
LITTLE   EXTENT   EXTENT
EXTENT

22. To what extent are there opportunities for alternative teaching strategies?

QUESTION IS:

___0. Unimportant
___1. Relatively Unimportant
___2. Moderately Important
___3. Important
___4. Extremely Important

D. SKILL DEVELOPMENT:

/ / / / / / /
0 1 2 3 4 5 6
NO OR   TO SOME   GREAT
LITTLE   EXTENT   EXTENT
EXTENT

23. To what extent are skills and skill development stressed?

QUESTION IS:

___0. Unimportant
___1. Relatively Unimportant
___2. Moderately Important
___3. Important
___4. Extremely Important

```
 |  /  /  /  /  /  /
 0  1  2  3  4  5  6
 NO OR    TO SOME    GREAT
 LITTLE   EXTENT     EXTENT
 EXTENT
```

24. To what extent do the materials accommodate the range of reading abilities of the students most likely to be using it?

QUESTION IS:
—0. Unimportant
—1. Relatively Unimportant
—2. Moderately Important
—3. Important
—4. Extremely Important

```
 |  /  /  /  /  /  /
 0  1  2  3  4  5  6
 NO OR    TO SOME    GREAT
 LITTLE   EXTENT     EXTENT
 EXTENT
```

25. To what extent are students required to employ rational thought in discovering and testing value positions?

QUESTION IS:
—0. Unimportant
—1. Relatively Unimportant
—2. Moderately Important
—3. Important
—4. Extremely Important

E. CONCLUSIONS:

```
 |  /  /  /  /  /  /
 0  1  2  3  4  5  6
 NO OR    TO SOME    GREAT
 LITTLE   EXTENT     EXTENT
 EXTENT
```

26. To what extent would this material be learnable?

QUESTION IS:
— 0. Unimportant
— 1. Relatively Unimportant
— 2. Moderately Important
— 3. Important
— 4. Extremely Important

```
 |  /  /  /  /  /  /
 0  1  2  3  4  5  6
 NO OR    TO SOME    GREAT
 LITTLE   EXTENT     EXTENT
 EXTENT
```

27. To what extent would this material be teachable?

QUESTION IS:
— 0. Unimportant
— 1. Relatively Unimportant
— 2. Moderately Important
— 3. Important
— 4. Extremely Important

```
 |  /  /  /  /  /  /
 0  1  2  3  4  5  6
 NO OR    TO SOME    GREAT
 LITTLE   EXTENT     EXTENT
 EXTENT
```

28. To what extent would you recommend this material be used?

QUESTION IS:
— 0. Unimportant
— 1. Relatively Unimportant
— 2. Moderately Important
— 3. Important
— 4. Extremely Important

```
 /1ST /2ND /3RD /4TH /5TH /
 CHOICE            CHOICE
```

29. How would you rank this textbook among those reviewed?

```
 |  /  /  |
 YES    NO
```

30. Is this material designed for students with reading disabilities?

```
 |  /  /  |
 BETTER  WORSE
```

31. Is this material better, worse, or about the same as the existing material?

347

E. COMMENTS:

Use this space for elaborating on your ratings of this book. Summarize your opinions, giving particular attention to the extent this material is consistent with department goals and educational platform.

SUPPLEMENTARY MATERIAL EVALUATION FORM

SUBJECT MOST APPLICABLE TO: _____

TITLE OF MATERIAL _____

COPYRIGHT DATE _____ AUTHOR (DEVELOPER) _____

PUBLISHER _____

TYPE OF MATERIAL (CHECK ONE) FILM _____ FILMSTRIP _____ TAPE _____

    FILMSTRIP/TAPE _____ SINGLE CONCEPT FILM _____ SLIDE/TAPE _____

    VIDEO/CASSETTE _____ TRANSPARENCY _____ SIMULATION/GAME _____

    MULTI-MEDIA KIT _____ INDEPENDENT TEACHING/LEARNING UNIT _____

OTHER _____

EVALUATOR _____

COST _____

Directions: Read each question slowly and thoroughly. To answer a question, mark an "X" over the number indicating your evaluation of the material.

SAMPLE:

To what extent does the title indicate the content of the material?

```
  /    /    /    /    /    /    /
0    1    2    3    4    5    6
NO OR      TO SOME      GREAT
LITTLE     EXTENT       EXTENT
EXTENT
```

1. To what extent is this material geared to the interests and abilities of the student who will use it?

```
  /    /    /    /    /    /    /
0    1    2    3    4    5    6
NO OR      TO SOME      GREAT
LITTLE     EXTENT       EXTENT
EXTENT
```

2. To what extent is the language used understandable to students using the material?

```
  /    /    /    /    /    /    /
0    1    2    3    4    5    6
NO OR      TO SOME      GREAT
LITTLE     EXTENT       EXTENT
EXTENT
```

3. To what extent are the instructional objectives of this material complimentary to your course goals and objectives?

```
  /    /    /    /    /    /    /
0    1    2    3    4    5    6
NO OR      TO SOME      GREAT
LITTLE     EXTENT       EXTENT
EXTENT
```

349

4. To what extent does this material aid in the development of skills?

```
 /  /  /  /  /  /  /
0   1   2   3   4   5  6
NO OR      TO SOME    GREAT
LITTLE     EXTENT     EXTENT
EXTENT
```

5. To what extent does this material require students to use higher processes?

```
 /  /  /  /  /  /  /
0   1   2   3   4   5  6
NO OR      TO SOME    GREAT
LITTLE     EXTENT     EXTENT
EXTENT
```

6. To what extent does this material require students to examine their personal values on a particular issue or situation?

```
 /  /  /  /  /  /  /
0   1   2   3   4   5  6
NO OR      TO SOME    GREAT
LITTLE     EXTENT     EXTENT
EXTENT
```

7. To what extent is this material conducive to small group instruction?

```
 /  /  /  /  /  /  /
0   1   2   3   4   5  6
NO OR      TO SOME    GREAT
LITTLE     EXTENT     EXTENT
EXTENT
```

8. To what extent is this material applicable to an individualized program of instruction?

```
 /  /  /  /  /  /  /
0   1   2   3   4   5  6
NO OR      TO SOME    GREAT
LITTLE     EXTENT     EXTENT
EXTENT
```

9. To what extent can the teacher depart from the instructional sequence of the material without impairing its effectiveness?

```
 /  /  /  /  /  /  /
0   1   2   3   4   5  6
NO OR      TO SOME    GREAT
LITTLE     EXTENT     EXTENT
EXTENT
```

10. To what extent does this material assist in the development of accurage concepts and generalizations?

```
 /  /  /  /  /  /  /
0   1   2   3   4   5  6
NO OR      TO SOME    GREAT
LITTLE     EXTENT     EXTENT
EXTENT
```

11. To what extent does this material tend to raise open questions?

```
 /  /  /  /  /  /  /
0   1   2   3   4   5  6
NO OR      TO SOME    GREAT
LITTLE     EXTENT     EXTENT
EXTENT
```

12. To what extent can this material be used to initiate inquiry?

/ / / / / / /
0   1   2   3   4   5   6
NO OR
LITTLE   TO SOME   GREAT
EXTENT   EXTENT   EXTENT

13. To what extent can this material be used in the application of concepts and generalizations?

/ / / / / / /
0   1   2   3   4   5   6
NO OR
LITTLE   TO SOME   GREAT
EXTENT   EXTENT   EXTENT

14. To what extent is this material applicable to more than one discipline?

/ / / / / / /
0   1   2   3   4   5   6
NO OR
LITTLE   TO SOME   GREAT
EXTENT   EXTENT   EXTENT

15. To what extent does this material require the replacement of specific parts (pieces, worksheets, group activity sheets, etc.)?

/ / / / / / /
0   1   2   3   4   5   6
NO OR
LITTLE   TO SOME   GREAT
EXTENT   EXTENT   EXTENT

16. To what extent is this material designed for students with reading deficiencies?

/ / / / / / /
0   1   2   3   4   5   6
NO OR
LITTLE   TO SOME   GREAT
EXTENT   EXTENT   EXTENT

17. To what extent would you recommend that this material be used?

/ / / / / / /
0   1   2   3   4   5   6
NO OR
LITTLE   TO SOME   GREAT
EXTENT   EXTENT   EXTENT

18. How would you rank this set of material among others reviewed?

/ 1ST / 2ND / 3RD / 4TH / 5TH /
CHOICE   CHOICE

19. *Comments:* Use this space for elaborating on your ratings. Summarize your opinions, giving particular attention to the extent this material is consistent with department goals and educational platform.

EVALUATING YOUR DEPARTMENT'S EDUCATIONAL PROGRAM

Granted that continuous and informal evaluation is the approach you most likely use to understand and improve your department's educational program. From time to time, however, it is desirable to conduct a full-scale formal evaluation. Such an evaluation is not to judge adequacy of individuals, or to summatively evaluate the department's program. Little is gained from voting up or down or rating a department's program on a ten-point scale ranging from awful to super. What is needed and intended is a formative evaluation strategy designed to increase understanding of the department's program offerings, to focus faculty attention more deliberately on what they believe in and are trying to accomplish, and to provide feedback on relative progress toward reaching these ideals. Program evaluation should be seen more holistically as a natural and interdependent component of the department's staff development and curriculum improvement activities.

In this section a description of an actual evaluation of an English department program is provided as a model for both discussion and example purposes. There is a danger in wholesale borrowing of evaluation approaches but the intent here is to suggest ideas to help you tailor an evaluation program to fit your department. The model provided is traditional in its format but incorporates features discussed in the concepts section of Chapters 9 and 10, such as defining goals and objectives broadly and evaluating unplanned events.

Assuming that one understands the formative nature of periodic and systematic evaluation of department programs, it is a good idea for departments and units throughout the junior and senior high school to be involved in a continuous evaluation rotation. In successive years, one department is selected for systematic annual review. A more ambitious rotation would ensure that each department and unit review of program is conducted systematically at least once every five years. Departments should solicit help from each other in planning, conducting, and making sense of the evaluation programs. In the example provided, the group which assumed major responsibility for the evaluation included four English teachers and one social studies teacher from the same school and one elementary school teacher.

Is evaluation costly in time and money? Yes, but the costs may well be greater where evaluation does not take place, when one considers the additional benefits likely to accrue from evaluation: building an effective program for students and the community. Is the thought of evaluation likely to conjure images of suspicion, interference, and repression in teachers? Yes, again, if evaluation is seen as something the system does to the teachers rather than something done *with* the teachers to the system. Program evaluation should be strictly formative and the slightest hedging from this position can endanger the credibility of all your evaluation effort for a long time.

The evaluation program that follows was conducted by Enoch Sawin and teachers from the school involved.

AN EVALUATION OF AN ENGLISH CURRICULUM*

It should be emphasized that the main purpose of the evaluation study was no merely to evaluate but rather to obtain information useful in improving the curriculum. For example, the study group was not interested in comparing the overall achievement of pupils in the district with norms. Such comparisons would yield only gratification or disappointment; they would not point to ways in which the curriculum could be improved. On the other hand, the members were much interested in *patterns* of achievement or lack of achievement, for these would point to areas of needed emphasis in the program.

The consensus of all concerned was that the new curriculum was working well and was accepted by most teachers and pupils. The problem was not one of finding out what was wrong; it was how to conduct an evaluation study that would yield information on how to make a good program even better. A second purpose was to provide the participants with in-service education on the use of evaluation techniques.

Special care was taken to clarify the purpose of the study, so that it would not be viewed as an attempt to check on the effectiveness of teachers or to pass judgment on individual students.

PROCEDURES

After the decision was made to evaluate the modified curriculum, the author was engaged as a consultant to assist in planning and conducting the study. In the early planning meetings the author met with school administrators and teachers interested in the project. Their interests and ideas were discussed, together with additional possibilities outlined by the author.

After the initial planning sessions, a work group was identified. It consisted of six volunteer teachers. They decided to meet for two hours once a week for the remaining half of the school term. The school board agreed to grant credit toward salary increments for the teachers who participated.

The first major task undertaken by the work group was to draw up specifications of what to evaluate. It was necessary to clarify the instructional purposes in terms of the kinds of changes in thinking, feeling, or acting that were desired. These statements of objectives provided the main part of the specifications for selecting and developing evaluation instruments.

It was agreed, however, that the evaluation study should not be limited to those *planned* outcomes set forth in the objectives. Sometimes *unplanned* effects of a program of instruction prove to be as important as attaining or failing to attain objectives of instruction. For example, it is likely that many teachers of English contribute a great deal toward logical habits of thought on the part of their students, even though their objectives do not include the teaching of logic. Another example, but of an unfortunate kind, is that students have sometimes been known to develop such a negative attitude toward the study of English that it has a seriously disabling effect on their mastery of the subject and on later use of what they have learned.

On the basis of this reasoning, the group planned to make provisions in certain instruments for identifying some of the unplanned effects that might be resulting from the English program. It was decided, however, that the first phase of the evaluation effort would be focused primarily on objectives because the number of things that could be evaluated was quite limited and because the objectives were actually rather broadly con-

*From *Evaluation and the Work of the Teacher,* by Enoch I. Swain (Belmont, Calif.: Wadsworth Publishing Company, Inc., 1969). Reprinted by permission of the publisher.

ceived. For these reasons, most of the specifications for instruments were in the form of objectives. It was believed that the best way of getting started on assessing unplanned effects was to include some items in the instruments that were "open ended"—that allowed students to express some of their own reactions and ideas. It was hoped that the results would yield clues on possibly important outcomes that could be used as leads in later, more systematic assessments of unplanned effects.

The specifications for selection and construction of instruments were formulated in terms of subject matter content, behavior (thinking, feeling, or action), and types of instruments likely to be used for assessing each type of outcome. An excerpt from the table of specifications follows:

CONTENT	BEHAVIOR	TYPES OF INSTRUMENT
"Main currents" of American literature and selected portions of world literature by eminent authors	Comprehends what the authors are trying to communicate	Objective test items, written exercises, and interviews
	Is able to identify some of the qualities of the selections that make them great literary masterpieces	Objective test items, written exercises, and interviews
	Enjoys reading or listening to the selections	Self-report questionnaires, interviews, and library records
	Reads literature of these kinds extensively for enjoyment and seeks opportunities to interact with literature of these kinds	Direct observation, interviews, and self-report questionnaires

The complete table of specifications is four pages long. The group felt that the process of analyzing the objectives for this purpose was a very worthwhile experience in itself. In addition to serving as the basis for evaluation, the clarifications achieved in the table of specifications made it useful for further curriculum development and instructional planning.

Examination of the completed table of specifications made it inescapably clear that even a fully comprehensive sampling of the outcomes of the program would be a huge task, but the only sensible thing to do was to make a beginning somewhere. It was noted that the table of specifications contained the following kinds of outcomes: (1) cognitive attainments (knowledge, understanding, and so forth); (2) actual performance (such as communication through writing); and (3) attitudes. It was considered important that each of these kinds of outcomes be represented in the initial results obtained. The group decided that the best way to get started was to find or construct one instrument to measure cognitive attainment, one instrument to obtain a sample of actual performance, and one instrument to assess attitudes. The instruments selected were a standardized test, a letter writing exercise with a diagnostic scoring system, and a sentence completion test.

Choosing the standardized test was a difficult task. Detailed comparison of the contents of a number of standardized tests showed that no single test even came close to covering all the cognitive outcomes in the table of specifications. Further analysis showed that it would be necessary to use portions of no less than *five* commercial standardized tests in order to cover, even fairly adequately, the cognitive outcomes. Time was not available for administering portions of five different tests, so the one test that seemed to be the best fit for the objectives was selected. This was the *California Achievement Test.*[1]

The checklist of actual performance was constructed by the group. The instrument will be found on pages 271 to 275. In this exercise the students were given an outline and some specific information that was to be contained in a letter. The instructions gave the students directions on how to write the letter and to use the outline and information provided. A special checksheet was prepared for teachers to use in evaluating the letters. The checksheet provided spaces for tallying errors in sentence structure, capitalization, punctuation, spelling, division of words, abbreviations, relationships among sentences, relationships among paragraphs, letter writing form, and accuracy in presenting the information the letter was supposed to contain. Use of the rating sheet in tallying the kinds of errors made by groups of students was planned to provide a diagnostic profile of attainments and deficiencies. The degree of specificity of the checksheet is indicated by the fact that it has 99 separate tally boxes. For example, it has boxes for six types of errors in capitalization and for eight types of errors in punctuation.

A serious attempt was made by the group to attain objectivity and uniform standards in the use of the checksheet. All members of the group jointly evaluated several letters and discussed differences. Good progress was made, but more joint sessions of this kind were probably needed.

It was recognized that the checklist could be used to assess only a narrow band of the kind of performance listed in the table of specifications. It was necessary, however, to limit the scope of the instrument in order to keep the size of the tasks of developing and using it from getting out of hand.

The sentence completion test, which was developed to assess attitudes, was presented to students as an exercise in writing complete sentences. In each item the students were given a few words to start a sentence, followed by a blank space which was to be filled in with words that would make a complete sentence. They were told that they could fill the blanks with any words they chose, so long as the result was a complete sentence. A few sample items are as follows:

4. To me, the subject of English is _____.
8. After I finish high school, my study of English will most likely _____.
15. Classwork on how to make good sentences is _____.
31. I wish my English teacher would _____.

Some items on history and arithmetic were included to make it less apparent that the instrument was aimed at attitudes towards English. There were 31 items in all. It was believed that student responses to this type of projective test would reflect attitudes toward English related to the objectives and possibly additional outcomes in the form of unplanned effects of the program.

Table D.1 shows the number of students who responded to each instrument, by grade level.

The sample for the standardized test was the total of students in Grades Nine, Ten, and Eleven who were in school on the day the test was administered, except for the students in English I Special (freshman remedial). In the other samples an attempt was made to draw as random a sample as possible. The situation, however, did not permit use of truly random samples. Table D.1 shows that most of the students in the samples were from Grades Nine, Ten, and Eleven. This was because the instruments were not ready to be administered until late in the school year and student time was not always available.

[1] Ernest W. Tiegs and Willis W. Clark, *California Achievement Test, Form W, Grades 9–12* (Los Angeles: California Test Bureau, 1957).

The samples available for testing were considered suitable for preliminary tryout of the new instruments and for at least exploratory analyses of results.

Before presenting the findings, the kinds of analyses made of the results will be summarized. The following scores were obtained on the *California Achievement Test*: capitalization, punctuation, word usage, total mechanics of English, and total language. The means and standard deviations[2] of each of these scores were computed for each grade level. In addition to these scores, mean scores were obtained on the 31 subareas of the test. This permitted the compiling of a highly specific diagnostic profile of students at each grade level. To facilitate interpretation, the means for all the subarea scores were converted to percents.

TABLE D.1. Numbers of students responding to instruments

| | GRADE LEVEL | | | | | | | | | |
Instrument	4	5	6	7	8	9	10	11	12	Total
Standardized test						151	128	117		396
Letter writing exercise						39	52	58		149
Sentence completion test		29		18	33	26	67	81		254

The tallies on the checksheets for the letter writing exercise were combined by grade level. In addition, separate compilations were made for those students in the college preparatory classes as compared to those in general English classes. When appropriate, the tallies were converted to percents for ease of interpretation.

A content analysis was made of all the responses to all the items on the sentence completion test. This was done by grouping all the similar responses to each item and tallying the number of students giving each type of response. Since there were 31 items in the sentence completion test, it was necessary to make 31 separate content analyses of the responses from the 254 students in the sample. The tallies were recorded separately by grade level.

The levels of statistical significance of results were not determined. One reason was that the study was a preliminary, exploratory one, with limited resources. In addition, there is a considerable amount of controversy about whether tests of statistical significance are necessary or appropriate in curriculum evaluation studies.[3]

FINDINGS

Standardized Test Results As shown in Table D.2, the means for each of the scores obtained on the *California Achievement Test* showed improvement from Grades Nine

---

[2] Standard deviation is an index of the amount of dispersion, or "scatter," in a set of scores. The greater the differences among the scores, the greater the standard deviation. The closer the scores are grouped around their average, the smaller the standard deviation.

[3] Herbert H. Hyman, Charles R. Wright, and Terence K. Hopkins, *Applications of Methods of Evaluation: Four Studies of the Encampment for Citizenship* (Berkeley: University of California Press, 1962), p. 70.

through Eleven. This is in accord with expectations, but the fact that there were no exceptions to the trend is noteworthy. In regard to Table D.2, it is important to point out that there are three "tracks" in Grade Nine (college preparatory, general, and remedial) but only two in Grades Ten and Eleven. Remedial students were *not* tested in Grade Nine. The two tracks in Grades Ten and Eleven included remedial students, who *were* included in the testing. The fact that remedial students were included in the testing of Grades Ten and Eleven but not in Grade Nine almost certainly made the trends of improvement from Grades Nine through Eleven look smaller than they actually were. The evaluation group had planned additional compilations of both Table D.2 and Table D.3 showing results separately for college preparatory and general English classes, but this was not completed because of lack of time and resources.

TABLE D.2. ACHIEVEMENT TEST RESULTS

Grade	CAPITALI-ZATION		PUNCTU-ATION		WORK USAGE		SPELLING		MECHANICS OF ENGLISH		TOTAL LANGUAGE	
	Mean	S.D.*	Mean	S.D.	Mean	S.D.	Mean	S.D.	Mean	S.D.	Mean	S.D.
11	33.5	5.5	26.8	7.9	39.8	10.8	14.5	6.1	100.1	22.0	114.5	27.2
10	32.3	5.9	23.7	7.4	37.5	10.2	12.4	5.2	93.5	20.4	106.4	23.0
9	31.9	6.8	22.1	7.7	37.2	10.1	12.3	4.2	91.3	21.9	104.2	24.6

*Standard deviation.

Analysis of the subarea scores showed that the greatest amount of progress from Grades Nine through Eleven was attained in the following subareas:

Capitalization:
Titles of literature and drama
First words of quotations

Punctuation:
Commas
Colons
Apostrophes
Quotation marks
Quotations within quotations
Overpunctuation

Word Usage:
Recognition of complete sentences
Classifying sentences as simple, complex, or compound

Some of the subarea scores *decreased* between Grades Nine and Eleven. The subareas in which this occurred are as follows:

Capitalization:
Days and months

Word Usage:
Differentiating between direct object and subject

357

Recognizing nominative case
Phrases and clauses
Tense

The trends for Grades Nine through Eleven for all subarea scores are shown in Table D.3.

TABLE D.3. MEAN SUBAREA SCORES EXPRESSED AS PERCENTS

	GRADE LEVEL		
SUBAREA SCORE	9	10	11
Capitalization			
Names of institutions	78	77	84
Titles of persons	92	92	93
Titles of literature and drama	86	89	95
First words of sentences	74	77	77
Names of persons	91	92	96
Names of places	74	75	77
Days and months	92	92	91
First words of quotations	57	58	67
Names of clubs	88	86	88
Names of languages	81	86	85
Overcapitalization	78	79	79
Punctuation			
Commas	63	68	75
Colons	52	57	74
Apostrophes	51	60	70
Quotation marks	46	54	59
Quotations within quotations	16	10	27
Overpunctuation	59	61	66
Word Usage			
Recognition of complete sentences	48	50	61
Classifying sentences as simple, complex, or compound	58	71	66
Differentiating between direct object and subject	81	78	80
Pronoun forms for subject and direct object	72	73	75
Differentiating between direct and indirect objects	63	64	66
Recognizing possessive case	56	52	62
Recognizing nominative case	68	71	63
Phrases and clauses	63	64	62
Classifying words as to parts of speech	70	70	73
Tense	72	71	71
Other verb forms	64	84	67
Agreement of subject with verb	57	60	63
Agreement of pronoun with antecedent	74	68	77
Miscellaneous	59	59	60

The magnitude of the percentages in Table D.3 reflects a combination of level of mastery of the subarea by the students and the relative difficulty of the items in the test. In other words, if the mean for a particular subarea is high, it may indicate either that the students acquired a high level of learning in this subarea or that test items in this subarea were easy—or both. In spite of this limitation, however, the magnitude of the percentages can be used to suggest hypotheses about areas of high achievement and low achievement. Subareas with relatively *high* means were differentiating between direct object and subject and capitalization of names of institutions, titles of persons, titles of literature and drama, names of persons, names of clubs, and names of languages. Subareas with relatively *low* means were punctuation involving quotation marks, quotations within quotations, and overpunctuation; and word usage involving recognition of complete sentences, classifying sentences as simple, complex, or compound, differentiating between direct and indirect objects, recognizing possessive case, recognizing nominative case, phrases and clauses, other verb forms, and agreement of subject with verb.

Letter writing exercise results The *trends* noted in the results from the letter writing exercise were as follows:

1. There was an increase in the number of run-on sentences between Grades Nine and Eleven.
2. There was a decline in the *proportion* of acceptable sentences of all types between Grades Nine and Eleven. For example, eleventh graders wrote a larger *number* of acceptable simple sentences, but the *proportion* of attempted simple sentences that were acceptable was smaller for eleventh graders than for ninth graders.
3. There was an increase in errors in capitalization involving both names of persons and overcapitalization from Grades Nine through Eleven. The standardized test results showed slight *improvement* in both these areas.
4. A great many more errors were recorded for tenth graders in capitalizing names of places than for either ninth or eleventh graders. No such trend was found in the results of the standardized test.
5. There was an increase in errors in the use of both commas and semicolons from the ninth to the eleventh grades. This result is in disagreement with the results on commas from the standardized test.
6. The number of spelling errors increased from Grades Nine through Eleven. A total of 33 errors in spelling were noted for ninth graders, 137 for tenth graders, and 111 for eleventh graders. This might be due to the fact that tenth and eleventh graders used more words—or more difficult words—in their letters than did ninth graders. The standardized test showed a slight improvement in spelling.
7. There was a decrease (improvement) in the amount of overabbreviation from the ninth through the eleventh grades.
8. A much larger number of deficiencies in transitions between paragraphs was noted for tenth graders than for either ninth or eleventh graders.
9. There was a decrease in errors in the form and content of headings from Grades Nine through Eleven, although more errors of this kind were recorded for tenth graders than for ninth graders.
10. More errors in indentations were noted for tenth graders than for either ninth or eleventh graders.

In contrast to the *trends* from Grades Nine through Eleven noted above, the following are the most frequent *kinds* of errors noted in the letters *for Grades Nine, Ten, and Eleven combined:*

1. Lack of conciseness in sentence structure
2. Lack of clarity in sentence structure

359

3. Lack of logic in sentence structure
4. Run-on sentences in attempts at compound sentences
5. Lack of agreement of subject with verb (especially for eleventh graders)
6. Errors in construction of compound sentences (only about half the compound sentences attempted were acceptable)
7. Errors in capitalization involving names of persons and names of places
8. Overcapitalization
9. Misuse of commas and semicolons
10. Errors in spelling
11. Overabbreviation
12. Failure to achieve purpose of usual paragraph pattern (lead-development-"clincher")
13. Lack of fluency or smoothness among sentences within paragraphs
14. Inadequate transitions between paragraphs
15. Inadequate form and content of letter headings
16. Fragments rather than complete sentences

It should be remembered that the types of errors listed above are less than half those checked on in evaluating the letters. The other types of errors listed on the checksheet were considerably less frequent. Discouragement should not, therefore, have resulted from noting the more frequent errors; this merely provided a basis for identifying areas that may have needed relatively more emphasis in instruction.

The results from the letter writing exercise were also examined for differences between college preparatory classes and general English classes. As would be expected, the college preparatory groups were generally superior in performance. There was one exception, however; the college preparatory group made considerably more errors in overabbreviation than did the general English group.

It should be borne in mind that the results from the letter writing exercise were obtained with an instrument being used for the first time. In addition, there probably were some differences in standards among the different teachers who used the checksheet to evaluate the letters in spite of determined efforts to eliminate such inconsistencies.

Sentence completion test results   The content analyses of responses to the sentence completion test indicated that more than half the students had rather favorable attitudes toward English. An important finding, however, was that there seemed to be a sizable minority of students who had a serious dislike for English. It was estimated that this group included approximately one-fourth the student body. It was gratifying to note that the attitudes reflected in the sentence completion test were clearly more favorable than unfavorable, but this did not remove the need for concern about the considerable number of students whose attitudes seemed so negative as to interfere seriously with their continuing mastery of the subject and, most importantly, with their actual use of their knowledge of English when they left school.

The following excerpts from the content analyses are provided to illustrate the kinds of results which showed both the generally favorable attitudes and those of the negatively inclined minority:

4. To me, the subject of English is _____.

STUDENT RESPONSES	NUMBER
not interesting, or boring	17
stupid, a waste of time, and so forth	13

very important, or useful	44
good, or nice	18
interesting	25

8. After I finish high school, my study of English will most likely _____ _____ .

STUDENT RESPONSES	NUMBER
come in handy, or help in my work	48
continue	14
be used regularly	5
be important	4
help me in college, or continue in college	8
discontinue entirely	28
be forgotten, or mostly forgotten	20
be dropped to a certain extent	8
be of little or no use	5

30. To me, reading and discussing stories and other works by famous authors is _____ .

STUDENT RESPONSES	NUMBER
boring	25
not interesting	8
not necessary	26
awful	4
not good	5
interesting	61
all right	11
enjoyable	40
good, or educational	16
important, or worthwhile	12

Another finding from the sentence completion test was that a considerable number of students found English difficult. They said they could not understand it or that it was confusing. This may have been a clue to why some students had negative attitudes toward the subject.

CONCLUSIONS AND RECOMMENDATIONS

The results from the standardized test and the letter writing exercise provided a considerable amount of specific information for teachers to consider as they made plans for further improving curriculum materials and instructional strategies. The evaluations were exploratory, but they did add a wealth of specific indicators to be combined with others routinely available and thus contributed to the accuracy of the assessments made and to the richness of the sources of clues on ways to increase student learning in the direction of desired goals. The evaluation of the curriculum should, of course, be expanded to include a wider variety of student learning outcomes and to provide further verification of the above results.

One significant finding was an unplanned effect—the dislike that some students felt for the subject of English. It should be noted, however, that this attitude was not due to the new curriculum alone. It was the cumulative product of all exposures to the study of English, including those that occurred before the new curriculum was introduced. Even though students with a strong dislike for English seemed to be in the minority, this still was accepted as an urgent problem. Without proper motivation, such students will not

361

learn effectively. Furthermore, a small number of disinterested and dissatisfied students can seriously interfere with the effectiveness of the teaching-learning process for other students who are interested and able to learn.

Perhaps the next most important steps to take regarding this dislike of English would be to learn more about the nature and causes of the negative attitudes and to find remedies for them. This could be done in part by analysis of attitudes in relation to levels of mental ability, presence or absence of language barriers, socioeconomic status, career plans, and other relevant factors. Intensive studies of a few students by the case method would also be of great value.

There are a number of other ways in which the present exploratory study could be continued and expanded. One would be to develop an attitude scale that would be more convenient to score than the sentence completion test. Another would be to develop a performance test on the use of English in speech. Finally, some of the instruments should be administered to high school graduates as a follow-up on changes taking place after graduation.

The remaining pages of Appendix D contain the letter writing exercise and the rating sheet used in the project. This exercise is an example of a device that can serve both as a learning exercise and as a means for obtaining evaluation data.

DIRECTIONS FOR LETTER WRITING EXERCISE

For this exercise you are to make believe that you and your father (or perhaps another member of your family) took a trip by car recently to Salt Lake City. On the way back, you and your father saw a car accident in the little town of Oasis, Nevada. Your father stopped, of course, but found that it was not a bad accident. No one was hurt; so after the police officer arrived, your father left his name and address and drove on.

Later on, however, a question came up as to who should pay for the damage to the cars. So, after you and your father returned home, a letter came asking your father to describe what he saw at the accident. The letter asked for a quick answer, because the case had to be settled before a certain date. Your father was asked to send a letter back very soon to Mr. O. B. Jones, who is the justice of the peace in Oasis, the small town in Nevada.

Your father began to prepare his letter. Since it was to be a very important letter, he first made a careful outline of what he planned to say and a list of the facts about the accident as you and he remembered them. He also drew a picture to help remember how the accident happened.

Now suppose that your father became sick and did not feel able to finish the letter. He asks you to write the letter for him, and then he could check it over and sign it. This is the only way that the letter can be mailed on time, *so the rest is up to you.*

You will find a copy of your father's outline, his list of facts about the accident, and his picture of the accident on the next page.

Be sure to set up the letter in the correct form with all the complete headings, paragraphing, and punctuation so that your father will not have to show you how to do it and so that you will not have to be asked to write the letter again.

Since your letter may be used to decide who must pay a lot of money for the damage to the cars, you should stick closely to the *facts* listed by your father. You want the letter to be like what your father would write, so you should follow his *outline* very closely, too.

You may begin the letter now. There should be three paragraphs. Write it on scratch paper first before making the final copy.

OUTLINE OF THE LETTER

I. Background
   A. Time and place of the accident
   B. How we happened to be in Oasis at the time of the accident
II. How things were just before the accident
   A. The crossroad where the accident happened
   B. The two cars in the accident
   C. The directions in which the cars were moving
   D. The position of our car when we saw the accident
III. What happened in the accident
   A. How the cars were moving
   B. Where each car was hit

FACTS TO USE IN THE LETTER

1. Time and place of the accident: 3:20 in the afternoon on March 29, 1961, Main Street and Elm Avenue, in the town of Oasis, Nevada.
   We were driving through Oasis on our way home from Salt Lake City.
2. A stop sign is at the crossroad for cars on Elm Avenue.
   The two cars in the accident were a tan 1958 Chevrolet two-door sedan and a light blue 1959 Ford station wagon.
   There were no other cars in or near the accident.
   The Chevrolet was headed north on Elm Avenue and was stopped in front of the stop sign just before the accident.
   The Ford was going east on Main Street.
   Our car was following about 100 yards behind the Ford.
3. The Chevrolet started to move out into the intersection but stopped again just before getting into the path of the Ford. The Ford slowed almost to a stop. Then both started up and ran together, the left front end of the Chevrolet hitting the right front fender of the Ford.

THE PICTURE OF THE ACCIDENT

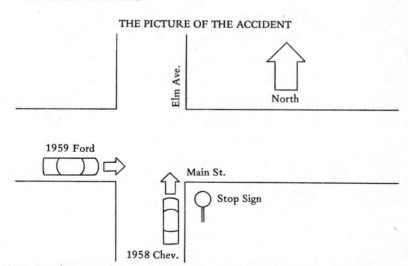

NOTE: You do *not* need to put the picture in the letter. The picture is to help you to see how the accident happened so that you can write about it in the letter.

EVALUATION OF AN ENGLISH CURRICULUM

NAME:_____ CLASS:_____

SCHOOL:_____ DATE:_____

_____

_____

_____

_____

_____

_____

_____

_____

_____

_____

_____

_____

_____

_____

_____

_____

_____

_____

_____

_____

_____

_____

_____

_____

_____

_____

_____

_____

_____

(If you need more space, turn sheet over.)

NAME_____ SCHOOL _____ GRADE_____ DATE_____

RATING SHEET
LETTER WRITING EXERCISE

DIRECTIONS: Apply items 1–10 to *one sentence at a time,* until all sentences have been evaluated. Then apply item 11 to *each paragraph, one at a time.* Finally, apply items 12–14 to the letter as a whole.

	FRAG-MENTS	SIMPLE SEN-TENCES	COM-PLEX SEN-TENCES	COM-POUND SEN-TENCES	COMPOUND-COMPLEX SENTENCES	TOTAL
1. Tally of number of each type attempted						
2. Use of criteria for sentence structure (tally violations)						
a. Lacks conciseness						
b. Lacks clarity						
c. Lacks logic within sentence						
d. Contains ambiguity						
e. Lacks unity—too many unrelated ideas						
f. Run-on sentences						
3. Rules of agreement (tally all violations)						
a. Subject with verb						
b. Pronoun with antecedent						
4. Tally of *acceptable* sentences of each type						

5. Tally of fragments that are

CLAUSES	PHRASES	SINGLE WORDS	TOTAL

6. Errors in capitalization (tally)

TITLES OF PERSONS	FIRST WORD OF SENTENCE	NAMES OF PERSONS	NAMES OF PLACES	DAYS AND MONTHS	OVER-CAPITALIZATION

7. Errors in punctuation (tally)

PERIOD	COMMA	QUESTION MARK	COLON	SEMI-COLON	APOS-TROPHE	QUOTES	OVER-PUNCTU-ATION

8. Errors in spelling (tally) [   ]

9. Errors in division of words (tally) [   ]

10. Errors in abbreviations (tally) [   ] OVERABBREVIATION

EVALUATION OF AN ENGLISH CURRICULUM

11. Relationships among sentences *within paragraphs*
    a. Lack of logical connectedness (tally) _____
    b. Lack of unity—too many unrelated
       ideas (tally) _____
    c. Does not achieve purpose of usual
       paragraph pattern (lead-development-
       "clincher") (tally) _____
    d. Lacks fluency or smoothness (tally) _____

12. Relationships *among paragraphs*
    a. Inadequate transitions between
       paragraphs (tally) _____
    b. Poorly chosen sequence of
       paragraphs (tally) _____
    c. To what extent does letter have
       overall unity or smoothness?   ___EXCELLENT ___GOOD ___FAIR ___POOR

13. Errors in letter writing form (tally)

CHOICE OF FORM	FORM AND CONTENT OF HEADINGS	SALUTATION	MARGINS AND POSITIONING	INDENTATIONS	COMPLIMENTARY CLOSE

14. Overall accuracy of information (compare with "Facts to Use in the Letter")
    CHECK ONE:
    _____ a. There were *very few* errors or omissions or none at all.
    _____ b. There were errors or omissions in *between one-fourth and one-half* of
             the facts.
    _____ c. There were errors or omissions in *at least half* of the facts, but at least
             one-fourth were accurate.
    _____ d. There were errors or omissions in *most or all* of the facts.

EVALUATING COGNITIVE LEVEL OF CLASSROOM ACTIVITIES

A number of taxonomies of objectives and activities were presented and discussed in the first section of this chapter. It was agreed that students should be exposed to ideas and learn to perform operations and intellectual tasks which certainly include the acquisition of knowledge but go beyond this level. Intellectual activity requires that a person not only know and understand but that he apply, analyze, synthesize, and evaluate concepts, relationships, and ideas.

In many classrooms, however, chairpersons will find that the variety of tasks required of students is limited and typically focuses on the acquisition and recalling of information. Teachers may very well intend to provide students with higher level experiences and often are not aware of the undue emphasis they give to knowledge-level objectives and activities.

In this section a self-evaluation form is provided which permits teachers to estimate, at least on one dimension, the sort of cognitive demands they are making on students. The form focuses on questions the teacher asks students and provides a method for sorting the questions into each of the categories of *The Taxonomy of Educational Objectives: The Cognitive Domain* as developed by Bloom and others.* Certainly other aspects of classroom activity need also to be considered in obtaining a complete picture but the use of questions is a common teaching technique and an evaluation technique which can provide important clues to cognitive level of classroom activity.

In using the self-evaluation form the teacher, either alone or with the help of the chairperson, collects and classifies the questions, and interprets the results. The teacher may focus on oral questions used in the normal course of classroom activity or on written questions asked of students. In the first case a tape recording will need to be made of the class sessions to be studied. In the second case, tests, assignments, workbooks, and other materials will need to be gathered for analysis.

Once the questions are collected, the next step is to classify them into each of the cognitive level categories. The form for classifying contains Part A for describing categories and Part B for recording and tallying questions. As each question is heard or read, compare it with the descriptions found in Part A. Place a tally mark in the corresponding section of Part B which provides the best match between the question and the descriptions provided. In classifying questions try to determine what is expected of the student. Is the student to remember, to criticize, to compare, to apply?

When all of the questions have been categorized, total the number of tallies and in each category determine the appropriate percentage. Refer to the concepts section of this chapter for further descriptions of each category.

---

*Benjamin S. Bloom, *Taxonomy of Educational Objectives: Cognitive Domain* (New York: David McKay Co., Inc., 1956).

SELF-EVALUATION FORM FOR ESTIMATING COGNITIVE LEVELS*

The Classification of Educational Goals in the Cognitive Domain
> "The cognitive domain . . . includes those objectives which deal with the recall or recognition of knowledge and the development of intellectual abilities and skills."

KNOWLEDGE

1. *Knowledge* of Specifics
  Terminology
  Specific Facts
 Knowledge of Ways and Means of Dealing with Specifics
  Conventions
  Trends and Sequences
  Classifications and Categories
  Criteria
  Methodology
 Knowledge of the Universals and Abstractions in a Field
  Principles and Generalizations
  Theories and Structures

INTELLECTUAL ABILITIES AND SKILLS

2. *Comprehension*
  Translation
  Interpretation
  Extrapolation
3. *Application*
4. *Analysis*
  Elements
  Relationships
  Organizational Principles
5. *Synthesis*
  Production of a Unique Communication
  Production of a Plan, or Proposed Set of Operations
  Derivation of a Set of Abstract Relations
6. *Evaluation*
  Judgments in Terms of Internal Evidence
  Judgments in Terms of External Criteria

---

*From Gary Munson and Ambrose Clegg, Jr., "Classroom Questions: Keys to Children's Thinking?" *Peabody Journal of Education*, March, 1970. Nashville: Peabody College for Teachers.

CATEGORY DESCRIPTION (PART A)				RECORDING FORM (PART B)	
CATEGORY NAME	EXPECTED COGNITIVE ACTIVITY	KEY CONCEPTS (TERMS)	SAMPLE PHRASES AND QUESTIONS	TALLY COLUMN	PERCENT OF TOTAL QUESTIONS ASKED
1. Remembering (Knowledge)	Student recalls or recognizes information, ideas, and principles in the approximate form in which they were learned.	Memory Knowledge Repetition Description	1. "What did the book say about . . .?" 2. "Define . . . ." 3. "List the three . . ." 4. "Who invented. . ."		
2. Understanding (Comprehension)	Student translates, comprehends, or interprets information based on prior learning.	Explanation Comparison Illustration	1. "Explain the. . ." 2. "What can you conclude. . .?" 3. "State in your own words. . ." 4. "What does the picture mean?" 5. "If it rains, then what . . . ?" 6. "What reasons or evidence. . .?"		
3. Solving (Application)	Student selects, transfers, and uses data and principles to complete a problem task with a minimum of directions.	Solution Application Convergence	1. "If you know A and B, how could you determine C?" 2. "What other possible reasons . . .?" 3. "What might they do with. . .?" 4. "What do you suppose would happen if . . .?"		
4. Analyzing (Analysis)	Student distinguishes, classifies, and relates the assumptions, hypotheses, evidence, conclusions, and structure of a statement or a question with an awareness of the thought processes he is using.	Logic Induction and deduction Formal reasoning	1. "What was the author's purpose, bias, or prejudice?" 2. "What must you know for that to be true?" 3. "Does that follow?" 4. "Which are facts and which are opinions?"		

369

	CATEGORY DESCRIPTION (PART A)			RECORDING FORM (PART B)	
CATEGORY NAME	EXPECTED COGNITIVE ACTIVITY	KEY CONCEPTS (TERMS)	SAMPLE PHRASES AND QUESTIONS	TALLY COLUMN	PERCENT OF TOTAL QUESTIONS ASKED
5. Creating (Synthesis)	Student originates, integrates, and combines ideas into a product, plan or proposal that is new to him.	Divergence Productive thinking Novelty	1. "If no one else knew, how could you find out?" 2. "Can you develop a new way?" 3. "Make up . . ." 4. "What would you do if . . .?"		
6. Judging (Evaluation)	Student appraises, assesses, or criticizes on a basis of specific standards and criteria (this does not include opinion unless standards are made explicit).	Judgment Selection	1. "Which policy will result in the greatest good for the greatest number?" 2. "For what reason would you favor . . .?" 3. "Which of the books would you consider of greater value?" 4. "Evaluate that idea in terms of cost and community acceptance."		
				Total Questions Evaluated =	Sum = 100%

CHAPTER ELEVEN

SUPERVISION AND EVALUATION OF TEACHERS

CONCEPTS

Traditionally teacher evaluation has meant the rating, grading, and classifying of teachers, using some locally standardized instrument as a yardstick. The instrument generally lists certain traits of teachers assumed to be important ("teacher has a pleasant voice") and certain tasks of teaching considered to be critical ("teacher plans well"). The evaluator usually writes in comments as, increasingly, does the teacher.

This evaluation instrument is filled out after a classroom observation of the teacher, often lasting for one-half to one period. The observation visit is usually preceded by a conference, the purpose of which varies from a brief encounter to a session where lesson plans, objectives, and teaching strategies are discussed. A post-observation conference follows, whereby comments and ratings are discussed and negotiated. Usually, the teacher evaluation procedure is concluded as both parties sign the instrument, which goes to the district archives. Typically this teacher evaluation procedure occurs once or twice a year for the tenured teacher and two to four times a year for novices.

This is the legally required personnel observation and evaluation procedure found in most secondary schools. This procedure, if done intelligently and with care, has merit and will likely remain an important part of a school's total evaluation plan. Nevertheless, many teachers, chairpersons, and administrators find this procedure alone to be inadequate to fulfill the school's evaluation needs. Further, the procedure occasionally becomes ritualistic and boring.

This traditional evaluation procedure can be made more effective for the school and more satisfying to teachers and administrators. A different kind of evaluation focuses less on rating a teacher's performance or measuring a program's output than on providing information to help that teacher grow or to help that program operate more effectively. In this context, evaluation experts make an important distinction between "formative" and "summative" evaluations.[1] The traditional teacher evaluation procedure can be classified as summative. Evaluation which emphasizes on-going growth and development would be considered formative.

Summative evaluation has a certain finality to it—it is terminal in the sense that it occurs at the conclusion of an educational activity. In evaluating a teacher's performance summative evaluation suggests a statement of worth. A judgment is made about the quality of one's teaching.

Summative evaluation is a legitimate and important activity which, if done carefully, can play a constructive role in a school's total evaluation strategy.

Formative evaluation is intended to increase the effectiveness of on-going educational programs and activity. Evaluation information is collected and used to correct and improve on-going activity.

With respect to teaching, formative evaluation is concerned less with judging and rating the teaching than with providing information which helps improve teacher performance.

In the strictest sense formative and summative evaluation cannot be separated for each contains aspects of the other, but it is useful nevertheless to speak of a formative focus and a summative focus to evaluation.

Summative evaluation is an important administrative responsibility which focuses legitimately on determining the value of educational programs and the performance of educational workers. No hard rules exist to help us decide how much responsibility the chairperson should assume for summative evaluation. Certainly the principal's responsibility is clear and the chairperson can be expected to assist the principal. But as much as possible, the chairperson's primary evaluation concerns should weigh heavily toward the formative side of this balance.

Formative evaluation, because of its concern more with improvement of on-going activity than with judgment of what has happened, is more akin to the staff development and supervisory responsibilities of the chairperson than it is to summative evaluation. This chapter begins with a discussion of formative focused evaluation, particularly as expressed through clinical supervision. Next are discussed the principles underlying the traditional, more summative, teacher evaluation process.

CLINICAL SUPERVISION

Clinical supervision, born in the real world of professional practice, evolved from a series of problems faced by supervisors as they worked with teachers and would-be teachers. As problems were faced, a set of practices emerged, at first sporadic, then incrementally, finally becoming a systematic form now known as clinical supervision. The essential ingredients of clinical supervision as articulated by Cogan[2] include the establishment of a healthy general supervisory climate, a special supervisory mutual support system called colleagueship, and a cycle of supervision comprising conferences, observation of teachers at work, and pattern analysis.

When compared with traditional rating and evaluating, clinical supervision is based on a number of different assumptions and prescribes a pattern of action which departs substantially from present practice. In clinical supervision it is assumed, for example, that the school curriculum is shown in what teachers do day by day; that changes in curriculum and in teaching formats require changes in how teachers behave in classrooms; that supervisors are not teachers of teachers; that supervision is a process for which teachers and supervisors are both responsible; that the focus of supervision is in teacher strengths; that given the right conditions teachers are willing and able to improve; that teachers have large reservoirs of talent, often unused; and that teachers want to increase competencies, for they derive satisfaction from challenging work.

 Clinical supervision is an in-class support system designed to deliver assistance directly to the teacher.

In practice, clinical supervision requires a more intense relationship between supervisor and teacher than that found in traditional evaluation, first in the establishment of colleagueship and then in the articulation of colleagueship through the cycle of supervision.

The heart of clinical supervision is an intense, continuous, mature relationship between supervisor and teacher with the intent being the improvement of professional practice.

THE CYCLE OF CLINICAL SUPERVISION

One cannot provide in a few pages all of the competencies needed for effective clinical supervision. Competency will come with practice as chairpersons learn the skills of clinical supervision. The intent here is to describe the cycle of supervision, to provide some basic principles and concepts underlying clinical supervisory practice, and to suggest some techniques and tools which chairpersons might find useful as they begin to develop competencies as clinical supervisors.

Cogan identifies eight phases to the cycles of supervision[3]:

 Phase 1 requires establishing the teacher-supervisor relationship.

This first phase is of particular importance for on its success rests the whole concept of clinical supervision. Teachers are markedly suspicious of evaluation in general and the intense sort of supervision prescribed by Cogan can be even more alarming. Further, the success of clinical supervision requires that teachers share with supervisors responsibility for all steps and activities. The chairperson, then, has two tasks in phase 1: building a relationship based on mutual trust and support, and inducting the teacher into the role of co-supervisor. Both tasks should be well advanced before the chairperson enters the teacher's classroom to observe teaching.

373

Phase 2 requires intensive planning of lessons and units with the teacher.

In phase 2 teacher and supervisor plan, together, a lesson, a series of lessons, or a unit. Planning includes estimates of objectives or outcomes, subject matter concepts, teaching strategies, materials to be used, learning contexts, anticipated problems, and provisions for feedback and evaluation.

 Phase 3 requires planning of the observation strategy by teacher and supervisor.

Together teacher and supervisor plan and discuss the kind and amount of information to be gathered during the observation period, and the methods used to gather this information.

 Phase 4 requires the supervisor to observe in-class instruction.

Only after careful establishment of the supervisory relationship and the subsequent planning of both the lesson or unit and the observation strategy does the observation take place.

 Phase 5 requires careful analysis of the teaching-learning process.

As co-supervisors, teacher and chairperson analyze the events of the class. They may work separately at first or together from the beginning. Outcomes of the analysis are identification of patterns of teacher behavior which exist over time, critical incidents that occurred which seemed to affect classroom activity and extensive descriptions of teacher behavior and artifacts of that behavior.

 Phase 6 requires planning the conference strategy.

The supervisor prepares for the conference by setting tentative objectives and planning tentative processes, but in a manner which does not overly program the course of the conference. He plans also the physical setting and arranges for materials, tapes, or other aids. Preferably the conference should be unhurried and on school time. It may well be necessary to arrange for coverage of a teacher's classroom responsibilities from time to time.

 Phase 7 is the conference.

The conference is an opportunity and setting for teacher and supervisor to exchange information about what was intended in a given lesson or unit and what actually happened. The success of the conference depends upon the extent to which the process of clinical supervision is viewed as formative focused evaluation intended to understand and improve professional practice.

☙ **Phase 8 requires the resumption of planning.**

A common outcome of the first six phases of clinical supervision is agreement on the kinds of changes sought in the teacher's classroom behavior. As this agreement materializes, the seventh phase begins. Teacher and supervisor begin planning the next lesson or unit, and new targets, approaches, and techniques to be attempted.

As one reviews the cycle of clinical supervision it appears as though it describes that which chairpersons have been doing all along. But a quick review of the assumption basic to clinical supervision, particularly the concept of co-supervisor, suggests that the resemblance is superficial. The supervisor works at two levels with the teacher during the cycle: helping him to understand and improve his professional practice, and helping him to learn more about the skills of classroom analysis needed in supervision. Further, while traditional classroom observation tends to be sporadic and requires little time investment, clinical supervision asks that the chairperson give two to three hours a week to each teacher. In large departments, the chairperson will need help. He can find some relief by involving only part of the faculty at a time—perhaps one-third for three months in rotation. Further relief can be expected as teachers themselves become competent in clinical supervision and assume increased responsibility for all phases.

CONCEPTS BASIC TO CLINICAL SUPERVISION

No single set of procedures exists for the supervisor to follow for each phase of clinical supervision. Indeed specific steps and procedures will depend upon the nature of classroom activity, the strengths of the teacher involved, and the inclinations of the chairperson. Some useful techniques are suggested in the practices section. Underlying clinical supervision are some basic ideas and concepts from which the chairperson may develop suitable practices for his unique situation.

Herbert Simon differentiates between natural and artificial sciences. "A natural science is a body of knowledge about some class of things—objects or phenomena—in the world: about the characteristics and properties that they have; about how they behave and interact with each other."[4] The artificial sciences, on the other hand, are created by human convention. The natural sciences are concerned with how things are; the artificial sciences with how things ought to be—with designing artifacts to attain goals. In Simon's words, "The thesis is that certain phenomena are 'artificial' in a very special sense: They are as they are only because of a system's being molded, by goals or purposes, to the environment in which it lives."[5] The study of human inventions or artifacts, such as formal organizations, the suburban family, and the professions (medicine, business, law and education for example), is the study of man's creations rather than of natural phenomena. The design of these artifacts depends largely on the goals which man seeks and on his view of reality. These are not objectives in a naturalistic sense but are a function of man's psychological self.

375

On a smaller scale the classroom is an artificial setting whose form and function is determined largely by the stated and inferred assumptions, beliefs, and intents of the teacher and by his attempts to adjust to his perception of a larger environment. This larger environment, equally as artificial, is composed of the expectations and other conventions found in the school as an organization, in parents, other professionals, the community and the society at large. Further, every other person involved in the life of that classroom lives in a behavioral world of his own, artificial in the sense that it is influenced by his goals, needs, and aspirations, and by his relationships with others.

 Clinical supervision is a planned intervention into the world of the artificial. Its objective is to bring about changes in classroom operation and teacher behavior.

The teacher's behavioral world is shaped and influenced by his stated and implied assumptions, beliefs and goals and therefore successful changes in the former require changes in the latter.

This world of the artificial is further complicated by the incompleteness of knowledge which one has about himself and the world in which he lives. "In actuality, the human being never has more than a fragmentary knowledge of the conditions surrounding his actions, nor more than a slight insight into the regularities and laws that would permit him to induce future consequences from a knowledge of present circumstances."[6]

 Clinical supervision is not only concerned with teacher behavior and the antecedents of this behavior but with the incompleteness with which most of us view our assumptions, beliefs, objectives and behavior.

EDUCATIONAL PLATFORMS OF TEACHERS

It is tempting to view the classroom enterprise as a rational set of activities, each generated in pursuit of clearly stated and understood objectives. From previous discussion of educational platforms applied to educational program development and evaluation, one is led to believe that classroom activity is a logical process of determining objectives, stating them in acceptable form, developing learning experiences, and evaluating the outcomes of these experiences in relation to the predetermined objectives. This view assumes that the teaching arena is objective and that teachers come to this arena with a clean slate, free of biases, willing and able to make rational choices.

In reality however, teaching is not nearly as antiseptic an enterprise as one might think. Indeed, teachers, supervisors, and others bring to the classroom a variety of agendas, some public, some hidden and probably most unknown, each of which has a telling effect on educational decision-making. Agenda items about teaching tend to fall into three major categories: what one believes is possible; what one believes is true; and what one believes is desirable. Together the three are the essential ingredients of one's *educational platform.*[7] A platform implies something that supports one's action and from which one justifies or validates his own actions.

Assumptions we hold help us to answer the question, What is possible? Assumptions are composed of our beliefs, the concepts we take for granted, and the ideas we accept without question about schools, classrooms, students, teaching, learning, and knowledge.

Assumptions help the teacher to define what classrooms are actually like and what is possible to accomplish within them. Assumptions are important to the decisions that teachers make for they set the boundaries on what information will or will not be considered and on possibilities at the onset.

 Theories we hold help answer the question, What is true? Theories are beliefs about relationships between and among assumptions we consider to be true. Theories form the basis for developing instructional strategies and patterns of classroom organization.

Beliefs about what is desirable in classrooms are derived from assumptions and theories which one holds regarding knowledge, learning, classrooms and students. What is desirable is expressed in the form of *aims and objectives.*

Consider, for example, a teacher whose educational platform includes the assumptions, "Little or no knowledge exists which is essential for everyone to learn," and, "Youngsters can be trusted to make important decisions." The two assumptions might well lead to the theory, "Students who are allowed to influence classroom decisions will make wise choices and will become more committed learners." That being the case, a corresponding aim for that teacher might be "to involve students in shared decision-making," or perhaps "to have students interact with subject matter in a manner which emphasized its concepts and structure rather than just information."

EXPLICIT AND IMPLICIT PLATFORM DIMENSIONS

In the world of the classroom the components of educational platform are generally not well known. That is, teachers tend to be unaware of their assumptions, theories, or objectives. Sometimes they adopt components of a platform that seem right, that have the ring of fashionable rhetoric, or that coincide with the expectation of important others. Teachers may adopt overtly a set of objectives but covertly or unknowingly hang on to contradictory assumptions and theories. Indeed teachers tend to be unaware that their behavior does not match their espoused platform.

A FRAMEWORK FOR CLINICAL SUPERVISION

It has been suggested that the classroom is an artificial setting where form and function is determined largely by the stated and implied assumptions, theories, and aims of the teacher. Together these beliefs form an educational platform which supports one's actions and from which one justifies or validates his actions. As has also been suggested, many aspects of one's platform are unknown or perhaps known but covert. When covert dimensions differ from espoused, the former are likely to comprise the operational platform for a given individual.

 The clinical supervisor needs to be concerned with two theories which the teacher brings to the classroom—an espoused theory and a theory in use.

As Argyris and Schön suggest, "When someone is asked how he would behave under certain circumstances, the answer he usually gives is his espoused theory of action for that situation. This is the theory of action to which he gives allegiance, and which, upon request, he communicates to others. However, the theory that actually governs his action is his theory in use, which may or may not be compatible with his espoused theory; furthermore, the individual may or may not be aware of the incompatibility of the two theories.[8]

When one's espoused theory matches his theory in use they are considered congruent. Congruence exists, for example, for the teacher who espouses that self-image development in youngsters is desirable in its own right and is related to student achievement and whose teaching behavior and artifacts of that behavior confirm this espoused theory. Lack of congruence between espoused theory and theory in use, when known, proposes a dilemma to the individual. Teacher B, for example, shares the same espoused theory regarding self-concept but his pattern of questioning, his use of negative feedback, his marking on the bell curve, and his insistence on standard requirements may reveal a theory in use incongruent with his espoused theory. The social studies teacher who believes in and teaches a course in American Democracy in a totalitarian manner represents another example of incongruency between espoused theory and theory in use.

The "Johari Window" might well be a useful model for understanding the educational platform underworld and its relationship to one's espoused theory and theory in use.[9] The nature of this underworld is illustrated in Figure 11-1. The Johari window in this case depicts the relationship between two parties, teacher and chairperson as clinical supervisor. The relationship revolves around aspects of the teacher's educational platform known to self and others, known to self but not others, not known to self but known to others, and not known to self or others.

In Cell 1 of Figure 11-1, *the public or open self,* what the teacher knows about his teaching behavior and other aspects of his professional practice corresponds with what the supervisor knows. This is the area in which communication occurs most effectively and in which the need for the teacher to be defensive, to assume threat, are minimal. The clinical supervisor works to broaden or enlarge this cell for the teacher.

In Cell 2, *the hidden or secret self,* the teacher knows about aspects of his teaching behavior and professional practice that the supervisor does not know about. Often the teacher conceals these aspects from the supervisor for fear that he might use this knowledge to punish, hurt, or exploit the teacher. Cell 2 suggests how important a general administrative and supervisory climate characterized by trust and credibility is to the success of clinical supervision. In clinical supervision the teacher is encouraged to reduce the size of this cell.

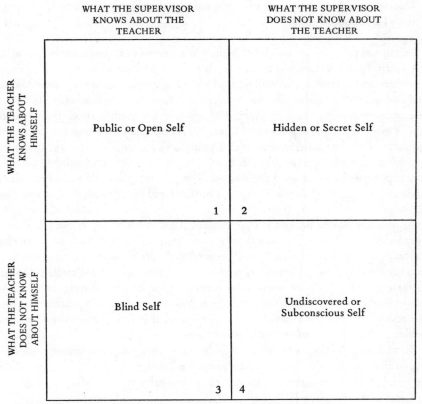

FIGURE 11-1. JOHARI WINDOW AND EDUCATIONAL PLATFORM

In Cell 3, *the blind self,* the supervisor knows about aspects of the teacher's behavior and professional practice of which that teacher is unaware. The teacher may be convinced that he encourages active student participation in the class but the supervisor knows from careful observation that the teacher talks about 90 percent of the time. Reducing the blind self is an important objective of clinical supervision but not an easy one to accomplish.

Cell 4, *the undiscovered or subconscious self,* contains aspects of teacher behavior and professional practice not known to either teacher or supervisor.

In Johari window language, clinical supervision works to help reduce the teacher's hidden self and blind self with respect to his educational platform and professional practice.

SURFACING DILEMMAS

Dilemmas surfacing is an important strategy for reducing a teacher's blind self and for creating the conditions for change.

Dilemmas surface as a result of one's learning that his theory in use is incongruent with his espoused theory.

Dilemmas promote an unsettled feeling in a person both cognitively and affectively. Affectively one's espoused theory tends to be linked with one's image of oneself. It is something important to that individual.[10] Yet learning of an incongruency between espoused and use theories also imposes a cognitive strain on an individual.[11] In each case this state of incongruency tends to precipitate a search for modification or change in either one's espoused theory or theory in use. This readiness for change is a critical point in the process of clinical supervision. At this point, an appropriate support system needs to be provided. Part of this support system will be psychological and will be geared toward accepting and encouraging the teacher. But part must also be technical and will be geared toward making available teaching and professional practice alternatives to the teacher.

Argyris and Schön point out that congruence is not a virtue in itself. Indeed a "bad" espoused theory matched to a theory in use may be far less desirable from the chairperson's point of view than a "good" espoused theory insufficiently matched. Change is very difficult in the former case, which may ultimately have to be resolved administratively in the form of a personnel action such as change of assignment. Teachers usually espouse theories in line with generally accepted concepts and practices. This probably results from the link between one's espoused theory and his self-esteem and the latter's relationship to esteem received from others.

By and large teachers are able to readily share their espoused theories about teaching, subject matter, discipline, young people as learners, and other aspects of professional practice. But theories in use tend not to be generally known. They are part of one's blind self and undiscovered self.

 The major job of the chairperson as clinical supervisor is to help construct theories in use from observation of classroom behavior and from collections of artifacts which are the products of this behavior.

Teacher plans, classroom organizational patterns, transcripts of dialogue, patterns of student influence, interaction patterns over time, curriculum materials, bulletin boards, student projects, homework assignments, teacher-made tests, grading practices, time logs, discipline procedures, reinforcement patterns, and video tapes of classroom activities are only some examples of behavior patterns and artifacts which might be analyzed carefully to construct an adequate teacher's theory in use.

As the teacher's theory in use is constructed (perhaps initially with the chairperson assuming the most responsibility but ideally constructed by chairperson and teacher together as co-supervisors) the chairperson should adhere to certain rules of feedback. Consider these examples offered by the National Training Laboratories.[12]

1. *When giving feedback to teachers, be descriptive rather than judgmental.* Clinical supervision is an expression of formative evaluation designed to help improve on-going activity, not summative evaluation designed to determine the value of a person

or program. For example, instead of saying to the biology teacher, "You are spending too much time in lecture and not enough time with students engaged in field work and laboratory work;" try, "Your time log shows that you've spent 85 percent of class time these past two weeks in lecture. Let's look at your objectives and plans for this unit and see if this is what we intended."

2. *When giving feedback to teachers be specific rather than general.* General statements tend to be misunderstood more than specific statements. Instead of saying to the teacher, "You interrupt students and tend not to listen to what they are saying," try, "When you asked John a question, you interrupted his response and seemed disinterested in what he had to say." A cassette transcript of the question, response attempt, and interruptions would be helpful.

3. *When giving feedback to teachers concentrate on things that can be changed.* A teacher may have little control over a nervous twitch or his voice quality, but much can be done about how seats are arranged, how students are grouped, how to improve balance between knowledge level and other objectives, or about how students are disciplined.

4. *When giving feedback to teachers consider your motives.* Often feedback is given to impress teachers with one's knowledge or for some other reason which implies self-gratification. Feedback is intended for only one purpose—to help the teacher know and understand his actual behavior.

5. *Give the teacher feedback at a time as close to the actual behavior as possible.* Details of events are likely to be forgotten easily. Further, fairly prompt attention is likely to upgrade and personalize the importance of clinical supervision.

6. *When giving feedback to teachers rely as much as possible on information whose accuracy can be reasonably documented.* Photographs of bulletin boards, audio and video tapes of teachers and students at work, a portfolio of classroom tests, a record of books borrowed from the class library, the number of students who return to shop during free periods or after school, a tally of questions asked by the teacher sorted into the hierarchy of educational objectives, are examples of documented feedback from which parts of one's theory in use can be constructed. It will not always be possible and sometimes not even desirable to provide this type of relatively objective feedback but its importance nevertheless as a technique for clinical supervision cannot be overestimated.

Figure 11-2 provides a schematic of clinical supervision, from identifying educational platform components to dilemma surfacing and back again. In actual practice the articulation of clinical supervision is likely to be much less predictable. Further, the ability to compartmentalize one's espoused theories and his theories in use will not be as pronounced. With Figure 11-2, one might view important bench marks in the process rather than a workflow model of linear steps and procedures. Indeed in practice the focus is likely to be on constructing theories in use, calling on espoused theories for contrast in a much more piecemeal fashion.

Now we review some assumptions basic to clinical supervision:

• A teacher's classroom behavior and the artifacts of that behavior are a function of assumptions, theories, and intents he brings to the classroom. Together these compose his educational platform.

381

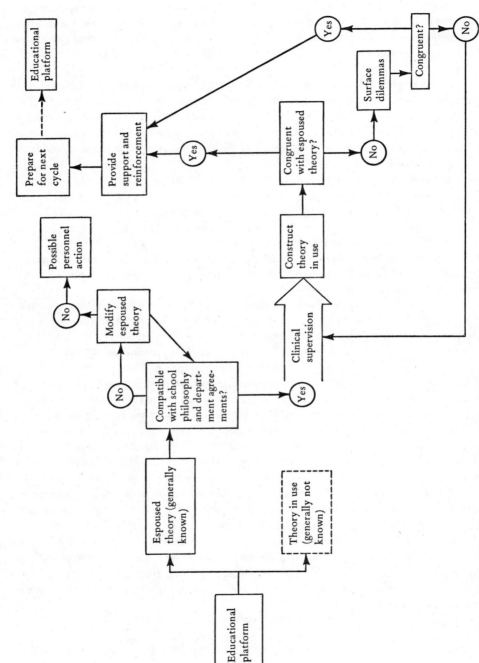

FIGURE 11-2. SCHEMATIC OF CLINICAL SUPERVISION. FROM T. SERGIOVANNI, "TOWARD A THEORY OF CLINICAL SUPERVISION," *JOURNAL OF RESEARCH AND DEVELOPMENT IN EDUCATION*, JANUARY, 1976.

- One's educational platform exists at two levels: what one says he assumes, believes, and intends (his espoused theory) and the assumptions, beliefs, and intents inferred from his behavior and artifacts of his behavior (his theory in use).

- Espoused theories are generally known to the teacher.

- Theories in use are generally not known to the teacher and must be constructed from observation of teacher behavior and artifacts of that behavior.

- Lack of congruence between one's espoused theory and one's theory in use proposes a dilemma to the teacher.

- Faced with a dilemma, a teacher becomes uncomfortable, and search behavior is evoked.

- Dilemmas are resolved by modifying one's theory in use to match one's espoused theory. It is possible that espoused will be modified to match theory in use but because of the link between espoused theory and self-esteem and self-esteem with the esteem received from others, the more common pattern will be as predicted.

In summary, clinical supervision is a process concerned with the whole teacher—his educational platform, his teaching behavior, and his classroom artifacts. The purpose of supervision is to increase effectiveness in teaching by surfacing dilemmas between one's espoused theory and one's theory in use. Granting the importance which the chairpersons must give to building and maintaining a healthy supervisory climate and to cultivating appropriate leadership and human resource development skills, the technical focus of clinical supervision is in working with teachers to construct theories in use and helping teachers to make explicit espoused theories for comparison. Equally important is the provision of an appropriate support system and the cultivation of adoptable alternatives as the teacher seeks to modify his theory in use. Specific suggestions, examples of teaching artifacts, and samples of information collecting instruments—all helpful in construction theories in use—are provided in the practices section of this chapter.

Summative Evaluation

Granting the importance of formatively focused evaluation, the necessity for more summative evaluation remains. In practice the two can never be fully separated and therefore, though we emphasize determining worth and value in the ensuing discussion, the quality of this evaluation will depend upon the overall contribution to the improvement of professional practice.

 Deciding who is a good teacher or what is good teaching is difficult but not impossible.

The key to evaluation is a clear statement of what is of value to a given department or school.

The root word in evaluation is *value* and indeed the process cannot be conducted without understanding and agreement on what is of value. An early step in developing an evaluation program is the development of a set of agreements, sort of an espoused theory for the department, general enough to permit individual expression from teachers but specific enough to provide a platform from which decisions about curriculum, students, and teaching are made and against which they can be evaluated. A general statement of beliefs such as "Students are worthwhile" or of objectives such as "Each student should become all he is capable of being" are of little practical use. But statements should not be so specific that they have little meaning or potency. A handful of potent statements of beliefs, objectives, or both, will serve better as a set of agreements than a list of a hundred or so fairly specific instructional, expressive, middle-range and informal objectives. These specific objectives are more appropriately developed by individual teachers at the lesson plan or unit level and validated against the more potent set of agreements.

What a set of agreements looks like for a given department or school, of course, depends upon the beliefs and values of those included. One example is provided below but it should not be adopted in whole or part by a department without discussion and commitment from the chairperson and teachers of that department.

SAMPLE SET OF AGREEMENTS

The set of agreements used in this example are for a social studies department. Assume that they are determined by the department faculty asking the questions, "all things being equal, one activity is more worthwhile than another when it. . . ?" The criteria for worthwhile activities which compose this set of agreements were suggested by James Raths.[13]

 A worthwhile educational activity is one which permits students to make informed choices in carrying out the activity and to reflect on the consequences of their choices.

Members of this department believe that students should accept responsibility for selecting objectives, and for making decisions from alternatives as to how objectives might be pursued.

 A worthwhile educational activity is one which assigns students to active learning roles rather than passive ones.

Members of this department believe that more often than not students should assume classroom roles as researchers, panel members, reporters, interviewers, observers, and participants rather than just listeners, ditto sheet responders and question answerers.

 A worthwhile educational activity is one which asks students to engage in inquiry into ideas, applications of intellectual processes, or current personal and social problems.

Members of this department believe that acquainting students with ideas that transcend traditional subject matter areas (truth, justice, self-worth), with intellectual processes such as hypothesis testing and identifying assumptions, and with writing opportunities which ask students to deal creatively and personally with social problems or human relationships are more worthwhile than focusing at the knowledge level on places, objects, dates, and names.

 A worthwhile educational activity is one which involves students with reality.

Members of this department believe that students should have hands-on experience with ideas. Field trips, projects, community surveys, real objects, and interviews are considered more worthwhile than just relying on books and classroom discussion.

A worthwhile educational activity is one which can be successfully accomplished by students at different levels of ability.

Members of this department believe that students should not be subjected to only a single level of accomplishment, that youngsters should work at their own levels of ability and that comparisons should be made in terms of individuals working to capacity.

A worthwhile educational activity is one which asks students to examine in a new setting ideas, applications, intellectual processes, and problems previously studied.

In Raths' words, members of this department believe "an activity that builds on previous student work by directing a focus into *novel* location, *new* subject matter areas, or *different* contexts is more worthwhile than one that is completely unrelated to the previous work of the students."[13]

A worthwhile educational activity is one which examines topics or issues that are not normally considered by the major communication media in the nation.

Members of this department believe that students should be generously exposed to such topics as race, religion, war and peace, the court system, fairness of the media, credibility in government, social responsibilities of public corporations, ethical standards for politicians, social class, immigration practices and effects on the economy, the representatives of lay governing groups such as school boards, labor-union practices, minority political parties, the self-interest of professional groups such as the AMA, NEA and Chamber of Commerce, student rights and responsibilities, drug use in professional athletics, and other topics often considered less than safe.

A worthwhile educational activity is the one which requires students to rewrite, rehearse, or polish their initial efforts.

Members of this department believe that students should not perceive assignments as chores but as worthwhile goals requiring high standards. Students should have the

385

opportunity to receive feedback and criticism of written work and oral work and of field projects as a means of formative evaluation. Opportunities should then be provided for revision and overhauling in light of this feedback. Fewer assignments well done are seen by this faculty as better than lots of tasks to be completed.

 A worthwhile activity is one which involves students in the application and mastery of meaningful roles, standards, or disciplines.

Members of this department believe that "using standards derived from students as well as authorities; panel discussions can be disciplined by procedures; reporting of data can be disciplined by consideration of control; essays can be regulated by consideration of style and syntax." Before students conduct interviews outside the supermarket for example, standards for a good interview should be established. Further, students should assume a key role in establishing these standards.

 A worthwhile educational activity is one which provides students with opportunities to share the planning, the carrying out of a plan, or the results of an activity with others.

Recognizing the importance of independent study projects and of other individualized education techniques, the members of this department nevertheless believe that cooperative group activity is important and that the group setting provides numerous learning opportunities beyond group tasks.

The ten criteria for worthwhile educational activities comprise the set of agreements for our sample social studies department. Your department might well decide on other criteria or perhaps might develop a set of agreements in the form of critical assumptions or perhaps a set of key potent objectives.

 In any event, it would be expected that lesson and unit plans, teaching behavior, classroom activity and teaching artifacts reflect this set of agreements.

Evaluation rating scales would be developed to relate instrument items with aspects of the set of agreements. In the example, perhaps an average of three items could be developed for each of the ten criteria listed.

Raths suggests that teachers keep a log which shows over a period of time the emphasis given to and the number of students exposed to each of the criteria valued by the department.[14] An example of such a log is shown in Figure 11-3.[15]

He also suggests that if log items were punched on a computer card, a program could be written to reveal the percentage of time a given teacher, or department, or even school, spent on each activity and in each *value* area and the number of students involved. Such an analysis would provide a profile of activity, a partial theory in use in the language of clinical supervision, to be contrasted against espoused theories.

386   Rating instruments and time logs should be supplemented by professional judg-

Subject:................Teacher's Name:..........................Unit:.........Dates: From..............To...........

(1) ACTIVITY NUMBER	(2) DATES	(3) TITLE OF ACTIVITY	(4) NUMBER OF STUDENTS COMPLETING ACTIVITY	(5) ESTIMATED NUMBER OF HOURS OF PARTICIPATION PER STUDENT	(6) JUSTIFIED BY CRITERIA (CHECK THOSE RELEVANT) 1 2 3 4 5 6 7 8 9 10 11 12
1	Jan. 8	Role playing a jury trial	15	4 hrs.	x x x x x

FIGURE 11–3. TEACHER'S LOG. ADAPTED FROM JAMES RATHS, "TEACHING WITHOUT SPECIFIC OBJECTIVES," *EDUCATIONAL LEADERSHIP,* VOL. 28, NO. 7, 1971, p. 719.

ments based on observation. Observations not backed up by more objective data are often considered suspect and subject to criticism ("That's just your opinion"). In a sense the demand for accountability and for objective measures of performance have eroded the confidence of educational professionals. It has been argued, however, that the work of education may be more akin to art than science and that professional judgment must be part of the overall evaluation strategy. The analogy of judging skating events or diving contests may well be appropriate. In each case judges, considered to be experts, view the performance and express their opinions through number ratings with remarkable agreement. A revival of professional judgment in evaluation is needed, focusing on understanding and rating the performance as a whole. As in skating or diving, however, a consensus judgment of two or more raters would be more credible.

 Linking rating instruments, time logs and consensus ratings to a set of department agreements establishes credibility to the evaluation strategy.

Using department agreements, or school agreements as the case may be, changes the focus of evaluation from judging the worth of a teacher in an absolute sense to judging the extent to which the teacher is "living up to" the agreed-upon criteria.

Only in rare cases of obvious neglect, mistreatment, incompetence, or insubordination is it possible to judge a teacher absolutely in a manner which permits personnel action such as pay penalty, change of assignment or dismissal. On the other hand, if hiring a person is contingent upon his willingness to abide by a set of agreements, then it seems reasonable to document his defaulting from the agreements. The intent, of course, is to help teachers meet and increase their commitments to professional practices and disciplinary action is reserved only for cases of consistent and woeful default.

A COMPREHENSIVE VIEW OF EVALUATION

An effective evaluation program is not limited to observation of teacher classroom activity. It seems reasonable to assume a school can expect that teachers *know how* to do their jobs, *can do* their jobs, *will do* their jobs, and *will grow* in job competencies. All four dimensions should have a part in a school's evaluation program. We have tended so far to focus on the *can do* aspects of evaluation whereby teachers demonstrate competencies under observation. Having successfully done so, the evaluator still has little knowledge of the depths of understanding which a person brings to his job, whether that person will continue to perform satisfactorily when not under observation, or whether that person is involved in continuous improvement of his competencies.

Know how refers to the extent a teacher understands the structure, concepts, and meanings of his academic discipline or area of specialization. A teacher who lacks insight into his teaching area often does trivial, mundane and anti-intellectual teaching. Further, teachers should possess a reasonable amount of *know how* in the professional practice areas (curriculum, evaluation, teaching methodology, principles of learning) and in understanding characteristics and problems of adolescence.

Chairpersons can encourage teachers to keep current and can improve teacher *know how* by asking questions, engaging in conversations about job-related matters, and by providing a forum for sharing ideas. Conversations about subject matter and professional practice should be in abundance in the informal and formal life of the department. Conversation, when it does occur, tends to focus on local events, sports, gossip, and popular discussion of kids. A starting point in highlighting the *know how* dimension is the chairperson showing interest in and conversing about the subject matter interests and professional practices of his staff, as well as important issues and current developments in the field.

Typically evaluation programs assume that if a teacher under observation demonstrates that he can do the job, all is well. But *can do* competence is not the same as continuous high-level performance when not under observation.

 Therefore a comprehensive evaluation program provides for judgments to be made by looking back at a teacher's performance over a period of time.

Looking back is based on the fallible assumption that what a teacher has done in the past, he is likely to continue to do. "Will he be on time?" is in part answered by his past record of promptness, and "Will he share ideas with colleagues?" is in part answered by evidence of his past history of sharing. Other items which could be considered might be the teacher's planning, willingness to give time to students, cheerfulness with which he accepts his share of undesirable assignments, attitudes toward administrators or perhaps parents, classroom control, and willingness to serve on department committees. These and similar items which seem important to a given department or school could be listed. The chairperson looking back over a period of time, perhaps one semester, checks his estimates of the teacher's performance on each item. Others familiar with the work of the teacher, and perhaps the teacher, too, could respond similarly. A checklist such as we describe goes well beyond a given observation and can provide valuable information.

 The chairperson who "gets around," who is visible in and out of classes, and who interacts with teachers frequently is likely to be in a better position to evaluate in this fashion than his less visible peers.

The *will grow* dimension is of evident importance. Every growing profession and professional undergoes continuous development and improvement. An effective department is one which has firm and clear expectations for all members to be engaged in continuous self-development.

Rubin identifies four areas of professional growth of teachers, each of which can be included in department evaluation efforts: growth in sense of purpose, philosophy, and meaning with respect to education in general and the secondary school in particular; growth in one's understanding of adolescents; growth in one's knowledge of subject matter; and growth in one's mastery of technique.[16]

In consultation with chairpersons or other supervisors, teachers should be engaged continuously in a cycle of target setting designed to improve competencies in each area of professional growth. Further, a tentative strategy needs to be developed which describes how the agreed-upon targets will be reached, and evaluation standards need to be developed to assess progress made toward reaching targets. Target setting overlaps with both supervisory and staff development activities and is an important tool for increasing department effectiveness.

TARGET-SETTING TIMELINE

Target setting might take a number of forms—one of which we suggest below in the form of a timeline.

August	Review district priorities, school goals, needs assessment data, and department objectives.
September	Review previous evaluation work and develop tentative department inservice needs and department objectives.
October	Meet with individual teachers to develop individual growth targets. Adjust department priorities, needs and objectives accordingly.
	Develop with individual teachers strategies and plans designed to achieve growth targets.
	Together determine standards and procedures for judging gains toward growth targets. This is a key step.
November	Implement plans.

389

December–March	Assist teachers in implementing plans by conferring, consulting, observing, correcting, suggesting and modifying.
	It is at this point the time line pattern for individual teachers may differ depending upon targets elected by teachers. Some targets may be more comprehensive or complex than others thus requiring an 18-month, two-year or longer cycle.
March	Complete evaluations where needed for spring deadline for notice of contract renewal.
April–June	Conduct yearly growth target setting evaluation conferences. Use results to revise existing department growth needs and priorities or to develop new ones. Incorporate conference results into general evaluation for the teacher or for the department as a whole.

SUMMARY

Supervision and evaluation of teachers represents an important responsibility which consumes a major share of the chairperson's time. The success of an evaluation program depends, of course, on the general supervisory climate in the department and on the educational leadership abilities of the chairperson. Without these, evaluation will not be much more than a ritual cautiously conducted by role players. But a healthy supervisory climate and strong educational leadership alone are insufficient. They in turn must be combined with a well-planned evaluation program.

Summative evaluation is necessary; properly conducted, it can be an asset to the school. The first step in this process is the establishment of a set of department agreements which stand as the value system of the department and the standard against which one is evaluated.

Good summative evaluation cannot substitute for formative evaluation. Formative evaluation focuses less on determining value than on providing feedback and assistance to teachers. The two cannot be clearly separated but the emphasis in evaluation should be formative.

ENDNOTES

1. Scriven, Michael, "The Methodology of Evaluation," Robert Stake, ed. *AERA Monograph on Curriculum Evaluation,* No. 1 (Chicago: Rand McNally, 1965).

2. Cogan, Morris, *Clinical Supervision* (Boston: Houghton Mifflin, 1973). Our discussion of clinical supervision follows closely that which appears in Thomas J. Sergiovanni, "Toward a Theory of Clinical Supervision." *Journal of Research and Development in Education,* January, 1976.

3. *Ibid.,* pp. 10–12.

4. Simon, Herbert A., *The Sciences of the Artificial* (Cambridge: The MIT Press, 1969), p. 1.

5. *Ibid.,* p. ix.

6. Simon, Herbert A., *Administrative Behavior: A Study of Decision-Making Processes in Administrative Organizations,* 2nd ed. (New York: The Free Press, 1957), p. 81.

7. Walker Decker, "A Naturalistic Model for Curriculum Development."*The School Review.* Vol. 80, No. 1, 1971, pp. 51–65.

8. Argyris, Chris, and David A. Schön, *Theory in Practice: Increasing Professional Effectiveness* (San Francisco: Jossey-Bass, 1974), p. 7.

9. Luft, Joseph, *Of Human Interaction* (New York: National Press Books, 1969).

10. Argyris, Chris, *Integrating the Individual and Organization* (New York: John Wiley, 1964).

11. Festinger, Leon, *Theory of Cognitive Dissonance* (Evanston, Ill.: Row, Peterson, 1957), and Rokeach, Milton, "A Theory of Organizational Change Within Value-Attitude Systems," *Journal of Social Sciences,* Vol. 24, No. 21, 1968.

12. *National Training Laboratories' Summer Reading Book* (Bethel, Maine: NTL Institute for Applied Behavioral Science, 1968).

13. Raths, James D., "Teaching without Specific Objectives," *Educational Leadership,* Vol. 28, No. 7, 1971, pp. 714–20.

14. *Ibid.,* p. 717.

15. *Ibid.,* p. 719.

16. Rubin, Louis, "The Case for Staff Development," in T. J. Sergiovanni (ed.), *Professional Supervision for Professional Teachers* (Washington, D.C.: Association for Supervision and Curriculum Development, 1975), pp. 33–49.

CHAPTER ELEVEN

PRACTICES

Supervision and evaluation of teachers remains a critical responsibility of chairpersons in secondary schools. As the present heavy reliance on summative evaluation gives way to formative evaluation, the standard teacher evaluation checklist must also give way to other methods and procedures. A number of alternatives are presented below:

Target setting and evaluation
Target setting work sheet
Cooperative-comprehensive evaluation plan
Interaction analysis: a formative evaluation technique
Preparing written evaluation reports
Teacher-focused evaluation through self-assessment
Personal assessment inventory
Keeping supervisory records

TARGET SETTING AND EVALUATION

The setting of targets, or supervision by objectives as some call it, is becoming a popular alternative to evaluation strategies which rely heavily on checklist rating scales in many secondary schools. Target setting *should not* be confused with using student-oriented behavorial objectives and evaluating teachers on the amount of pupil gain demonstrated for each objective. Widespread as this particular practice may be, particularly in California with the advent of the Stull Act, the practice is regarded with suspicion by leading evaluation experts and is totally unacceptable as the primary or exclusive evaluation strategy. Refer to the concepts section of Chapter 10 (pp. 324–28), for an elaboration of this discussion.

As the pressure builds for staff development in education, target setting increases in importance as an evaluation strategy. Our profession is presently characterized by stability in turnover of teachers and by a generally youthful teaching force. The teachers now employed in your school are very likely to remain for ten, fifteen, and even twenty or more years. Effective teaching in the years to come will depend largely upon the continuous growth and development of teachers. Target setting is one way to focus attention on the necessity for growth.

Some school districts link the entire teacher evaluation system around the target-setting strategy and others (more appropriately in the view of this book) see target setting as a critically important component of a more comprehensive evaluation strategy. Either alone or in combination with other approaches, the target-setting strategy is a powerful means for linking teacher evaluation and supervision to continuous staff development.

Target setting is subject to abuses and has short-comings which if ignored, can seriously undermine the development of an effective evaluation strategy. The most serious problems arise from supervisors' rigid adherence to prespecified targets and autocratic imposition on teachers of targets. Rigidly applying the system unduly focuses the evaluation and blinds individuals to many important events and activities not originally anticipated or stated. Teachers may focus all their concerns and energy on the targets at issue, and neglect other areas not presently targeted. Target setting is meant to help and facilitate, but rigid application can actually hinder teacher growth.

With regard to the second problem, target setting should not be seen as a system of management control (although for weak teachers who show little or no capability for self-improvement, it might legitimately be used as a management system of close supervision) but as a cooperative system of self-improvement. Supervisors and teachers together should discuss events and participate in the development of targets, with the teacher assuming the primary role, the supervisor an influential but supporting role.

The sample Target-setting worksheet, with teacher targets and chairperson comments, is provided as an illustration of a target-setting procedure. Steps to be followed in implementing the procedure are:

Step 1. Target Setting. Based on last year's observations, conferences and summary report, and on self-evaluation, the teacher develops targets in his job's critical areas. Targets should be few and within reach—rarely exceeding eight or ten, preferably three to six. Estimated time frames are provided for each target. Targets are then submitted to the chairperson.

Step 2. Target-Setting Review. The chairperson reviews each target and estimated time frame and provides the teacher with a written reaction. A copy of both is forwarded to the principal for his review and comments. A conference appointment is made with the teacher.

Step 3. Target-Setting Conference. The teacher and chairperson meet together to discuss targets, time frames and reactions, and to revise them if appropriate. A written summary of the conference is prepared.

Step 4. The Appraisal Process. This begins at the conclusion of the target-setting conference and continues in accordance with the agreed-upon time frame. The specific nature of the appraisal process depends upon each of the agreed-upon targets and could include formal and informal classroom observation, an analysis of classroom artifacts, videotaping, student evaluation, interaction analysis. The teacher participates in this step by suggesting appraisal methods and by periodically conferring with the chairperson.

Step 5A. Summary Appraisal Form. The chairperson prepares a summary appraisal form commenting on each of the targets and confers with the teacher.

Step 5B. Summary of Appraisal Procedures. In addition to the summary appraisal form the chairperson completes a summary of appraisal procedures which details dates and frequency of contacts with the teacher, a general review of targets and progress noted, a summary of help given to the teacher, an indication of the comprehensiveness of the appraisal and recommendation. This form is also discussed in conference, Step 5A, with the teacher.

TARGET-SETTING WORKSHEET*

NAME__Margaret Shills_____   DATE___Sept._____

SCHOOL YEAR_____   DEPT. __Science_____

CRITICAL AREAS	SPECIFIC TARGETS	ESTIMATED TIME FRAME
Professional Skills	1. Improve my short and long-range planning. 2. Tighten up my class management techniques. 3. Find more appropriate materials for my low-achieving class.	1. 2nd semester. 2. Now to end of year. 3. Next three months.
Professional Growth	1. Take a special "probabilities" class at the university to fill a gap in my training.	1. 2nd semester.
Personal Qualities and Relationships	1. Try to improve my relationships with parents who are difficult to work with. 2. See if I can cut down my lateness this year by finding a way to reschedule my morning time table and those of my children. Maybe arrange a car pool for my two elementary school age children.	1. Now to end of year. 2. Now to end of year.
Other (specify)		

_____   _____
TEACHER'S SIGNATURE   DATE

DEPARTMENT CHAIRPERSON'S COMMENTS:

_____   _____
DEPT. CHAIRPERSON   DATE

PRINCIPAL'S COMMENTS:

_____   _____
PRINCIPAL   DATE

*This worksheet is adapted from one developed by the Homewood-Flossmoor, Illinois, High School.

Department Chairman's Comments

The targets seem appropriate. I am pleased that you are putting as much emphasis as you are upon the improvement of instruction. In this connection, I think greater use of the cumulative records and tests results for some of your students will help. Also, I suggest you visit with the Director of Guidance or your area counselor. Class management improvement is a good target. I will give as much help as I can. We can talk about this in our conferences. I have some ideas too about the problems you have been having with some of the parents. I have no additional goals to suggest.

DATE	DEPT. CHAIRPERSON

Principal's Comments

I am in general agreement with you as to the appropriateness of the goals. Obviously, I think you are wise to put the major emphasis upon instructional improvement. You have many assets which haven't been put to the best use yet. I shall be glad to confer with you and offer specific suggestions on the instructional targets listed. Your last target is important. *Being more punctual in the morning is important so that adequate planning can be done for the day.* I think this will help with the management problem. We can talk more about this as time goes on. Your targets are frank and realistic. We will help you reach them in every way we can.

DATE	PRINCIPAL

CONFERENCE REPORT

DATE _____

TEACHER'S NAME Margaret Shills   CHAIRPERSON Peter Martinez   DEPT. _____

Chairperson's Comments:*

      In our conference, some points were discussed which could be selected as targets for the year. We both agreed that most often you have good rapport with your classes. You observed that at times you do need to establish more clearly some routines that help the learning situation. Starting on time, being better organized with handout materials, giving directions more clearly — there were a few areas we agreed could warrant attention. Improving your organization of each class is related to your over-all planning. As you indicated, some of your tardiness has resulted in hurried starts and in devoting more time to some aspects of the course than originally planned. We also spent some time discussing the difficulties with attempting to have both the intermediate and advanced classes use the same materials.

      Two additional areas discussed were working with parents of students and considering taking additional courses.

      I feel that our conference was beneficial to both of us. I look forward to working together with you this year.

Teacher's Comments: Use this space to react to the comments above.*
(A reaction is optional.)

      I believe the conference did help clarify some areas I need to work on this year. It was a help to be able to discuss these areas.

Signatures: (Signature indicates completion of appraisal: not necessarily agreement)

_____ / _____   _____ / _____
    CHAIRPERSON   DATE   TEACHER   DATE

_____ / _____
    PRINCIPAL   DATE

SUMMARY APPRAISAL REPORT

TEACHER'S NAME _____Margaret Shills_____   DATE_____

DEPT. ___Science_____   _____

Dept. Chairperson's Comments (*) Use this space to evaluate the teacher's performance with reference to the achievement of targets.
_____

Evaluation of job targets:

1. *Planning*   Improvement over last year, but there is some inconsistency still in your procedures.
2. *Class management*   You are improving. At times you are too rough on pupils and at other times too lax.
3. *Materials*   You have achieved good results in this area and you are more effective with slower-moving pupils this year.
4. *University class*   Apparently this was a worthwhile activity and you certainly will feel more secure in the area of statistics as it relates to your advanced science seminar.
5. *Parent-relations*   You have made substantial improvement in your insights and skills in working with parents, especially those who are difficult.
6. *Tardiness*   You achieved your goal quite well.

If as much improvement is made next year as this, I see no reason but to believe that you can be recommended for continuing contract when you have obtained the appropriate certificate.

Teacher's comments: (*) Use this space to react to the comments above.
(A reaction is optional - not required.)
_____

No comments

Signatures (Signature indicated completion of appraisal; not necessarily agreement.)
   (*) If more space is needed, use separate sheet

TEACHER _____ __   DATE_____

DEPARTMENT CHAIRPERSON _____   DATE_____

PRINCIPAL _____   DATE_____

SUMMARY OF APPRAISAL PROCEDURE

Sample

NAME OF TEACHER __Margaret Shills_____ DEPARTMENT _____

(This form is to be used to record a resume of appraisal contacts made with teacher.)

I. DATES OF OBSERVATIONS/CONTACTS:

September 19, November 14, December 12, February 27 and March 14

II. GENERAL STATEMENT OF PROBLEM: (including strengths and weaknesses)

In her first year, she encountered more than the usual problems of a first year teacher. She had a tendency to "plan as she taught." This resulted in trouble. Class management was a severe problem before the year was over. She also found some of the parents difficult to deal with and tended to avoid discussing with them the problems their youngsters were having. This usually happened after report cards went home. Her tardiness was higher than normal her first year. She takes criticism reasonably well and accepts supervision gracefully but fails to follow through as consistently as she should.

Her job targets this year have been relevant to her major problems. She has done much better and her follow-through is encouraging.

III. SUMMARY OF HELP GIVEN:

Have observed her five times, long enough each time to feel knowledgable about her performance. Follow-up conferences have been held after the visitations. An interim appraisal conference was held at the end of the first semester. In order to help her with difficult parent conferences, she and I did some role playing as a means of anticipating some of the problems the parents might bring up. She said that these sessions were helpful. One three-way conference was held with her and the principal. Succeeded in getting her to come to me for advice before she took action with some of her difficult discipline problems. This was a better procedure than last year, when she acted and then "sought advice." Our rapport has improved.

IV. COMPREHENSIVENESS OF OBSERVATIONS

In addition to regular classroom observations I have reviewed and discussed with this teacher:

	YES	NO
1. Daily and unit lesson plans including intents, proposed activities, evaluation procedures, and provision for identifying outcomes not originally intended.	_____	_____
2. Decisions, plans, activities, and outcomes as they relate to the department's educational platform.	_____	_____
3. Actual student classroom, homework and project assignments including teacher intents, grading practices and uses, and teacher feedback in the form of written comments and student conferences.	_____	_____

V. RECOMMENDATIONS:

Give her careful supervision next year and if her performance continues to improve at current rate, I believe that she will be a satisfactory teacher. We need to look carefully for evidence that the potential for and commitment to *long-range* growth and development exists. Ms. Shills is aware that a satisfactory rating is acceptable for a tenure appointment only if accompanied by indications that the teacher can and will work continuously at professional improvement.

VI. SIGNATURE OF DEPARTMENT CHAIRPERSON _____

DATE SUBMITTED _____

SIGNATURE OF TEACHER _____ DATE _____

SIGNATURE OF PRINCIPAL _____ DATE _____

AN EXAMPLE OF A COOPERATIVE-COMPREHENSIVE EVALUATION PLAN

In this section a detailed set of evaluation procedures and criteria currently operational in a five-high school suburban school district is presented for illustrative purposes. This example is not meant to be imitated "as is" but rather, to suggest ideas, provoke discussion, stimulate, raise questions and otherwise assist as you think about, evaluate, and revise your own procedures.

The illustrated plan is *cooperative,* in that it was developed by a teacher evaluation committee composed of teachers and administrators and has become a part of the written agreement between the teacher organization and the school board. Further, the teacher evaluation committee continuously evaluates and monitors the plan. The most recent evaluation (a summary of which is also provided) has resulted in not only a revision of the procedures but in a commitment by teachers and administrators to focus staff development efforts more deliberately on improving the use of the procedures.

The illustrated plan is comprehensive in that while overall judgments are made in the form of a rating-scale checklist, provisions are made for self-evaluation and target setting. Further, wide latitude is afforded teacher and supervisor as they develop methods and select techniques for determining ratings. Further, the evaluation procedures carefully specify evaluative criteria in important areas, including the general attitude of the teacher toward his job, the instructional process, evaluation, and professional interest and growth. Noteworthy about this list is that it represents a set of agreements, determined cooperatively among professionals, as to what constitutes appropriate performance and behavior for this group of high schools.

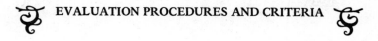

TOWNSHIP HIGH SCHOOL DISTRICT 211
Palatine-Schaumburg Townships, Illinois

Created and Approved by the Teacher Evaluation Committee—1972
Revised by the Teacher Evaluation Committee—1975

THE EVALUATION PROCESS

Preparation

Annually, prior to observation, all teachers and evaluators shall be oriented to the evaluative procedures, criteria and standards. This orientation shall include a copy of this evaluation document followed by open discussion between the teachers, or evaluators, and their immediate supervisors concerning the meaning of the document. This document and the school code shall be the basis for evaluation procedures.

Observation

Evaluation involves an analysis of the total involvement of the teacher with the District educational program throughout the school year and involves observations in a variety of situations in addition to the classroom. Thus, the evaluator probably will not evaluate all criteria at one time. Following a series of observations, an evaluator shall meet with the teacher to discuss the evaluation and to plan to eliminate problems. Further observations may be confined to problem areas previously identified.

Evaluators and Evaluations

The teacher shall:

1. conduct a self-evaluation. This evaluation should include some of the following: observations of peers, evaluations by students, observations by peers and micro-teaching;
2. develop objectives to remediate problems identified by evaluation and
3. work to fulfill objectives.

The department chairperson shall:

1. discuss evaluative criteria with his teachers;
2. evaluate teachers through observations and comparisons of these observations with District 211 standards;
3. review the results of class visitations and evaluations with the teacher in a private conference, and either party may request the presence of another staff member as a silent observer;
4. discuss with the teacher the process used for his self-evaluation;
5. advise teacher in defining objectives in problem areas and continue to evaluate performance;
6. submit the written results of the evaluation to the principalship,* and
7. discuss the results of the evaluation with the principalship.

*Principalship: the principal or his designee.

The principalship shall:

1. discuss evaluation criteria and procedures with department chairperson;
2. evaluate teachers through observations and comparisons of these observations with District 211 standards;
3. initiate discussion with the department chairperson to seek consensus on evaluations in order to produce a combined evaluation (Form A);
4. discuss the class visitations and evaluations with the teacher (the teacher may request the department chairperson to be present at this time); and
5. submit the combined evaluation (Form A) to the District office.

A district administrator shall:

1. discuss evaluation criteria and procedures with the principal and his designees;
2. review evaluations;
3. evaluate problem areas at the request of the principal, department chairperson, or teacher; and
4. make recommendations to the Board of Education.

TIME LINE—TENURED TEACHER

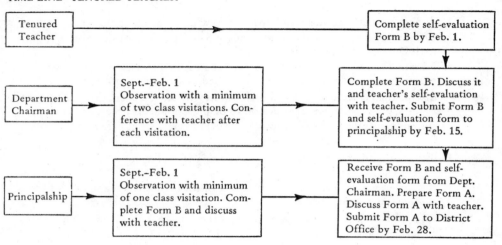

Tenured Teacher → Complete self-evaluation Form B by Feb. 1.

Department Chairman → Sept.–Feb. 1 Observation with a minimum of two class visitations. Conference with teacher after each visitation. → Complete Form B. Discuss it and teacher's self-evaluation with teacher. Submit Form B and self-evaluation form to principalship by Feb. 15.

Principalship → Sept.–Feb. 1 Observation with minimum of one class visitation. Complete Form B and discuss with teacher. → Receive Form B and self-evaluation form from Dept. Chairman. Prepare Form A. Discuss Form A with teacher. Submit Form A to District Office by Feb. 28.

TIME LINE—NON-TENURED TEACHER

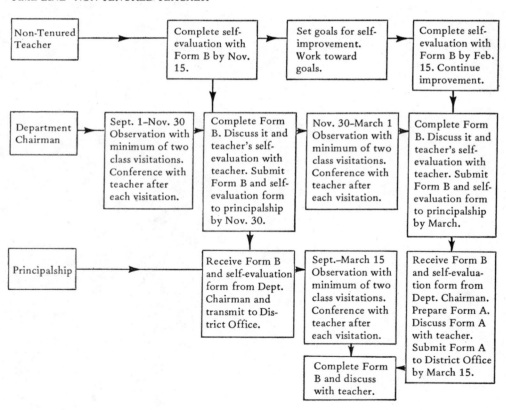

Non-Tenured Teacher → Complete self-evaluation with Form B by Nov. 15. → Set goals for self-improvement. Work toward goals. → Complete self-evaluation with Form B by Feb. 15. Continue improvement.

Department Chairman → Sept. 1–Nov. 30 Observation with minimum of two class visitations. Conference with teacher after each visitation. → Complete Form B. Discuss it and teacher's self-evaluation with teacher. Submit Form B and self-evaluation form to principalship by Nov. 30. → Nov. 30–March 1 Observation with minimum of two class visitations. Conference with teacher after each visitation. → Complete Form B. Discuss it and teacher's self-evaluation with teacher. Submit Form B and self-evaluation form to principalship by March.

Principalship → Receive Form B and self-evaluation form from Dept. Chairman and transmit to District Office. → Sept.–March 15 Observation with minimum of two class visitations. Conference with teacher after each visitation. → Complete Form B and discuss with teacher. → Receive Form B and self-evaluation form from Dept. Chairman. Prepare Form A. Discuss Form A with teacher. Submit Form A to District Office by March 15.

EVALUATION SUMMARY A

	MEETS OR EXCEEDS 211 STAN-DARDS	NEEDS IMPROVE-MENT	UNAC-CEPTABLE
Overall Effectiveness			
Department Chairperson			
Administrative Evaluation			
Self-Evaluation			
Final Appraisal by Principalship			

I have read and discussed the above document with a Building Administrator and have received a copy.

☐ If checked — see teacher comments attached

_____
SIGNATURE OF TEACHER

_____
SIGNATURE OF PRINCIPAL OR DESIGNEE

Comments (list any plans for improvement the teacher is undergoing)

Recommendations

EVALUATION WORKSHEET B — TEACHER

TEACHER _____ SITUATION _____

DATE _____ EVALUATOR _____

SCHOOL _____ TITLE _____

	MEETS OR EXCEEDS 211 STAN- DARDS	NEEDS IMPROVE- MENT	NEEDS IMMEDIATE ATTENTION
I. ATTITUDE			
A. Punctuality			
B. Cooperativeness			
C. Relationship with Colleagues			
D. Personal Conduct			
E. Acceptance of Responsibility			
Overall			
II. THE INSTRUCTIONAL PROCESS			
A. Planning Instruction			
1. Develops Instructional Objectives			
2. Relates Objectives to Goals of Course			
3. Relates Objectives to Student Needs			
4. Aims Toward a Variety of Results			
B. Implementing Instruction			
1. Correlates Learning Activities w/Objectives			
2. Correlates Learning Activities w/Student Needs			
3. Demonstrates Subject Matter Competency			
4. Motivates Students in a Positive Direction			
5. Exhibits Respect for and Understanding of Students			
6. Maintains Appropriate Student Conduct for Type of Learning Activity			
7. Demonstrates Self-Control and Poise			
8. Uses Classroom Time Efficiently			
9. Efficiently Manages Classroom Facilities			
C. Evaluating Instruction			
1. Relates Evaluation to Objectives			
2. Relates Evaluation to Student Ability			
3. Uses Evaluation to Improve Learning and Instruction			
Overall			

III. PROFESSIONAL INTERESTS AND GROWTH
   A. Dedication to Education
   B. Willingness to Keep Abreast of Change
   C. Willingness to Share Successes with Others
   D. Accepts Criticism Profitably in a Mature Manner
   E. Incorporates Material From Other Academic Fields

   Overall

Any category checked "Needs Immediate Attention" requires that the teacher and department chairperson jointly develop objectives in this area to be reviewed by the principal or his delegate.

At the evaluation conference, an appropriate time line shall be established for the development of objectives and their subsequent review.

Any category checked "Needs Improvement" suggests similar action.

I have read and discussed the above document with my department chairperson or building administrator and have received a copy of this form and any attachments.

TEACHER'S SIGNATURE	DATE	DEPT. CHPN.'S/ADM.'S SIGNATURE	DATE

_____If checked, see attached statement of teacher.

_____If checked, see attached statement of evaluator.

Evaluative Criteria: Attitude

The attitude a teacher might have for his job is often reflected in his approach to teaching. School is a community which is affected by the attitudes of its members. The following items are regarded as essential indicators of a person's attitude.

PUNCTUALITY. In accordance with current policy and rules, the teacher is expected to be in the classroom and ready for class before it begins. This situation also applies to meetings and the start of school. Frequent tardiness shall be regarded as below the district standards of punctuality.

COOPERATIVENESS. A cooperative teacher is one who can work with colleagues to accomplish certain goals, one who is willing to compromise when necessary to attain agreed-upon goals, one who uses positive methods and appropriate channels to initiate change. Cooperativeness is not synonymous to being a "yes man," for a cooperative teacher can be a critical thinker and an initiator of change. The means he uses to attain his goals are the key to cooperativeness, rather than the specific goals in which he believes.

Occasionally a teacher will be called on to perform some additional task requiring extra effort, perhaps at a personal inconvenience. The truly professional teacher will accept this responsibility as a portion of his duty which is necessary to allow the enterprise to function. It is recognized, however, that there are limits beyond which it would be unreasonable to ask.

RELATIONSHIP WITH COLLEAGUES. The teacher should assume the basic objective of working with his colleagues in a way that will best serve the needs of the students. The teacher must be aware that a positive attitude and a willingness to work harmoniously with fellow teachers are in the best interest of education and group morale. The success of the total educational plan is dependent upon the spirit of cooperation.

PERSONAL CONDUCT. Because the teacher deals with the young during an impressionable time in their lives, the teacher is expected to be exemplary in his daily personal conduct, which includes demeanor, habits, and dress.

407

ACCEPTANCE OF RESPONSIBILITY. As an educator, the teacher is charged with assuming the responsibility of assisting in the moral, physical, and intellectual growth of the child. A professional teacher will also recognize his responsibility in guiding the student in his emotional growth, in the development of social consciousness, and in building a positive self-image. The assumption of this responsibility is an inherent task in the teaching process, and the teacher must be willing to meet this commitment. During the course of professional activities, the teacher must accept implied responsibility in the areas stated above as basic to teaching, in addition to teacher responsibilities which are specifically stated.

The Instructional Process

PLANNING INSTRUCTION
1) *Develops instructional objectives:* Does the teacher develop specific as well as general instructional objectives for the course and units within the course? Written objectives are preferred; in their absence an evaluator may request a discussion of these objectives.
2) *Relates objectives to goals:* Are the objectives developed by the teacher appropriate to the goals of the course as outlined by the district philosophy, curriculum committee, approved courses of study and/or departmental agreement?
3) *Relates objectives to student needs:* Are the objectives appropriate for the students for whom they are designed? The abilities, backgrounds and ages of the students should be major factors in determining objectives. There should be an individualization of objectives where feasible.
4) *Aims toward a variety of results:* Do the objectives aim at a variety of learning results in the various areas of psychomotor skills, the cognitive domain and the affective domain? These objectives must be planned according to the nature of the discipline involved. Wherever appropriate, the high cognitive and affective domains should be included.

IMPLEMENTING INSTRUCTION
1) *Correlate learning activities with objectives:* Are the learning activities which are provided compatible with the objectives which have been set?
   A. Teachers should make students aware of the relationship between objectives and learning activities.
   B. The teacher should manage a variety of learning activities skillfully.
   C. Learning activities should provide enough direction to students to progress toward objectives.
   D. Additional direction should be provided by making clear to the students how and upon what they will be evaluated for the purpose of determining grades.
2) *Correlates learning with student needs:* Are the needs of the students being considered in the learning activities which are occuring in the classroom? These needs encompass not only the teacher's feelings as to the subject matter needs of the students, but also such needs as remediation of deficiencies in prior learning, the need of each individual to achieve some element of success, interests of the students, and goals of students.

3) *Demonstrates subject matter competency:* Is subject matter presented accurately? The teacher should present material responsibly, in appropriate detail and context, and whenever possible from several points of view.

4) *Motivates students in a positive direction:* Is there evidence that the students are actively involved in the activities which the teacher has intended for the class to pursue?

5) *Exhibits respect for and understanding of students:* Does an atmosphere of mutual respect and empathy exist in the classroom? Reciprocity is a key concept here; positive attitudes toward learning and true respect from students, will be gained only if the teacher strives to uphold and enhance the self-concept of each of his students. Opportunities for positive reinforcement of student responses should be seized; student opinions should be respected; the effort should be made to understand the feelings and concerns of the student and to look at the course and the classroom through the eyes of the student.

6) *Maintains appropriate student conduct for type of learning activity:* Does the teacher consistently maintain a level of student conduct appropriate for the learning activity taking place? Poise, competence, consistency and a positive attitude toward students all contribute to the maintenance of appropriate conduct. The kind of conduct which is appropriate varies according to the learning activity taking place. Informality is more appropriate in some settings than in others. The basic standard is: Can *that* learning activity proceed smoothly? An unnecessarily rigid, deadening environment can be just as damaging to learning as one which is inappropriately "loose."

7) *Demonstrates self-control and poise:* Does the teacher exhibit the necessary self-control and poise in a given situation? The teacher should maintain a composure based upon self-confidence, understanding of adolescents, and trust in students. The usual expression of feelings and emotions should be in a manner which respects other persons and improves interpersonal relationships.

8) *Uses classroom time efficiently:* Does the "business of the classroom" proceed efficiently with a minimum of wasted time? The teacher should handle such routine tasks as attendance, announcements, and assignments in an efficient manner. Students are expected to be involved for a maximum amount of time in activities which are appropriate to the objectives.

9) *Efficiently manages classroom facilities:* Does the teacher efficiently and effectively use the classroom facilities to aid in the achievement of instruction objectives? The organization of classroom facilities should depend upon the type of learning activities. The seating arrangement, lighting, use of chalkboard, audio-visual equipment, and other teaching aids should vary in relationship to the objectives being sought.

EVALUATING INSTRUCTION

1) *Relates evaluation to objectives:* Is evaluation correlated with course and unit objectives? Whatever the form evaluation may take, it should be correlated in both content and form with the objectives as well as with the way material has been presented in the course. The attainment of some objectives, however, such as certain affective objectives, can be evaluated only by inference from observed behavior.

2) *Relates evaluation to student ability:* Does the teacher employ techniques which challenge all students while permitting success for each? The teacher should attempt where feasible to develop different methods of evaluation to

allow for individual differences (for example, some students can better indicate their competence through such activities as projects, role playing, and laboratory analysis). The teacher should also attempt to measure the achievement of the individual student relative to his own growth and abilities and not solely to those of his classmates.

3) *Uses evaluation to improve learning and instruction:* Is evaluation used to improve learning and instruction? Evaluation should be used to help students recognize and correct areas in their education where they are weak. At the same time, as a result of evaluation, the teacher may select for future use those portions of his teaching which lead to student success and revise techniques which have been unsuccessful.

Criteria for the Measurement of Professional Interest and Growth

A certain degree of professional interest is necessary if a teacher is to meet even the minimum requirements for acceptability as an educator. Obviously, a teacher who perceives his primary goal as being nothing more than engaging in a daily routine of making assignments, explaining subject matter, and grading papers in order to draw a paycheck is unprofessional in attitude and action. The least that should be expected of a teacher in the area of professional interest is that he set as his main objective the education of students—that he see himself as an agent of constructive behavioral and attitudinal change in other human beings. The measurement of this quality in a teacher, like so many others in education, must of necessity be subjective; it is no less than an assessment of the general bearing, orientation, and kind of personal interaction through which the teacher engages in his daily work. Such an assessment can only be made by observing and working with the teacher in a variety of settings, both inside and outside of the classroom.

Beyond this minimum requirement in the area of professional interest, other criteria may be established which have as their aim the measurement of professional growth. These criteria would be among those that separate the good or excellent educator from the merely acceptable teacher. Measurement in this area must also be rather subjective in nature; any attempt to quantify standards of professional growth (number of organizations joined, number of meetings attended) carries with it the danger that the criteria so established will only ostensibly be indicative of what the evaluator hopes to measure. The following criteria for professional growth are listed, then, with the understanding that different teachers might exhibit them in a wide variety of ways:

1) The teacher pursues and shares, with both colleagues and students, knowledge, ideas, and meaningful values as a continuing enterprise.
2) The teacher keeps abreast of changes both in his academic field and in the field of education.
3) The teacher incorporates material from other academic fields into his own.
4) The teacher shares his successes with others so that instruction in general may be improved.
5) The teacher is receptive to considering the successes of others so that his own instruction may be improved.

TEACHER EVALUATION COMMITTEE REPORT

Township High School District 211
Administrative Center

For the past several months the Teacher Evaluation Committee has been meeting to study and review our present evaluation document and procedures. Our committee was requested to perform this task by the association/administrative council. Throughout our study we have attempted to solicit faculty opinion on this subject through formal surveys and informal discussions.

As a result of our findings, we have revised worksheet B to allow for more meaningful comments, thus strengthening the evaluation process.

As we studied and reviewed the current evaluation document it became apparent to us that the true potential of the document has not been realized. The main purpose of the current document is to improve instruction, and we believe the document can be helpful in achieving this goal. The areas of concern seem to center on attitude and procedures rather than on any inherent defect in the document.

We are recommending the organization, development, and implementation of in-service training programs which would:

1) Acquaint teachers with the ways of maximizing the value of the self-evaluation phase.
2) Provide in-service training for evaluators so that they can more effectively use the document to improve instruction.
3) Provide programs which would clarify the evaluation process in regards to the results being sought, what to expect, the objectives of evaluation, time-lines, and other related matters.

We believe the above programs, if properly designed and implemented, will bring about improved attitudes toward evaluation. More importantly, they should be instrumental in creating a climate where professional growth is maximized through teamwork and cooperation. The improvement of instruction is a goal shared by all teachers and administrators and its achievement is essential to the educational progress of our students.

The teacher evaluation committee recommends the formation of an evaluation committee at each building. We feel these committees could review the above suggestions and devise appropriate methods for implementation, idea sharing, and evaluation. The ways used to achieve the in-service goals could include, but would not be limited to:

1) Faculty meetings
2) Revolving meetings
3) Department meetings
4) Panel discussions
   a) Teachers
   b) Administrators
   c) Evaluation Committee Members
   d) Combinations of the above
5) Multi-media presentations
6) Outside consultants
7) Intra-district consultants
8) Formation of idea books
9) Administrators meet with their respective departments prior to observation and evaluation.

Each building committee shall submit a report covering its activities to the March meeting of the association/administrative council.

We urge that our suggestions be implemented for the 1975–76 school year. In order to do this, the planning phase must begin this spring.

Respectfully submitted.

B. H. Altergott, Chairperson

INTERACTION ANALYSIS: A FORMATIVE EVALUATION TECHNIQUE

As a tool for observing classroom interaction most chairpersons are at least noddingly acquainted with interaction analysis. A number of techniques and systems exist; in this section we discuss perhaps the most well-known—Flanders Interaction Analysis.* This system assumes that one important key to understanding what goes on in the classroom is the verbal interaction which takes place between teacher and students and among students. The system focuses only on this aspect of classroom functioning, recognizing that other such aspects as nonverbal interaction, movement, grouping patterns, must also be considered to get a complete picture.

As one views the ebb and flow of verbal interaction, the system provides for categorizing in a way which helps one to understand the amount of teacher talk and nature of teacher influence, and the amount of student talk and nature of student influence.

The categories are summarized in Table 11–1. Notice that the categories are broadly grouped into teacher talk (categories 1–7) and into student talk (categories 8 and 9). A separate category, silence or confusion, is provided to record anything else which is not teacher talk or student talk. Within the teacher talk grouping, categories 1–4 represent indirect influence on the part of the teacher and categories 5–7 represent direct influence. As exercised by the teacher, direct influence restricts the freedom of students to respond; indirect influence maximizes the freedom of students to respond.

TABLE 11–1. SUMMARY OF CATEGORIES FOR INTERACTION ANALYSIS[a]

TEACHER TALK I

Indirect Influence A

1* *Accepts feeling:* accepts and clarifies the feeling tone of the student in a non-threatening manner. Feelings may be positive or negative. Predicting or recalling feelings is included.

2* *Praises or encourages:* Praises or encourages student action or behavior. Jokes that release tension, not at the expense of another individual: nodding head, or saying "uh huh?" or "go on" are included.

3* *Accepts or uses ideas of students:* Clarifying, building or developing ideas or suggestions by a student. As teacher brings more of his own ideas into play, shift to category five.

*This discussion follows closely Edmund J. Amidon and Ned A. Flanders, *The Role of the Teacher in the Classroom: A Manual for Understanding and Improving Classroom Behavior* (Minneapolis: Association for Productive Teaching, 1971). See also Ned Flanders, *Analyzing Teacher Behavior* (Reading, Mass.: Addison-Wesley, 1971). For additional interaction systems see Anita Simm and Gil Boyer, *Mirrors for Behavior: An Anthology of Classroom Observation Systems* (Philadelphia: Research for Better Schools, 1970).

4* *Asks questions:* answering a question about content or procedure with the intent that a student answer.

Direct Influence B

5* *Lectures:* giving facts or opinions about content or procedures; expressing his own ideas, asking rhetorical questions.

6* *Giving directions:* directions, commands, or orders with which a student is expected to comply.

7* *Criticizing or justifying authority:* statements intended to change student behavior from unacceptable to acceptable pattern; bawling someone out; stating why the teacher is doing what he is doing, extreme self-reference.

STUDENT TALK II

8* *Student talk-response:* talk by students in response to teacher. Teacher initiates the contact or solicits student statement.

9* *Student talk-initiation:* talk by students which they initiate. If "calling on" student is only to indicate who may talk next, observer must decide whether student wanted to talk. If he did, use this category.

10* *Silence of confusion:* pauses, short periods of silence, and periods of confusion in which communication cannot be understood by the observer.

---

[a] From Edmund J. Amidon and Ned A. Flanders, *The Role of the Teacher in the Classroom*, p. 12.

*There is NO scale implied by these numbers. Each number is classificatory; it designates a particular kind of communication event. To write these numbers down during observation is to enumerate—not to judge a position on a scale.

Within the student talk grouping, category 8 provides for student talk initiated by the teacher and category 9 refers to student-initiated responses.

Examine each of the categories and elaborations provided in Table 11–1. Now consider each of the following *teacher* statements[†] and assign each a number representing the most appropriate category.

_____ 1 "I think I understand what you are saying. Are you saying that if we work the problem this way, although it is not the way I showed you, we shall still come out with the correct answer?"
This statement should be assigned a 3 because the Teacher restates and clarifies the pupil's contributions and has given no indication of his personal feelings about the pupil's statement.

_____ 2 "What steps do you think we ought to take now in order to finish our group project?"
This statement should be assigned a 4 because the teacher asks a question about class procedure with the intent that the class answer.

_____ 3 "I am willing to listen to what you have to say."
This statement should be assigned a 1 because the statement accepts the feelings of the student.

_____ 4 "I don't particularly believe either one of them, really. Mr. X said that

[†]Excerpted from Amidon and Flanders, *op. cit.,* pp. 5–11.

there would be new natural resources coming up, but I think he left one thing out."
This statement should be assigned a 5 because the teacher gives an opinion on content and expresses his own idea.

_____ 5 "I don't like what you have been doing. Don't do it anymore."
This statement should be assigned a 7 because the statement intends to change student behavior from unacceptable to acceptable pattern.

_____ 6 "That's a good idea; I like what you said."
This statement should be assigned a 2 because the statement praises the behavior or action of the student.

_____ 7 "Please sit down, Johnnie."
This statement should be assigned a 6 because directions tell the student what to do.

_____ 8 "How many of you, I wonder, know what Billy means when he says that we ought to subtract 3 from 6 to see if we get the same answer?"
This statement should be assigned a 3 because the statement uses Billy's idea.

_____ 9 "I understand that this upsets you."
This statement should be assigned a 1 because the teacher accepts student's feelings.

_____10 "Open your books to page 14."
This statement should be assigned a 6 because the teacher directs students and expects them to comply.

_____11 "Van Gogh was a Dutch painter who lived in the 19th century. I think he was a very good painter because he expressed his ideas in a creative, individualistic way."
This statement should be assigned a 5 because the teacher gives opinions and expresses his own ideas.

_____12 "Johnnie, why don't you listen to me?"
This statement should be assigned a 7 because the statement intends to change student behavior or to scold Johnnie.

_____13 "Mary, you've really done an excellent job on your English notebook."
This statement should be assigned a 2 because the teacher praises student action.

_____14 "Do you know what the story is about?"
This statement should be assigned a 4 because the teacher asks students a question on content with intent that students answer.

In observing a class or in listening to an audio tape of a class in action, the rater jots down a number to represent each of the categories of interaction which takes place. Flanders recommends recording numbers at three-second intervals but for formative evaluation purposes every four or five seconds will do as well. The number ten always begins and ends the recording of numbers. Specific rules for recording numbers are provided in the Amidon and Flanders book, *The Role of the Teacher in the Classroom: A Manual for Understanding and Improving Classroom Behavior.* One rule, for example, requires that you record changes in interaction patterns which take place within the three- to five-second interval. If a question and answer occurs within this time, both a 4 and 8 are recorded. Our discussion in this section will only introduce you to the technique. *You will need to refer to this or another reference which more completely describes the technique before you try it.*

A one-minute record of numbers might look like this:

10
6
5
5
4
8
8
9
9
2
3
5
5
10

The numbers now need to be plotted into an interaction matrix as shown in Table 11–2. This requires that numbers be arranged in overlapping pairs in order to permit plotting into the matrix. The numbers are paired as follows:

$$\begin{pmatrix}10\\6\end{pmatrix}\begin{pmatrix}5\\5\end{pmatrix}\begin{pmatrix}4\\8\end{pmatrix}\begin{pmatrix}8\\9\end{pmatrix}\begin{pmatrix}9\\2\end{pmatrix}\begin{pmatrix}3\\5\end{pmatrix}\begin{pmatrix}5\\10\end{pmatrix}$$

An interaction matrix is provided in Table 11–2 (Table 11–3 contains an additional matrix for your use). In plotting numbers into the matrix, the first number in the pair (10 in our case) is located as the vertical side of the matrix and the second number (6) on the horizontal side. Find the square within the matrix where lines drawn from each of the numbers in the pair intersect and record a tally mark. The second number in the first overlapping pair (6) now becomes the *first* number of the second over-

TABLE 11-2. INTERACTION MATRIX

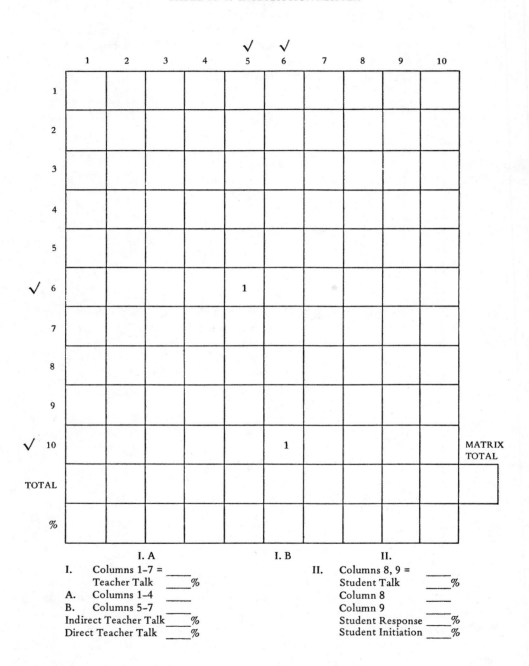

	I. A			I. B		II.	
I.	Columns 1–7 = ____				II.	Columns 8, 9 = ____	
	Teacher Talk ____%					Student Talk ____%	
A.	Columns 1–4 ____					Column 8 ____	
B.	Columns 5–7 ____					Column 9 ____	
	Indirect Teacher Talk ____%					Student Response ____%	
	Direct Teacher Talk ____%					Student Initiation ____%	

TABLE 11-3. INTERACTION MATRIX

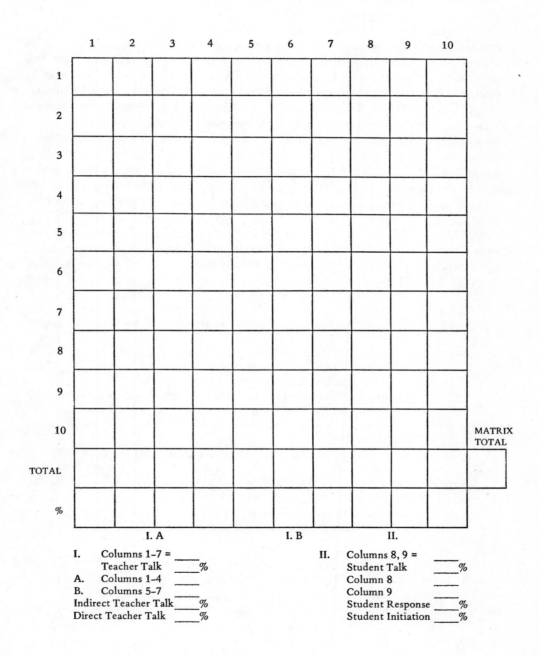

I. A   I. B   II.

I.	Columns 1–7 = _____		II.	Columns 8, 9 = _____
	Teacher Talk _____%			Student Talk _____%
A.	Columns 1–4 _____			Column 8 _____
B.	Columns 5–7 _____			Column 9 _____
	Indirect Teacher Talk _____%			Student Response _____%
	Direct Teacher Talk _____%			Student Initiation _____%

lapping pair. The six is located on the vertical side and a five is located on the horizontal side. The point at which lines drawn from each of these positions is identical and a tally mark is placed in that square, and so on until all of the pairs are recorded.

Table 11–4 illustrates a completed interaction matrix. Two hundred tallies were recorded on the matrix, each representing a category of classroom interaction. Columns numbered one through ten across the top represent each of the interaction analysis categories. Column totals represent the number of times interactions were placed in that category. Thus in this example, three of the 200 interactions recorded (or 1.5 percent) were in category 1 "accepts feelings"; thirty (or 15 percent) were in category 3 "uses ideas of students"; sixty-eight (34 percent) in category 5 "lectures" and so on. By grouping columns, one is able to identify the "amount of time" or *more appropriately* the amount of emphasis given to teacher talk (70 percent) as opposed to student talk (28 percent); indirect teacher talk (31 percent) as opposed to direct teacher talk (39 percent); student response talk (31 percent) as opposed to direct teacher talk (39 percent); student response talk (15 percent) as opposed to student initiated talk (13 percent); and other combinations of interest.

The concentration of tally marks on the grid can also be used systematically to understand a particular classroom better. In addition to areas A, B, C, & D, areas E to L are illustrated in Table 11–5. Concentration of tally marks in each of these areas can be interpreted as follows:

Area E   represents the emphasis given to using student ideas and extending student statements. This area suggests extended indirect influence by the teacher.

Area F   represents the emphasis given to criticism and directing behavior. This area suggests a heavy focus on teacher authority.

Area G   represents the emphasis given to student responses. The first four columns in this area represent indirect responses to teacher comments and the next three direct responses.

Area I   represents prolonged student talk by one student or sustained talk by several students.

Area K   represents indirect statements made by the teacher intended to stimulate student talk.

Area L   represents direct statements made by the teacher intended to stimulate student talk.

Area J   represents the emphasis given by the teacher to content and evidenced by the teacher lecturing and questioning of students.

This interaction analysis technique can provide teachers with a great deal of useful information. But it should be understood that the technique is not very suitable, or readily accepted by teachers, for summative evaluation purposes. Indeed before judgments can be made about whether a particular matrix profile is "good" or not, one needs to know what the teacher intended and what pattern of action is best for that purpose. Teachers themselves are in the best position to make this sort of judgment; for that reason, the interaction analysis technique is much more suitable for self-evaluation.

TABLE 11-4. INTERACTION MATRIX

	1	2	3	4	5	6	7	8	9	10	
1	2	1									
2		5		2							
3			8		2						
4		1		18				1			
5					55	2			4		
6					11	3		1	1		
7							3			2	
8			12				2	26	10		
9	1	3	10					1	10		
10								1	1	1	MATRIX TOTAL
Total	3	10	30	20	68	5	5	30	26	3	200
%	1½	5	15	10	34	2½	2½	15	23	1½	

	I.A			I. B		II. C		D
I.	Columns 1–7	141			II.	Columns 8, 9	56
	Teacher Talk =	70%				Student Talk =	28%
A.	Columns 1–4	63				Column 8	30
B.	Columns 5–7	78				Column 9	26
	Indirect Teacher Talk =	31%				Student Response =	15%
	Direct Teacher Talk =	39%				Student Initiation =	13%

419

TABLE 11-5. MATRIX ANALYSIS*

CATEGORY		1	2	3	4	5	6	7	8	9	10
TEACHER TALK — INDIRECT INFLUENCE	ACCEPTS FEELINGS	1									
	PRAISE	2	AREA E — Teacher use of student ideas, acceptance of student feelings						AREA K — Indirect teacher talk producing student talk		AREA H — Kind of talk followed by silence or confusion
	STUDENT IDEAS	3									
	ASKS QUESTIONS	4									
TEACHER TALK — DIRECT INFLUENCE	LECTURES	5				AREA J — "Content Cross" Extent of emphasis on content			AREA L — Direct teacher talk producing student talk		
	GIVES DIRECTIONS	6				AREA G — How the teacher motivates and controls	AREA F — Teacher use of authority				
	CRITICISM	7									
STUDENT TALK	STUDENT RESPONSE	8							AREA I — Uninterrupted student talk		
	STUDENT INITIATION	9									
	SILENCE	10									
	Total		AREA A — Indirect Teacher Talk				AREA B — Direct Teacher Talk			AREA C — Student Talk		Area D — Silence

*From Amidon and Flanders, *op. cit.*

420

At a given time most any matrix profile might be constructed in observing a given teacher. But over a period of time, say twenty-five observations each for fifteen minutes over a semester, one should be able to notice a definite pattern emerging for that teacher. Does interaction analysis really work? Fred Wilhelms has been familiar with the interaction analysis movement since its inception and has made a careful study of the viability of this technique. Consider his answer to that question below.*

1. When teachers have practice in analyzing teaching and get feedback on their own teaching performance, most of them do tend to build what they learn into their daily behavior. This is "the big one." They do change. Their patterns of teaching behavior do shift (though the permanence of the changes is still in need of study). Various studies have quantified the degree of change on particular variables. There is no way to quantify the changes as a whole. But it can be said that the changes reported in studies are generally clearly significant.

2. Teachers experienced in interaction analysis become more responsive to the ideas of their pupils and use a wider variety of questions to evoke those ideas. There is some evidence that as this occurs the proportion of pupil-initiated or free and creative student response also rises.

3. There is evidence that many teachers tend to move in the direction of a more "indirect" style. That is, they exert their influence less by direct control and tend to create a more "open," supportive, and flexible classroom. This statement must not lead one to expect huge quantitative shifts. What interaction analysis measures most directly is the amount and proportion of time teachers and pupils spend in various categories of verbal behavior. If one looks at the report matrices of a group of "indirect" teachers and compares them with those of a group of "direct" teachers, he may not find any great differences in the amount of "lecture" (information-giving), in the number of questions asked, or even in the amount of praise given. The differences are likelier to be subtle, low-percentage shifts in the recognition of feelings, in accepting and building upon student contributions, in asking more questions of higher orders, and in using brief "lectures" that are highly responsive to student "moves." The important thing is that such quantitatively small shifts apparently have a disproportionate impact on total classroom climate.

The inevitable question, then, is whether such a spectrum shift toward the indirect is "good." The question is a real one, for many teachers and laymen alike are fearful of the results of a lessening of direct control and straightforward, businesslike task-ordering by the teacher.

The general answer is pretty clearly yes. For most typical teachers, a shift toward more "indirect" patterning will prove productive. (This has to be taken in measured terms. Certainly any crude conclusion that everything indirect is good and everything direct is bad is silly. The best "indirect teachers" use a great deal of "direct" process. And there are teachers who are so weakly "permissive" and lacking in strong initiative that they produce nothing much but chaos and confusion.)

The evidence is of two sorts. First, many studies have started by first identifying small groups of teachers judged in various ways to be unusually effective or unusually ineffective. When the classroom practices of these teachers are then

*Fred T. Wilhelms, *Supervision in a New Key.* Washington, D.C.: Association for Supervision and Curriculum Development, 1973, pp. 18–19. Italics added.

analyzed, a high incidence of indirectness will be found in the better group and a high incidence of directness in the poorer group. In her somewhat differently measured study, Marie Hughes, for example, found the poorer teachers using mostly "closed" questions and responses, while the better ones used more "open" tactics. A thoughtful move toward indirectness, one may say then, is a move in the direction of what superior teachers already tend to do.

Second, there is a body of criterion-referenced studies which have correlated pupil results with teaching patterns. There is considerable variability in detail among such studies. But, by and large, the answer comes out clear: "indirect teaching" tends to produce both a better affective tone and greater cognitive learning. On the logic, one is forced (at least, I am forced) to believe also that it will generate more desirable personal qualities in learners (for example, autonomy, independence, creativity).

In short, the systematic analysis of teaching behaviors, including one's own, and the repeated use of sophisticated feedback on one's own styles may well produce changes which tend to be to the good. Learning to apply one or more systems of analysis may well be the cornerstone of planned progress in a teacher's long-term growth.

PREPARING WRITTEN EVALUATION REPORTS

The preparation of written reports, either those limited to classroom observation or those more inclusive of the full range of a teacher's activities, is unfortunately not common practice among chairpersons and other supervisors in today's secondary schools. But interest in this technique is increasing, particularly as dissatisfaction with traditional checklist rating scales increases.

What are the advantages and disadvantages of using written reports as an evaluation technique? On the debit side, it should be understood that carefully prepared written reports are very time-consuming not only in preparation but in extensive classroom observation and general contacts with teachers.

Unless supervision and evaluation is seen as a critical task area for the chairperson, not only by him but by his principal and other administrators, and therefore unless this area is accorded a high priority, time will likely be unavailable and the less desirable but more common checklist rating scales are likely to predominate. A further disadvantage is that the written report technique requires more competence and skill from the chairperson in understanding subject matter structures and concepts, classroom practices, class observation, and actual report writing. The quality of a written report reveals much more about the chairperson's abilities as a supervisor then do his checks on a rating scale. In this sense, many chairpersons may see the written report technique as a potential threat.

On the positive side, this technique is more related to the actual problems, issues, and events faced by the teacher. With respect to specific classroom observation, the evaluation does not focus on generalizations such as "The teacher has planned well" but on the actual events which take place in that class at that time. Further, rather than globally indicating for each category the extent to which the teacher is superior, satisfactory, or needs improvement, specific incidents are discussed and specific suggestions are provided. In this sense, the carefully-prepared written report is teacher centered rather than instrument centered and has the potential for providing more practical suggestions to teachers.

Written reports collected over time seem more useful than checklist rating scales as records of professional improvement. In this sense, they are better able to serve as information or "data" banks from which self-improvement targets might be selected, in-service programs might be developed, and as a means for charting an individual's professional growth over time. Potential benefits also exist for the supervisor in that the technique forces him to be more concerned with instructional matters and staff development needs in the department; and provides him with visible evidence that he is performing supervisory and educational leadership functions. Further, the written report technique seems to be a more effective means of sharing with the principal information about what is actually going on in classrooms and about the actual professional growth of staff members than the more customary checklist rating scales.

The written report may take a number of forms, several of which are illustrated later in this section. Regardless of how the reports are organized, they should share certain characteristics*:

> *An effective report emphasizes formative rather than summative evaluation.* It is designed primarily to improve teaching, to help teachers grow. While negative comments should be included if appropriate, the emphasis is on positive, supportive commentary. When negative comments are included, they should always be accompanied by suggestions for improvement.

> *An effective report is selective rather than comprehensive.* The report focuses on a few basic areas. Detailed recommendations for improvement are provided but not in overwhelming numbers. Recommendations are clear, definite, and realizable. If it is necessary that all areas be included in an evaluation, use a more comprehensive rating scale technique. Perhaps supplement that technique with a more focused written report.

> *An effective report is addressed to the teacher.* You are not writing the report to impress the teacher or others, such as the principal, with your knowledge but to help the teacher. In evaluating *your* report, you and the principal should ask, "To what extent does this report help the teacher?"

> *An effective report is considered as an interdependent part of previous and future reports.* The report should refer to previous reports and be written in a fashion which facilitates future referrals. Several reports viewed together should represent a record of progress or growth for a particular teacher. Further, they should facilitate the setting of growth targets and the suggesting of staff development needs.

> *An effective report is based on an extensive observation of the teacher at work.* At the very least, a full-period observation is recommended. Observing two or more consecutive days of the same class is preferable. Ideally, several random visits as a teacher works on a particular unit with the same class can result in several useful written reports, all linked together.

*The characteristics are suggested by Francis Griffith, *A Handbook for the Observation of Teaching and Learning.* Midland, Mich.: The Pendell Publishing Company, 1973, pp. 142–144.

Four written reports, one each for Mathematics, Social Science, English, and Business Education, are presented as examples of report writing. The reports are not perfect, and differ in format and organization, but each represents a fairly descriptive and effective attempt at helping teachers. A critique follows each of the written reports.*

*This material is excerpted from Francis Griffith, *A Handbook for the Observation of Teaching and Learning.* Midland, Mich.: The Pendell Press, 1973, pp. 145–155.

June 4, 1977

Dear Miss Salem:

It was a pleasure to visit your geometry class and to witness the fine professional job of teaching that you are doing. Your subject matter competency was quite evident in the way you developed your lesson and in the way you answered questions in the classroom. Your explanations were consistently accurate, clear, and easily comprehensible.

I particularly liked the way you responded to the student who made an erroneous conjecture about the measure of angles in circles after you proved the inscribed angle theorem. You did not tell him immediately that he was wrong, but instead you cleverly used the indirect method of proof through a series of questions to show that his assumption could lead to a contradiction of a previously proven theorem. Such a response stimulates critical thinking, encourages students to ask questions and make conjectures without embarrassment or fear of ridicule. Most importantly it was a lesson in itself of the type of logical and analytical thinking you are trying to instill in your students. There is also the element of fun, suspense, and interest which aids students to learn through self-discovery. Such a resourceful method of handling unexpected questions is commendable.

In the previous evaluation of the use of your class time in geometry, we discussed ways of using your time and student time more effectively. If you recall, it was noted that approximately one-third of your class time was taken up by having students write their homework proofs on the chalkboard. While this activity was going on, other students had little to do. While you did spend some time answering questions during this interval, each question seemed to be of interest only to the individual asking it. Many were of the type, "Is my proof done correctly?" I suggested during our discussion that students write their homework problems on acetates for presentation by an overhead projector. You adopted this suggestion and it seems to be working quite well. I noticed that students appeared eager to display their solutions and that most assignments were done neatly. They were easier to read than chalkboard presentations. I also noticed that students concentrated on each problem and did not let their minds wander off to a future one. Getting students to work cooperatively and share responsibilities is important in a geometry class. You have made a significant improvement in the use of class time by this method of discussing homework.

You seem more appreciative of the potential of the overhead projector. You had prepared the figures and diagrams you needed in advance and they were available at your fingertips. These prepared transparencies will also be of value to you for review work or summarizing concepts.

In our conference I said that you would communicate more effectively if you projected your voice. There is a tendency on your part to speak too softly and monotonously so that even the best students are induced to daydream. Your explanations are excellent and too valuable to be wasted on "tuned-in eyeballs" and "tuned-out ears." Perhaps, through practice, you will learn to use your voice more effectively. Maybe the speech teacher could make some suggestions that would be of value. I will let you know after the next observation whether I can detect any improvement in the strength and tonal quality of your voice.

In our discussion we agreed that some time in the lesson should be set aside for a summary of key ideas and theorems. Not only is there a normal tendency to forget new ideas quickly, but it is also possible to lose sight of the total picture and the relationship of many theorems. For example, you might want to ask the class to name all the ways of establishing that two angles are congruent, two lines are parallel, two lines are perpendicular, etc. You might want to indicate at the end of each unit what was accomplished. Perhaps a brief summary of the previous day's work should be of value at the start of the lesson; such a summary would be of particular help to students who were absent.

While we did not discuss the homework assignment, I would like you to consider the following criteria when planning future assignments:

1. Does the assignment arise out of the lesson?
2. Is it clear and definite?
3. Is it understood by the students?
4. Is it related to student needs?
5. Does it challenge student interest and efforts?
6. Is provision made for individual differences?

During the one year that you have been with us, I have been quite impressed by your professional growth and by your attitude toward your work. Your active participation at our department meetings and your valuable help in developing our math department philosophy are greatly appreciated.

Yours truly,

Edward Remington
Chairperson, Mathematics Department

CRITIQUE.   The recipient of this report, a new staff member, undoubtedly found it constructive. Its tone is friendly and encouraging, and its recommendations are basic.

The supervisor is aware that successive reports should be articulated. In this report he observes that class time was used more efficiently than in his previous visit, and he is pleased to note that the suggestion he made has worked out well. His report looks backward to the last observation and forward to the next. ("I will let you know after the next observation whether I can detect any improvement in the strength and tonal quality of your voice.") Presumably, too, he will focus on the homework assignment in his next visit.

Consciously or unconsciously Miss Salem had applied Bruner's discovery principle, and the supervisor commends her for it. It is a safe conjecture that she will seek other applications of the same principle in succeeding lessons.

The supervisor recommends that key ideas be summarized and he supports his recommendation with sound reasons. Since Miss Salem now understands the rationale behind the recommendation, it is more than likely that she will put it into practice.

Although the teacher's voice is apparently a major shortcoming, the supervisor offers little specific assistance other than to say that she may improve with practice or that the speech teacher may be able to help. In this case the vocal monotony and lack of force are probably psychological in origin. If they are indeed caused by diffidence or fear, the supervisor can help the teacher grow in confidence and poise. He can recommend that she attend a university course in voice and diction or even a course in dramatics. He can also suggest that she video-tape a lesson and later evaluate it, paying special attention to her use of voice. If Miss Salem's vocal problem has a physical origin, he can refer her to a university speech clinic for diagnosis and treatment. In any case, he should take positive steps rather than the vague ones he suggested.

Why doesn't he invite Miss Salem to observe one of his own lessons? She would undoubtedly be receptive to such an invitation, since she is eager to improve, and she might learn a great deal from his demonstration, particularly if it is followed up by a conference in which she is encouraged to discuss what she observed.

TEACHER: Mr. Charles J. Hines
SCHOOL: John Philip Sousa High School
GRADE: 11
OBSERVER: Thomas Fleming
THE LESSON: March 23, 1977

Dear Charlie:

You have your work cut out for you. It will take some doing to equal or surpass your lesson of Tuesday.

This was one of the most fascinating lessons that I have ever seen in a social studies class. Your use of family histories made this culmination of the topic of immigration a highlight that will long be remembered by most of the students.

The assignment and presentation could easily have turned out to be a rambling, unrelated affair, but your careful planning and guidance were clearly evident. Your division of the reports into the topics of "The Old Country," "Reasons for Leaving," "The Trip," and "The Arrival and Early Experiences" gave the lesson form and meaningful direction.

The past came even more alive with the impressive display of documents, photographs, letters, passports, toys, and other artifacts.

You did well to relate the individual family histories to the general concepts learned in earlier lessons, especially the economic, religious, political, and social motivations for emigration from the native lands.

Your manner was quiet, sure, firm. You were completely in control, but had the perception and sensitivity to make your touch light. There was fine rapport evident, and your questioning was subtle and skillful. The arrangement of desks in a circular fashion certainly facilitated communication and learning.

In lesser hands, this lesson could have been a major letdown for the students considering the amount of family interviewing that must have been standard for yourself and the department.

The Conference: March 24, 1977

This is intended primarily as a memorandum concerning the items discussed and agreed to in our conversation after the lesson described above. We agreed that. . .

1. The bulletin board could be utilized by posting maps and cards with the students' names to show both the lands of origin and locations of their first homes in America.
2. Many of the family papers and objects should be arranged in the display case near the Social Studies Department classrooms.
3. Various words and phrases used during the lesson, such as acculturation, assimilation, pogrom, "black-and-tans," and "greenhorn," might be listed on the chalkboard, perhaps by a student assistant.
4. The family interview technique might well be utilized for other units for such things as experiences during the depression and the Second World War, remembrances of presidents and other outstanding persons, and opinion polls on current issues.
5. You would explain the methods involved in your lesson at the next department meeting.

Sincerely,

Thomas Fleming
Chairperson

CRITIQUE.   The organization of this report is unique. First, details of time, place, grade, and the names of the teacher and observer are listed; next, there is a personal letter about the lesson; finally, the post-visit conference is summarized.

The letter is enthusiastic but unmistakeably sincere. Specific features are commended in generous terms, as they apparently deserve to be. The agreements reached in the conference, held the day following the lesson, are sound.

The report is good not because the teacher is a creative artist and the lesson imaginative but because the observer is perceptive. He recognizes and commends specific excellences and offers thoughtful suggestions. More importantly, he makes arrangements for this master teacher to discuss his methods at a department meeting so that others may benefit from his expertise.

English M31 March 15, 1977 Mr. M. Simons

The teacher began by saying that the class was going to talk about something new, namely the theatre. He asked how many had been to the theatre and how many watched television. He questioned the students about their favorite TV shows. When a preference was shown for shows with action, he explained melodrama as a type of drama. He developed the meaning of other types of plays as follows: comedy, tragedy, fantasy, and farce.

Comment

1. The first question we must ask ourselves when we teach any lesson is: What changes are we trying to bring about in our students and how does this lesson help bring about these changes?

You taught this slow class the meaning of five dramatic terms. Why? Are these labels important? Do they help students enjoy their reading?

The primary reason for teaching literature—drama, poetry, fiction, essays, biography—is enjoyment. An appreciation lesson should be, above all, enjoyable. Students should leave the lesson with pleasurable emotional reactions and look forward to more such pleasant experiences. Tags such as melodrama and fantasy are relatively unimportant. When students complain about their school work being irrelevant, this is what they mean.

Why not start by reading a one-act play aloud? You have had dramatic experience and your students will undoubtedly enjoy and profit from hearing you interpret the various roles. You can bring the play to life with your dramatic reading. Later, involve the students in oral reading. Better yet: let them act out the play under your direction. Since the registration in this class is small, you can stage dramatizations with not too much difficulty.

After the students have read aloud or enacted several one-act plays, you may introduce the terms which describe them. ("What is the difference between such-and-such a play and such-and-such a play? This one is called a comedy. Why? The other is called a fantasy. Why?") In other words, definitions should follow, not precede, direct experiencing.

Our ultimate aim, as I said above, is to develop a love of literature—in this class, the drama particularly—so that students will read plays on their own, go to the theatre to see good plays, listen to good drama on television, and be able to make sound critical judgments about what they read, see, and hear.

2. Arrange your board work with underlined headings so that it becomes a summary of the lesson which is easy to read and understand.

3. You were pleasant with the boy who used "you know" at the end of every sentence. I think he will remember the correction when he begins to say it again. You also quietly corrected a grammatical error made by one boy: "It don't make no sense."

Margaret Driscoll
Chairperson, English Department

Conference held: March 17, 1977

429

CRITIQUE. The supervisor's point of view about the teaching of literature is valid. Her philosophy accords with that of every modern authority on English education, including the National Council of Teachers of English. It is surprising that the teacher in this instance is concerned with teaching definitions to a group of slow students instead of helping them to experience enjoyment through literature.

The final paragraph is an afterthought as if the supervisor had cudgelled her mind to find something favorable to say about a nondescript performance. It is a sop, a transparent effort to find at least one matter worthy of commendation. It is better omitted.

October 31, 1977
Stenography 3-3

Dear Elsie Collins:

As usual I enjoyed the fine esprit de corps in your class during the third period today. Your cheerfulness set the tone. When an error was made by a student, your appeal to use common sense brought the correct interpretation of outlines.

Your fine drive was in evidence throughout the period. No wonder a brave soul complained that her hand was falling off! However, I approve. The only way to become a good stenographer is to take quantities of dictation daily. You did not waste one second of the period. Good!

During our conference I emphasized that ALL the students should have the feeling of success. One thing I did not make clear, however. Your drive for high speed with rates varying from 85-110 wpm, while too difficult for a daily diet, would be excellent for one or even two days a week. I predict you will eventually get more fast writers with a little more encouragement now. The letters are difficult. This alone makes the speed more difficult to attain. You could dictate a series of short, easy letters with which to build speed at the beginning of the period. Then dictate homework letters at a lower rate, and finally new letters at a speed within their scope provided they are straining to take the dictation. At no time do I want a feeling of comfort except for a few short, easy letters at the beginning. This gives them confidence. Then move to faster, more difficult dictation.

I liked your week's assignment on the chalkboard. However, it should have been in shorthand. Scold in shorthand! I enjoyed your directive to be sure to call up the absentees and give them the assignment. This is all excellent teaching. Every good teacher makes a youngster stretch in order to reach a goal.

This is your first term teaching beginning transcription. This grade is most important, since it is a meshing of skills. Make a drive to increase the English vocabulary as well as the shorthand vocabulary. Your board lacked shorthand outlines and spelling words. Because the class can spell FINAL it does not mean they can spell FINALLY. This is the crucial grade where good or bad habits are established. You are the model. Get the class to think shorthand. Subject matter becomes alive when the student feels the dictation is INSIDE an office.

With your pep, enthusiasm and interest in every student, I expect a crop of super-excellent stenographers! Keep up your fine work!

Sincerely,

Amy L. Walter
Chairperson
Secretarial Department

CRITIQUE.   Here is a breezy, almost colloquial, reaction to a lesson taught by a teacher who, though experienced, has never before taught this grade of stenography. The report is characterized by good sense, sincerity, and informality. Although it is a bit hortatory, it is also down-to-earth and encouraging, the kind of report a teacher is pleased to receive and glad to act upon.

The supervisor mingles genuine praise with practical suggestions. One suspects that she is a friendly energizer and that the members of her department respond affirmatively to her leadership because they recognize her concern for them and their students and acknowledge her competence.

The emphasis is on production, as it should be in every business education class but too often is not.

Teacher-Focused Evaluation Through Self-Assessment

Self-Assessment strategies are often included as parts of a school's comprehensive evaluation program but rarely do they assume the central role in the program. This Personal Assessment Inventory includes suggestions for its use as the central or focal point for your evaluation program.

The items which comprise the inventory are presumed to represent a set of agreements which teachers accept, value and consider as standards toward which they work. (For this reason the items provided in this example may well need careful study and perhaps revision by your staff before they meet the acceptance requirements.)

Periodically, perhaps twice a year, all teachers respond to the inventory. Teachers are expected to provide examples or otherwise support or clarify their self-assessment ratings for each category studied in the inventory. Support may take the form of lesson and unit plans, student groups, assignments and examinations, audio and audio-visual tapes of classroom activity, observations by other teachers, student rating forms, invited observations by the chairperson, or work of students.

In working with non-tenured teachers, the inventory ratings and support data are reviewed in conference with the chairperson and perhaps with others designated by the chairperson. You might try inviting each tenured teacher to select any three members of the professional staff in the school to serve as a review committee for himself with you serving informally as a member of all review committees of teachers in the department. After the ratings and supporting data are reviewed, the committee prepares a brief written report (see Preparing Written Evaluation Reports) summarizing the conference and providing suggestions for the teacher. Such a report could well serve as a source document for the identification and setting of targets by the teacher and the procedure outlined here serves well as a complement to target-setting evaluation strategies such as outlined earlier in this chapter.

Personal Assessment Inventory

To what extent are students involved in planning my classes?

1. In my classroom, students are involved in the formulation of goals and in the selection of activities and instructional strategies.
    Hardly ever   1   2   3   4   5   Almost always
2. I can provide evidence that students in my classroom are involved in the assessment of curriculum outcomes.
    Hardly ever   1   2   3   4   5   Almost always

Give examples to support and clarify your ratings:

To What Extent Are My Classes Relevant?

1. The central focus of the curriculum of my classroom revolves principally around enduring social issues.
    Hardly ever   1   2   3   4   5   Almost always
2. In my classroom a wide variety of materials are used to accommodate a variety of student reading and interest levels.
    Hardly ever   1   2   3   4   5   Almost always
3. In my classroom the curriculum being studied focuses upon problem solving and the decision-making process.
    Hardly ever   1   2   3   4   5   Almost always
4. Controversial issues such as racism, poverty, war, and pollution are dealt with in my classroom.
    Hardly ever   1   2   3   4   5   Almost always

5. In my classroom opportunities are provided for students to meet, discuss, and work with each other.

   Hardly ever   1   2   3   4   5   Almost always

6. I can provide evidence that students in my classroom gather data from sources outside the classroom (with the community for example) as well as in the classroom.

   Hardly ever   1   2   3   4   5   Almost always

Give examples to support and clarify your ratings.

To What Extent is the Content of My Classes Accurate?

1. I can provide evidence in my classroom that current knowledge, theories, and interpretations are used and consistent with modern thinking.

   Hardly ever   1   2   3   4   5   Almost always

2. I can provide evidence in my classroom that textbooks and other instructional resources are carefully evaluated for up-to-date scholarship.

   Hardly ever   1   2   3   4   5   Almost always

3. In my classroom extensive up-to-date references are readily available for use in the curriculum.

   Hardly ever   1   2   3   4   5   Almost always

4. I can provide evidence that up-to-date methods of inquiry and processing data are utilized in my classroom.

   Hardly ever   1   2   3   4   5   Almost always

Give examples to support and clarify your ratings:

To What Extent are my Classes' Goals Clear?

1. In my classroom goals are defined for students to enable them to clearly understand what is expected of them.

   Hardly ever   1   2   3   4   5   Almost always

2. I can provide evidence that needs of students in my classroom are considered in the selection and formulation of goals and objectives.

   Hardly ever   1   2   3   4   5   Almost always

3. In my classroom community resource people are consulted in the planning of long- and short-range goals.

   Hardly ever   1   2   3   4   5   Almost always

4. I can provide evidence that a variety of means are employed in my classroom to assess needs and accomplishments of the students.

Hardly ever   1   2   3   4   5   Almost always

5. In my classroom goals and objectives are related to each of the following areas: knowledge, skills, and abilities, valuing.

Hardly ever   1   2   3   4   5   Almost always

6. In my classroom attention is given to discovering goals, objectives, and outcomes not anticipated before a lesson or unit.

Hardly ever   1   2   3   4   5   Almost always

Give examples to support and clarify your ratings:

To What Extent Are My Students Involved in Class?

1. In my classroom students have access to a variety of learning resources appropriate to the goals and objectives of educational program.

Hardly ever   1   2   3   4   5   Almost always

2. I can provide evidence in my classroom that students are active in the planning process.

Hardly ever   1   2   3   4   5   Almost always

3. I can provide evidence in my classroom that students are involved in the selection of goals and play a vital role in assessment and evaluation of the curriculum.

Hardly ever   1   2   3   4   5   Almost always

Give examples to support and clarify your ratings:

To What Extent Are My Learning Strategies Varied and Broad?

1. I can provide evidence to indicate that in my classroom a variety of learning material is available for use in the educational program.

Hardly ever   1   2   3   4   5   Almost always

2. In my classroom materials for various academic ability levels and interest levels are available.

Hardly ever   1   2   3   4   5   Almost always

Give examples to support and clarify your ratings:

How Do I Evaluate Student Progress?

1. I can provide evidence in my classroom that goals and objectives are considered and provide focus for planning, development, and evaluation of the program.

   Hardly ever   1   2   3   4   5   Almost always

2. In my classroom I have evidence that data is gathered in an attempt to evaluate each student's progress, both cognitively and affectively.

   Hardly ever   1   2   3   4   5   Almost always

3. I can provide evidence in my classroom that a variety of evaluation techniques are used to evaluate learnings (cognitive and affective) in the curriculum.

   Hardly ever   1   2   3   4   5   Almost always

4. I can provide evidence in my classroom that evaluation procedures and progress of students are reported frequently to both the pupil and the parent.

   Hardly ever   1   2   3   4   5   Almost always

Give examples to support and clarify your ratings:

Keeping Supervisory Records

Record keeping associated with the evaluation of teachers is often limited to reports of the evaluation. Obviously a collection of thoughtful reports which span several evaluation time frames can be invaluable in charting professional growth and in planning future growth activities. However, the actual evaluation report records should be supplemented by a brief, simple accounting system which indicates with whom the chairperson has worked, the nature of his supervisory activity, and the time spent with each teacher and on each activity. This accounting, combined with the more substantive evaluation reports, can help you to plan your own supervisory activities, assist in your calendaring, and more efficiently manage your time. This accounting provides a permanent record for legal purposes if such a need should arise. And such a record can help demonstrate to your principal and other administrators how time-demanding the process of supervision is, and thus could help you argue for additional resources such as a secretary, assistant chairperson, or a reduced teaching assignment. Finally, if you are involved in the process of identifying critical task areas and setting supervisory targets, as suggested in Chapter 8, this record can help provide some indication of the extent to which you are reaching certain targets.

An example of a simple accounting system is provided in the Supervision Record form below. A record should be kept for each teacher and the example form provides for listing the kind of supervisory activity engaged in with the teacher, and the approximate hours spent each month on that activity. Simple totaling permits one to review hours spent in all types of supervision for each month and in each activity for the year.

SUPERVISION RECORD

TEACHER _____   YEAR _____

CHAIRPERSON _____

NATURE OF ACTIVITY	INDICATE APPROXIMATE HOURS	A	S	O	N	D	J	F	M	A	M	J	TOTAL
1. Target Setting													
2. Conferences													
3. Classroom observation													
4. Lesson and unit planning													
5.													
6.													
TOTAL													

INDEX

441